W9-ARH-207

Buddhism:
A History

by
Noble Ross Reat

ASIAN HUMANITIES PRESS
Berkeley, California

ASIAN HUMANITIES PRESS

Asian Humanities Press offers to the specialist and the general reader alike, the best in new translations of major works and significant original contributions, to enhance our understanding of Asian literature, religions, cultures and thought.

Library of Congress Cataloging-in-Publication Data

Reat, N. Ross, 1951-
　　Buddhism : a history / by Noble Ross Reat.
　　　　p.　　cm.　　—　　(Religions of the world)
　　Includes bibliographical references and index.
　　ISBN 0-87573-001-9. — ISBN 0-87573-002-7 (paper)
　　1. Buddhism—History.　I. Title.　II. Series.
BQ266.R43　　1994
294.3'09—dc20
　　　　　　　　　　　　　　　　　　　　　　93-1792
　　　　　　　　　　　　　　　　　　　　　　CIP

Contents

Series Editor's Foreword

As the first volume in the Religions of the World series, this book establishes several principles and practices that will operate throughout the series. The guiding editorial principle of this series is to provide readable, reliable and comprehensive books that are accessible to the general reader. It is not necessary to have any prior knowledge of the religions examined in order to understand and profit fully from any book in this series. The series as a whole is intended to fill the widening gap between single-volume treatments of all the world's religions and whole libraries of specialized literature on the religions of the world. The extent and sophistication of this specialized literature is now so great that no single-volume treatment of the world's religions can adequately prepare one for it.

We divide our treatments of each of the the major religions into two volumes — one on history and one on beliefs and practices — in recognition of the separate methods and goals of historical studies on the one hand and doctrinal studies on the other. This practice also allows our authors and readers to concentrate upon a single object of study without being constantly distracted by digressions and explanations that are better pursued in a separate volume. Nonetheless, this volume, like every other volume in the series, is intended to stand on its own. Depending upon their interests, readers can derive full benefit from any volume in this series quite independently of any other volume. Together, the *Introduction* and *History* of any given religion are designed to cover the material normally taught in a semester-long University course in that religion.

Each book in the series is designed to provide a thorough foundation for further reading and study in its area, in this case the history of Buddhism. Having digested this book, the reader should not be entirely mystified by any other book or article on the history of Buddhism. In addition, the thorough glossaries and indexes in these books will make them useful as reference works. The editor and publisher take responsibility for our series policy of minimizing footnotes. Further research is facilitated instead by including in each volume of the series an extensive Suggestions for Further Reading section. These sections are organized according to the chapter divisions of each book, so that readers may readily perceive pathways for extending their knowledge in whatever areas they find interesting.

Author's Preface

To undertake a comprehensive history of Buddhism in one volume is admittedly an ambitious project. Some would call it foolhardy. Nonetheless, the need for such a volume is apparent. Other than this book, beginning students of Buddhism have no alternative but to plunge into a small library of difficult works dealing with various areas, aspects and eras of Buddhist history. To take this plunge is a rewarding experience for those with the time and determination to persevere. It is also a daunting prospect which deters many who would like to be better informed about the history of one of the world's major religions.

This book is designed on the one hand for those who are interested but do not have the time or inclination to dedicate a significant portion of their lives to the study of Buddhism. On the other hand, it is also intended to serve as a starting point for those who may discover that they do wish to pursue further study of Buddhism. More advanced students of Buddhism may find the book useful because it condenses into one volume an overview of the major events and personalities in the history of Buddhism.

Among the several methods currently employed in religious studies, this book may be classified as traditional, Western-style history. This approach is consciously adopted in the interests of serving its intended readership, the majority of whom will have little or no stake in academic trends and counter-trends such as deconstructionism. To say that this book is a traditional, Western-style history indicates in essence that it attempts to present a coherent narrative based on facts, insofar as it is possible to determine facts that occurred in the distant past or in distant cultures.

In the service of this purpose, the present book approaches Buddhism as a coherent and comprehensible historical phenomenon. Other treatments justifiably deal with "Buddhisms" in the plural, emphasizing the diversity of that which bears the name "Buddhism" rather than the relatedness of its various forms. Characteristically and quite validly, such treatments emphasize the gaps and inconsistencies in the history and manifestations of the phenomenon known as Buddhism. This "deconstructionist" approach may or may not describe history more accurately than the present, narrative approach. However, one has to start somewhere, and narrative history still provides the most straightforward basis for further study and critical reflection. For those who do not go on to further study, this narrative approach will provide a reliable basic knowledge of the history of Buddhism. For those who do go on to further study, this approach provides a convenient starting point.

In the space allowed, I cannot possibly mention all of the many people and institutions that have assisted in the research and writing of this book. Professor Karl Potter, editor of the Encyclopedia of Indian Philosophies, called upon me to write part of the introduction to the volume on Buddhism. He was gracious in readily agreeing, on behalf of the publishers, that I could without concern cover the same ground in Chapters I-III of the present book. Professor Lewis Lancaster of the Department of East Asian Languages at Berkeley was extremely helpful in exerting influence to secure for me accommodation in Berkeley and access to the magnificent library facilities of the University of California during two long periods of research there. On both occasions, I stayed at the Institute of Buddhist Studies, and I wish to thank them for providing excellent accommodation. Of the many who read parts of the manuscript and offered expert advice, I wish to thank in particular Drs. Rod Bucknell, Martin Stuart-Fox and John Weik of the University of Queensland; Bruce Williams and Sung-taek Cho of the University of California at Berkeley; Ven. Silavimalla and Dr. Richard Payne of the Institute of Buddhist Studies in Berkeley, and Frank Tedesco of the University of Maryland. I wish to thank also my copyeditor, Jane Townsend, and my proofreader Jac-Aileen De Marco. Having acknowledged this assistance, I hasten to add the obvious: that I alone am responsible for any errors and defects in the book. Finally, I wish to thank my own institution, the University of Queensland in Brisbane, Australia, for generously supporting this project by allowing me three semester-long study leaves over a period of ten years.

Introduction

For readers entirely unfamiliar with Buddhism and its history, a few introductory points may be useful. The founder of Buddhism, the Buddha or "awakened one," lived and taught in northern India approximately 500 years before Jesus founded Christianity along the shores of the Mediterranean Sea. Westerners traditionally count time from the birth of Jesus, employing the designations B.C. and A.D. to locate events before or after this point in time. Others, of course, traditionally count time differently, and start from different points. Buddhists, for example, usually count from the birth of the Buddha, although the timing of this event is not widely agreed upon. The Christian calendar has been widely adopted throughout the world, and for the sake of convenience it is used in this book. In recognition of other religions and modes of counting time, however, this book employs the increasingly widespread designations BCE and CE — meaning "before common era" and "common era" — as more neutral versions of the designations B.C. (before Christ) and A.D. *(anno domini)*. The latter, which means "in the year of our lord," i.e. of Jesus Christ, can be particularly uncomfortable for non-Christians. Dates marked BCE and CE correspond exactly to dates elsewhere marked B.C. and A.D.

While on the subject of time, it should be noted that many cultures have been less concerned than Western culture with recording the dates of events and individual persons. The ancient cultures of India and Southeast Asia fall into this "non-historical" category. For this reason, precise dates, sometimes even approximate dates, of ancient events and persons in Asia are often difficult to determine. Because this is an introductory book, it seeks to avoid entering into disputes regarding dating and adheres to the dates most widely accepted by Western scholars. Though every attempt is made to indicate where important differences of opinion exist, in most cases no attempt is made to resolve such differences. This practice provides readers with a starting point from which to evaluate scholarly debates, should they care to do so. It also allows the narrative to proceed smoothly for those who only want an overview of the history of Buddhism. In general, the present book attempts to indicate where uncertainties and disagreements exist regarding the history of Buddhism, but its primary purpose is not to resolve such problems. Its primary purpose is to tell the story of Buddhism in such a way that Western readers may begin to comprehend and appreciate the beauty, coherence and continuing significance of the religion.

In addition to dates, languages may present confusion for the general reader. In the first place, for the first two or three centuries of Buddhism's existence, until about 250 BCE, writing was virtually unknown in India, and no Buddhist scriptures were written down until the beginning of the common era. Instead, Buddhist teachings were retained by memory and passed on orally for about five hundred years. This situation, of course, creates uncertainty regarding the original teachings of the Buddha, even though oral traditions can be very accurate. Most historians of India accept that ancient Indian oral traditions were particularly accurate, and so when this book mentions the probable dates of the composition of "scriptures" in India prior to the first century CE, it refers to oral rather than written composition.

Although Buddhism originated in India, it spread throughout the Eastern world and came to be recorded in several languages. The historical Buddha — a term used in contrast to the Buddha of legend and mythology — spoke a dialect of Sanskrit, the classical language of ancient India. It is not clear which dialect or dialects he spoke. The several dialects of ancient India, known as Prakrits, stood in relation to Sanskrit somewhat as the Romance languages — Italian, French, Spanish, etc. — once stood in relation to Latin. Like Latin, Sanskrit was a formal, literary language used almost exclusively by the elite of society. An extensive record of the Buddha's teachings survives in the ancient Indian dialect known as Pāli. This record forms the scriptural basis of one of the two major branches of contemporary Buddhism, the Theravāda, which is practiced in Sri Lanka and Southeast Asia. The scriptures of the other major branch of Buddhism, the Mahāyāna, were originally written in Sanskrit, as were the scriptures of some extinct schools related to the Theravāda. Some of this Sanskrit written material may well be based upon earlier material in the several dialects or Prakrits of ancient India. Very little of this Sanskrit written material survives, but as Buddhism spread across the Eastern world, most of it was translated into Chinese and Tibetan. These four languages — Pāli, Sanskrit, Chinese and Tibetan — are the most important scriptural languages of Buddhism today. The conventions used in this book to render foreign names and terms into Roman script are explained in the Pronunciation Guide toward the back of the book.

The geography of Buddhism is also somewhat complex. Like several other religions that once flourished in India, Buddhism was eventually absorbed by Hinduism and has all but ceased to exist in the land of its birth. Despite its virtual disappearance from India, however, Buddhism enjoyed enormous success throughout Asia. As Buddhism spread beyond India to the east, the Theravāda branch of Buddhism became dominant in the southern lands of Sri Lanka and Southeast Asia (Burma, Cambodia,

Laos, and Thailand), while Mahāyāna Buddhism became dominant in the northern regions of China, Korea, Vietnam, Japan, Tibet, and Mongolia. For this reason, Theravāda is sometimes referred to as southern Buddhism, and Mahāyāna is sometimes called northern Buddhism. Buddhism also spread westward from India into Central Asia, roughly the area of present-day Pakistan, Afghanistan and far western China. In this area, Buddhism was supplanted by Islam and no longer exists. Nonetheless, Buddhism played an important role in the history of Central Asia, and contemporary archaeology and research in this area is producing a constant stream of new material relating to the history of Buddhism.

In addition to being an important religion in its own right, Buddhism's influence in Asia is evident in its influence upon several other religions, each of which must be considered in the course of recounting the history of Buddhism. Though Hinduism supplanted Buddhism in India, the two religions developed to maturity in constant contact, and they exerted considerable influence upon one another. As a result, Buddhism left an indelible mark upon Hinduism, and this influence of Buddhism does survive in India. In China, Buddhism encountered Daoism (Taoism; see Pronunciation Guide) and Confucianism. For many centuries, Buddhism itself was the dominant religion of China, and it remained an important element of Chinese religion — in the form of a synthesis with Daoism and Confucianism — until the communist period in the twentieth century. In Japan, Buddhism absorbed the native Shintō religion to the extent that the two religions became virtually inseparable in the spiritual life of the Japanese. Similarly, in Tibet Buddhism encountered and absorbed the indigenous Bon religion. Today, Buddhism itself, with about 500 million followers, is usually counted as the fourth largest of the world's religions, after Christianity, Hinduism and Islam. Because of its strong influence upon the enormous populations of China and India, however, one may safely say that Buddhism has directly or indirectly touched more human lives than any other religion or ideology in history.

CHAPTER I

The Buddha in Legend and History

The story of Buddhism begins with the life and times of its founder, the Buddha or "awakened one" (approximately 560-480 BCE — see Abbreviations). Given his enormous historical significance, remarkably few Westerners are even vaguely acquainted with the Buddha or the religion he founded. A few comparisons with figures better known in the West may help set the stage for the story which is to follow. In terms of influence upon human history, the Buddha can be compared with only two historical individuals: Jesus and Muḥammad, the founders of Christianity and Islam. As with Jesus and Muḥammad, little is known of the early life of the Buddha, but in his later years as a teacher he stands out as one of the first figures ever to be recorded in history as a real, recognizable human personality rather than as a two-dimensional character in a mythologized narrative. In this sense, he is comparable to the Greek philosopher Socrates (fifth century BCE) and to some of the figures in the *Hebrew Bible* or *Old Testament.*

This is all the more remarkable given the generally non-historical character of Indian thought, which does not normally emphasize the dates and details of individual events and personalities. The early Buddhist scriptures provide our first glimpse of daily life and historical events and figures in ancient India. Of these early Buddhist scriptures, those in the Pāli language survive most extensively. Only this Pāli canon, the scriptural basis of Theravāda Buddhism, survives complete in its original language. On the basis of this material, it is possible to construct a coherent account of the broad outlines of the life of the historical Buddha and the early history of the religion he founded. Chapters II and III explain why the Pāli canon, as opposed to other relevant sources, forms the starting point of this narrative. At this point, inclusion or reasoned elimination of material from other sources would only delay the beginning of the story.

For example, even the dating of the Buddha's life is a complex problem. On the basis of diverse sources, scholarly estimates of the years of the Buddha's birth and death vary by more than a century. The most common dates given are 563-483 BCE. This estimate is based on the so-called "long chronology" contained in the Pāli sources. Other estimates based on these same sources vary by as much as a decade. A "short chronology" based on Sanskrit and Chinese sources moves these dates forward by 118 years to approximately 445-365 BCE. It is safe and for most purposes sufficient to say that the historical Buddha lived in the decades surrounding 500 BCE.

In this period occurred what is arguably the most profound and widespread intellectual and spiritual transformation the world has ever seen. In China, Confucius and Lao Zi (Lao Tzu — see Pronunciation Guide) were formulating the principles of Confucianism and Daoism (Taoism), systems of ethics and religion which would guide nearly one quarter of the human race into the present century. Zoroaster (the founder of Zoroastrianism) in Persia, and a few decades later Socrates in Greece were laying the ideological foundations of the empires that dominated the classical history of the Western world, the Persian, the Greek and the Roman. Following the Babylonian exile of the Jews (586-538 BCE), Jeremiah and Second Isaiah, author of most of the book of Isaiah in the Hebrew Bible, were formulating the principles of universal monotheism, the philosophical basis of Judaism, Christianity and Islam. In India at the time of the Buddha, composition of the principle *Upanishads* (between 800 and 300 BCE), the first scriptures of classical Hinduism, was in mid-course.

In India at this time, the *Upanishads* and the teachings of the Buddha represent separate attempts to synthesize elements of the two ancient cultures which ultimately account for Indian civilization. One of these — known as the Indus Valley civilization because it was centered on the Indus River — was indigenous to the Indian subcontinent. The other was a warlike, nomadic people known as Indo-Europeans. As the name Indo-European suggests, the migrations and conquests of these people exerted influence right across Europe and Asia from the Atlantic to the Pacific Ocean. Today, the result of this influence is most apparent in the relationship of modern languages spoken from Europe through to India. Examples of languages belonging to the Indo-European family are English, Greek, Latin and the modern Romance languages, the Germanic languages, Russian, Persian, the Urdu language of Pakistan, and the languages of northern India, such as Hindi and Bengali. In order to appreciate the Buddha's contribution to Indian thought, it is necessary to consider briefly the mingling of the Indus Valley and Indo-European cultures in India long before the time of the historical Buddha.

Indian Proto-history: The Background of Buddhism

Two thousand years before the Buddha's time, in approximately 2500 BCE, the area now known as Pakistan harbored an advanced civilization in the valley of the Indus River. The two major cities of this civilization, Mohenjo Daro and Harappa, rivaled any cities known to humankind at that time and for millennia afterward. Both cities were designed around an orderly grid of streets lined with brick town houses whose connected facades blocked the noise and dust from the street. Under the streets ran an extensive network of sewers, so that these ancient cities were probably more hygienic than European cities were before the nineteenth century. Both Mohenjo Daro and Harappa had ample granaries, where emergency food supplies were stored, and numerous large municipal buildings and complexes which appear to have been palaces, assembly halls, government houses, and even perhaps schools and universities.

Aside from the vague but impressive picture that archaeological ruins divulge, the details of this ancient culture remain a mystery, for the Indus Valley civilization had vanished entirely from human memory until Mohenjo Daro and Harappa were unearthed early in the twentieth century. Because of this four-thousand-year disappearance, the Indus Valley writing system is a puzzle. Much written material survives on clay tablets, but efforts to decipher this material have failed thus far. Without access to written material, the precise nature of the Indus Valley religion remains a matter of speculation. Nonetheless, a few tentative conclusions about the religion of the Indus Valley are possible. These conclusions, which help explain the backgrounds of Buddhism, are based not so much upon the positive evidence of archaeological relics from the Indus Valley as they are upon negative evidence forthcoming from another source of knowledge about the religions of ancient India. This source is the *Rig Veda*, a scripture containing sacred hymns of the Indo-Europeans who began to arrive in India in approximately 2000 BCE. Like many nomadic peoples, these Indo-Europeans were illiterate, and maintained their sacred traditions and hymns in a memorized, oral tradition. Due to their domination of India, the art of writing disappeared there for some fifteen hundred years. During this period, not only the *Rig Veda,* but all of the religious traditions of India had to be maintained and passed on by means of memorized, oral traditions.

Until the rediscovery of the long-forgotten Indus Valley civilization, the *Rig Veda* was the only source of knowledge about religion in India prior to approximately 1000 BCE. According to Hinduism, the *Rig Veda,* gradually compiled between 2000 and 1000 BCE, is the fountainhead of all the sacred knowledge of India. Hindus regard all subsequent Indian religious thought, including Buddhism, as elaboration upon or deviation from the eternal truths enshrined in the obscure hymns of the *Rig Veda*. Until the rediscovery of the Indus Valley civilization it seemed likely that all subsequent religious thought in India did indeed derive ultimately from the *Rig Veda,* even though this hypothesis left several major problems unresolved. The essence of these problems is that the hymns of the

Rig Veda exhibit very few of the prominent characteristics of Hinduism or of other Indian religions. Few if any of the major deities of classical Hinduism have convincing counterparts in the *Rig Veda*, nor is there any real foreshadowing of the almost universal Indian beliefs in an immortal soul, multiple rebirths of the soul determined by one's karma (moral action), and spiritual release of the soul *(moksha)* from rebirth. Instead, the hymns of the *Rig Veda* petition the Vedic deities for material benefits in this life and for an afterlife in heaven, characterized as the blissful abode of the ancestors. Alternatively, the *Rig Veda* mentions a hell of "blind darkness." Whether heaven or hell, the *Rig Veda* envisions only one earthly life and a single afterlife determined primarily on the basis of whether or not one has been scrupulous in performing the proper rituals.

Before the rediscovery of the Indus Valley civilization, on the basis of the *Rig Veda* alone, it was difficult to explain how belief in a soul, rebirth and spiritual release from rebirth came to be so prominent in all of the several religions which developed in India. It was similarly difficult to discern any convincing similarities between the Vedic deities and the deities of classical Hinduism. Discovery of the Indus Valley civilization solved these problems by providing evidence that Indian culture and religion had not developed out of the Vedic religion alone, but rather from a combination of Indo-European and Indus Valley elements. For example, the popular Hindu deity Krishṇa, meaning literally "the dark one," might have found his way into the Hindu pantheon as a representative of the dark-skinned, indigenous inhabitants of India. There is evidence too of an Indus Valley deity associated with asceticism and wild animals, possibly a prototype of the Śiva of classical Hinduism, the favored deity of Hindu practitioners of yoga.

In all of its several forms, including Buddhist forms, yoga involves introspective, meditational discipline intended to *release* the *soul* from *rebirth*. Release from rebirth is desirable because rebirth is regarded as a tedious and pointless repetition of suffering, illness, old age and death. Evidence of an Indus Valley deity similar to Śiva suggests that the yogic triad of belief in souls, rebirth and release derives from indigenous Indian religion rather than from the *Rig Veda*. This possibility is strengthened by the existence of two religious traditions in ancient India which claim to predate and to be independent of the *Rig Veda*, namely the Jains and the Ājīvakas. Both systems, which already existed at the time of the Buddha, are purely yogic in that they are solely concerned with release of the soul from rebirth. All of this evidence suggests that both Buddhism and Hinduism are products of a synthesis of Vedic and yogic religion which occurred during the first millennium BCE.

Such a synthesis explains the sudden appearance of apparently non-Vedic material in the principal *Upanishads,* Hindu scriptures composed between 800 and 300 BCE. These scriptures contain the first clear expressions of many of the fundamental doctrines of classical Hinduism. These Upanishadic expressions occur in terms which attempt to harmonize the theistic concerns of the *Rig Veda* with yogic concerns regarding release of the soul from rebirth. The *Upanishads* accomplish this by emphasizing a relatively minor Vedic theme which appears in only a few late hymns of the *Rig Veda* — the question of the origin of the universe. According to these hymns, the single, ultimate source of the universe is an insoluble mystery, beyond the comprehension of humans or gods. The *Upanishads* propose to solve this mystery by dovetailing Vedic cosmology with the yogic triad of soul, rebirth and release. The Upanishadic solution is that the origin of the universe is comprehensible through yogic introspection. Such introspection, they say, reveals that the source of the universe (*brahman*) is in fact one's own innermost soul (*ātman*). In the last analysis, this doctrine implies that the universe is an illusion, a dream in which all consciousness participates. According to the *Upanishads,* just as all the objects and beings in one's dreams — even those that appear alien and repulsive — originate from one's own mind, so do all things and beings in the universe originate from the innermost source of one's consciousness, which is identical to the supreme being. Release from rebirth is construed as an awakening from this dream and a realization of one's identity with all consciousness and with the universe itself.

Though an ingenious means of harmonizing Vedic and yogic religious concerns, this Upanishadic doctrine created several conceptual problems. In the ancient Indian context, the worst problem was related to the theory of karma and rebirth. If one's innermost soul is the source of the universe, it is difficult to imagine how the soul could be reborn in that same universe. Moreover, if one is divine in one's innermost essence, one is thereby beyond the categories of good and bad, and so the theory of karma becomes nonsensical. To get around these problems, the Upanishadic sages constructed elaborate theories of various layers of the soul. According to these theories, the lower layers of the soul are reborn according to one's merit, but the upper layers remain unaffected. The topmost level of the soul is identified with ultimate reality, the source of the universe. While these theories of the layers of the soul were religious in origin, they also involved a great deal of analytical, psychological insight regarding the nature of the human mind. Much like modern Western psychologists, the Upanishadic sages attempted to identify and define various levels and aspects of the human mind. Some of their conclusions are remarkably similar to modern psychological concepts such as ego, superego, subconscious and unconscious. These Upanishadic psychological discoveries appear to have influenced the teachings of the historical Buddha, who also proposed a multi-layered theory of the mind.

The historical Buddha refused to speculate upon the origin of the universe, preferring to concentrate on gaining release from rebirth. In this sense, Buddhism belongs to the pre-Vedic, yogic tradition of India. The Buddha, however, denied the existence of the soul, a decidedly non-yogic position. Instead, he incorporated and refined the psychological insights of the Upanishadic sages and offered an analytical theory of the mind which remains remarkably valid even in the modern secular world. Again like the Upanishadic sages, the Buddha held that the attainment of release from rebirth entails realization of the ultimate nature of reality. This position too is more Upanishadic than yogic. The Buddha's notion of ultimate reality, however, was quite contrary to that of the Upanishadic sages, for the Buddha was skeptical regarding any ultimate source of the universe.

These Buddhist doctrines will be discussed further in Chapter III. The point here is to locate the Buddha in his historical and philosophical context. The foregoing material indicates that he was a critical and creative participant in a movement to synthesize the ancient, traditional worldviews that vied for the collective heart of India in his time. By the time of the Buddha, this attempt to create a coherent unity from the religious and intellectual heritages of two great peoples had become widespread and urgent. The Buddha's contribution to this transition in ancient India made him, without a doubt, the most influential historical figure of India. In the centuries following the life of the Buddha, the spread of Buddhism throughout East and Southeast Asia made him arguably the most influential historical figure of the entire Eastern world. Indeed, the Buddha was one of the most influential individuals in all human history.

Early Life of the Buddha: Birth to the Great Renunciation

In approximately 250 BCE, the Indian emperor Aśoka erected an inscribed granite pillar at the birthplace of the Buddha, a village called Lumbinī in what is today southern Nepal. Unfortunately, Aśoka's inscription does not specify how many years had passed since the Buddha's birth. As a result, the Buddha's birthplace is more certain than his birth date, which is most likely somewhere around 560 BCE. The Buddha was a member of the Śākya clan, and is often referred to as Śākyamuni, the "Sage of the Śākyas." His family name was Gotama (sometimes spelled

Gautama), and his given name is said to have been Siddhattha (Sanskrit: Siddhārtha), which means "goal-accomplished." The word "Buddha" (meaning literally "the awakened one") is a title, and it is technically improper to apply it to Siddhattha Gotama before his experience, at the age of thirty-five, of full and final enlightenment, regarded by Buddhists as the greatest achievement possible for human beings and even for gods. Before this enlightenment, the Buddha should be referred to with his given name or as "the bodhisatta" (Skt. bodhisattva), which means "Buddha to be," or literally "enlightenment-being."

The voluminous scriptures which purport to contain the teachings of the Buddha provide little credible information regarding his early life. A few passages preserved in the Pāli canon of Theravāda Buddhism, however, record plausible information concerning the early life of the Buddha. One such passage indicates that Siddhattha's father was at least minor royalty, and that the young prince lived in luxury in three different palaces, one for each of the three Indian seasons: winter, summer and monsoon (A1:145-46).[1] This same passage, corroborated by another (M1:163), also indicates that the prince was inspired to abandon this privileged life for the austere life of a wandering seeker of truth because of deep concern regarding the affliction of humankind by old age, sickness and death. Several passages indicate that Siddhattha's parents opposed his decision to become a wandering holy man and resisted it with tears and pleadings (M1:163, etc.).

There is no reason to doubt this basic scenario of the Buddha's early life: that he was a sensitive, intelligent and privileged young man who, like many in his day, rejected the comforts of the household life in favor of the rigorous but unattached life of the mendicant seeker of truth. Legends of the Buddha's life recorded in the Pāli canon and elsewhere amplify extravagantly upon this credible historical scenario. These legends add little if anything to our knowledge of the historical Buddha's life, but they are themselves important elements in the history of Buddhism. The following legendary account of the early life of the Buddha is based primarily upon the *Nidāna-kathā* of the Pāli canon, probably the earliest surviving, continuous legend of the life of the Buddha. The *Nidāna-kathā*, in turn, appears to derive primarily from two suttas (Skt. sūtra) or discourses in the Pāli canon. Both of these suttas — the "Acchariyab-bhuta-dhamma Sutta" (M3:118-24) and the "Mahāpadāna Sutta" (D2:1-54) — are of doubtful authenticity, but they reveal how early and how widespread was the tendency to mythologize the life of the Buddha. Later Mahāyāna scriptures dealing with the life of the Buddha — most notably the *Mahāvastu,* the *Lalita-vistara,* and the *Buddha-carita* — further magnify and expand upon the basic Pāli account.

Universally, Buddhist legends portray the Buddha's father Suddhodana as a mighty ruler of unimaginable wealth. During pregnancy, his
mother, the beautiful Queen Māyā, is said to have received auspicious
omens heralding the exalted status of the child she bore, most notably a
dream of a white elephant entering her abdomen when the prince was
conceived. The birth is said to have occurred not in the royal palace at
Kapilavatthu, but in a nearby park at Lumbinī, while Queen Māyā was on
a pleasure outing. This detail may well be historical fact, but accounts of
the birth itself can scarcely be accepted as history. According to these
traditional accounts, the infant prince issued miraculously from his mother's side, took three steps, and proclaimed his supremacy in all the world.
This miraculous infant, it is said, bore thirty-two major and eighty minor
marks upon his body. These marks vary in different accounts, but always
include wheel symbols on the soles and palms, a protuberance on the
crown of the head *(ushnīsha)*, and a circle of hair between the eyebrows
(ūrṇā), all of which are common features of Buddha images.

On the basis of these marks, King Suddhodana's ministers predicted
that the child was destined to supreme greatness, either as a universal
monarch — a *cakravartin* or "wheel turner" of the mythical wheel of
universal dominion — or as the spiritual savior of humankind. The ministers warned that if the child ever came in contact with human suffering,
he would be overcome with compassion and would abandon the prince-
ly life and embark single-mindedly on a quest for spiritual release, thereby becoming the savior of the world rather than its ruler. The king, of
course, wished for his son to follow in his own royal footsteps and rule
the world as its righteous monarch, and so he is said to have constructed
three magnificent palaces within which to isolate the young prince from
any contact with the sufferings of the outside world.

According to legend, Prince Siddhattha lived out his youth entirely
within the walls of these pleasure palaces. He quickly gained superhuman proficiency in all of the respected arts of the day, intellectual, military and amorous. He enjoyed a large company of adoring concubines,
and in addition, at the age of sixteen he married the most beautiful woman in the land, Princess Yasodharā, who bore him a son named Rāhula.
Throughout his youth, Prince Siddhattha was never allowed to experience or even witness disease, old age, death, or indeed any form of
suffering whatsoever. In his twenty-ninth year, however, the gods themselves conspired to bring the bodhisatta in contact with the "four great
visions" which inspired him to embark on the quest for enlightenment.
These experiences are said to have occurred when the prince contrived
to escape the palace for a pleasure outing, driven by his faithful charioteer Channa. On this surreptitious outing, he encountered for the first

time in his life the sight of an old person, a diseased person, a corpse, and finally a radiantly serene, mendicant holy person.

As predicted by the king's ministers, the first three visions preoccupied the prince with the unavoidable sufferings of 'mundane life. The fourth vision, the holy person, inspired in him the resolution to renounce material well-being and enter the austere path of spiritual enlightenment. As noted above, the Pāli suttas record the Buddha himself as indicating that contemplation of the universal misery of old age, disease and death inspired his search for truth. In order to pursue this search, Siddhattha contrived with his charioteer to flee the palace forever. The two friends escaped on the prince's faithful horse Kanthaka and traveled to the bank of a nearby river, where Siddhattha cut off his hair, changed his fine garments for rags from a rubbish heap, and set forth penniless on the path of the seeker of truth. Bearing the sad news of Siddhattha's departure, the charioteer returned to Kapilavatthu on foot, for the prince's faithful horse had died of a broken heart.

From the Great Renunciation onward, one can begin to speak of the Buddha as a real historical personage. The Pāli suttas do not specifically seek to give a connected account of the Buddha's life, and they clearly contain much exaggeration. Nonetheless, they include a surprising amount of material which appears to capture actual historical events and people in remarkable detail for literature of such an early age. These suttas reveal that when the bodhisatta Siddhattha set out on the open road he entered a rich and stimulating subculture of spiritual aspirants. This subculture included naked and rag-draped ascetics wandering the countryside alone or in groups, seeking or claiming to have found ultimate truth. Some of these were quite mad, while others were members of the foremost families of the day. Some, like the Jains and Ājīvakas, represented the ancient, indigenous yogic religion of India. Others, like the Upanishadic sages, were respected albeit renegade members of the orthodox priestly establishment of the Indo-Europeans. Though living off alms and the fruits and nuts of the jungle, these wandering ascetics were honored by kings while associating also with the lowest elements of society.

Even the legendary and mythological content of the Pāli suttas is revealing of the ethos of the time. Spiritual saviors were expected to emerge from the ranks of wandering, penniless ascetics. These ascetics were thought to perform miracles and consort with deities almost as a matter of course. Ultimately though, their exalted task was to discover and teach the spiritual path that leads beyond the relentless insecurity of mundane life to a realm beyond suffering and death. In this task, deities were merely assistants and well-wishers, for the spiritual salvation of humankind was widely thought to depend not upon divine intervention, but upon remarkable human beings like Siddhattha Gotama.

The Quest for Enlightenment

The Pāli canon records only words of the Buddha spoken after his realization of enlightenment. However, the Pāli suttas record him as making occasional reference to his earlier life. The following account is reconstructed from these scattered references, primarily the "Ariya-pariyesana" and "Mahā Saccaka" Suttas (M1:160-75 and 237-51). While this account cannot be historically verified, there is little reason to doubt its basic truthfulness. Notations in parentheses after the following paragraphs indicate the scriptural source of the information in each paragraph.

After Siddhattha left home, he studied meditation under two teachers, first Aḷāra Kālāma and then Uddaka Rāmaputta. Under them he mastered the uppermost meditational levels of consciousness *(jhāna)*. Buddhism retains eight of these meditational states as important spiritual exercises, but Siddhattha did not accept them as final enlightenment and release from the suffering of human existence. For Siddhattha, as for many if not most people in India at the time, final enlightenment and release entailed escape from the relentless round of birth, death and rebirth known as saṃsāra. Experience of the *jhānas,* though sublime, he regarded as still confined to the mundane world. Dissatisfied with his attainments under these two teachers, Siddhattha set out to seek enlightenment on his own. He soon attracted five followers, and with them undertook severe ascetic practices involving self-mortification and starvation. Such austerities were common among seekers of enlightenment in his day, and were intended to liberate the immortal soul from the mortal body. (M1:163-66; 171)

The following purports to be the Buddha's own description of the ascetic discipline he imposed upon himself.

> I was unclothed, indecent, licking my hands. . . . I took food only once a day, or once in two or seven days. I lived under the discipline of eating rice only at fortnightly intervals. . . . I subsisted on the roots and fruits of the forest, eating only those which fell [of their own accord]. I wore coarse hempen cloth . . . rags from a rubbish heap . . . clothes of grass and of bark. . . . I became one who stands [always] refusing to sit. . . . I made my bed on thorns. . . . The dust and dirt of years accumulated on my body. . . . I subsisted on the dung

of suckling calves. . . . So long as my own dung and urine
held out, I subsisted on that. . . . Because I ate so little, my
limbs became like the knotted joints of withered creepers, my
buttocks like a bullock's hoof, my protruding backbone like
a string of beads, my gaunt ribs like the crazy rafters of
a tumble-down shed. My eyes were sunken deep in their
sockets. . . . My scalp was shriveled. . . . The hair, rotted at
the roots, fell out if I stroked my limbs with my hand.

M1:77-80 (abridged, following PTS edition)

Many of these austerities, as extreme as they may seem, are still practiced by ascetics in India. The Pāli suttas record that after some six years
of these rigorous ordeals, the Buddha concluded that self-mortification
would not lead him to the ultimate goal of enlightenment and spiritual
liberation. In the midst of his self-inflicted torment, he is said to have
recalled that as a child he had entered spontaneously into a tranquil
meditational state later known as the first *jhāna*. Upon experiencing this
recollection, he resolved to pursue a more natural and wholesome means
of spiritual development and to practice a moderate, middle path between self-indulgence and self-mortification. Later the term "Middle Path"
would name and epitomize the entirety of Buddhist doctrine and practice. First as a prince, and then as an ascetic, the bodhisatta Siddhattha
had known the extremes of self-indulgence and self-mortification. He
now rejected both as inhibiting spiritual progress, and developed the
moderate daily routine that governs the lives of Buddhist monks to the
present day. His five companions regarded this change as backsliding,
and abandoned him in disgust. (M1:246-47)

Siddhattha then carried on alone, going on an alms round in the morning, eating one moderate meal a day before noon, and spending the
afternoon and evening in meditation, often late into the night. His
progress was swift, and before long he is said to have realized enlightenment beneath the fabled Bodhi tree ("tree of enlightenment"), a descendant of which still stands at Bodh Gaya, near Patna in the modern state of
Bihar in northern India. Interestingly, the Pāli suttas make no reference to
the Bodhi tree, although all forms of Buddhism agree in identifying the
tree of enlightenment as an Aśvattha or *Ficus religiosa*. On the night of
the Great Enlightenment, it is said that Siddhattha sat beneath the Bodhi
tree and resolved not to stand until he had attained final spiritual release.
Buddhist legend depicts the events of that night as a titanic struggle between Siddhattha's quiet resolve and the onslaughts and temptations of
Māra, the Buddhist equivalent of Satan. Siddhattha's triumph over Māra's

attack may be taken as representing mythologically the triumph of meditational discipline over the terrors and temptations of mundane existence. Māra's demon armies and seductive daughters were unable to dis-
turb Siddhattha's meditation, and when he stood in the morning, he had
realized the ultimate attainment of humans and gods: Buddhahood.

From this point, when Siddhattha was approximately thirty-five, it is
proper to speak of him as the Buddha, "the Awakened one." Those who
subsequently follow in the footsteps of the Buddha and accomplish the
same "awakening" *(bodhi)*, are known as arahats (also spelled arhat, arhant and arahant) or "deserving ones," fully enlightened followers of the
Buddha. Buddhist doctrine emphasizes that the specific content of the
Buddha's experience on the night of enlightenment — or the equivalent
experience of an arahat — can never be conveyed by mere words. Sutta
accounts say that the Buddha experienced the "three knowledges":
remembrance of his past rebirths in detail, ability to discern the past and
future rebirths of other beings, and knowledge that he himself was free of
all faults and illusions and would therefore never be reborn again. The
"third knowledge" is synonymous with the realization of nirvāṇa (P.
nibbāna — see Abbreviations). (M1:248-49)

Because of the inexpressibility of nirvāṇa and the difficulty of the path
thereto, the Buddha is said at first to have despaired of ever being able to
convey his discovery to others. Various deities are said to have intervened and encouraged him to teach the dharma ("truth," P. *dhamma)*
and "open the door of deathlessness" to gods and humankind. The gods
themselves informed him that the most capable recipients of his new
teaching, his previous teachers Aḷāra Kālāma and Uddaka Rāmaputta, had
died. The Buddha then concluded that the people best qualified to
understand his profound and subtle discovery were the five ascetics with
whom he had undergone austerities. He is said to have been able to
perceive with his miraculous "divine eye" that they were then staying at
Sarnath, near Varanasi (Benares) in the modern Indian state of Uttar
Pradesh. Having journeyed to Sarnath, the Buddha was able to overcome
the initial resistance of the five ascetics who had rejected him for
abandoning the ascetic path, and thus he gained his first followers.
(M1:168-70)

The Pāli canon preserves what purports to be a record of the words
the Buddha spoke to these first five followers at Sarnath. This, the first
discourse or sutta of the Buddha, is known as the "Turning of the Wheel
of Truth" (S5:420-24). Ironically, Prince Siddhattha had become, as his
father desired, a *cakravartin,* a "Wheel Turning Monarch," but the
wheel he had set in motion with this first discourse, rather than the
mythical, world-conquering wheel of universal monarchy, was the death-

conquering wheel of truth. For the next forty-five years — from his enlightenment at age thirty-five until his death at the age of eighty — the Buddha wandered northern India on foot, preaching his message and attracting an ever-growing band of followers.

The Buddha and his Followers

In the course of recording the sermons of the Buddha, the Pāli suttas also record incidentally a good deal of information regarding the daily life of the Buddha and his followers. Essentially, the Buddha taught a lifestyle and spiritual discipline whereby others could follow in his footsteps and realize for themselves the enlightenment and liberation he had gained under the Bodhi tree. The fundamental principle of this lifestyle and discipline is following a "middle path" between self-indulgence and self-mortification. The most devoted followers of the Buddha became monks or nuns and were expected to abstain entirely from sex, intoxicants, and all harmful, abrasive or frivolous conduct. In addition, the Buddha and his following of monks and nuns avoided all luxuries of attire, accommodation and diet. Like their teacher, the monks and nuns possessed only a robe and begging bowl, and they moved constantly from place to place lest they become attached even to such rudimentary shelter as a certain tree or cave.

These monks and nuns rose early in the morning, sometimes sitting in meditation before going on their daily alms rounds in a nearby village. They ate only one meal a day, before noon. If the opportunity arose, in the afternoon or evening they would listen to sermons by the Buddha or his foremost disciples, and then put the teachings into practice by meditating, often long into the night. In addition to monks and nuns, these afternoon and evening sermons were attended by lay followers of the Buddha, interested and sometimes hostile followers of other religious persuasions, and the merely curious. Through these sermons by the Buddha and his chief disciples, the following of this new spiritual path grew steadily in numbers.

Increasingly, the Buddha attracted wealthy and even royal followers who made lavish arrangements to host his sermons. The most colorful of these patrons was without doubt Ambapālī, reputedly the most sought after courtesan in India. Princes are said to have purchased a night with Ambapālī by paving her garden with gold coins. The support of wealthy and royal patrons no doubt further increased the Buddha's following among the rank and file. The Pāli suttas may exaggerate when they claim that audiences of up to twenty-five hundred attended some sermons, but it is not unlikely that several hundred may have gathered on some occasions to hear the person who was probably the best known religious teacher in India at the time. In spite of this fame, the Buddha and his followers maintained a simple routine of wandering about the countryside with a minimum of possessions and accepting only minimal hospitality — in the form of almsfood, robes and medicines — from their lay supporters. (D2:95-8)

During the monsoon season, this wandering lifestyle became impractical, and Buddhist monks and nuns were allowed to take continuous shelter for a period of about three months. As more followers of the Buddha joined the Saṅgha — the order of Buddhist monks and nuns — specific centers for assembling during the monsoon came to be recognized. At first these were caves and groves of trees, but as the lay following of the Buddha increased in numbers and wealth, permanent shelters for the monsoon retreats sprang up across the countryside. These were the beginnings of the first monasteries in which it is now customary for Buddhist monks and nuns to dwell permanently. During the Buddha's life and for several generations afterward, however, monks and nuns wandered the countryside alone or in small groups for most of the year. In addition to the communal retreats of the monsoon season, monks and nuns were expected to gather fortnightly on the *uposatha* days of the new and full moon in order to hear confessions and punish lapses of discipline. The worst offenders were expelled from the order, but most lapses required only a public apology. As the number of rules governing the Saṅgha increased, the practice developed of reciting the code of monastic conduct at the conclusion of the *uposatha* ceremonies. These communal recitations were the beginning of an oral tradition that endures to the present day.

During these monsoon and *uposatha* gatherings, novices had an opportunity to gain instruction in the teachings of the Buddha from their elders, and a recognized canon of teachings attributed to the Buddha and his foremost disciples began to form. These recognized teachings were eventually recorded in collections of scripture known as the Sutta Piṭaka, which contains the sermons of the Buddha and his foremost disciples, and the Vinaya Piṭaka, which contains the rules governing the Saṅgha. At the time of the historical Buddha, however, writing was virtually unknown in India, so that his teachings could be preserved only through memorization by his followers. These teachings were transmitted orally for some five hundred years, until they were written down in Sri Lanka at the beginning of the common era, i.e. at about the time of Jesus. The resulting corpus of literature, known as the Pāli canon, is the scriptural basis of Theravāda Buddhism.

Five hundred years, of course, is a long time to maintain an oral tradition. This raises doubts as to the accuracy of the Pāli canon. Such doubts concerning the Sutta Piṭaka are crucial, in that this purports to be the repository of the doctrines taught by the historical Buddha. On the positive side, the literary form of the Pāli suttas suggests that they are indeed a record of an oral tradition. There is a great deal of repetition from one sutta to another, not only in terms of the doctrines expressed, but also in terms of extensive verbatim repetition of much material. Individual suttas, moreover, often have a repetitive, easy to memorize structure — like songs with choruses. This suggests that the Sutta Piṭaka is a sincere attempt to record memorized versions of individual sermons rather than an edited compilation of doctrine. Individual suttas usually identify the location at which the sutta was preached. They always identify the speaker of the sermon — who is sometimes not the Buddha but one of his chief disciples — and they often provide details about the audience and the circumstances surrounding the discourse. Though the Pāli suttas obviously exaggerate and mythologize the qualities and deeds of the Buddha, they have every appearance of constituting for the most part a faithful and reasonably accurate record of his teachings.

Despite this immediate appearance of reliability, doubts regarding the historical accuracy of the teachings preserved in the Pāli suttas have been raised by modern Western scholars of Buddhism, most notably Edward Conze.[2] These scholars correctly point out that in addition to the Pāli suttas of Theravāda Buddhism, other quite different accounts of teachings ascribed to the Buddha survive and form the basis of Mahāyāna Buddhism. They point out too that none of the literature purporting to contain the authentic teachings of the Buddha was actually written down before the beginning of the common era, approximately five hundred years after the death of the Buddha. Because of such considerations, it will probably remain forever impossible to determine with historical certainty the precise content of the Buddha's original teachings. The following chapter, however, considers the schism of Buddhism into the Theravāda and Mahāyāna and the available evidence bearing upon their respective claims to preserve accurately the teachings of the historical Buddha. On the basis of this evidence, it is possible to provide in Chapter III a reasonably confident account of at least the broad outlines of the original teachings of the historical Buddha.

CHAPTER II

The Death of the Buddha
and
Schism in the Sangha

For the duration of the Buddha's life, his supreme authority within the Saṅgha prevented any serious doctrinal or procedural disagreements among his followers. The "Mahā Parinibbāna Sutta" or "Sutta of the Great Decease" (D2:72-167) indicates that such disagreements began to develop almost immediately after the Buddha died, in about 480 BCE. The "Mahā Parinibbāna Sutta" is not a historical document, but it survives in several reasonably consistent versions. The following plausible historical outline of the last days of the Buddha is based on the Pāli version of the sutta.

According to the Pāli sutta, the Buddha spent the last rainy season of his life at Beluva, a small village near the city of Vesālī, in the modern state of Bihar. Eighty years old at the time, he became gravely ill but recovered through a determination to take leave of the Saṅgha before dying his final death. Shortly after emerging from the monsoon retreat, however, the Buddha contracted food poisoning and died in a grove of trees near the city of Kusinārā (Skt. Kuśinagara), without having had an opportunity to address the assembled Saṅgha. The "Mahā Parinibbāna Sutta" fleshes out and clothes this historical skeleton with a fabric of supernatural events and hyperbole. Trees bloom out of season and shower the dying Buddha with flowers. Muddy water becomes clear for him to drink. The kings of the gods vie with one another in uttering hymns of praise to the Exalted One. The Buddha announces that if he had so desired he could have chosen to live on until the end of the eon and gives instructions for a cremation befitting a king of kings. The earth quakes and thunder rolls through the sky as the Buddha utters his last words:

All things are impermanent. Work out your own salvation with diligence.

D2:156

The First Buddhist Council

According to universal Buddhist tradition, shortly after the Buddha's death an authoritative gathering of monks was convened by the senior monk Mahā Kassapa in order to establish agreement concerning the content of the Buddha's teachings. Most sources agree that this gathering, known as the First Council, was held at Rājagaha, a village in the modern state of Bihar, and was attended by 500 arahats, enlightened followers of the Buddha. The traditions of all schools of Buddhism agree that at this gathering two collections of teachings, the Sūtra (P. Sutta) and Vinaya Piṭakas, were recited and standardized. [Because the scriptures of some schools of early Buddhism were recorded in Sanskrit rather than Pāli, it is conventional to use Sanskrit rather than Pāli terminology — for example "sūtra" rather than "sutta" — when referring generally to all or several schools of early Buddhism.] In addition to agreeing that the Sūtra and Vinaya Piṭakas were finalized at the First Council, all of the early schools of Buddhism included in their Sūtra Piṭakas discourses of doctrinal significance and in their Vinaya Piṭakas rules for monks and nuns. Different schools, however, included variant material in their respective versions of the Sūtra and Vinaya Piṭakas. Moreover, accounts of the First Council vary in details from school to school. For these reasons, the historicity of the First Council is debated by modern scholars, and will probably remain in doubt forever. In the course of such debate, however, it must be remembered that members of the Saṅgha were accustomed to gathering on a fortnightly and yearly schedule, and that the death of the Buddha would have provided occasion for a special convocation. Whether there was any single assembly as large or as authoritative as the First Council is not as important historically as the point that soon after the death of the Buddha, if not already within his lifetime, a corpus of his teachings regarded as authentic began to take shape.

The *Cullavagga* of the Theravāda Vinaya Piṭaka contains in chapters 11 and 12 the best known and most frequently cited account of the First Council and of a Second Council which occurred a hundred years later. The surviving Vinayas of five other schools of early Buddhism provide varying details for these councils, but all agree that some such gatherings occurred. According to the *Cullavagga* and most of the other Vinayas, at the First Council the entire Vinaya Piṭaka was recited from memory by the monk Upāli, and the entire Sūtra Piṭaka by Ānanda, the Buddha's constant attendant. The existing Pāli Sutta Piṭaka contains about twenty-five volumes, and the Vinaya Piṭaka contains five large volumes. Such prodigious feats of memory are difficult to believe, but one should not be overly skeptical. In the first place, these collections were no doubt smaller at the time of the First Council, as indeed some of the Vinaya accounts of the First Council suggest. In addition, it is possible that Ānanda and Upāli actually presided over a recitation to which several monks contributed. Writing was virtually unknown in India at the time, and knowledge had to be passed on orally from one generation to the next. Even after the advent of writing, oral transmission and memorization of scripture remained sacred activities. As a result, even in modern India one encounters people who can recite entire volumes of scripture from memory.

It is significant that the *Cullavagga* account of the First Council does not mention at all the Abhidhamma (Skt. Abhidharma) Piṭaka, a third collection of scripture containing seven books in about a dozen large volumes of highly abstruse philosophical and psychological material. Some of the other schools of early Buddhism do mention the Abhidharma Piṭaka in their accounts of the First Council. This implies two things: 1) the lateness of the Abhidharma Piṭaka, and 2) the basic truthfulness of the *Cullavagga* narrative. Orthodox Theravāda Buddhism, like most other forms of Buddhism, holds that the Abhidharma Piṭaka is the word of the historical Buddha. Nonetheless, omission of any mention of the Abhidharma Piṭaka in the Theravādin account of the first two councils implies that the Abhidhamma Piṭaka was unknown for at least a century after the death of the Buddha. At any point in the hundreds of years of oral and written transmission of the *Cullavagga,* insertion of a mere sentence — stating that the Abhidharma Piṭaka had been recited at the First and Second Councils — would have sufficed to validate the orthodox Theravādin position. The fact that the oral transmitters and the compilers of the written *Cullavagga* did not insert such a sentence indicates that they were remarkably reliable historians for such an ancient age.

The Second Council and the Mahāsaṅghika Schism

According to most sources, about a century after the death of the Buddha a Second Council, held in the city of Vesālī, resulted in a schism between the Sthaviravāda — in Pāli the Theravāda, the "School of Elders" — and the Mahāyāna, the "Great Vehicle." Since the Second Council was the occasion of a schism, it is not surprising that the historical details of the Second Council vary in different sources. Some such event probably occurred in about 350 BCE, but further details may never be confirmed. The six surviving Vinayas representing early schools of Buddhism give conflicting accounts of the Second Council, and the situation is further complicated by Mahāyāna versions of the event. All accounts must be suspected of sectarian bias.

The major disparity between the Theravāda and Mahāyāna accounts of the Second Council concerns the circumstances that made the convening of a council necessary. According to the Theravāda version, the Elders Yasa and Revata called for the assembly because many monks had become lax concerning ten points of discipline. The most important of the alleged lapses were accepting money in lieu of almsfood, eating after noon, and following improper procedures at meetings. According to Mahāyāna accounts, a monk named Mahādeva initiated the Second Council by raising five criticisms against the supposedly enlightened arahats who dominated the Saṅgha at that time. According to the Mahāyāna accounts, Mahādeva's criticisms of those who claimed to be arahats were that they 1) had not fully conquered passion because they still had wet dreams, 2) were not omniscient because they often had to ask for directions, etc., 3) were still subject to doubts, and 4) had gained their knowledge through others rather than through their own experience. The fifth point is obscure, but seems to have to do with making verbal exclamations during meditation. The reasons for the calling of the Second Council will probably remain forever doubtful, if indeed there was one rather than several councils. At any rate, most accounts agree that about a hundred years after the death of the Buddha a large group of monks — known as the Mahāsaṅghika or "majority group" — rejected the authority of the Elders, and that as a result a major schism in Buddhism occurred.

The Mahāsaṅghikas are generally acknowledged as the forerunners of Mahāyāna Buddhism. The Elders — the Sthaviras or Theras — came to be called the Sthaviravāda or the Theravāda. Sthaviravāda in Sanskrit and Theravāda in Pāli mean exactly the same thing — "Doctrine of the Elders." Conventionally, however, Sthaviravāda is the term used to refer to the very archaic school. This ancient school spawned several different schools — traditionally seventeen in addition to the Mahāsaṅghikas — before emerging finally as the Theravāda, the sole surviving school of the Elders. The degree to which the Theravāda resembles the ancient Sthaviravāda is an issue of considerable scholarly disagreement.

Before dealing with this issue, a further clarification of terminology is necessary. Mahāyānists typically refer to the seventeen ancient schools of non-Mahāyāna Buddhism with the derogatory term "Hīnayāna," which means "small, inferior vehicle" as opposed to Mahāyāna, which means "great, glorious vehicle" As a collective term for non-Mahāyāna Buddhism, the term Hīnayāna can be convenient, but it should never be used as a synonym for Theravāda. This terminology, though common, is both offensive and inaccurate. Alternatives to the term Hīnayāna are "Nikāya Buddhism" or "Āgama Buddhism," which name the non-Mahāyāna schools after groupings of scripture that they all employed — the Nikāyas or Āgamas. Since no living Buddhists consider surviving Āgamas to be authoritative, this book employs the term "Nikāya Buddhism" instead of the derogatory term Hīnayāna.

Most of the disagreements among the seventeen schools of Nikāya Buddhism appear minor in retrospect, and in most cases are hopelessly obscure.[3] Differences among the schools of Nikāya Buddhism are certainly insignificant compared to the divergence of Mahāyāna Buddhism from all of them. The initial rift represented by the Mahāsaṅghika schism widened into a chasm separating traditions of scripture and formulations of doctrine so divergent that one can scarcely imagine they originated with the same historical person. No one denies responsibly that a historical Buddha existed, but a widespread skepticism among scholars of Buddhism casts doubt upon the possibility of discovering even the broad outlines of his original teachings.

The most viable means of moving toward resolution of this uncertainty is comparison of the surviving scriptures of the various early schools of Buddhism. When scriptural material is preserved in two or more independent traditions, one may reasonably conclude that the agreeing material predates the parting of the traditions in question. Such circumstantial evidence does not constitute definite proof, but it is probably the best available starting point for establishing a chronology of the development of early Buddhism. Unfortunately, the only entire canon of early Buddhism which survives is the Pāli canon of the Theravāda. Fortunately, the surviving portions of the scriptures of other schools of Nikāya Buddhism — which exist in Chinese translations — together make up an entire canon, more or less. Comparison of these two corpuses is a first step toward clarification of the nature of original Buddhism. It also provides an occasion to introduce the surviving literature of Nikāya or Āgama Buddhism.

The Scriptures of Nikāya Buddhism

Other than the Pāli canon of the Theravāda, the only extensive literature to survive from any of the schools of Nikāya Buddhism is the Sarvāstivāda canon, which is preserved almost in its entirety in Chinese translations. Those texts which are missing from the Chinese Sarvāstivāda canon can usually be found in Chinese translations of texts from other schools. In general, Chinese translations of the Sarvāstivāda scriptures are in reasonably good agreement with their Theravāda counterparts. This agreement establishes a common tradition regarding the teachings of the

Buddha going back to approximately 250 BCE, when the Sarvāstivāda split from the Sthaviravāda, the ancient school of Elders represented now by the Theravāda. The following, more detailed comparison of the Sarvāstivāda and Theravāda canons illustrates the extent of this agreement and provides an outline of the basic scriptures of Nikāya or Āgama Buddhism.

As discussed above, the Theravāda scriptures are organized into three major sections known as "collections" or *piṭakas.* These are the Vinaya, Sutta and Abhidhamma Piṭakas. Together they comprise the Tipiṭaka (Skt. Tripiṭaka) or "Three Collections." The Vinaya Piṭaka, containing the rules of monastic discipline, is further subdivided into three sections: the *Sutta Vibhaṅga,* the *Khandhaka,* and the *Parivāra.* The *Sutta Vibhaṅga* contains the *pāṭimokkha* rules governing the Saṅgha. Each of the 227 rules for monks and 311 rules for nuns is accompanied by a commentary explaining the rule, a story which purports to describe the circumstance which made the rule necessary, and cases in which the rule was judged to apply or not to apply. These stories and cases provide delightful glimpses of day-to-day life in ancient India. The *Khandhaka* section of the Vinaya is devoted to procedural rules for the conduct of the affairs of the Saṅgha. The *Khandhaka* is further divided into the *Mahāvagga* and the *Cullavagga,* the latter of which contains accounts of the First and Second Councils discussed above. Finally, there is a supplement to the Theravādin Vinaya Piṭaka known as the *Parivāra.* In addition to the Theravāda Vinaya, the Vinayas of the Sarvāstivāda and four other early schools are preserved in Chinese and Tibetan translations. These vary in arrangement and details, particularly in the procedural sections (*Skandhaka* in Sanskrit) and in their supplements. The actual rules governing the monks and nuns, however, are remarkably consistent.

From the standpoint of early Buddhist doctrine, by far the most important section of the Tripiṭaka is the Sūtra Piṭaka, which contains the sermons of the Buddha and his foremost disciples. In the Theravāda canon, these discourses are divided into five groups known as Nikāyas. These are the *Dīgha,* the *Majjhima, Saṃyutta, Aṅguttara,* and *Khuddaka Nikāyas.* The *Dīgha Nikāya* or "Long Group" contains the longest sermons. The *Majjhima Nikāya* or "Middle-length Group" contains the shorter discourses. The *Saṃyutta Nikāya* or "Connected Group" contains short discourses arranged according to their subject, and the *Aṅguttara Nikāya* or "Numerical Group" contains material grouped according to the number of items discussed. The *Saṃyutta* and *Aṅguttara Nikāyas* appear to be derivative, mnemonic rearrangements of material found in the *Majjhima* and *Dīgha Nikāyas.* Finally, there is the *Khuddaka Nikāya,* or "Minor Group," containing miscellaneous material.

The first four Theravādin Nikāyas correspond to similar groupings known as Āgamas in the other schools of Nikāya Buddhism. The actual content of the *Dīgha* and *Majjhima Nikāyas* in Pāli agrees relatively well with that of the corresponding Āgamas of the Chinese canon. This agreement is particularly important in the case of the Middle-length groups — the *Majjhima Nikāya* and the *Madhyama Āgama* — because the latter is a Sarvāstivāda Āgama. As noted above, agreement between Theravāda and Sarvāstivāda scriptures suggests a common scriptural tradition predating the first schism of Nikāya Buddhism in about 250 BCE.[4] The Pāli *Saṃyutta* and *Aṅguttara Nikāyas* are less similar to their Chinese counterparts, as might be expected given that these Nikāyas or Āgamas appear to have been later compilations derived from the "Long" and "Middle-length" discourses. Such compilations may themselves have been the beginnings of sectarian divisions in Buddhism.

The Theravādin *Khuddaka Nikāya* or "Minor Group" is comprised of several miscellaneous works — some short, some long, some purporting to be the word of the Buddha, some composed by disciples, some very early, and some relatively late. Though labeled "minor," this group of texts contains some of the most revered scriptures of Theravāda Buddhism. The Chinese canon also contains a fifth section of miscellaneous material translated from Sanskrit scriptures representing several schools of Nikāya Buddhism. This section is not called an Āgama, but is known instead as the *Avadāna*. As might be expected, the material in the *Avadāna* does not correspond well to material in the Theravādin *Khuddaka Nikāya*.

The third section of the Theravāda canon, the Abhidhamma Piṭaka (Skt. Abhidharma), also has a Sarvāstivādin counterpart, but aside from a general similarity of the ideas expressed, the actual content of the two corpuses is dissimilar. Both contain seven books, but the Theravādins ascribe their composition to the Buddha himself, whereas the Sarvāstivādins ascribe them to seven different disciples of the Buddha. In both cases, it is clear that the Abhidharma represents a scholastic development within Buddhism quite some time after the death of the Buddha. In fact, the content and interpretation of Abhidharma material seems to have been the primary basis of disagreement among the various schools of Nikāya Buddhism.

The foregoing comparisons of the Pāli and Chinese versions of the canon of Nikāya Buddhism suggest distinct stages in the development of the oral tradition of early Buddhism. The *Saṃyutta* and *Aṅguttara Nikāyas* and the corresponding *Āgamas* appear to record early attempts to organize doctrine in a systematic form. This may indicate that these Nikāyas were something of an innovation, albeit a very conservative innovation, involving rearrangement rather than alteration of the core teachings contained in the *Dīgha* and *Majjhima Nikāyas*, the basic collections of long and middle-length discourses. It is almost certain that parts of the Theravāda *Khuddaka Nikāya*, the Chinese *Avadāna* and the Abhidharma Piṭaka as a whole, represent doctrinal developments in Theravāda and Sarvāstivāda Buddhism beyond what the historical Buddha taught.

The next stage in this development is recorded extensively only in the Theravāda tradition in a large number of commentaries and sub-commentaries which offer detailed, word-by-word explanations of the texts of the Tipiṭaka. It should be noted, though, that the Sarvāstivāda Abhidharma seems to have played partly the role of a commentary upon earlier scriptures. The Theravādin commentaries were composed originally in the indigenous Sinhalese language of Sri Lanka. For the most part, these commentaries were probably written works composed after the Pāli canon itself had been written down, near the beginning of the common era. They were translated into Pāli by the great scholar Buddhaghosa in the fifth century CE. These commentaries confine themselves to expounding the texts of the Tipiṭaka, but in so doing they interpret, extrapolate, systematize, and thereby modify the doctrines found in the Theravāda suttas and Abhidhamma Piṭaka. Buddhaghosa's great manual, the *Visuddhimagga* or *Path of Purity*, provides an admirable summary of the commentarial tradition in Theravāda Buddhism. This tradition — which is based upon the Pāli commentaries as compiled and systematized by Buddhaghosa — represents a marked development beyond the ancient doctrines expressed in the Sutta Piṭaka. This specific interpretation of the Pāli scriptures is the doctrinal basis of modern Theravāda Buddhism.

The Mahāyāna canons, by contrast, exhibit no such tendency to categorize scriptures and thereby to isolate doctrinal innovations. On the face of it, early doctrinal developments in Mahāyāna Buddhism are incorporated into the sūtras themselves. Parts of some Mahāyāna sūtras appear to be very old, but these are augmented with material that appears to represent doctrinal development and innovation. The conservative Theravādins appear to have been reasonably careful, though perhaps not absolutely scrupulous, in separating new or doubtful material from their most ancient texts. This isolation appears to have occurred first in the *Khuddaka Nikāya*, then in the Abhidhamma Piṭaka, and finally in the commentarial literature. The Sarvāstivādins apparently did the same, but the only commentarial literature surviving from this school — other than the commentarial content of their Abhidharma Piṭaka — relates to Vinaya and Abhidharma texts. Later on, starting with the great scholar Nagārjuna in the second century CE, the Mahāyāna also developed an extensive commentarial literature, but in the early period of their development they appear to have been content to incorporate new ideas and interpretations into the sūtras themselves.

The Question of Original Buddhism

The evidence considered thus far suggests that the *Majjhima* and *Dīgha Nikāyas* of the Pāli canon and the corresponding Āgamas of the Chinese canon contain the most reliable surviving records of the teachings of the historical Buddha. General agreement between these independent records representing rival schools confirms that the basic doctrines of Nikāya Buddhism were in place by the time of Aśoka, about 250 BCE, when the Sthaviravāda (P. Theravāda) and Sarvāstivāda schools separated. Even though these two schools disagreed upon the interpretation of the Buddha's words, they agreed substantially upon the words themselves. No such independent corroboration is available for Mahāyāna scriptures at such an early date. By and large, the Mahāyāna scriptures exhibit almost no direct similarity to the scriptures of Nikāya Buddhism, and there appear to have been no early, rival schools of Mahāyāna Buddhism whose scriptures might be compared. However, by 250 BCE — the date established through comparison of Theravāda and Sarvāstivāda texts — about a century had passed since the Mahāsaṅghika schism that gave rise to the Mahāyāna. It is possible that during this century Nikāya Buddhism as a whole had drifted as far as Mahāyāna Buddhism from the teachings of the historical Buddha. Some scholars of Buddhism maintain precisely this position, but several considerations suggest otherwise.

On the surface, the form and content of Mahāyāna literature suggest that it is later in origin than the scriptures of Nikāya Buddhism. The Pāli suttas and their Chinese counterparts are formulaic and repetitive, like songs with choruses — relatively easy to memorize, pleasant to hear, but somewhat tedious to read. They appear to be the end product of a pre-literate, oral tradition. Mahāyāna scriptures are more literary in form. They appear to be the products of a literate age in which works were composed and transmitted in writing. Many Mahāyāna sūtras contain complex narratives and elaborate descriptive passages which would have been extremely difficult to memorize and pass on orally.

The content of Mahāyāna sūtras also suggests that they are later in origin than the Pāli suttas and their Sarvāstivādin counterparts. On the one hand, some Mahāyāna scriptures contain sophisticated philosophical concepts that appear to have developed out of earlier ideas found in the Pāli suttas. On the other hand, Mahāyāna sūtras in general exhibit a great deal of highly fanciful mythological content. The Pāli suttas also contain myth and miracle, but the Mahāyāna sūtras are extravagant in this regard. In particular, the process of divinizing the Buddha, begun in the Pāli suttas, is dramatically advanced in the Mahāyāna sūtras. Many of the Mahāyāna sūtras, for example, claim to have been delivered to the gods in various heavens, tacit admissions that they do not record historical events.

Nonetheless, most Mahāyānists believe sincerely that their sūtras do record accurately the teaching of the historical Buddha. Most Mahāyānists do not deny that the Theravāda suttas were also taught by the Buddha, but they assert that these were inferior teachings for those with inferior intelligence. Mahāyānists typically assert that their own scriptures contain teachings which had been reserved for the spiritual elite among the Buddha's followers. With all due respect, this does not seem likely. Moreover, the agreement throughout Mahāyāna Buddhism that the historical Buddha did indeed deliver the teachings preserved by Nikāya Buddhism is a clear recognition that Nikāya Buddhism's scriptures are reasonably accurate accounts.

In a few instances, this rudimentary corroboration may be enhanced by direct comparison of Mahāyāna scriptures with those of Nikāya Buddhism. In most cases, such comparisons are fruitless because surviving scriptures of the two major branches of Buddhism are so dissimilar. A few Mahāyāna sūtras surviving in Tibetan and Chinese, however, do yield fruitful comparisons. Most notable among these is the *Śālistamba* or "Stalk of Rice" Sūtra.[5] This text appears to have been an important Mahāyāna sūtra in its day, for it is extensively quoted in several important Mahāyāna commentarial texts that actually survive in Sanskrit. By matching these quotations against the Tibetan and Chinese translations one can reconstruct reliably approximately ninety percent of the original Sanskrit text of the sūtra.

Though the *Śālistamba Sūtra* is a Mahāyāna scripture, it bears much general similarity to Theravāda suttas and contains numerous passages directly paralleled in the Pāli texts. The *Śālistamba Sūtra* is only about twenty pages long, and its scope is limited to elucidating a particular Buddhist doctrine of causation. Nonetheless, its general agreement with the doctrines of Nikāya Buddhism, enhanced by several directly parallel passages, suggests that Mahāyāna doctrine and literature diverged gradually from an original corpus that was similar to the Long and Middle-length collections of the Theravāda and Sarvāstivāda canons. This evidence does not establish the historical accuracy of the Theravāda and Sarvāstivāda collections as a whole. It does, however, constitute corroboration that several fundamental doctrines were universally accepted as part of the teaching of the historical Buddha before the Mahāsaṅghika schism. Most estimates, ancient and modern, place this event about a hundred years after the death of the historical Buddha.

The following chapter considers in some detail the nature of the teachings that can be verified as very early on the basis of comparison of the *Śālistamba Sūtra* with Theravāda material in the Pāli canon. For now, it is sufficient to note that there is considerable evidence suggesting that the Long and Middle-length collections (*Majjhima* and *Dīgha Nikāyas*) of the Theravāda canon contain a reasonably accurate record — in an original language probably spoken by the historical Buddha — of the basic doctrines of very early Buddhism. These collections may contain embellishments, but there is no compelling reason to doubt that their basic doctrines were taught by the Buddha himself.

The Rise of Mahāyāna Buddhism in India

Starting in the reign of the emperor Aśoka in approximately 250 BCE, the development of Buddhism becomes clearer, as does the history of India as a whole. Only from the time of Aśoka, who ascended the throne of India in about 270 BCE, can one begin to speak of India as a political entity, for it is he who conquered and united for the first time a large part of the landmass that constitutes present-day India. Before Aśoka's time, the Indian subcontinent was divided into numerous small kingdoms. Aśoka subdued these kingdoms in a ruthless and bloody campaign, but once he had become the undisputed emperor of all India, he became one of the most benevolent and progressive monarchs of history. Buddhists assert that this transformation from ruthless warmonger to benign lover of peace was due to Aśoka's conversion to Buddhism. Be that as it may, it is clear that the emperor chose Buddhism as the religion with which to unify his realm ideologically. It is also clear that he ruled wisely by promoting peace, harmony, and justice in the name of Buddhism, while decreeing tolerance toward all religions.

In addition to unifying India under a benign and progressive regime, Aśoka also reintroduced the art of writing on a wide scale after more than a millennium of illiteracy in India. He left a legacy of scores of high-minded edicts carved into rocks and on great granite pillars erected throughout his empire. These edicts are the first surviving examples of writing in India after the still undeciphered Indus Valley writings which came to a halt in about 1500 BCE. Aśoka's edicts are thus the earliest decipherable written source of Indian history. The Aśokan edicts do not mention any specific sectarian divisions within Buddhism, though they do frequently encourage unity within the Saṅgha and express concern over schism. They mention a few Buddhist texts by name, but none of these can be identified confidently with a specific school of Buddhism. The edicts also mention Buddhist missions sent to lands beyond Aśoka's realm. At least one of these, the mission to Sri Lanka, certainly appears to have been Theravādin, for Sri Lanka continued to be the bastion of Theravāda Buddhism long after the Mahāyāna had become dominant in India.

A Third Buddhist Council, supposed to have been convened under the auspices of Aśoka, is recorded in Theravāda sources written in Sri Lanka. These chronicles, the *Mahāvaṃsa* and the *Dīpavaṃsa,* were compiled in the fourth and fifth centuries of the common era. Being Theravādin, they regard the Third Council as validating once again the conservative teaching of the Elders (Sthaviras or Theras), the forebears of Theravāda Buddhism. Mahāyāna sources do not mention a Buddhist council under Aśoka, nor does the Theravādin *Cullavagga*, further indication that the text of the *Cullavagga* was frozen before the time of Aśoka and not subject to sectarian corruption thereafter. At any rate, it is not unlikely that Aśoka would have convened an authoritative Buddhist council in order to standardize the state religion of his empire.

Whether or not Aśoka initiated a Third Council, most indications are that he favored the conservative school of Elders. The most persuasive evidence is that the mission he sent to Sri Lanka established Theravāda Buddhism firmly on the island. Nonetheless, despite Aśoka's apparent Theravādin orientation, it was he who established the environment that would result eventually in the ascendancy of Mahāyāna Buddhism in India. Aśoka transformed Buddhism overnight from one of the many non-Vedic sects in India into a mass religion, the state religion of one of the greatest empires on earth. In addition, he inaugurated one of the greatest ages of religious freedom and free thinking that the world has ever seen. The pressure for doctrinal development, innovation, and popularization was much greater in the cosmopolitan environment of post-Aśokan India than in the relative isolation in which Theravāda Buddhism thrived on the island of Sri Lanka. As noted above, the Mahāyānists tended to incorporate doctrinal developments into their sūtra literature. As a result, the Mahāyāna sūtras eventually came to contain an exposition of Buddhism that is scarcely recognizable from the Theravāda point of view. In addition to creating new scriptures purporting to be the word of the Buddha, Mahāyānists developed new and divergent doctrines on the basis of these scriptures. In particular, they introduced supernatural savior figures into the originally self-reliant religion of the historical Buddha. All of these innovations may be regarded as parts of a program to transform Buddhism into a religion readily accessible to a mass following such as it enjoyed after the conversion of the emperor Aśoka.

CHAPTER III

The Teachings of
the Historical Buddha

As much of the foregoing material indicates, the content of the historical Buddha's teachings is a matter in dispute among both Buddhists and
scholars of Buddhism. To summarize briefly, the issues in this dispute are
as follows. At present there are two major branches of Buddhism, the
Theravāda and the Mahāyāna, both of which claim to record accurately
the teachings of the historical Buddha. Neither branch actually committed
to writing any record of the Buddha's teachings until approximately five
hundred years after his death. From a historian's point of view it is clear
that the Mahāyāna scriptures are highly embellished accounts of historical
events, if indeed they record historical events at all. The Theravāda scriptures appear to be less embellished, but this in itself does not prove that
the Theravāda scriptures are more accurate than their Mahāyāna counterparts as a record of the teachings of the historical Buddha. General agreement between Theravāda and Sarvāstivāda scriptures indicates that in
about 250 BCE Nikāya Buddhists agreed concerning most of the content
of the Long and Middle-length discourses of the Buddha. Though early,
250 BCE is still about two centuries after the death of the Buddha. Moreover, a consensus among Nikāya Buddhists concerning the content of the
Buddha's teachings still does not account for the different versions of
these teachings preserved by the Mahāyāna. Since Mahāyāna Buddhism
developed from the Mahāsaṅghika schism of approximately 350 BCE,
agreement between Mahāyāna sūtras and those of Nikāya Buddhism
would indicate material which probably predates that schism. By and
large, such corroboration is impossible because the Mahāyāna scriptures
differ so radically from the scriptures of Nikāya Buddhism. This radical
difference between the scriptures of the two major branches of Buddhism
has led some modern scholars to conclude that the actual teachings of the
historical Buddha have been lost forever.[6]

At least one text, however, the *Śālistamba Sūtra* noted in Chapter II,
provides a starting point for reaching reasoned historical conclusions
concerning very early Buddhist doctrine. The *Śālistamba's* status as an
authoritative Mahāyāna sūtra is attested by the fact that it is quoted extensively in several of the most important commentarial works of Mahāyāna
Buddhism.[7] Because these commentarial works survive in Sanskrit, it is

possible to make direct comparisons, in the original languages, between parts of the *Śālistamba Sūtra* and suttas of the Pāli canon. When this is done, it becomes clear that much material in the *Śālistamba Sūtra* is remarkably similar to material found in Theravāda texts and in Nikāya Buddhism in general. In the case of the Pāli canon, which survives in its original language, even direct parallels in wording can be established. This substantial agreement between a Mahāyāna sūtra and scriptural material of Nikāya Buddhism constitutes evidence that certain fundamental doctrines of Nikāya Buddhism date back to at least 350 BCE, to within a hundred years of the historical Buddha himself. These doctrines are no longer prominent in classical Mahāyāna Buddhism, but apparently they were prominent in early Mahāyāna Buddhism. The *Śālistamba Sūtra* appears to represent a period in the development of Buddhist literature before the Mahāyāna and Nikāya accounts of the historical Buddha's teachings had diverged significantly. Moreover, the *Śālistamba Sūtra* reads more like a Theravāda or Sarvāstivāda text than like a Mahāyāna text. This suggests that Mahāyāna scriptures developed over the centuries from early texts which were similar to those of Nikāya Buddhism. This in turn suggests that a critical reading of the Long and Middle-length discourses of the Pāli canon — corroborated where possible by independent traditions — is our best source of knowledge concerning original Buddhism.

The following outline of the probable teachings of the historical Buddha attempts to maintain such a critical reading without losing sight of its primary purpose: to be informative to the general reader. This discussion takes corroboration between the *Śālistamba Sūtra* and the Long and Middle-length collections of the Pāli canon as its starting point. Given this starting point based on direct evidence, it becomes clearer that even though the doctrines of classical Mahāyāna Buddhism differ significantly from those of the Theravāda, these two major branches of Buddhism actually agree concerning much that is fundamental to all Buddhism. Where the Mahāyāna and the Theravāda agree, there is little reason to doubt that we are dealing with the original teachings of the Buddha. The following discussion also considers evidence provided by the *Upanishads*— early Hindu texts roughly contemporary with the Buddha — as well as doctrines of the Jains and Ājīvakas, yogic sects which predate Buddhism. Where Buddhist doctrines are similar to Upanishadic teachings or the doctrines of the Jains and Ājīvakas, there is additional reason to regard them as genuinely ancient. Where such similarities occur, one may reasonably conclude that one is dealing with ideas that were common in India at the time of the historical Buddha, and therefore likely to have been employed by the Buddha.

Having applied these criteria, the following treatment attempts to present a coherent framework of doctrine that convincingly prefigures the remarkable diversity of subsequent Buddhist thought. This treatment is certainly deficient, in that arguably original teachings have been omitted for lack of specific evidence. Other arguably original teachings have been omitted because they are tangential, and their inclusion would not advance the purpose of the present historical account. This purpose, once again, is to relate the development of Buddhism in all its diversity as a coherent historical phenomenon deriving intelligibly from the teachings of its founder.

Philosophical Teachings

The *Śālistamba Sūtra* is a straightforward treatment of a twelvefold formula known as "conditioned arising" *(pratītyasamutpāda)*. This formula, a theory of cause and effect, will be considered later in this chapter. At this point, it is sufficient to note that the *Śālistamba's* treatment of conditioned arising would be somewhat surprising to an orthodox Theravādin at a few points, but nowhere objectionable. Though not prominent in Mahāyāna Buddhism, the twelvefold formula of conditioned arising is central in Nikāya Buddhism. As a result, in the course of its exposition of the formula the *Śālistamba Sūtra* touches upon many important points of basic Buddhist doctrine as recorded in the Theravāda and Sarvāstivāda versions of the Long and Middle-length discourses.

On the basis of agreement between the *Śālistamba Sūtra* and material found in the Pāli canon, one may say with confidence that the essence of the historical Buddha's teachings was the Four Noble Truths: 1) Mundane existence is suffering (P. *dukkha,* Skt. *duḥkha).* 2) Desire is the cause of suffering. 3) Nirvāṇa (an awakening or enlightenment like that of the Buddha) is the cessation of suffering. 4) There is a practical method for realizing this awakening. This method is the Noble Eightfold Path comprised of right view, right thought, right speech, right action, right livelihood, right effort, right mindfulness, and right concentration. No form of Buddhism denies the authenticity of the Four Noble Truths and the Eightfold Path. The eight-spoked wheel, probably the most universally acknowledged symbol of Buddhism, represents this Eightfold Path. All Nikāya Buddhism and most Mahāyāna Buddhism may be regarded as elaboration upon these fundamental doctrines, all of which are specifically corroborated in the *Śālistamba Sūtra.*

The first Noble Truth is often rendered in English as "suffering," a literal translation of the Pāli *dukkha* or the Sanskrit *duḥkha.* "Unsatisfactoriness," however, is a more adequate rendition of the term in its Buddhist context. Buddhism recognizes readily that existence can sometimes seem pleasant. The apparent pleasantness of existence is in fact regarded as the chief disincentive to the pursuit of a spiritual life. The first Noble Truth of Buddhism asserts that all mundane things — from the most trivial to the most sublime — are impermanent (P. *anicca,* Skt. *anitya*) and doomed to pass away in time. According to Buddhism this impermanence applies to our selves as well, and consequently there is no soul (P. *atta,* Skt. *ātman*). All beings in the universe — from the most trivial to the most sublime — are also doomed to pass away in time. The doctrines of impermanence and no soul thus form the two complementary facets of the most fundamental of Buddhist doctrines, the doctrine of universal unsatisfactoriness. These three together — *anicca* (impermanence), *anatta* (no soul), and *dukkha* (unsatisfactoriness) — constitute the "three marks" of existence. Recognition of these three essential characteristics in all things is held to be tantamount to penetration of the true nature of reality.

Most religious thinkers of any age or place would accept the Buddhist doctrine of impermanence enthusiastically and without reservation. The doctrine of no soul, however, set Buddhism apart from contemporary Indian religions in the age of the historical Buddha, and it continues to set Buddhism apart from and at odds with all other major religions. Belief in rebirth and in the soul as the vehicle of rebirth had become practically axiomatic among Indian religions at the time of the Buddha. In the ancient Indian context, denial of the soul was tantamount to denial of an afterlife. Nevertheless, as discussed later in this chapter, the Buddha affirmed rebirth by means of a novel dovetailing of causal theory and morality. The Buddha's denial of the soul also had the effect of trivializing any and all deities. Though the Buddha did not deny the existence of deities, they too, according to the no soul doctrine, are doomed eventually to pass away. According to early Buddhism, there is no creator or ruler of the universe, and no unchanging metaphysical principle undergirding it.

In the place of a supreme deity or metaphysical principle, early Buddhism's ultimate reality and goal was nirvāṇa (P. *nibbāna*), the cessation of rebirth and thereby of suffering. The term nirvāṇa means literally "blown out." This literal meaning probably referred to extinction of the consuming flame of desire and ignorance that keeps one entangled in saṃsāra, the mundane realm of repeated death and rebirth. There is some indication too that the term connoted extinction of the "flame" of consciousness, which according to early Buddhism is the medium in which the process of rebirth takes place.

The spiritual ambition to bring an end to rebirth and thus to mundane consciousness as we know it was common in Indian religions of the Buddha's time. Common too were the beliefs that achieving release from rebirth entailed cessation of individual consciousness, that the cessation of individual consciousness involved realization of and participation in the ultimate nature of reality, and that both the experience of spiritual release and the ultimate reality thus encountered were utterly beyond the scope of words or thought.[8] The Buddha, however, was more explicit and systematic than any of his recorded forebears or contemporaries in denying that one could in any way express or conceive of ultimate reality. In the course of this denial, the Buddha formulated the famed *catush-koṭi,* — the "four-cornered negation" or "tetralemma" — which has served ever since as the basis of Buddhist logic. In particular, the four-cornered negation is fundamental and pervasive in the philosophy of Mahāyāna Buddhism.

According to the *catush-koṭi,* any proposition entails four logical possibilities: 1) It is; 2) It is not; 3) It both is and is not; and 4) It neither is nor is not. In some instances, in response to questions regarding the nature of ultimate reality, the Pāli suttas record the Buddha as denying all four logical possibilities. For example, the Buddha denies that a person who has realized nirvāṇa exists, does not exist, both exists and does not exist, or neither does nor does not exist (S4:400). Reasoning based on the *catush-koṭi* underpins the philosophical characterization of Buddhism as the "Middle Path," a characterization universally accepted throughout Buddhism. In one sense, the term Middle Path refers to the spiritual discipline taught by the Buddha, a moderate practice mid-way between the two extremes of self-indulgence and self-mortification. In another sense, Middle Path refers to the Buddhist philosophical position of avoiding the two extremes of nihilism on the one hand and belief in an everlasting soul or metaphysical principle on the other.

Reasoning based on the *catush-koṭi* is also integral to the Buddhist doctrine of rebirth without a soul. No aspect of Buddhism has been so poorly understood and so often misrepresented in the West, possibly because of failure to come to grips with the reasoning behind the four logical possibilities recognized in Buddhism from its inception. Be that as it may, the doctrine of no soul is universally recognized, if not always emphasized, in all forms of Buddhism. There can be no serious doubt that it formed an integral part of the original teachings of the Buddha. Nor can there be any doubt that in conjunction with this doctrine the Buddha taught that one is morally accountable for one's actions (karma) through the mechanism of rebirth.

The apparent contradiction in affirming rebirth while denying that there is a soul is not a contradiction at all from the standpoint of *catush-koṭi* reasoning. From this standpoint, there both is and is not rebirth, and there neither is nor is not something which is reborn. The classical Theravādin statement on rebirth is that the being as which one will be reborn is "not oneself and not another" *(na ca so, na ca añño)*. This statement is not canonical, but encapsulates admirably the position expressed at S2:19-20, where the Buddha, again resorting to the *catush-koṭi,* denies that one's suffering is caused by oneself, by another, by both or "arisen by chance," i.e. that it is caused neither by oneself nor by another. The *Śālistamba Sūtra* employs a direct parallel to this Pāli passage in the course of expounding the process of rebirth.[9]

Catush-koṭi reasoning renders intelligible these multiple denials as well as the doctrine of rebirth without a soul. For example, one *is not* reborn, because no permanent entity survives death. On the other hand one *is* reborn in the sense that one's actions and experiences in this life will affect causally a consciousness reinstated in another life. By way of illustration, even in a single lifetime, one may observe that one both does and does not survive from day to day and from year to year. In one sense an infant develops into an adult through the mechanism of cause and effect operating both mentally and physically. In another sense, the infant's physical body, desires, motivations and intentions perish utterly through this same mechanism. The infant both does and does not survive infancy.

This universally observable process of identity in difference — whether in one lifetime or across many lifetimes — is summarized in the Buddhist doctrine of *pratītyasamutpāda* or "conditioned arising." The *Śālistamba Sūtra's* extensive treatment of the twelvefold formula of conditioned arising leaves little doubt that the classical formula as frequently expounded in the Pāli suttas goes back to within a hundred years of the historical Buddha himself. The classical, twelvefold *pratītyasamutpāda* formula, which incorporates many of the terms and concepts already discussed, runs as follows: 1) Ignorance conditions 2) mental formations. Mental formations (in turn) condition 3) consciousness. Consciousness conditions 4) name-and-form *(nāma-rūpa)*. Name-and-form conditions 5) the six senses (including mind). The six senses condition 6) sensual contact. Sensual contact conditions 7) feeling. Feeling conditions 8) desire. Desire conditions 9) grasping. Grasping conditions 10) existence. Existence conditions 11) birth (i.e. rebirth). Birth conditions 12) ageing and death.

Even a preliminary explanation of these twelve items and their interrelations would involve more speculation than would be justified within the boundaries of this discussion of verifiable doctrines of early Buddhism. The twelvefold formula, however, is only a particular expression of the more general Buddhist theory of causation. At its most general, this theory is expressed in the *Śālistamba Sūtra* and in numerous Pāli suttas with the phrase "This being, that occurs; from the arising of this, that arises,"[10] which means that effects always come about as results of specific causes. According to this Buddhist theory of causation, moreover, the laws of cause and effect operate just as inexorably in the moral realm as they do in the physical world. Like the *Śālistamba Sūtra*, the Pāli suttas employ the simile of a seed growing into a plant to illustrate this point.[11] If one plants a seed, and various conditions are met, a plant will grow. The plant is not the seed, and yet it is not other than the seed. It is a *result* of the seed. Obviously, the type of seed sown determines the type of plant that will result. Similarly in the moral realm, if one performs an action (karma), a result *(vipāka)* similar in nature to the action performed will accrue to the one who performed the action.

In the physical realm a result does not always follow its cause immediately. For example, a drought at the time of planting a seed may result later in a stunted plant. Similarly, in the moral realm there may be a delay between an action and the moral result of that action. During this delay, there may well have been a considerable change in the person who initially performed the action in question. He or she may well have aged by several years. Thus, the person who suffers or enjoys the result of the previously performed action would be "not the same, and yet not another." For example, one may suffer as an adult for actions performed as a teenager. Both the plant and the person in these examples may suffer or profit from causes and conditions which themselves occurred and vanished long ago. According to Buddhist moral and causal theory, both the plant and the person as such are at any given time the sum total result of many causes and conditions which have occurred in the past. The constant operation of cause and effect brings about constant change in both conscious beings and inanimate objects. The effect of any given cause — whether immediate or delayed and whether occurring in the physical or moral realm — often operates upon a thing or being that has changed in a minor or major way since the occurrence of the cause in question. Whether or not the thing or being "deserves" the result which occurs is a moot point, for the laws of cause and effect are impersonal and inexorable, whether operating in the physical or the moral realm.

In the physical realm, the constant changing of things, resulting from the operation of cause and effect, is denoted by the term *anicca* (Pāli) or *anitya* (Sanskrit), meaning "impermanence." The constant change in sentient beings gives rise to the term *anatta* (P.) or *anātman* (Skt.), meaning "without soul." Thus far, the Buddhist theory of karma (action) and its results *(vipāka)* is empirical, which is to say that it may be tested and verified through experience. It is a fact of life that one may suffer as an adult for actions performed as a teenager, and that the adult who suffers is not the teenager who performed the action. Buddhist moral doctrine, of course, also includes the concept of rebirth, whereby one may suffer or prosper in a future lifetime as a result of actions performed in a past life that one does not remember at all.

Some may not accept the doctrine of rebirth, but as noted above, rebirth was all but axiomatic in India at the time of the historical Buddha. It was one of those commonly held, antecedent beliefs upon which all great religions have been built. Though the Buddha accepted the general theory of rebirth current in his day, this acceptance was by no means uncritical. On the contrary, the Buddha's teaching of rebirth without a soul appears to have been an attempt to resolve contradictions in existing concepts of rebirth that were based on belief in the soul. Pre-Buddhist theories of rebirth regarded the soul as the innermost essence of one's identity. As such, the soul was usually regarded as sublime and unchanging.[12] On the other hand, the soul was universally regarded as the agent ultimately responsible for evil as well as good actions. That which does not change, however, cannot act; and that which is sublime cannot be evil. Such contradictions in the existing theories of the soul and rebirth were not lost upon the forebears of the Buddha. The Upanishadic sages, some of whom definitely predated the Buddha, conceived of the innermost soul in various ways, but most regarded it as the eternal, sublime, unchanging essence of one's being. They recognized the contradiction in asserting that such an entity could meaningfully be said to suffer or benefit from actions occurring in the mundane world, or indeed that such an entity could conceivably be responsible for relatively "good" or "bad" actions. In order to overcome such problems, religious thinkers predating the Buddha, some of them recorded in the *Upanishads,* devised various hierarchies of aspects and faculties of the soul. These hierarchies depicted the soul as a complex, layered phenomenon rather than as a unitary entity. The Upanishadic sages suggested that karma and rebirth affected only the soul's lower, less essential aspects, which were somehow shed by the essential, eternal soul at the point of release.[13]

The several Upanishadic theories of multiple layers of the soul involved a remarkable degree of psychological observation and deduction. The available textual evidence suggests that before the historical Buddha, the Upanishadic sages had recognized the five empirical senses — sight, hearing, taste, touch, and smell — as conduits of information to the mind *(manas),* and postulated yet deeper levels of consciousness remarkably similar, though perhaps not identical, to modern psychological concepts such as mind *(manas)*, consciousness *(vijñāna)*, ego *(ahaṃkāra)*, and superego *(buddhi* or *prajñā)*. The best known of these layered theories of the soul is the *Taittirīya Upanishad's* doctrine of the five "sheaths" of the soul, the material *(anna)*, the vital *(prāṇa)*, the mental *(manas)*, the pure conscious *(vijñāna)* and the blissful *(ānanda)*.[14]

There is every indication that the historical Buddha expanded upon an existing fund of psychological observation and deduction in order to formulate his own systematic analysis of the individual human being into the "five aggregates" *(pañca khandha,* Skt. *skandha)*, again a doctrine conspicuously treated in the *Śālistamba Sūtra.* According to this doctrine, that which we typically experience as the individual self is in fact divisible into at least five "aggregates." These are: 1) body *(rūpa)*, 2) feelings *(vedanā)*, 3) perceptions *(saññā)*, 4) mental formations *(saṅkhārā)* and 5) consciousness *(viññāṇa)*. Together these form a constantly fluctuating conglomerate which only gives the appearance of an abiding personal identity. Each aggregate can be further analyzed into constituent components. Body, like all material phenomena, is composed of the elements earth, air, fire, and water. Feelings, perceptions and consciousness all occur as results of the activity of the five senses and the mind *(manas)* as *sensus communis,* the "common sense" into which all of the other senses feed information. Thus there may be visual feelings, perceptions of sound, or consciousness of smells, and so on up to eighteen basic types of feeling, perception and consciousness — i.e., six senses (including mind) multiplied by three aggregates.

These basic types of feeling, perception, and consciousness may be analyzed further according to the nature of the aggregate in question. Feelings, the most primitive level of experience, occur in three categories: pleasant, unpleasant, and neutral. Perceptions represent more refined experiences normally denoted by adjectives, such as red, round, smooth, fragrant, etc. At this point, a specific idea or identification regarding the object in question may be formed at the level of the "mental formations" aggregate. By way of illustration, pleasant visual, tactile and olfactory *feelings,* along with similar *perceptions* of "red, round, smooth and fragrant," may give rise to the *mental formation* "an apple." On the basis of further experience, this mental formation may be revised to, say, "a pomegranate." Also at the level of mental formations occur volitional, karmic reactions such as desire (e.g., for an apple) or aversion (e.g., to pomegranates). Similar processes of perception and volition occur throughout one's waking life, and presumably in sleep and dreams as well. Incessantly they impinge upon and influence the quality of consciousness, the fifth aggregate, which represents the sum total functioning of feelings, perceptions and mental formations.

In addition to analyzing the structure and functioning of consciousness, the Pāli suttas repeatedly assert the interdependence of consciousness and the objects of consciousness, the implication being that material
objects may not be real.[15] The following passage is a notable example. In
this passage, material form "comes to be" as a result of having been seen,
just as vision arises on the basis of seeing a material form.

> When, sir, the internal eye is intact, external forms come with-
> in its range and there is appropriate attention, then there is
> appearance of the appropriate type of consciousness. What-
> ever is the form *(rūpa)* of what has thus come to be is called
> the grasping aggregate of form.
>
> M1:190

The implication of this passage is that one never experiences "external" objects as such. One only experiences *apparent* objects with an
admixture of subjective bias. On the other hand, one's subjective consciousness is influenced by the objects with which it comes in contact. In
other words, consciousness influences the objects of consciousness, just
as objects influence consciousness. An angry mind will see an ugly world,
whereas a happy mind looking at the same world will see beauty.

Such psychological insights and theories in the Pāli suttas provide a
convincing basis for later developments in Mahāyāna Buddhism. The
most prominent of these developments are the Madhyamaka dialectic
and Vijñānavāda metaphysics, both of which will be discussed more fully
in Chapter IV. Briefly, in terms of the Madhyamaka dialectic, there can
be no self-existent knower, no self-existent thing known, and no self-
existent act of knowing, because all of these are interdependent. An object cannot occur without a subject. In terms of Vijñānavāda metaphysics,
the entire universe is nothing but consciousness. All objects are illusory,
like the objects in dreams. In highlighting the necessary subjective component in any experience of an object, the Pāli suttas pave the way for
discarding the objective referent of consciousness altogether in Mahāyāna
Buddhism.

Moral Teachings

Virtually all forms of Buddhism agree concerning the moral requirements of the religion. This allows an easing of the requirements of verifi-
cation which dominated the previous section. Buddhism's across-the-
board agreement concerning the principles of morality, however, is not

always apparent. This is because of a persistent Mahāyānist characterization of Theravāda Buddhism — and indeed, all forms of Nikāya Buddhism — as selfish. In essence Mahāyānists claim that their own moral ideal — the bodhisattva — is superior to Nikāya Buddhism's ideal of the arahat. The bodhisattva ideal will be discussed at length in Chapter IV. Briefly, however, according to the Mahāyāna the bodhisattva renounces nirvāṇa in order to remain in saṃsāra (the mundane world) and work for the welfare of deluded, suffering beings. Mahāyānists typically claim that the arahat abandons suffering humanity by accepting nirvāṇa, and for this reason Nikāya Buddhism may be characterized as selfish. The present section of this chapter illustrates the contrary — that compassion for one's fellow beings is an integral part of Nikāya Buddhism. Drawing upon the Pāli scriptures of Theravāda Buddhism, this section also shows that the admirable morality of Mahāyāna Buddhism — like the philosophy of Mahāyāna Buddhism — is convincingly foreshadowed in Nikāya Buddhism.

The foregoing analytical philosophy and psychology of Theravāda Buddhism, in addition to countering *ignorance* of the true nature of reality, is intended to counter *desire* as well. By virtue of its position as the second Noble Truth — that desire is the cause of all human suffering — desire may appear to be regarded in early Buddhism as a graver fault than ignorance. In fact, ignorance is regarded as the obverse of desire. The two are inseparable. According to early Buddhist doctrine, and much of later Buddhist doctrine as well, if one were truly to comprehend the impermanence of all phenomena, including oneself, one's desires would automatically cease. Conversely, if one did not desire that things be other than what they are, ignorance of how things actually are would automatically fade.

In addition to ignorance and desire, the third grave fault, according to the Pāli suttas, is hatred. Desire, hatred and ignorance, when considered together usually occur in the Pāli suttas as *lobha, dosa* and *moha,* or in Sanskrit as *rāga, dvesha* and *moha,* a triad which occurs in the *Śāli-stamba Sūtra* and is well attested throughout Buddhism. These three faults constitute the "roots of unwholesomeness" *(akusala-mūla).* Their opposites — generosity, benevolence and wisdom — are the roots of wholesomeness *(kusala-mūla).* Buddhist morality in general, whether early or late, is based upon a distinction between the wholesome and the unwholesome rather than between good and evil. This is so because Buddhism posits no God who might decree what is good and what is evil. Instead, within the realm of karma and rebirth, thoughts and actions truly conducive to the immediate as well as the ultimate relief of suffering, both one's own and that of others, are wholesome. Thoughts and actions that cause suffering for oneself or others are unwholesome. From its inception, Buddhist morality has always been founded upon compassion toward one's fellow beings. The *Sutta Nipāta,* a very ancient Theravādin text, summarizes admirably the basis of all Buddhist morality:

> As I am, so are they. As they are, so am I. Comparing others
> with oneself, one should not harm or cause harm.

Sutta Nipāta, vs. 705

The compassionate attitude enjoined by Buddhism from its inception is held to be practically validated by the mechanism of karma and rebirth. The term karma, whether in the Buddhist context or in other Eastern contexts, is often misunderstood in the West, and therefore requires brief explanation. Literally "karma" means "action." In most Indian contexts, and particularly in the Buddhist context, karma implies "volitional action or thought." Emphatically, karma is not like some sort of blessing or curse hovering around one. One does not *have* good or bad karma, one *performs* good or bad karma. The *result* of a volitional action or thought is *karma-vipāka* or *karma-phala,* "the maturing or fruit of karma." If one stubs one's toe, that misfortune is not bad karma, it is the *result* of bad karma. Karma is volitional action or thought itself, nothing more. Volition, moreover, is the essence of karma. Unintentional actions are not regarded as morally relevant, even though they may cause great benefit or harm to others.

With these fundamental concepts in mind, it becomes clear that the Noble Eightfold Path — right view, right thought, and so on — deals primarily with Buddhist morality. The Eightfold Path, moreover, is recognized as a teaching of the historical Buddha in virtually all schools of Buddhism, thus meeting the historical criterion of consensus. It therefore serves admirably as a framework within which to exhibit the moral teachings of early Buddhism. This Eightfold Path is traditionally divided into three categories known as pillars *(khandha):* wisdom *(paññā),* ethics *(sīla)* and meditation *(samādhi).* According to the traditional enumeration of the limbs of the Path, the twofold wisdom pillar comes first, its components being 1) right view and 2) right thought. Right view *(sammā diṭṭhi)* is consistently equated in the suttas with acceptance of the Four Noble Truths, and thus may be regarded as entailing understanding of and agreement with the analytical, doctrinal material considered in the previous section of this chapter. The second limb of the Path, however, *sammā-saṅkappa,* "right thought" or "right intention," relates more to morality than to analytical philosophy. In the Pāli suttas, *sammā-*

saṅkappa is consistently said to involve thoughts or intentions of 1) renunciation, 2) benevolence and 3) nonviolence *(nekkhama, avyāpāda* and *avihiṃsā;* D2:312). These three "right thoughts" constitute the volitional underpinnings of early Buddhist morality rather than a philosophical position. This point is fundamental to a sympathetic understanding of early Buddhist morality, which otherwise may appear to be merely a set of rules designed to insure one's karmic welfare in this and future lives.

The second pillar of the Eightfold Path puts forward specific rules for wholesome conduct, conduct which will harm neither oneself nor others. These three limbs of the path — 3) right speech, 4) right action and 5) right livelihood — correspond roughly to the "five precepts" *(pañca-sīla* or *sikkhā-pada)* enjoined upon the Theravāda Buddhist layperson. These five precepts are avoidance of 1) violence toward anything that breathes, 2) taking that which is not freely given, 3) false, harsh or harmful speech, 4) sexual misconduct, and 5) abuse of drugs or alcohol. Again, however, traditional Theravāda doctrine is not strictly borne out in the early texts, for only four of the traditional "five precepts" are included in sutta treatments of the Eightfold Path. Though it is clear that the Buddha did not approve of alcohol and drugs (A1:261; S2:167), abstinence from intoxicants is not included in elucidations of "right action" in the Pāli suttas. As at D2:312, the suttas normally mention only abstinence from 1) violence toward living creatures *(pāṇātipāta)*, 2) taking what is not given *(adinnādāna)*, and 3) sexual misconduct *(kāmesu micchācāra)*, as constituting "right action." "Right speech" is consistently defined as abstaining from falsehood, slander, verbal abuse and idle chatter (D2:312; A5:205).

With regard to "sexual misconduct," as the term *kāmesu micchācāra* is usually understood, it should be noted that the term actually implies immoderate behavior motivated by sensual desire *(kāma)* of any kind, e.g. desire for excessive comfort or possessions (M1:85). With regard to sexual misconduct as such, monks and nuns are forbidden any sort of sexual contact. The specific prohibition for laypeople, however, is remarkably liberal, though cast in terms which give women little guidance. The Pāli suttas consistently enjoin men to refrain from having sex with women who are "under the protection of" *(rakkhitā,* i.e. supported by) parents, relatives or a husband (M1:286; S5:264). Presumably, women too should have sexual dealings only with men who support themselves — assuming in either case, of course, that no violence or dishonesty is involved.

To summarize the material considered thus far, the third and fourth limbs of the Eightfold Path, right speech and right action, comprise four

of the "five precepts" — excluding abuse of intoxicants. The fifth limb of
the path (right livelihood) prohibits professions which would entail
wrong speech or action — for example work on the killing-floor in a
slaughterhouse — and professions which would encourage wrong
speech or action in others — for example the manufacture of weapons
or poisons.

With the sixth limb of the Path, "right effort" *(sammā vāyāma)*, begins
the section or "pillar" of the Path traditionally regarded as pertaining to
meditation. The standard definition of right effort, however, also pertains
to morality as cultivation of the wholesome *(kusala)* and rejection of the
unwholesome *(akusala)*. The "roots of unwholesomeness," it will be
remembered, are desire, hatred and ignorance. Their opposites — generosity, benevolence and wisdom — are the roots of wholesomeness. In
exerting right effort, one is enjoined to 1) eradicate existing unwholesome states of mind, 2) prevent the arising of other unwholesome states
of mind, 3) cultivate existing wholesome states of mind, and 4) encourage the arising of other wholesome states of mind (D2:312).

Thus five limbs of the Eightfold Path — limbs two through six — all
bear directly upon morality, even though the second limb is classified in
the pillar of wisdom and the sixth limb is classified in the pillar of meditation. This overlapping illustrates the pervasiveness of morality in the
teachings of Nikāya Buddhism. The natural confluence of Buddhist
morality and meditation is nowhere better illustrated than in the well-
known verse 183 of the Pāli *Dhammapada* (also occurring at D2:49), a
verse which is said to encapsulate the essence of the Buddha's teaching:

> Avoidance of all evil *(pāpa)*,
> Cultivation of the wholesome *(kusala)*,
> Purification of one's mind,
> This is the teaching of the Buddhas.

This natural overlapping of morality and meditation within the Eightfold Path lends credence to the *Brahma-vihāra* meditations as an original
part of Buddhism. According to this contemplative practice, which is
prominent in the Pāli suttas, one is to cultivate and extend to all beings a
mental attitude of benevolence *(metta)*, compassion *(karunā)*, sympathetic joy *(muditā)* and equanimity *(upekkhā)*. As the verifiably ancient
Sutta Nipāta states at verse 148:

> Just as a mother would protect her only child at the risk of her
> own life, even so one should cultivate a boundless heart
> toward all beings.

This prominent attitude of compassion and benevolence in the Pāli suttas is extended rather than altered in the bodhisattva ideal of Mahāyāna Buddhism, whereby all of one's actions are to be motivated by a sincere desire to relieve all beings of their sufferings. This situation in no way diminishes the moral excellence of the bodhisattva ideal. It does, however, belie the Mahāyānist position that Nikāya Buddhism is inherently selfish. Moreover, as in the case of Buddhist philosophy, so in the realm of Buddhist morality — the scriptures of Nikāya Buddhism provide an adequate basis for the development of Mahāyāna Buddhism.

Meditational Teachings

It is with regard to meditational teachings that the greatest doubt concerning the teachings of the historical Buddha exists. In the first place, given the prominence of meditational practice in the early Buddhist spiritual path, remarkably little space in the Pāli Sutta Piṭaka is dedicated to these practices. Such explanations as exist are normally formulaic and sweeping in scope, treating the stages of a lifetime's meditational practice in a paragraph or so. On the other hand, the Pāli suttas — as well as a few other texts of Nikāya Buddhism — are far more informative regarding the actual practice of meditation than are other contemporary texts, most notably the *Upanishads*. The general scarcity of precise information about meditation in ancient Indian texts probably reflects the fact that the details of meditational practice were considered an individual affair to be worked out between teacher and pupil.

In the context of early Buddhism, the two final items of the Eightfold Path pertain directly to meditation. These are: 7) right mindfulness *(sammā sati)* and 8) right concentration *(sammā samādhi)*. Two suttas of the Pāli canon — the "Satipaṭṭhāna" of the *Majjhima Nikāya* and the "Mahā-satipaṭṭhāna" of the *Dīgha Nikāya* — deal specifically with mindfulness and define it precisely as continuous and systematic attention to the body *(kāya)*, the feelings *(vedanā)*, the mind *(citta)*, and certain points of doctrine *(dhammā)*. These two suttas indicate clearly that like "right effort," mindfulness is to be practiced at all times, not only during formal meditation sessions. What is required of the practitioner, moreover, is objective observation — not evaluation or conscious modification — of 1) the composition, postures and activities of the body, 2) the pleasant, unpleasant or neutral nature of the feelings, and 3) the emotional and moral quality of the mind. Even with regard to the fourth specified object of mindfulness — aspects of doctrine — the meditator is enjoined merely to note the presence or absence of certain wholesome and unwholesome states of mind specified in the teachings of the Buddha, and to note when other aspects of the teachings are verified in experience.

Right concentration involves the ability to attain "mental one-pointedness" *(cittassa ekaggatā)*. It is consistently defined as cultivation of four *jhānas* or meditational states. These meditational states are only minimally defined as involving the presence or absence of certain positive and negative mental characteristics. Four higher meditational states, the "formless" *(arūpa) jhānas,* are not described at all, but are evocatively named as 1) the sphere of infinite space, 2) the sphere of infinite consciousness, 3) the sphere of nothingness, and 4) the sphere of neither perception nor non-perception. Chapter I noted that the Buddha is said to have learned the last two *jhānas* from his teachers Āḷāra Kālāma and Uddaka Rāmaputta, and to have rejected them as falling short of final enlightenment and release. A ninth *jhāna,* however, the "cessation of perception and feeling" *(saññā-vedayita-nirodha),* also known as "the attainment of cessation" *(nirodha samāpatti),* appears to be regarded as an integral part of the realization of nirvāṇa.[16] The following characterization of this *jhāna* indicates that it involves suspension of all mental activity.

> The monk who has attained *saññā-vedayita-nirodha,* his bodily activities, verbal activities and mental activities have been stopped, have subsided, but his vitality is not destroyed, his (body) heat is not allayed, and his senses are purified. This, sir, is the difference between a dead thing, passed away, and that monk.
>
> M1:296

A passage in the *Dīgha Nikāya* suggests that development of the ninth *jhāna* may have been regarded in some circles as being itself tantamount to the realization of nirvāṇa, which is normally a synonym of the term *nirodha.*

> To one standing at the summit of consciousness [after realization of the eight *jhānas*] it may occur: "To think at all is inferior. It would be better not to think. . . . So he stops thinking or willing, and perception ceases. . . . He touches cessation *(nirodhaṃ phussati).* Thus, Poṭṭhapāda, does the gradual and deliberate attainment *(samāpatti)* of cessation *(nirodha)* occur.
>
> D1:184

This poses a problem with regard to the concept of nirvāṇa in the Pāli suttas. On the one hand spiritual release appears to be regarded as the result of intellectual comprehension of the true nature of reality and a consequent penetration of the reality of things "as they are" *(yathā-bhūta)*. On the other hand, the actual realization of nirvāṇa appears to be regarded as involving a meditational cessation of even the most rudimentary mental activity. Part of this apparent confusion may be due to an attempt to reconcile a conflict in early Buddhist practice by integrating two distinct meditational endeavors: on the one hand the cultivation of *jhānas* by developing tranquility *(samatha)* and concentration *(samādhi)*, and on the other hand the cultivation of insight *(vipassanā)* and intuitive wisdom *(ñāṇa* or *paññā)*.

The general thrust of the Pāli suttas is that if anything, insight and wisdom are more essential than tranquility and concentration. The "Satipaṭṭhāna Sutta" and the "Mahā Satipaṭṭhāna Sutta," the suttas most explicitly dedicated to elucidating meditational practice, both suggest that enlightenment and release are possible without cultivation of the *jhānas* at all. In addition, it must be remembered that the Buddha mastered the seventh and eighth *jhānas* under his two teachers, and that he regarded these meditative absorptions as falling short of final release from suffering. To a considerable degree, this rejection of meditative absorption as an end in itself is the basis of the distinction between Buddhism and other contemporary spiritual paths.

Nonetheless, the Pāli suttas are ambivalent concerning the relative importance of meditative absorption via tranquility and concentration on the one hand, and meditative cultivation of insight and wisdom on the other. Both absorption and insight were held to entail meditation, but they appear to have been regarded in some circles as distinct goals involving different techniques of practice. One passage (A3:355) records traces of an outright dispute between two factions of monks: the *jhāyins,* who cultivated meditative absorption via the *jhānas,* and the *dhamma-yoga* monks, who concentrated upon development of insight and wisdom. The passage in question attempts to quell this disagreement without deciding in favor of either side, but given such a dispute, various passages in the Pāli suttas appear to weigh in on one side or the other. Most passages favor the cultivation of wisdom and insight, but not all. For example, the *Dīgha Nikāya* asserts that even before the Buddha there were two types of recluse, the meditators *(jhāyin),* and an inferior group incapable of the rigors of the meditational regimen (D3:93-4). The existence of passages that place priority upon meditative absorption, in conjunction with the great importance that the Pāli suttas place upon on the ninth *jhāna,* indicates that there were real differences of opinion among early Buddhists regarding the proper techniques and goals of meditation.

Even though the Pāli suttas are ambivalent concerning the relative importance of two distinct types of meditation — one aimed at absorption and the other aimed at insight — orthodox Theravāda Buddhism is decisive in its emphasis upon insight. Again, the fact that the suttas record ambivalence where orthodox Theravāda doctrine is unequivocal indicates that these suttas themselves did not suffer excessive sectarian revision at the hands of their preservers and compilers. If they had been subject to biased revision, a few words omitted here and a few added there would have expunged all traces of inconsistencies in the meditative practices of early Buddhists. As it is, one may note that two types of meditation, as well as tensions between their practitioners, are well attested in the Pāli canon.

Whereas the Theravāda tradition eventually came to emphasize insightful penetration of the analytical teachings of Buddhism, the early Mahāyāna tended to emphasize the non-conceptual, concentrative side of meditation. Starting with the *Prajñā Pāramitā* or "Perfection of Wisdom" literature (first or second century BCE), as systematized in the Madhyamaka school of Nāgārjuna, Mahāyāna Buddhism exhibited a conspicuous mistrust of doctrine, and tended to regard enlightenment as a purely intuitive, non-conceptual, meditative attainment. The *jhāyins* or *"jhāna*-cultivators" of the Pāli suttas appear to survive in the Dhyāna or "Meditation" school of Mahāyāna Buddhism. *Dhyāna* is the Sanskrit equivalent of the Pāli term *jhāna*, and names an important school of Mahāyāna Buddhism transmitted from India to China and then to Japan under the name of Zen.

In contrast to the Mahāyāna, the Theravāda and Sarvāstivāda traditions — and apparently other schools of Nikāya Buddhism as well — tended to emphasize the analytical content of the historical Buddha's teachings in their meditational as well as their intellectual endeavors. The Theravāda and Sarvāstivāda — and presumably other forms of Nikāya Buddhism as well — developed in their respective Abhidharma corpuses rigorously systematic guides to the practice of meditation. Such systematization did not, however, preclude participation in the spontaneous and intuitive side of Buddhism, as is amply demonstrated by the *Theragāthā* and *Therīgāthā*, the inspirational "Songs of the Monks and Nuns" enshrined in the Pāli canon. On the other hand, although the Mahāyāna tended to emphasize the intuitive side of Buddhist meditation, no one would suggest that Mahāyānists have lacked the inclination or the talent for rigorous doctrinal systematization.

All of the foregoing material regarding the historical Buddha, the affairs of his Saṅgha, and the probable nature of his original teachings, indicates that Buddhism began as a spiritual path in which the intellect, morality and meditation play mutually supportive roles. Later, divergent forms of Buddhism emphasized one or another of these fundamentals, but throughout Buddhism, each is thought necessary and none alone sufficient for enlightenment and spiritual release. The diversity of sincere and legitimate developments that have arisen from the basic teachings of the historical Buddha testify both to the genius of the religion's founder and to the ingenuity of his followers in adapting these teachings to a wide range of cultures and temperaments.

CHAPTER IV

The Development of Mahāyāna Buddhism

On first impression, the exuberance of Mahāyāna Buddhism appears to be incompatible with the austere practices and minimal doctrine of Nikāya Buddhism. Closer examination reveals that the elaborate doctrines and mythology of the Mahāyāna actually justify forms of Buddhist practice more readily accessible to the average person. Philosophical analysis and meditation remain important in Mahāyāna Buddhism, but they are augmented with the hope that supernatural savior figures may intervene to help relieve one's sufferings and to guide one along the spiritual path. Historical evidence bearing directly upon the emergence of Mahāyāna Buddhism is scarce, but what evidence there is indicates that the Mahāyāna developed naturally and comprehensibly from the teachings preserved in the scriptures of Nikāya Buddhism. To understand this development, one must return in one's imagination to the time of Aśoka, approximately 250 BCE.

In many ways, life in Aśoka's India was similar to life in India today. Then as now, the mass of the population was scattered in villages isolated from the major urban centers. Even within the cities, the majority of people toiled for a living and had little access to the artistic and intellectual circles of the elite. Though average working people may well have admired the discipline and ideals of the community of Buddhist monks, they had little opportunity to actualize those ideals in everyday life. The philosophy and ascetic discipline of Nikāya Buddhism was then, as it is now, beyond the reach of the rank and file. As one may observe today of Theravāda Buddhism in Sri Lanka and Southeast Asia, so in Aśoka's time the gods and rituals of popular religion had no place in the official doctrine of the Elders of Nikāya Buddhism.

Despite its inaccessibility to the common people, during Aśoka's reign Buddhism gained rapid ascendancy over the other religious beliefs and practices of India. In many if not most cases, the so-called "religions" of Aśokan India did not even have names. It must not be imagined that the masses of India in those days were Hindu in any meaningful sense of the term. The priestly religion of the Indo-Europeans — known as "Brahman-ism" in order to distinguish it from the classical Hinduism into which it eventually developed — was a powerful force in pre-Aśokan India. It was largely inaccessible to the masses, however, because of its caste discrim-ination and the financial burden of participating in its elaborate rituals. Many religious teachers in addition to the Buddha taught various ascetic paths no doubt admired by the masses, but nevertheless beyond their practical reach. Then as now, the vast majority of Indians lived under the lofty canopy of a highly sophisticated spirituality, but contented them-selves with a simple religion focused upon a variety of supernatural beings believed to exert influence upon their day-to-day lives.

Shortly after Aśoka made Buddhism the state religion of India, the religious aspirations of the masses began to exert influence upon the canonical scriptures of Indian religion. The first surviving evidence of this emergent populism in Indian religion is the sudden appearance of *bhakti* — loving devotion to a savior figure — in the scriptures of Buddhism and Hinduism. Regardless of its validity, loving devotion to a savior deity is a form of religion that is readily accessible to the rank and file. The *Bhagavad Gītā,* composed between 200 BCE and 200 CE, is the first Hindu text to incorporate *bhakti,* and given the central importance of *bhakti* in Hinduism, it is thereby arguably the first representative text of classical Hinduism. What is often overlooked, however, is that devotion-alism began to appear in the scriptures of Mahāyāna Buddhism at about the same time it began to appear in Hindu scriptures like the *Bhagavad Gītā.* Chapter V examines in greater detail the historical situations sur-rounding the incorporation of *bhakti* into Indian religions. It is sufficient here to note that both Buddhism and Hinduism began to incorporate forms of devotionalism — apparently in a bid to gain the allegiance of the masses — at about the same time, shortly after or perhaps during the reign of Aśoka.

Hinduism as such began to emerge from Brahmanism in a recogniz-able form during this rise to prominence of popular devotionalism. Because of its roots in sacrificial Brahmanism, this emergent Hinduism recognized easily and naturally the exalted status of various deities. The Brahmanic priests and their followers already worshipped many deities. These deities were different from the deities of classical Hinduism, and they do not appear to have been objects of loving devotion. Nonetheless, the theistic and ritualistic predisposition of Vedic Brahmanism made the absorption of *bhakti* a natural development. Nikāya Buddhism, by contrast, was not in a position to participate in this devotional trend. Its doctrines clearly condemn rituals and portray the various popular deities as being deluded or as being followers of the Buddha. Buddhism appears to have reacted to the rise of popular devotionalism in two ways. The conservative Elders of Nikāya Buddhism appear to have reacted by incorporating the practices of the masses as a lower form of Buddhism, marginally acceptable and of limited spiritual benefit, but ultimately invalid and to be transcended as soon as possible. These sacrificial and devotional practices appear to have been regarded as a sort of spiritual kindergarten, as indeed they are today in the Theravāda Buddhism of modern Southeast Asia and Sri Lanka.

By contrast, Mahāyāna Buddhism appears to have been determined to incorporate popular devotionalism into the very fabric of Buddhist doctrine. In order to do this, appropriate Buddhist objects of devotion were needed to serve in place of the popular deities that were incorporated into emergent Hinduism and grafted onto the bottom of Nikāya Buddhism. In pursuing this incorporation, the Mahāyānists resorted to a radical reinterpretation of two ideal figures prominent in early Buddhist scriptures: the bodhisattva and the Buddha. An examination of this reinterpretation reveals the continuity underlying the apparently vast divergence between Mahāyāna and Theravāda Buddhism.

Development of the Bodhisattva Concept

The term "bodhisattva" appears first as the title the Buddha used to refer to himself before he realized nirvāṇa. The *Jātaka Tales,* popular scriptures of Theravāda Buddhism, extend the concept of bodhisattva to include previous lives of the Buddha before he was born as Siddhattha Gotama. These texts recount hundreds of fanciful stories about previous lives of the Buddha before he was born as Prince Siddhattha. Since he was not yet enlightened in these previous lives, he is known in these stories as the bodhisatta, Pāli for bodhisattva. Along with the writings of Aesop, these stories of the Buddha's previous lives are the most ancient existing examples of the literary genre of the fable. Aesop's fables and the *Jātaka Tales* are in fact compilations drawn from the extreme western and eastern ends of a common fund of orally transmitted fable literature current throughout the entire ancient world. In the *Jātaka Tales,* otherwise unrelated stories are artificially tied together by identifying the protagonist, whether human or animal, as the Buddha in a previous life. Already on the path to Buddhahood, the bodhisatta (Skt. bodhisattva) in these stories exhibits many of the qualities of a Buddha, most notably a selfless desire to serve others regardless of the consequences for himself.

In Theravāda Buddhism, these tales of the bodhisattva's exploits remained children's stories, though their moral ideal of selfless service is enjoined upon adults as well. Mahāyāna Buddhism, by contrast, seized upon the concept of the bodhisattva as one of its most important spiritual ideals. Followers of Mahāyāna Buddhism are expected to take and repeatedly reiterate the "bodhisattva vow," a promise to dedicate one's life to the welfare of other beings and to forgo final realization of nirvāṇa until all beings have been led to release. In essence, the bodhisattva vow replaces nirvāṇa, the supreme goal of Theravāda Buddhism, with the supreme goal of Mahāyāna Buddhism: Buddhahood. In seeking to realize nirvāṇa, Theravāda Buddhists seek to become arahats. In Theravāda Buddhism, there is no distinction in spiritual status between the Buddha and an arahat, one who has realized nirvāṇa by following the Buddha's teachings. The distinction between Buddha and arahat is instead a historical distinction, the title Buddha being reserved for the first arahat of the present age. In Mahāyāna Buddhism, by contrast, the arahats of Nikāya Buddhism are portrayed as selfish beings, preoccupied with their own salvation, and hence not truly enlightened.

It is inconceivable, according to Mahāyāna Buddhism, that a bodhisattva who had dedicated countless lifetimes to serving others would vanish into nirvāṇa soon after attaining enlightenment, just when there is greatest scope for truly serving and saving others by continuing to teach. Thus, they reasoned, a being truly dedicated to service of others would postpone nirvāṇa and continue to exist in saṃsāra in order to guide others to enlightenment and liberation. Such continuing enlightened service to others would constitute the best imaginable karma, and would result in increasingly exalted status within saṃsāra. By continuing to serve others selflessly, one would eventually gain the highest celestial status, from which one could exert enormous compassion and power in the service of suffering beings everywhere.

Such celestial beings — also known as bodhisattvas because technically they had not yet realized nirvāṇa and thereby become Buddhas — were incorporated by Mahāyāna Buddhism as appropriate objects of specifically Buddhist devotionalism. The celestial bodhisattvas could replace the popular deities worshipped by the masses and accepted only as inferior objects of religion in the conservative Buddhism of the Elders. Mahāyāna scriptures depict the celestial bodhisattvas as radiant beings seated upon jewel-encrusted thrones and surrounded by entourages of adoring heavenly attendants. Like the various Hindu deities, the different bodhisattvas appeal to a wide variety of temperaments. Of the many named celestial bodhisattvas of Mahāyāna Buddhism, Avalokiteśvara, the bodhisattva of compassion, and Mañjuśrī, the bodhisattva of wisdom are the best known. Wisdom and compassion, the two cardinal virtues of Buddhism, are known as the "wings of enlightenment," so that Mañjuśrī and Avalokiteśvara personify the ideal human qualities.

Accordingly, in addition to providing objects of devotion, the bodhi-sattva concept also supplies Mahāyāna Buddhism with the foundation of its morality. Mahāyāna Buddhism urges its followers to begin immediate-ly to be motivated by the same selfless desire to serve others that charac-terizes the bodhisattva's motivation. Also in imitation of the bodhisattvas, Mahāyāna Buddhists are expected to forswear nirvāṇa, promising to con-tinue to be reborn in saṃsāra to work for the welfare of its countless suffering beings. Theravādins typically applaud the noble sentiments behind the bodhisattva vow, but regard it as unrealistic. According to the Theravāda, the realization of enlightenment and the realization of nirvāṇa are two sides of the same coin. Regardless of one's inclination, one sim-ply cannot have one without the other. One who has realized enlighten-ment may teach others for the duration of one's life, but when such a one dies, the realization of final nirvāṇa is automatic and inevitable. Nirvāṇa as an utter and final escape from the realm of rebirth remains the spiritual ideal of Theravāda Buddhism.

In Mahāyāna Buddhism, by contrast, nirvāṇa loses all practical urgen-cy and becomes only theoretically important as the ultimate goal of spiritual practice. Having taken the bodhisattva vow, one must postpone one's own realization of nirvāṇa until all sentient beings in the universe have been led to nirvāṇa. In the context of the Buddhist worldview, whether Theravāda or Mahāyāna, the universe contains infinite numbers of worlds inhabited by infinite numbers of beings. To lead all of them to nirvāṇa is an infinite task. Theoretically, nirvāṇa remains ultimately desir-able in Mahāyāna Buddhism, but construed as liberation for all beings, it becomes such a distant goal as to lose all urgency.

This Mahāyāna interpretation of the bodhisattva's responsibilities and its consequent devaluation of nirvāṇa poses obvious problems concern-ing the historical Buddha. The Buddha is the original inspiration of the bodhisattva ideal, and yet he himself did realize final nirvāṇa. He realized nirvāṇa, moreover, while there were still countless suffering beings in saṃsāra. The Mahāyāna overcomes these and other dilemmas through a reinterpretation of what it is to be a Buddha and to realize nirvāṇa. In the course of this reinterpretation, dharma (truth) replaces nirvāṇa as the ultimate goal and ideal of Mahāyāna Buddhism, and the Buddha is identified with dharma through the concept of the Dharma-kāya or "Truth-body" of the Buddha.

Mahāyāna Developments of the Concept of the Buddha

Dharma, of course, is a central concept in Theravāda as well as Mahāyāna Buddhism. In Buddhism as a whole, the essential meaning of dharma is "truth." In a closely related sense, dharma signifies the teaching of the Buddha, which is held to enshrine this truth. Most often both of these meanings are implied together when the word "dharma" is used. For example, an often repeated passage in the Theravāda scriptures describes dharma as being "eternal, verifiable, and onward-leading — to be known individually by the wise" (M1:265). Another well-known passage states that "whether or not Tathāgatas [Buddhas] arise, this world remains the same, with constancy of dharma, normativeness of dharma" (S2:25-6). In both passages, dharma is clearly an ultimate value. According to Nikāya Buddhism, the realization of nirvāṇa and the full realization of dharma — both as "truth" and as "teachings" — occur together.

The Mahāyāna, by contrast, emphasizes the realization of dharma, and de-emphasizes nirvāṇa. In doing so, Mahāyāna Buddhism overcomes the apparent conflict between its bodhisattva ideal and the life story of the Buddha. The Mahāyāna came to regard the essential Buddha not as a human being, but as the omnipresent truth (dharma) manifest in all things. To emphasize this distinction, Mahāyāna Buddhism refers to the Dharma-kāya or "truth-body" of the Buddha as opposed to the Nirmāṇa-kāya or "physical body" of the historical Buddha. The Nirmāṇa-kāya of the Buddha was limited in space and time, whereas the Dharma-kāya Buddha is omnipresent and eternal. Though this abstract characterization of the Buddha is alien to Theravāda Buddhism, its roots are apparent in the Pāli suttas.

The Theravāda scriptures record the story of the monk Vakkali, who was on his deathbed and desired to glimpse the Buddha before he passed away. The Buddha — who is consistently portrayed in the Theravāda scriptures as resisting the development of a personality cult centering upon himself — consented, but regretted his disciple's behavior saying, "Enough, Vakkali. What is the use of seeing this vile body? Whoever, Vakkali, sees dharma, he sees me. Whoever sees me, he sees dharma" (S3:120). In context, the obvious intent of this statement is that it is more important for one's spiritual well-being to practice the Buddha's teachings (dharma) and thereby see truth (dharma) than it is merely to see the person of the Buddha.

Taken out of context, however, the Buddha's statement can be understood as asserting that the Buddha is identical with dharma, and therefore is much more than a mere historical person. If the Buddha is equated with dharma as eternal truth, the implication is that the Buddha is also eternal. Interestingly, the *Śālistamba Sūtra* interprets the foregoing passage in precisely this way. Put simply, the truth (dharma) is everywhere at all times; it is a question of whether or not one sees it. Even a lie manifests truth, if one is but capable of seeing it. If it is literally true that "whoever sees the truth sees the Buddha," then it is possible to see the Buddha everywhere at all times. This is tantamount to saying that the Buddha is omnipresent and eternal, precisely what Mahāyāna Buddhism asserts with its doctrine of Dharma-kāya Buddha.

If, however, as the Mahāyāna asserts, the Buddha remains ever present in saṃsāra, a new understanding of nirvāṇa is required. The great Mahāyāna philosopher Nāgārjuna expressed this new understanding in his doctrine of the identity of saṃsāra and nirvāṇa, perhaps the most important doctrinal formulation in Mahāyāna Buddhism.

> There is no distinction of saṃsāra from nirvāṇa.
> There is no distinction of nirvāṇa from saṃsāra.
>
> *(Madhyamaka Kārikā 25.19)*

This doctrine is an outright rejection of the Theravāda concept of the radical duality of "this world" (saṃsāra) and the "other world" (nirvāṇa). In Mahāyāna Buddhism, nirvāṇa and saṃsāra become two aspects of the same reality, the same dharma. If one looks at the universe and sees the truth, that is nirvāṇa. If one fails to see the truth, it is saṃsāra. The universe does not change merely because it is perceived differently in the deluded and enlightened states. The universe remains eternally a manifestation of the Dharma-kāya, whether it is seen as saṃsāra or nirvāṇa. The final passing of the historical Buddha is similar. If one is capable only of seeing the physical body of the Buddha, one may believe that the Buddha has abandoned saṃsāra. If one sees the Dharma-kāya everywhere and at all times, one knows that the Buddha remains present in saṃsāra. The *Lotus Sūtra,* parts of which contain some of the earliest Mahāyāna literature, foreshadows this new doctrine of the Buddha and of nirvāṇa as follows.

> The life of the Tathāgata so long ago enlightened is unlimited; he is everlasting. Without becoming extinct, the Tathāgata makes a show of nirvāṇa, on behalf of those needing guidance.
>
> *Saddharma Puṇḍarīka Sūtra,* section 15

The Buddha's "making a show" in this passage represents an instance of *upāya* or "skillful means," the final structural element in the conceptual foundation of Mahāyāna Buddhism's devotionalism. The Pāli suttas often record the Buddha as noting that one has to teach in accordance with the ability of one's audience. For example, when one tells an eight-year-old that atoms are like bricks, one is not really lying, although one is not being altogether truthful either. Out of compassion, one skillfully presents part of the truth in a way that the pupil can grasp. When the child is twelve, one may again employ *upāya* and say that atoms are actually like swarms of billiard balls, another skillful untruth. In the passage above, the *Lotus Sūtra* suggests that even the death of the Buddha was only an *upāya,* an educational ruse for the benefit of those who are determined that there must be a goal for which to strive, in this case, nirvāṇa.

By integrating the concept of Buddha and the concept of dharma in this way, the Mahāyāna was able to provide for the masses appealing objects of religious devotion that remained appropriately Buddhist. This integration made possible a proliferation of Buddhas and bodhisattvas personifying various Buddhist ideals such as wisdom (Mañjuśrī bodhisattva), compassion (Avalokiteśvara bodhisattva), and benevolence (Maitreya Buddha). Each of these personifications developed its own individual mythology and iconography — reflecting its own particular *upāya* — so as to appeal to the various temperaments of different devotees. And yet all of them are thought to resolve ultimately into the supreme, eternal, omnipresent Dharma-kāya. In the last analysis, all of the various Buddhas and bodhisattvas of Mahāyāna Buddhism are but facets of the one ultimate truth, the dharma.

The incorporation of supernatural savior figures into the originally self-reliant religion of the historical Buddha is an outright heresy from the standpoint of Nikāya Buddhism. Mahāyāna Buddhism appears to have undertaken this radical departure from earlier Buddhism in order to enhance the popular appeal of the religion. Despite this popular appeal, however, Mahāyāna Buddhism did not abandon the philosophical rigor of early Buddhism. In the vigorous and sophisticated intellectual forum of post-Aśokan India, Buddhists were pressed more than ever to defend their doctrines philosophically against numerous rivals. In the course of this defense, the two main philosophical branches of Mahāyāna Buddhism took shape. These were the Madhyamaka or "Dialectical school" and the Vijñānavāda or "Consciousness school." Both of these schools, in different ways, provided philosophical underpinnings for Mahāyāna devotionalism by arguing that all phenomena are illusory and must necessarily resolve into an absolute which alone is real, and which can be identified with the supreme Dharma-kāya Buddha. In working out their respective philosophical doctrines, the Madhyamaka and Vijñānavāda schools of Mahāyāna Buddhism again built upon aspects of early Buddhism that are prominently recorded in the Theravāda scriptures.

Madhyamaka Philosophy

Madhyamaka philosophy is based on the doctrine of *śūnyatā*, or "emptiness." According to this doctrine, all things are empty in that they are devoid of self-existence *(svabhāva)*. This is to say each thing exists only by virtue of the existence of other things which themselves are not self-existent either. The Madhyamaka holds that careful analysis of any phenomenon will reveal its metaphysical emptiness, its lack of grounding in anything permanent. Paradoxically, Dharma-kāya Buddha as ultimate truth represents precisely this emptiness, this absence in all things of any metaphysical basis. All things are Buddha in the sense that each and every thing is utterly empty of self-existence, utterly devoid of any metaphysical basis. The Buddha — the truth which we seek — is everywhere, yet when found it is not found, for there is nothing to find. To seek and to find nothing is to find the true Buddha.

15. Those who describe in detail the Buddha — who is unchanging and beyond all description — are defeated by description, and do not perceive the Tathāgata.
16. The self-existence of the Tathāgata is the self-existence of the world. The Tathāgata is without self-existence, and the world is without self-existence.
Madhyamaka Kārikā 24.15-6

In the course of defending philosophically the doctrine of emptiness, two schools of thought developed within Madhyamaka Buddhism. These are known as the the Svātantrika and the Prāsaṅgika schools. Though these schools disagree, the origins of both lines of argument may be discerned in the scriptures of Nikāya Buddhism.

The philosophical position of the Svātantrika school is foreshadowed in Theravāda Buddhism's justification of its doctrine of impermanence. In Theravāda Buddhism, a doctrine of radical impermanence is the philosophical basis of the first Noble Truth, universal unsatisfactoriness *(dukkha)*. According to the Theravāda scriptures, all things are results of causes and conditions which are themselves caused and conditioned. Anything that depends upon causes and conditions must necessarily pass away when the conditions of its existence are no longer fulfilled. The Svātantrika school expanded upon the Theravāda doctrine of impermanence to establish the Madhyamaka doctrine of metaphysical emptiness.

Consider, for example, a simple chair. We normally say and think that a chair *has* a back, *has* a seat and *has* legs. Actually, however, there is no such thing as a chair apart from an assemblage of these components. There is no "chair" which could possess a back, seat or legs. Take away the back, and the "chair" becomes a stool. Take away the legs, and the "stool" becomes a slab of wood. The assembly of components is the condition for the "existence" of the chair. There is no self-existent thing which corresponds to the idea of "a chair." Moreover, when a "leg" is removed from a chair or stool, it is no longer a leg. It is just a stick of wood. Hit someone with it, and it becomes a club. Burn it, and it becomes first fuel, and then a pile of ashes. Even the components of a chair lack self-definition and self-existence. They are one thing when they are part of a chair, but quite another when not part of a chair.

Theravāda Buddhism was content to establish the impermanence of all phenomena. The Svātantrika school of Madhyamaka Buddhism extended the reasoning behind the Theravāda doctrine of the *impermanence* of all phenomena to establish the Mahāyāna doctrine of the *emptiness* of all phenomena. According to the Svātantrikas, a thorough analysis of causes and conditions — as in the example above of a chair — will establish that nothing in the universe exists in and of itself. This absence of self-existence *(svabhava)*, this metaphysical emptiness of all things *(śūnyatā)*, is itself ultimate truth (dharma), is itself the ultimate, Dharmakāya Buddha according to the Svātantrika school.

The Prāsaṅgika school rejected this positive demonstration of universal emptiness. The Prāsaṅgikas held that emptiness — being equivalent to Dharma-kāya Buddha and thereby to ultimate reality — cannot be comprehended or expressed through a mere philosophical theory. Instead, they held that emptiness represents the failure of all theories to capture truth. The Prāsaṅgikas claimed that the causal mechanism whereby the Svātantrikas attempted to establish emptiness is itself devoid of self-existence or self-definition. To prove this, the Prāsaṅgikas offered a comprehensive refutation of the entire concept of causation, attempting to prove that it is impossible to maintain that things are caused by themselves, caused by something else, caused by both or by neither. That is to say that they are not x, not non-x, not both x and non-x, and not neither x nor non-x.

Though the details of the Prāsaṅgika philosophical critique of causation are beyond the scope of the present historical treatment, it should be clear that this critique is based upon the *catush-koṭi* or "four-cornered negation" presented in Chapter III as a verifiable feature of early Buddhism. In their critiques of conceptual theories, the Prāsaṅgikas attacked Buddhist theories as vigorously and as often as they attacked other theories, but the origin of their critical stance is apparent in the scriptures of Nikāya Buddhism. For example, at several points the Pāli suttas mention the Buddha's refusal to answer certain questions. When confronted with these questions — essentially, "Is the universe finite in extent? Did the universe have a beginning? And does one who has realized nirvāṇa exist after death?" — the Buddha is said to have refused to affirm any of the four alternatives that the *catush-koṭi* entails for each question. When asked to explain his refusal to answer, the Buddha replied:

> [To affirm any of these alternatives] is holding a speculative view. . . . It is accompanied by anguish, distress, misery, and fever. It is not conducive to renunciation, dispassion, stopping, calming, knowledge, awakening, or nirvāṇa. I, Vacca, beholding this is a peril, do not approach any of these speculative views. . . . Speculative views have been abandoned by the Tathāgata.

> M1:486

Nāgārjuna's famous statement in verse 29 of his *Vigraha Vyāvartanī* is practically a paraphrase of the preceding passage:

> If I were to make any proposition whatsoever, then I would be in error, but I make no proposition, and therefore I am not in error.

Of course, the Prāsaṅgika rejection of doctrines and concepts is far more thoroughgoing than the historical Buddha's. The Prāsaṅgikas wished finally to demolish the possibility of any valid knowledge whatsoever. It must be remembered, however, that the Prāsaṅgika dialectic is not mere philosophical skepticism. Instead, by refuting all aspects of conceptual thought, the Prāsaṅgikas were attempting to validate *śūnyatā*, the metaphysical emptiness of all things, which is identified with the omnipresent and eternal Dharma-kāya Buddha. The concept of Dharma-kāya, in turn, is the basis of Mahāyāna devotionalism. Both the Svātantrika and the Prāsaṅgika branches of Madhyamaka Buddhism built upon old lines of argument evident in Nikāya Buddhism in order to buttress philosophically the new and specifically Mahāyāna devotion to savior figures.

Vijñānavāda Philosophy

Like the Madhyamaka, the Vijñānavāda or "Consciousness school" — the second major branch of Mahāyāna Buddhism — is in essence an attempt to defend philosophically the devotional orientation of the Mahāyāna as a whole. As in Madhyamaka, so in Vijñānavāda philosophy, this enterprise hinged upon validating the concept of Dharma-kāya Buddha by establishing the emptiness of all phenomena. Again like the Madhyamaka, the Vijñānavāda school enlarged upon a prominent theme of Nikāya Buddhism in formulating its philosophical position. This theme was analysis of the relationship between consciousness and its objects — a theme pursued in Nikāya Buddhism primarily through the doctrine of conditioned arising. The previous chapter showed how the Theravāda suttas exhibit ambiguity regarding the objective existence of phenomena. They hold that consciousness and its objects are mutually interdependent. This is to say that the nature of the perceiving mind influences how objects and events will appear, just as objects and events shape the perceiving mind. The position of the Pāli suttas, though non-committal, is implicitly critical regarding the objective reality of the "external" world. The Vijñānavāda philosophers took the quasi-immaterialist position of the Pāli suttas one step further and proclaimed confidently that all reality is "consciousness only" *(citta mātra).*

According to Vijñānavāda philosophy, all we can know about reality is confined to the content of a stream of mental images that is unique in each individual mind. Most of us, for example, think we know what a tree looks like. All we really have to go on, however, is a tiny, inverted image of a tree on the retina of the eye, and even this is invisible or distorted unless the entire mechanism of visual consciousness is working properly. The situation is similar with regard to the other senses as well. We know of the "external" world only that which is accessible to the mind as some sort of mental image deriving from sight, hearing, taste, smell, or touch. We experience this internal stream of images as an enormous external universe in which we live and move as subjects. In most cases we uncritically assume that there really is such a universe and that it is the same for others.

According to the Vijñānavāda, both of these assumptions — that others experience the same universe and that any external universe actually exists — are unwarranted assumptions. All that one ever actually experiences is a stream of mental images in one's own mind. According to the Vijñānavāda, this stream of mental images is reality itself. The objective, "external" world is a projection, an illusion, as in a dream. If, however, the objective universe is an illusion, then subjectivity must also be an illusion, because the subjective can only be defined with reference to the objective. If there is no "external" world, there can be no "internal" world either. According to this reasoning, both the illusion of an objective universe and the illusion of a subjective self originate from the imaginary bifurcation of simple, non-dual streams of mental images. These streams of images, in themselves, are neither subjective nor objective, neither material nor immaterial, neither conscious nor non-conscious. They are unadulterated reality itself. Deluded people only imagine that there is an objective, material universe over against which they define themselves as conscious subjects. Purified consciousness is devoid of objects, and therefore devoid of the illusion of a subjective self as well. As the great Vijñānavāda philosopher Vasubandhu wrote:

27. As long as one places something before oneself, taking it as an object and saying: "This is only a mental image," so long does one not dwell in that (mental image) alone.
28. But when cognition no longer apprehends an object, then it stands firmly in consciousness only, because where there is nothing to grasp, there is no more grasping.
29. It is without thought, without bias, and is the supra-mundane cognition. . . .
30. This is the element without defilements, inconceivable, wholesome and stable, the blissful body of liberation, the Dharma-kāya of the Great Sage.

Trimśikā, vs. 27-30

Thus the Vijñānavāda, like the Madhyamaka, seeks to render the Mahāyāna doctrine of the omnipresent Buddha philosophically reasonable. In doing so, it attempts to validate the basis of devotionalism in Mahāyāna Buddhism. The present historical study cannot go further into the intricacies of Madhyamaka and Vijñānavāda philosophy, fascinating though they are. It should be clear, however, that both of the philosophical branches of Mahāyāna Buddhism built upon concepts evident in early Buddhism as represented by the Pāli canon. By retaining these roots in early Buddhism, they are able to integrate popular devotionalism into the very fabric of Buddhism without becoming indistinguishable from the Hindu devotionalism that was developing at the same time in India. This conceptual continuity between Nikāya Buddhism and Mahāyāna Buddhism, though often obscured, is the fundamental basis upon which one is justified in speaking of "Buddhism" rather than various "Buddhisms."

CHAPTER V

The Development of
Buddhism in India

The foregoing chapters have examined the development of Buddhism in India from its inception (about 500 BCE) until the time of Aśoka, approximately 250 BCE. This chapter concentrates upon the development of Buddhism in India from Aśoka through to its virtual disappearance from the land of its birth by about 1200 CE. This same period — 250 BCE-1200 CE — also witnessed several crucial stages in the development of Hinduism. Because Buddhism and Hinduism developed in close proximity over such a long period of time, their histories are intertwined. Therefore, while concentrating upon Buddhism, this chapter will also consider developments in Hinduism and the mutual influence these two religions exerted upon one another.

One often encounters the supposition that Hinduism is an older religion than Buddhism and that Buddhism is an offshoot from Hinduism. Even scholars often assume that devotionalism *(bhakti)* in Buddhism was imported from Hinduism. These notions are unfounded. The essential scriptural and doctrinal basis of Hinduism was not completed until the composition of the *Bhagavad Gītā*, which probably occurred between 200 BCE and 200 CE. Clearly, it is misleading to speak of Hinduism as such before its scriptural and doctrinal basis was in place. Just as the *Bhagavad Gītā* established *bhakti* — loving devotion to a supernatural savior figure — as a fundamental element of Hinduism, so did the earliest Mahāyāna scriptures — composed during this same historical period — establish *bhakti* within Buddhism. There is no evidence to suggest that Buddhism absorbed *bhakti* from Hinduism.

During most of the period between 250 BCE and 250 CE — when fundamental scriptures of both Hinduism and Buddhism were being composed — India was a Buddhist country in that its most influential rulers espoused Buddhism as their state religion. During the final third of this period, the politically dominant forces in India were not only Buddhist, but were also foreign converts, bringing outside influences — possibly including *bhakti* — to both Buddhism and Hinduism. After this formative period, over the next thousand years, Buddhism and Hinduism developed side by side in India into roughly the religions we know today. Each influenced the other and neither can be said to derive from the other.

Instead, as discussed in Chapter I, what evidence there is suggests that both Buddhism and Hinduism built upon an overall Indian religious worldview with dual origins in the Vedic and yogic traditions. In order to distinguish it from classical Hinduism, the Vedic religion that was brought into India by migrating Indo-Europeans is commonly known as Brahmanism. Examples of the pre-Vedic, yogic tradition of India are the Jain and Ājīvaka religions. Aspects of Indo-European Brahmanism — for example the caste system and certain rituals — survive in classical Hinduism, but classical Hinduism also incorporates a large admixture of the pre-Vedic, yogic tradition that was indigenous to India. Most notably, this admixture includes the doctrine of rebirth. Buddhism developed primarily out of India's yogic tradition, but it also incorporated elements that appear to be based primarily upon Vedic antecedents. Most notable is Mahāyāna Buddhism's incorporation of a highly abstract, metaphysical principle (Dharma-kāya Buddha) in its philosophical justification of Buddhist devotionalism.

The latest hymns of the *Rig Veda* and the earliest sections of the *Upanishads,* both of which came to be Hindu scriptures, contain the first recorded concepts of a metaphysical absolute in Indian religion. However, the first systematic philosophical expression of absolutism — belief in an impersonal, ultimate reality which pervades and explains the entire universe — was the Buddhist Nāgārjuna's exposition of the doctrine of *śūnyatā* in the second century CE. About six hundred years later, the Hindu philosopher Śaṅkara created Hinduism's first systematic formulation of absolutism. Devotionalism *(bhakti),* which appears to have neither Indo-European nor yogic roots, appeared in both Buddhism and Hinduism around the beginning of the common era. *Bhakti* was not fully integrated into classical Hindu doctrine, however, until the writings of Rāmānuja in the eleventh century and Madhva in the thirteenth century. By this time, Mahāyāna Buddhist devotionalism had been fully developed for almost a thousand years, and Buddhism as a whole had matured, flowered, declined and disappeared in India, and had spread throughout East Asia. Thus, though Buddhism eventually disappeared from the land of its birth, for many centuries it was the preëminent religion of India.

The Ascendancy of Buddhism in India: 250 BCE to 250 CE

Toward the middle of the third century BCE, Aśoka (r. circa 270-230 BCE), the first monarch to rule over a united India, inherited the throne of the powerful Maurya dynasty of the northern Indian kingdom of Magadha. From this power base, he waged extensive military campaigns, and by about 270 BCE he had conquered the numerous states of the Indian sub-continent and forged them into a vast empire that included most of the territory of present-day India. Aśoka may be justly regarded as the founder of India, since before him, India did not exist as a political entity.

According to Buddhist tradition, Aśoka's father Bindusāra had favored the Ājīvaka religion. His grandfather Candragupta is said to have favored Jainism. Aśoka himself, like his father, favored the Ājīvakas in the early years of his reign, although all of these monarchs honored the Brahmanic or "priestly" forebears of Hinduism. These observations illustrate the religious diversity prevalent in India at that time. Not only did Hinduism as such not yet exist, even the orthodox Brahmanism deriving from the *Vedas* and the *Upanishads* was only one of many more or less equally influential religious alternatives in India.

Aśoka covered his realm with numerous edicts carved into stones, cave walls, and free-standing granite pillars. These edicts — which are the first examples of writing in India after the demise of the Indus Valley civilization in about 1500 BCE — record that approximately ten years into his reign, around 260 BCE, Aśoka converted to Buddhism. After this point, Aśoka's edicts reflect his growing aversion to war and bloodshed and his determination to govern his realm according to Buddhist principles of non-violence and justice for all. These edicts reveal Aśoka's concern with preserving religious freedom on the one hand, and with promoting Buddhism on the other. Doubtless, this imperial patronage, which continued throughout the remaining eighty years of the Maurya dynasty, had a profound effect upon the religious orientation of the Indian masses. In effect, Buddhism was the first state religion of India, since India as such did not exist before Aśoka.

Aśoka's contributions to Buddhism are legendary and have been emulated by countless major and minor rulers throughout Asia for almost two thousand years. He and his heirs in the Maurya dynasty erected Buddhist monasteries and monuments throughout the realm. Surviving examples of Aśokan architecture indicate that the technical skill of his stonecutters remains unsurpassed throughout history. He is said to have presided over a third Buddhist Council to standardize the canon and purify the Saṅgha (the community of monks and nuns) of divisive and dissolute elements. He dispatched Buddhist missions to lands beyond his realm. On Buddhist principles, he forbade animal sacrifices throughout his realm and stopped the slaughter of animals for the royal kitchen. It is probably with Aśoka that vegetarianism became widespread in India. In addition to his Buddhist construction projects, he built facilities for other religions and public works such as roads, rest houses, wells and reservoirs for the benefit of the general populace. Finally, he reintroduced writing to India on a wide scale after over a thousand years of illiteracy. The unification of India alone would have made Aśoka one of history's great monarchs. These other high-minded accomplishments make him arguably the most progressive ruler the world has ever known. He died in approximately 230 BCE.

As is often the case following a truly great leader, Aśoka's heirs were unable to maintain his political legacy for long. In about 185 BCE the Maurya dynasty, reduced in strength and territory, gave way to the Śuṅga dynasty, which endured for about a hundred years. The Śuṅgas claimed descent from the legendary Vedic sage Bharadvāja, and thus favored Brahmanism over Buddhism. Buddhist legend remembers the century of Śuṅga rule as a time of persecution against Buddhism. Archaeological evidence indicates, however, that Buddhist architecture flourished in India during the Śuṅga period. It is therefore doubtful that the fall of the Maurya dynasty had any catastrophic effects upon Buddhism. Even if the Śuṅgas were as hostile toward Buddhism as Buddhist legend asserts, they did not exert anywhere near the geographical, political or military influence of Aśoka. Several other kingdoms vied with the Śuṅgas for control of the vast territory once ruled in its entirety by Aśoka, and there is no indication that Buddhism suffered under any of these kingdoms. By and large, Buddhism continued to thrive throughout India during the Śuṅga period, enjoying the aftereffects of the advantages it had gained under Aśoka and the Mauryas.

In the course of conflicts with rival Indian kingdoms, the territory of the Śuṅga dynasty dwindled into the northwestern corner of present-day India and Pakistan. This territory too was contested and finally dominated by Greeks from beyond the Indus river in the west. These Greeks, the aftermath of Alexander the Great's triumphal march across Asia in the fourth century BCE, had been driven from northern India by Aśoka's grandfather Candragupta, and were held at bay throughout the Maurya dynasty. For these Greeks, Buddhism was the primary religion of India, and when they were dominant in India, the Greeks showed great respect for Buddhism. In fact, the Greeks of northwestern India are given credit for manufacturing the first Buddha images in the first century BCE. The foremost of the Greek kings of India, Menandros (known as Milinda in Pāli), ruled from approximately 155 to 130 BCE. According to a Theravāda Buddhist text known as the *Milinda Pañha,* "The Questions of King Milinda," Menandros actually converted to Buddhism. This may be an exaggeration, but surviving coins minted by Menandros bear on their backs an imprint of the Buddhist wheel of dharma, indicating that Buddhism was promoted in his kingdom, and possibly that it was the state religion. After the Greeks, other invaders from Central Asia and Persia, known as Śakas (Scythians) and Pahlavas (Parthians), became dominant in northwest India, but they too appear to have treated Buddhism with respect. Though specific evidence is scarce, most indications are that Buddhism continued to thrive after Aśoka — albeit on a more even footing with other yogic sects and Vedic Brahmanism — until it entered its next great phase of expansion under the Kushan dynasty.

The Kushans, though often regarded as an Indian dynasty, were actually refugees from border areas of far western China. In the third century BCE the Chinese had begun to build the Great Wall of China to protect China's heartland from marauding hordes known as the Xiong Nu (Hsiung Nu). The Kushans, known to the Chinese as the Yue Zhi (Yüeh Chih), found themselves on the outside of the Great Wall, beyond the protection of imperial China and vulnerable to the random violence of the ferocious Xiong Nu. As a result, they migrated south, encountering and conquering the Greek kingdoms to the northwest of present-day India. The Kushans thus found themselves occupying what amounted to a buffer zone between the Persian empire to the west and the relatively weak states of northern India to the east. In this situation, they naturally exerted their own territorial ambitions upon their weaker neighbors to the east. Eventually, under the first great Kushan emperor Kanishka — who ruled from 78 to 123 CE or thereabout — they became dominant across a broad swath of territory including present-day Afghanistan, Pakistan and northern India. Kanishka was also influential, if not dominant, among the Central Asian states on the Silk Road, the gateway to China. The Kushans, who ruled northern India until about 225 CE, thus maintained Chinese, Persian, Greek and Central Asian contacts. They were, however, predominantly Buddhist.

Kanishka, the founder of the Kushan dynasty, is remembered among Buddhists as the Mahāyānist equivalent of Aśoka. It is clear, however, that he encouraged Nikāya Buddhism, particularly the Sarvāstivāda, as well as Mahāyāna Buddhism. Kanishka is said to have convened a fourth Buddhist Council in order to collect and systematize the scriptures and doctrines of Mahāyāna Buddhism, but this is doubtful. Kanishka appears to have been, like Aśoka, tolerant and pragmatic regarding religious belief in his empire, preferring harmony to sectarian strife. Some of his coins bear images of the Buddha, but others bear Brahmanic and even Persian and Greek deities. Given this eclecticism, it seems unlikely that Kanishka himself strongly favored one form of Buddhism over another. Nonetheless, as the "Mahāyānist Aśoka," Kanishka is credited, rightly or wrongly, with a dramatic upsurge and spread of Mahāyāna Buddhism. Whether or not the emperor was responsible for this upsurge, around the time of

Kanishka, Mahāyāna Buddhism began to thrive in India and spread throughout Central Asia. It was around this time too that Buddhism, primarily Mahāyāna, began to spread in earnest into imperial China.

Mahāyānists generally associate Aśvaghosha, the first great Mahāyāna scholar, with Kanishka, though Aśvaghosha is a shadowy historical figure and may have lived slightly before or after the monarch. Aśvaghosha is popularly but dubiously credited with having written *The Awakening of Faith in the Mahāyāna*, a work which is probably the product of a much later age. Aśvaghosha did, however, write the *Buddha-carita* or "Life of the Buddha," which is universally regarded as one of the greatest epic poems in Sanskrit or any other language. Aśvaghosha's *Buddha-carita* is a sophisticated and polished work, the culmination of what was by his time a highly developed literary genre — inspirational biography of the divinized Buddha.

Veneration of the Buddha was not confined to Mahāyāna Buddhism. By the time of Kanishka, several schools of Nikāya Buddhism had incorporated mythologized versions of the life of the Buddha into their Vinaya Piṭakas, in addition to the rules for monks and nuns which constitute the bulk of Vinaya literature. Some schools of Nikāya Buddhism had included mythological biographies of the Buddha in the "Miscellaneous" sections of their Tripiṭakas. The Sarvāstivādin Sangharaksha, believed to be one of Kanishka's teachers, wrote his own biography of the Buddha under the emperor's auspices, a work also called the *Buddha-carita,* which survives in Chinese. The *Mahāvastu,* the only complete text of the Mahāsanghikas to survive in Sanskrit, is also an inspirational account of the life of the Buddha and his previous lives as a bodhisattva. Buddha images were common in Kanishka's reign, and it is possible that the Buddha was the most popular object of religious devotion in India at the time.

By this time the popular deities of classical Hinduism were also gaining widespread recognition among the masses as a result of publicly performed works such as the *Bhagavad Gītā*. Such works, recounting the exploits of kings, heros and gods, had been for centuries a popular form of entertainment performed for the masses by roving bards. The *Bhagavad Gītā* probably was not completed until about the time of Kanishka, however, and it is the first known work to encourage religious devotion *(bhakti),* toward a classical Hindu deity, namely Krishna. Figures such as Krishna were probably well known among the masses well before this time, but they were known as epic heroes, not as objects of religious devotion.

With regard to the origins of devotionalism in India, what little evidence there is justifies only the general conclusion that *bhakti* gained widespread popularity across the religious spectrum of India between the reigns of Aśoka and Kanishka. This scant evidence certainly does not justify the conclusion that *bhakti* developed first in Hinduism or that Buddhist devotionalism derived from Hindu devotionalism. There is no real indication that the appearance of *bhakti* in Indian religion was anything but a spontaneous, indigenous development within India. If *bhakti* was an import, it was most likely introduced from Zoroastrian Persia via Buddhism. Zoroastrianism is a dualistic religion positing a saving deity of light, Ahura Mazda, opposed to an evil deity of matter, Angra Mainyu. According to Zoroastrianism, which originated in the sixth century BCE, the responsibility of human beings is to transcend the material world and align themselves with the spiritual light of Ahura Mazda. Because of its devotional content and Persia's proximity to India, Zoroastrianism is often cited as a possible source of Indian *bhakti*. The several non-Indian cultures which influenced India after the reign of Aśoka — the Greeks, the Śakas, the Pahlavas, and the Kushans — were all in contact with Persia and all favored Buddhism among the religions of India. Therefore, if *bhakti* was imported from Persia, it probably entered India first in a Buddhist guise. During the period in which *bhakti* appeared in India, Hinduism as we know it was only beginning to emerge from the orthodox Brahmanism that had been eclipsed by Buddhism since the time of Aśoka, a period of some three to four centuries.

In addition to the incorporation of *bhakti,* the other major development in Mahāyāna Buddhism by the end of the Kushan period was the beginning of its systematic philosophy, which attempted to forge consistent doctrine out of the exuberant insights of the Mahāyāna scriptures. Two of the foremost systematic philosophers of Mahāyāna Buddhism, Nāgārjuna and Āryadeva, probably belong to the Kushan period. Of the great philosophers of Mahāyāna Buddhism, Nāgārjuna, the founder of the Madhyamaka school of "emptiness" *(śūnyatā),* was undoubtedly the greatest. Nāgārjuna's date is uncertain, but he and his pupil Āryadeva are usually assigned to the second century CE, toward the end of the Kushan period.

The appearance of Nāgārjuna marks the beginning of Mahāyāna Buddhism's classical philosophical formulation. In Nāgārjuna's time there were already a fair number of Mahāyāna sūtras presenting quite different versions of the Buddhist teachings. Nāgārjuna concentrated on the class of sūtra known as *Prajñā Pāramitā* or "Perfection of Wisdom." These range from a very long sūtra in 100,000 verses to the "Perfection of Wisdom in One Letter," the letter "a". As the latter suggests, these sūtras concentrate upon the inexpressibility of ultimate truth and the necessity of intuitive knowledge to grasp it.

Of the many works attributed to Nāgārjuna, the most important and the one most certain to be actually his, is the *Madhyamaka Kārikā*, the "Verses on Madhyamaka," which attempts to establish metaphysical emptiness *(śūnyatā)* on the one hand, and the falsity of all concepts and beliefs on the other. As noted in Chapter IV, the Madhyamaka school of Buddhism split into two branches after Nāgārjuna. The Prāsaṅgika or "dialectical" branch, which attempted to disprove all philosophical positions, is associated with Nāgārjuna's pupil Āryadeva and almost certainly represents Nāgārjuna's own thought most faithfully. The Svātantrika school of Madhyamaka did not emerge until the fifth century, when the logician Bhāvaviveka, attempted to establish metaphysical emptiness on positive logical grounds. In the sixth century, Candrakīrti in effect settled the dispute decisively in favor of the Prāsaṅgikas with his famous commentary the *Prasannapadā*, which is now regarded among Buddhists as the definitive interpretation of Nāgārjuna and the definitive formulation of Madhyamaka as a whole. Candrakīrti's interpretation, however, is a conservative restatement and elaboration of Nāgārjuna's original position, so that Nāgārjuna himself is justly regarded as the founder of the Madhyamaka school in the second century CE.

In addition, Nāgārjuna may be regarded as the founder, or at least the first major figure, of the Mahāyāna academic tradition. Virtually unanimous Buddhist tradition associates Nāgārjuna with the great Buddhist university of Nālandā, the imposing ruins of which still stand in the modern Indian state of Bihar. This second century date may be a bit early for the foundation of an actual university at Nālandā, but the location of Nālandā is associated with Buddhist scholarship from very early times. Tradition has it that the followers of Sāriputta (Skt. Śāriputra), one of the foremost disciples of the historical Buddha, often gathered there for study. By the fifth century, reliable accounts by Chinese pilgrims record that the library at Nālandā was housed in three multi-story buildings and that the university had an enrollment of several thousand monk-students, representing all schools of Buddhism and governed by strict admission procedures and academic standards.

If it was indeed founded in the Kushan dynasty, Nālandā qualifies as one of the world's first institutions of higher education. It is also one of history's longest running universities, since it did not cease to exist until about 1200. Nāgārjuna and Āryadeva almost certainly lived during the Kushan period. Their surviving works indicate that by 250 CE, Mahāyāna Buddhism had reached adulthood if not full maturity and that Buddhism as a whole was already similar in scope to the religion we know today.

From the time of Aśoka, approximately 250 BCE, until the breakup of the Kushan dynasty, which may be roughly dated at about 225 CE, all indications are that Buddhism was the dominant creed in India. Jainism, Ājīvakism, Vedic Brahmanism, and cults devoted to Vishṇu and Śiva — who would become the favored deities of classical Hinduism — all existed during this period on a more or less equal footing as secondary religions, each of which occasionally enjoyed state patronage in limited geographical areas. Toward the end of the Kushan period, Hinduism as we know it began to emerge with confidence and identity from its primary source, the progressive Brahmanism which first appears in the principal *Upanishads* (800-300 BCE). The first truly representative scripture of classical Hinduism, the *Bhagavad Gītā*, was probably completed by the end of the Kushan period. Hinduism itself, however, did not begin to gain ascendancy in India until the founding of the Gupta dynasty in 320 CE.

The Completion of Classical Buddhism: 250-500 CE

The intervening century between the collapse of the Kushan dynasty and the founding of the Gupta dynasty was a complex period of numerous kingdoms about which little historical information survives. The coinage of this period, which bears a preponderance of Zoroastrian deities, suggests that Persian influence was strong during the third century in India, but there is no indication during this period of any large-scale alteration in the existing religious orientation of India, an orientation which appears to have been primarily Buddhist.

The Gupta dynasty is generally regarded as the first great Hindu dynasty of India. It must be remembered, however, that Hinduism as such was still in its formative stages during the Gupta period. The Guptas dominated northern India from the coronation of Candragupta I in 320 until the dynasty collapsed before an onslaught of the Huns in approximately 500. Throughout this period, Buddhism continued to flourish in India. During the Gupta period, in fact, the formulation of classical Mahāyāna philosophy, which began under Nāgārjuna, reached its completion under Asaṅga, Vasubandhu and Dignāga.

The brothers Asaṅga and Vasubandhu, in the fourth century, are generally credited with the founding of the Vijñānavāda or "Consciousness school" of Mahāyāna Buddhism. Asaṅga and Vasubandhu concentrated on sūtras that emphasize the illusory nature of the material universe. They formulated the philosophical position that reality consists of "mind only" *(citta mātra),* the doctrinal basis of Vijñānavāda Buddhism. Because of its emphasis upon meditation to overcome the illusion of an objectively existing world, the Vijñānavāda school is also known as the Yogācāra or "Yoga-practice" school. The primary scriptural

texts of this school are the *Sandhinirmochana Sūtra* and the better
known *Laṅkāvatāra Sūtra*. Vasubandhu's major works, the *Vimśikā* and
the *Trimśikā* (the "Twenty Verses" and the "Thirty Verses"), provide the
philosophical basis for the Vijñānavāda school of Buddhism.

In addition to his Vijñānavāda works, Vasubandhu also wrote an
important treatise, the *Abhidharma Kośa*, on the Abhidharma literature of
the Sarvāstivāda school of Nikāya Buddhism. For this reason Mahāyāna
tradition maintains that his brother Asaṅga was responsible for converting
him from Nikāya Buddhism to the Mahāyāna. For this same reason,
Western scholars of Buddhism often assert that there may have been two
different Vasubandhus living at about the same time. It is just as likely
that a single Vasubandhu was simply a versatile, open-minded scholar
capable of elaborating sympathetically the doctrines of different schools
of Buddhism.

Though it remained influential in its own right, the Vijñānavāda school
exerted its most important influence upon Buddhism and upon Indian
thought in general by developing within its ranks Buddhist logic. The
founder of Buddhist logic is generally held to be Dignāga, a pupil of
Vasubandhu, who thus must have operated around 400 CE. His most
important work is the *Pramāṇa Samuccaya*. With the advent of Dignāga,
the fundamental outlines of classical Mahāyāna thought became established. Buddhaghosa, the great systematizer of Theravāda doctrine in
Sri Lanka, will be discussed below in Chapter VI, but it is significant to
note here that he was a contemporary of Dignāga, operating in the
fifth century.

Thus, with the exception of Tantric Buddhism, which is discussed in
the following section, classical Indian Buddhism as we know it was fully
in place by the fifth century. The doctrinal developments that followed
were elaborations and refinements of the basic positions established by
this time. These basic doctrinal positions were: the seventeen schools
of Nikāya Buddhism, primarily Theravāda and Sarvāstivāda, on the
one hand, and on the other hand the Mahāyāna divided into the two
Madhyamaka schools (Svātantrika and Prāsaṅgika) and the Vijñānavāda
school, which also encompassed Buddhist logic.

The Medieval Period: 500-1000 CE

Following the establishment of its fundamental philosophical schools,
the final important development in Indian Buddhism was the advent of
Tantric or esoteric, magic-oriented Buddhism. Tantric practices appear to
have gained widespread popularity in both Buddhism and Hinduism in

the sixth and seventh centuries. The backgrounds of this sudden appearance of Tantrism in India are something of a mystery. Perhaps this should not be surprising, given Tantrism's emphasis upon secrecy and initiation. Tantric practices could have been around for centuries without having been recorded in the surviving literature of main-stream religious traditions. In this surviving literature, there are some enticing leads, but they remain inconclusive.

The Pāli suttas, for example, disapprovingly record various magical practices that could be construed as forerunners of Tantrism. Some scholars claim to discern the origins of Tantra, both Buddhist and Hindu, in the magical practices of the *Atharva Veda*. Though reckoned as the fourth Veda in orthodox Hinduism — after the genuinely ancient *Rig, Sāma* and *Yajur Vedas* — the text of the *Atharva Veda* is probably post-Upanishadic for the most part. Nonetheless, the beliefs and practices it depicts could be extremely ancient. These beliefs and practices appear to have both Vedic and non-Vedic roots. Hindu Tantrism is associated with the god Śiva, who was noted in Chapter I as possibly having roots in the Indus Valley civilization. When Tantric Buddhism arrived in Tibet — beginning in the eighth century — Himalayan shamans claimed that its magical beliefs and practices were already familiar to them. Himalayan Kashmir was an important source of Śiva worship and Hindu Tantrism, which gives some credence to these claims. South India too, however, claims convincingly to be an ancient source of Śiva worship and Tantrism.

Lacking conclusive evidence regarding the origins of Tantrism, the most defensible position is that Tantrism was an undercurrent throughout the Indian sub-continent and the Himalayas from very ancient times, and that it began to gain widespread "official" recognition in the sixth century. Unlike Buddhist *bhakti*, Buddhist Tantrism did borrow demonstrably from Hindu Tantrism, and Tantric practices appear to have gained recognition in main-stream Hinduism slightly before they were accepted in main-stream Buddhism. The first concrete evidence of a Tantric tradition in Buddhism is a fifth century Chinese translation of a Buddhist Tantric text from India, the *Ratnaketudhāraṇi*.[17] The first clear indication of a significant Tantric infiltration of the Buddhist establishment in India is the philosopher Dharmakīrti's criticism of the use of *mantras* (incantations) in the seventh century. By the eighth century, Indian monks were vigorously exporting Tantric Buddhism to China and Tibet, as will be discussed below in the relevant chapters.

Though common, it is ethnocentric and misleading to propose that Tantric Buddhism with its sexual and magical practices was responsible for a moral decay of Indian Buddhism. Despite these practices, which are primarily symbolic, Tantric Buddhism has always exhibited a high degree of morality, if not perhaps the prim propriety some Western writers naively associate with religion. Nonetheless, it may be fair to say that the prominence of Tantrism in Buddhist India after the sixth century was symptomatic of dissatisfaction with the arid scholasticism which otherwise characterized Indian Buddhism of this time.

The great monastic universities — most notably Nālandā, Vikramaśilā and Uddaṇḍapura — were dominated by sectarian scholar-monks debating the relative merits of increasingly arcane academic positions. The diaries of Chinese pilgrims indicate that Buddhists representing the various schools co-existed peacefully in Buddhist institutions throughout India and Central Asia. They existed, however, in a constant state of scholarly debate. The primary scholastic positions represented in these institutions were the several schools of Nikāya Buddhism — primarily the Sarvāstivāda — and the Madhyamaka and Vijñānavāda schools of Mahāyāna Buddhism. The prevalence of the Sarvāstivāda is surprising since virtually all other Buddhist schools opposed them. Most of the Mahāyāna philosophical critiques of Nikāya Buddhism are in fact directed specifically against Sarvāstivāda positions. The Theravāda and other schools of the Elders opposed them on virtually the same points, primarily their diluting of the doctrine of impermanence with the doctrine of "everything exists." One important school, the Sautrāntikas or "those concerned only with the sūtras," broke away from the Sarvāstivāda specifically, but rejected the Abhidharma and commentarial literature of all schools of Buddhism. Another group, the Pudgalavādins or "those who affirm the person," came so close to affirming a soul that they were regarded as heretics by all other schools of Buddhism. Nonetheless, according to the accounts of Chinese pilgrims, they were numerous.

The existence of the Sautrāntikas, "those concerned only with the sūtras," is particularly illustrative of the state of main-stream Buddhism in the medieval period. They represent a significant group of monks who had tired of the academic quibbles among the various schools of Nikāya and Mahāyāna Buddhism. Originally they wished to return as best they could to the teachings of the historical Buddha as recorded in the sūtras, whether those of Nikāya Buddhism or Mahāyāna Buddhism. In the scholastic atmosphere of the medieval period, however, even the Sautrāntikas felt compelled to produce academic treatises defining and defending their philosophical positions. Mahāyāna scholars of the medieval period produced the great commentarial works which finalized and finessed the positions advanced by the founders of the Madhyamaka and Vijñānavāda schools. Of these scholars, the foremost were Candrakīrti (seventh century) of the Madhyamaka school and Dharmakīrti (seventh century) of the Vijñānavāda school. Both were rigorous, technical philosophers dedicated to establishing and defending their school's doctrines vis-à-vis all opposition and alternatives. Inspirational works, such as the *Bodhi-caryāvatāra* and *Śiksbā Samuccaya* of Śāntideva (eighth century) were not unknown in the medieval period, but were the exception rather than the rule.

In this dry, scholastic atmosphere, Tantric Buddhism seems to have provided an avenue of spiritual release, offering as it did the prospect of enlightenment in this very lifetime through esoteric, secret practices. Having themselves turned Buddhism into a series of academic disciplines, the scholar-monks of India apparently began to seek out the non-rational spiritual alternatives of Tantrism, which promised direct and immediate benefits. The most colorful among these monks was Nāropa, who resigned as abbot of Nālandā (some sources say Vikramaśilā) in 1057, reputedly at the behest of an old peasant woman, to seek his predestined Tantric master. In doing so, he became a major figure in the continuing destiny of Buddhism, which by this time lay beyond India. We will encounter Nāropa again in the context of Tibetan Buddhism.

Toward the end of the fifth century the Gupta dynasty succumbed to the ferocious Huns, whose westward expansion plagued the Romans at about this time. The Huns in India are remembered as persecutors of Buddhism specifically, but were no doubt regarded as such by virtually all Indians. As the later Turkish conquest of northern India reveals, however, Buddhism was particularly vulnerable to the depredations of barbarians. The Huns dispersed from India within a century, as much by their own accord as by the efforts of various would-be liberators. This left a power vacuum eventually filled by the last great Indian emperor, Harsha, who was also India's last great patron of Buddhism.

Harsha reigned from about 606 to 647, and after a series of campaigns eventually dominated most of northern India. Luckily, the latter part of this period is relatively well documented in the travelogue of the great Chinese pilgrim Xuan Zang (Hsüan Tsang — see Pronunciation Guide). Xuan Zang was an honored guest and close personal associate of Harsha, and thus witnessed the best face that Indian Buddhism could show. Nonetheless, his account depicts Buddhism already in decline, with many monasteries and sacred sites abandoned or neglected, particularly in central and southern India. Interestingly, Xuan Zang, though himself a Mahāyānist, indicates that Nikāya Buddhism was still stronger than Mahāyāna Buddhism in most parts of India and Central Asia in the seventh century. Emperor Harsha himself is reputed to have been partial to Nikāya Buddhism before his conversion to the Mahāyāna by Xuan Zang.

In 637, during Harsha's reign, the Arab armies of Islam had already conquered Ctesiphon, capital of the Persian empire, thereby unleashing forces that would eventually destroy Buddhism in India. No one in India could have known of the coming disaster at the time, but it is almost as if Buddhism began to shrink eastward away from its nemesis. After the death of Harsha, Buddhism's center of gravity shifted to the northeastern corner of India under the auspices of the Pāla dynasty, which ruled present-day Bihar and Bengal from about 650 to 950. By 711, Muslims had occupied territory in present-day Pakistan, but without perpetrating the religious persecution that would characterize the Islamic blitz of northern India in the thirteenth century. Meanwhile, the internal conditions that would facilitate the demise of Indian Buddhism were well under way in the form of an upsurge of populist Hinduism.

Of the historical figures involved in this upsurge, the first and foremost was Śaṅkara, who probably lived in the eighth century. Though Śaṅkara had intellectual forebears in Hinduism, he is generally regarded as the founder of the school of Hinduism known as Advaita or "non-dual" Vedānta. The term Vedānta, meaning literally "culmination of the Vedas" refers to a movement within Hinduism that was based upon the *Upanishads,* the *Bhagavad Gītā,* and a third scripture known as the *Brahma Sūtras.* According to the Vedāntists, these three texts reveal more explicitly the hidden meaning of the Vedas, the most authoritative scriptures of Hinduism. The meanings of these three texts, however, are also obscure, mutually contradictory, and open to interpretation. Śaṅkara's interpretation, based primarily on the *Upanishads,* proceeded from the proposition that there is no difference, no duality, between the essence of human consciousness and the essence of the universe, hence the name "Advaita" or "non-dualist" for his school.

Despite Śaṅkara's opposition to Buddhism, his concept of ultimate reality corresponds so closely to that of Nāgārjuna that Śaṅkara's Hindu rivals referred to him as a "surreptitious Buddhist." Given this similarity to Nāgārjuna, and Śaṅkara's relatively late date, it is almost certain that Śaṅkara was significantly influenced by Madhyamaka Buddhism, which was fully formed and well known throughout India by Śaṅkara's lifetime in the eighth century. According to both Śaṅkara and Nāgārjuna, mundane reality is subsumed and negated by an ultimate reality that pervades everything but is beyond verbal or mental conceptualization. According to both, introspective meditation is the only means of realizing this ultimate reality, and this realization results in a negation of the individual self and a cessation of rebirth forever. According to both, this is the supreme spiritual achievement and entails not only transcendence of the mundane world, but transcendence of the gods and all heavenly worlds as well.

The only important philosophical difference between Śaṅkara and Nāgārjuna is that for Śaṅkara ultimate reality *(brahman* or *ātman)* is the source of the self and the universe, whereas for Nāgārjuna ultimate reality is the emptiness *(śūnyatā)* of all things and the self. Given that both thinkers reject the validity of verbal and conceptual formulations of the nature of ultimate reality, it is difficult if not impossible to distinguish meaningfully between Śaṅkara's ultimate "something" and Nāgārjuna's ultimate "nothing," especially since both thinkers would reject the labels "something" or "nothing" as being far too crude to characterize accurately the ultimately real. The difference between Śaṅkara and some early Vijñānavāda Buddhists is even more difficult to specify, since both assert that ultimate reality is a pure form of consciousness.

Before moving on to examine the decline and disappearance of Buddhism from the land of its birth, these similarities between Śaṅkara's Advaita Vedānta and Mahāyāna Buddhism merit pause for thought. Though a rival of Buddhism, Śaṅkara was almost certainly influenced significantly and directly by Buddhism. As a result, in a peculiar way Buddhism did survive and indeed thrive in India to the present day in the form of Advaita or non-dualist Vedānta. Religious bias on the parts of both Buddhists and Hindus resists this proposition, but it is notoriously difficult to point out any real differences between the Advaita Hindu and Mahāyāna Buddhist concepts of ultimate reality and the spiritual path and goal of humankind. Both Mahāyāna Buddhism and Hindu Advaita urge introspective meditation aimed at disclosing the illusoriness of the world and the individual self. Both systems encourage their followers to augment meditational practice with devotion toward a number of deities, all of which are regarded as aspects of and avenues to the ultimately real. Regardless of their philosophical disagreements regarding the nature of ultimate reality, both systems agree that ultimate reality itself remains forever elusive of the words or concepts of religious doctrine. In the course of the following examination of the spread of Buddhism beyond India, it will become clear that several of the forms of Buddhism which developed in east Asia and which survive to the present day are actually further removed from the original insights of the historical Buddha than is Advaita Hinduism. Even though Buddhism as such did not survive in India, its influence certainly did.

The Decline of Buddhism in India

The disappearance of Buddhism as such from the land of its birth remains something of a mystery. The conquest of India by Turkish Muslims, which began in earnest in the tenth century, is often blamed for the destruction of Buddhism in India. In Muslim eyes, not only were

Buddhists idolators and polytheists, but worse and inconceivably, they were also ultimately atheists. Moreover, the distinctively dressed monks, all concentrated in large monasteries, were an easily identifiable target for Muslim zealotry. There is no doubt that the Muslims persecuted Buddhists, massacred monks, and destroyed Buddhist monasteries, universities and libraries. Even accounts written by Muslim witnesses and historians depict a sickening spectacle of unrepentant barbarism, particularly against "the religion of Budd," though Hinduism was by no means spared. Nonetheless, the advent of Islam — ruthless as it was — cannot be blamed entirely for the disappearance of Buddhism from India. Hinduism, after all, survived the Muslim conquest and some five centuries of Muslim domination.

Both the survival of Hinduism and the demise of Buddhism appear to be due partly to the work of the Hindu systematists — primarily Śankara. Their success in establishing Hinduism among the masses cannot be denied, nor can Buddhism's retreat into its monasteries and universities. Equally important, the distinction between Buddhism and Hinduism had become blurred, once again as a result of the work of the Hindu systematists, particularly the Advaitin followers of Śankara. By the tenth century virtually everyone in India — Buddhist or otherwise — worshipped a variety of deities with the understanding that they represented collectively a single ultimate reality which is beyond human comprehension. The average person could not have cared much whether the deities worshipped were Buddhist or Hindu, particularly when Buddhists were being singled out for persecution. No doubt, the advent of Tantrism in both Buddhism and Hinduism further obscured the differences between the two religions.

By the time of the Muslim conquest, the separate identity of Buddhism resided primarily in its great monasteries and universities. Once these were destroyed and the educated monks killed or driven away, Buddhism had lost the core of its identity. Hinduism, by contrast, had no identifiable heart at which to strike. It had succeeded in pervading Indian society while Buddhism had become increasingly isolated in monasteries and universities. Traditionally, the destruction of Nālandā in 1197 and of Vikramaśilā in 1203 by Muḥammad Ghūrī marks the end of Buddhism in India. The Muslims never succeeded in dominating all of India, however, and Buddhism probably survived for some time before being absorbed completely into Hinduism.

Well before the destruction of Nālandā and Vikramaśilā, the cream of India's learned monks had joined an exodus to Tibet, China, Southeast Asia, Korea, and Japan. This exodus had begun as a trickle in the early eighth century, as perceptive monks began to see that the future of Buddhism lay beyond the land of its birth. This perception could have been only partly due to the threat posed by the advance of Islam. More immediately, it appears that Indian kings and the laity gradually lost interest in financing Buddhism's expensive monastic institutions. At least by the time of Emperor Harsha, the fortunes of these institutions appear to have been tied to the fortunes of Indian monarchies. In addition to the rise of Hinduism, the general decline of Indian monarchies was detrimental to Buddhism. Muslim persecution, harsh as it was, was only the final blow.

For a time after the Muslim conquest, Indian style Buddhism persisted in the southern, eastern, and northern extremities of India, beyond the reach of Muslim zealotry. Pockets of Buddhism may have survived to the present day in the northeast, in the area now comprising Bangladesh and the several far eastern states of India. Most of the Buddhism that now exists in this area, however, appears to have relatively recent origins in the form of immigration from Burma, which began in the eighteenth century. The small amount of Buddhism which now exists in the far eastern states of India is so heavily influenced by the Burmese Theravāda tradition just across the border that ancient Indian roots would be difficult if not impossible to establish.

Buddhism does appear to survive — uninterrupted from ancient times to the present — in some of the more remote mountain states and kingdoms on the Indian side of the Himalayas. These include Ladakh in the modern Indian state of Jammu and Kashmir, Lahaul Spiti and Kinnaur in Himachal state, the Indian state of Sikkim, and the independent kingdoms of Nepal and Bhutan. Of these, however, only the primarily Hindu kingdom of Nepal harbors a form of Buddhism which can be said to have maintained even tenuous links to its Indian ancestry. Buddhism in the other regions mentioned has become so closely aligned with Tibetan Buddhism that traditional histories usually associate the introduction and development of Buddhism in these areas with the introduction and development of Buddhism in Tibet. For this reason, these regions will be considered below in Chapter XII on Tibetan Buddhism beyond Tibet.

The Himalayan region of Kashmir, however, merits brief consideration at this point. Kashmir has a long and documented history of Buddhism, possibly going back to Aśoka himself. Ultimately, the history of Buddhism in Kashmir followed the Indian pattern of decline vis-à-vis Hinduism and finally disappearance following Muslim persecution. In Kashmir, however, Islam was held at bay until the fourteenth century, and Buddhism based on Indian precedents survived into the fifteenth century. Moreover, Kashmir played an important role in the transplantation of Indian-style Buddhism to Tibet.

Buddhism in Kashmir

The modern Indian state of Kashmir, officially known as Jammu and Kashmir, covers an ill-defined area of northwestern India which is disputed and partially controlled by Pakistan. According to chapter twelve of the *Mahāvaṃsa* chronicle of Sri Lanka, Aśoka sent the monk Majjhantika to introduce Buddhism to Kashmir and the neighboring state of Gandhāra. Aśokan ruins at Taxila in present-day Pakistan confirm his influence in this area.

After Aśoka, the Greek king Milinda or Menandros (r. 155-130 BCE) is supposed to have hosted in or near Kashmir his famous debate with the Buddhist monk Nāgasena, as recorded in the *Milinda Pañha* or "Questions of King Milinda." Around the beginning of the common era, the first Buddha images were produced under Greek influence by craftsmen in Gandhāra. Kanishka (r. 78-123 CE), founder of the Kushan dynasty, is widely believed to have convened a fourth Buddhist Council in Kashmir, though it is doubtful that he convened a Buddhist council at all. Although doubtful, this tradition is recorded by the Chinese pilgrim Xuan Zang (602-64 CE) and the Tibetan historians Tāranātha and Bu sTon (see Pronunciation Guide), indicating at least the importance of Kashmir as a Buddhist center during the Kushan dynasty (78-225 CE).

After the Kushan period, Buddhism in Kashmir appears to have begun a slow but steady decline vis-à-vis emergent Hinduism. There were certainly periods of revival during this decline, and many great Buddhist scholars are said to have come from or worked in Kashmir. The most notable of these is Kumārajīva, founder in the fifth century of the classical Chinese tradition of Buddhist translation and scholarship, who studied in Kashmir for three years. Kashmiri monks also played an important role in the spread of Buddhism to Central Asia and Tibet.

In the early sixth century, the same onslaught of Huns suffered by India wreaked terrible destruction upon the monks and monasteries of Kashmir. Thereafter, Buddhism was unable to recover under a series of Hindu kings who were indifferent or hostile toward Buddhism. As in India, there were exceptions, but in Kashmir the anti-Buddhist reigns of Kshemagupta (r. 950-58), and later of Harsha (r. 1089-1101 — not to be confused with the Buddhist Indian monarch, r. 606-47), resulted in a severe decline of Buddhism. Buddhism enjoyed a brief period of resurgence in Kashmir before the advent of Islam and its final demise. This resurgence, like a similar resurgence in Nepal at about this time, is probably due to a northward migration of Buddhists fleeing Muslim persecution in India. After Harsha, a series of rulers collectively known as the second Lohara dynasty (1101-1339) encouraged or at least tolerated

Buddhism. During this period, in the twelfth century, the great Kashmiri historian Kalhaṇa wrote his *Rājataraṅgiṇī* or "Succession of Kings," which remains the classical history of Kashmir. Though himself a Hindu, Kalhaṇa was clearly sympathetic toward Buddhism. This attitude in Kalhaṇa probably reflects the attitude of the majority of Kashmiris during his time.

The history of Buddhism in Kashmir ended symbolically in 1339 with the enthronement of Shah Mizra, the first Muslim ruler of Kashmir. References to later attacks — and rare favors — visited upon Buddhism by subsequent Muslim rulers indicate that Buddhism survived up to a hundred years beyond this symbolic point. This surviving Buddhism, however, was thoroughly mixed with Hinduism, so that the final demise of Buddhism in Kashmir may probably be located in the reign of Sikander (1389-1413), who finally drove Hinduism — along with its Buddhist admixture — from the area. Buddhism did survive in the northern-most region of present-day Kashmir, known as Ladakh, but this was a form of Buddhism introduced from Tibet, and so it will be discussed in Chapter XII.

Well before its final disappearance from Kashmir in the fifteenth century, Indian Buddhism's center of gravity had begun to shift to Tibet. As one of the last havens of Indian Buddhism, Kashmir played a significant role in this transfer. This transfer, however, represents a transformation of Indian Buddhism by way of absorption into an increasingly distinct Tibetan expression of the religion. Indian-style Buddhism in Kashmir did not survive to participate in this new expression of Buddhism.

Buddhism in Central Asia

In addition to Kashmir, it is necessary to consider briefly a closely related region which has only recently been widely recognized as significant in the history of Buddhism. This is the ill-defined region known as Central Asia. Roughly speaking, this inhospitable area includes the Karakoram, Hindu Kush and Pamir mountain ranges of Kashmir and northern Pakistan and Afghanistan, Tadjikistan and Uzbekistan to the Aral Sea, and thence east across the Tian Shan (T'ien Shan) mountains and the Takla Makan Desert of far western China. Today, this area is almost uniformly Muslim. Throughout the first millennium, however, Indian forms of Buddhism thrived in the region. Poised on the Silk Road into China and its tributary branch into India, Central Asia played an important role in the transmission of Buddhism from India to China. In addition to a surprisingly rich legacy of Buddhist textual and archaeological remains preserved by the desert sands of Central Asia, accounts of several Chinese pilgrims allow a distant appreciation of the role Central Asia once played in the history of Buddhism.

Aśokan ruins and inscriptions in present-day Pakistan and Afghanistan indicate that Buddhism was known in Central Asia by the third century BCE.[18] After the demise of the Mauryan dynasty of Aśoka, first Greeks, then the Iranian Śakas (Scythians) and Pahlavas (Parthians) dominated the Central Asian territory to the northwest of India. Throughout, Buddhism in Central Asia survived, and in some periods thrived, most notably in the reign of the Greek king Milinda (r. 155-130 BCE). In the first century CE, the Kushan empire under Kanishka (r. 78-123 CE) facilitated the spread of Buddhism across the present-day territory of eastern Afghanistan, Tadjikistan, Uzbekistan, and parts of Xinjiang (Hsin-chiang) in far western China. Around this time too, Buddhism began to spread in earnest from Central Asia into imperial China, as will be discussed in Chapter VIII. Neither Kanishka nor the Kushans as a whole appear to have been as thoroughly Buddhist as tradition depicts them, but stability and religious tolerance throughout their vast empire fostered an early and dramatic spread of Buddhism to the north and west of India.

In the third century, Iranian invaders encroached upon and eventually overthrew the Kushan empire. As they appear to have done in northern India, these Iranians tolerated and even encouraged the continuation of Buddhism in western Central Asia. Some of the most impressive Buddhist ruins of western Central Asia — such as the great rock-hewn Buddha at Bamian and the Jaulian stūpa at Taxila — date from this post-Kushan age. In eastern Central Asia, the fall of the Kushan empire left the way open for the prosperous independence of several mercantile city states along the northern and southern branches of the Silk Road skirting the Takla Makan Desert. Among these, Khotan in the south, Kashgar in the west, and Kucha and Turfan in the north were preëminent. Because of their reliance upon trade, these cosmopolitan city states tolerated a variety of religions, including Zoroastrianism, Mithraism, Hinduism and Christianity. For most of the first millennium, however, they were primarily Buddhist.

In the fifth century, the same ferocious Huns who destroyed the Gupta dynasty in India did great damage to Buddhism in western Central Asia as well as in Kashmir. Muslim invaders began to dominate western Central Asia from the eighth century. Nonetheless, Buddhism appears to have survived in the region until about 1000 CE. Eastern Central Asia was not as adversely affected by the Huns, and Islam did not become dominant there until the ninth century. Buddhism survived several more centuries in eastern Central Asia, but it does does not appear to have prospered there much beyond 1000 CE, roughly the same time as its demise in western Central Asia. Kashgar and Khotan had Muslim rulers by the tenth century, and finally the ruler of Turfan assumed the Islamic title of sultan in 1469. This date symbolically marks the end of Buddhism in Central Asia, and corresponds roughly with the final demise of Buddhism in Kashmir. Thus, after a history of some two thousand years, the fifteenth century witnessed the final gasp of Indian-style, Sanskrit-based Buddhism as a living tradition.

The Modern Buddhist Revival in India

Despite the disappearance of India's own ancient tradition of Buddhism, surprising recent events indicate that Buddhism may be on the verge of a revival in the land of its birth. The total number of traditional Tibetan-style and Burmese-style Buddhists within India's northern and eastern frontiers, though not precisely known, is less than a million. Since independence in 1947, however, the total number of Buddhists in India has jumped to approximately five million due to conversions by members of India's lowest castes, the so-called "untouchables."

Ultimately, this development may be traced to the advent of European influence in India, the consequent decline of Muslim influence, and the challenge to India's caste system posed by Western democratic ideals. European influence in India began with the Portuguese conquest of Goa in 1510. Within a century, the British had displaced the Portuguese as the dominant European power in India and by the nineteenth century were imperial masters of the entire sub-continent. Though British imperialism was deeply resented in India, British ideals and institutions paved the way for the emergence of the world's most populous democracy.

This latter development transformed India's seventy million downtrodden untouchables into a potentially significant political force. Part of the expression of this political potential has taken the form of organized conversion to Buddhism. In Hindu society, the untouchables are regarded as being by birth so inferior that higher caste Hindus literally must not come into contact with them, even indirectly — for example by sharing the same well. The highest castes will avoid contact even with the shadow of an untouchable. Buddhism rejects the entire caste system, so that conversion to Buddhism can be a potent symbolic protest against the inequities of Hindu society. Some Buddhists, notably those of Sri Lanka, do observe caste distinctions, but scriptural Buddhism is adamant in its rejection of hereditary social status.

Dr. Bhimrao Ambedkar — Ph.D. (Columbia, 1916), Minister of Law in the first government of independent India and "father of the Indian constitution" — perceived and acted upon Buddhism's potential as a rallying point for the untouchables. Although himself an untouchable, Ambedkar pursued with remarkable talent and tenacity the educational opportunities afforded in British India. As a prominent figure in India's independence movement, he opposed Mahatma Gandhi's policy of re-forming rather than outlawing India's caste system. While serving in the government of Jawaharlal Nehru, India's first prime minister, Ambedkar became thoroughly disillusioned with attempts to reform Indian society from within. In 1950 he opted out of the caste system entirely by declaring his conversion to Buddhism. Ambedkar urged his political constituency to follow him in rejecting the religion and society that rejected them, and in 1956 he presided over a mass conversion to Buddhism of several thousand untouchables in Nagpur, a city in the state of Maharashtra. Later the same year Ambedkar died.

Though lacking in comparable leadership after the death of Ambedkar, India's "new Buddhism" remains significant as a potential political force, particularly in and around Maharashtra. The slow growth in numbers of the movement is partly due no doubt to the Indian government's policy of withholding from Buddhist converts the educational and economic advantages granted to other members of the "scheduled castes." This policy represents a backhanded, albeit official recognition that conversion to Buddhism is a viable way to opt out of the caste system. Of course, these neo-Buddhists are still rejected by caste Hindus, so that untouchables have little to gain at present by conversion to Buddhism. In addition, the movement remains almost entirely a political movement, so that conversion to Buddhism in this context represents little in the way of ideological change, nor does it present as yet an opportunity to participate in a fully functioning religious and social community. As a result of such considerations, Buddhist converts remain a small proportion of India's total population of seventy million untouchables. Nonetheless, any movement among the untouchables, who constitute almost ten percent of India's population, is noteworthy.

Shortly after the death of Ambedkar, the Chinese repression of Tibetan Buddhism in 1959 sparked the flight of some 100,000 Tibetan refugees into India. This migration has actually had a more pronounced effect than Ambedkar's movement in re-establishing Buddhism in India. Though relatively few in number, these Tibetans have established thriving refugee communities throughout India and a highly visible presence in the modern world as a whole. In contrast to its poor treatment of untouchable Buddhist converts, India remains the world's foremost benefactor of

Tibetans in exile. As a result, India is the primary haven for that form of Mahāyāna Buddhism which among all others most faithfully preserves its Indian origins. Once again, as in the heydays of Nālandā and Vikramaśilā, people from distant lands travel to India to study with Buddhist masters, albeit Tibetan Buddhist masters in exile. This international attention, the survival of Buddhism on India's frontiers, and the interest in Buddhism shown among a massive population of untouchables, are all indications that Buddhism is by no means a spent force in India. The continuous, living tradition of Indian Buddhism has been broken, but Buddhism shows several promising signs of a resurgence in the land of its birth.

CHAPTER VI

The Development of Buddhism in Sri Lanka

Buddhism was introduced into Sri Lanka — the large tear-shaped island off the southern tip of India — in approximately 250 BCE by a mission sent by Emperor Aśoka of India. Sri Lanka thus claims the honor of preserving the world's most ancient verifiable and continuous practice of Buddhism. In addition, Sri Lanka is the acknowledged homeland of Theravāda Buddhism, the most ancient surviving form of the religion. Of all the Theravādin nations — which include Burma, Cambodia, Laos and Thailand — Sri Lanka provides the richest resources for the early history of Buddhism. These include not only the Sri Lankan historical chronicles, the *Mahāvaṃsa, Cūlavaṃsa* and *Dīpavaṃsa*, but also the voluminous Sri Lankan commentaries on the Pāli suttas. These commentaries, which were written before the fifth century, contain numerous scattered references relevant to the early history of Buddhism. Sources on the early histories of the other Theravādin countries are deficient by comparison. For this reason, and also because the island of Sri Lanka is recognized as the enduring heartland of Theravāda Buddhism, Sri Lanka is treated at greater length than the Theravādin countries of Southeast Asia, which are examined in Chapter VII.

Long before the advent of Buddhism, the island of Sri Lanka was inhabited by a dark-skinned, tribal race known as Veddas. The *Mahāvaṃsa* relates that the first human inhabitants of Sri Lanka arrived on precisely the day on which the Buddha passed away, and that before this time the island was inhabited only by demons, probably a reference to the primitive Veddas. These first human inhabitants were led by one Prince Vijaya, who was himself supposed to have been only part human, the product of a sexual dalliance between a lion and an unnaturally lustful Indian princess. The *Mahāvaṃsa* states too that the Veddas of Sri Lanka are descendants of a sexual liaison between Vijaya and a she-devil. This legendary material suggests that Indo-European settlers arrived in Sri Lanka sometime in the first millennium BCE, and that they established some sort of truce with the aboriginals on the island and intermarried with them to some degree. It is not clear why Indo-Europeans from northern India rather than the Dravidian population of south India became dominant in Sri Lanka.

After the arrival of the Buddhist mission sent by Aśoka in approximately 250 BCE, the traditional history of Sri Lanka becomes much more reliable. This mission established contact with one Tissa, supposedly a descendant in the royal line established by Vijaya, who maintained his capital at Anurādhapura. Anurādhapura eventually became a great capital, the stately ruins of which survive to the present day. At that time, however, the "capital" was little more than a village of mud huts, as the *Mahāvaṃsa* intimates in its account of the difficulty Tissa had in finding suitable accommodations for his honored visitors. It is somewhat unlikely that Tissa was at the time widely recognized as the king of all Sri Lanka, but after his alliance with Aśoka, his ascendancy on the island was assured. Apparently, Aśoka himself ordered and provided for a second coronation of Tissa, conveying upon him the title "Devānampiya," a traditional title of Indian royalty meaning "Dear to the Gods."

Thus Devānampiya Tissa became the first historical king of Sri Lanka — and the island itself became a political entity — as a direct result of the introduction of Buddhism under Aśoka. The traditional histories reveal that Brahmanism, Jainism and Ājīvakism were known in Sri Lanka before the arrival of Aśoka's mission, while pretending that Buddhism was entirely unknown. This is clearly part of an attempt to dramatize the arrival of Aśoka's mission and to emphasize the role Buddhism played in the resulting diplomatic connection between Sri Lanka and the mighty Indian monarch.

Supposedly, Aśoka's mission was headed by his own son, the monk Mahinda. Later, Aśoka's daughter, the nun Saṅghamittā, is supposed to have brought to Sri Lanka a cutting from the original Bodhi tree, under which the Buddha realized enlightenment. The tree that grew from this cutting, planted in the capital Anurādhapura, lives to the present day. As a result it has the oldest recorded history of any living thing on earth. This tree is without a doubt the most venerated plant in the world, and it remains in the popular imagination of Sri Lanka a preëminent symbol of the nation and its religion. In the nineteenth century, when British archaeologists ascertained that the great Hindu temple at Bodh Gaya in India had originally been a Buddhist temple marking the site of the Buddha's enlightenment, a cutting was taken from the tree in Anurādhapura and re-established at the original site of the Bodhi tree, where it grows to the present day.

Aśoka may have had many children by several wives, so the tradition that his own son and daughter established the Saṅgha of monks and nuns in Sri Lanka may not be an exaggeration. Given that Aśoka's might and Buddhism were probably well known on the island before the arrival of his mission, the traditional accounts of the rapid conversion of the entire population to Buddhism may also be accurate. The *Mahāvaṃsa* is probably accurate again in recording the receipt of holy relics from Aśoka and the dedication and completion of several major Buddhist construction projects during the reign of Devānampiya Tissa. Obvious exaggerations aside, the general picture of the events surrounding the arrival of Aśoka's mission appears to be accurately sketched in the *Mahāvaṃsa*. Under the auspices of Buddhism, this relatively backward island culture was rapidly transformed into a well organized, prosperous and autonomous state under Aśoka's great empire.

Of the construction projects initiated in the reign of Devānampiya Tissa, the most significant was the Mahāvihāra or "Great Monastery," established in a royal park near Anurādhapura as a residence for Mahinda and his companion monks. Even as the Bodhi tree took root in Sri Lanka, the Mahāvihāra took root and became the recognized world center of Theravāda Buddhism. Headquartered at the Mahāvihāra, Theravāda Buddhism thrived in Sri Lanka while it declined and disappeared in India and the other lands to which Buddhism spread. Surviving primarily in its Sri Lankan stronghold, Theravāda Buddhism eventually made a comeback in the early centuries of the second millennium, when it staged a revival in Southeast Asia, now a second abiding home for the most ancient branch of Buddhism. The fact that we have any knowledge at all of the original teachings of the historical Buddha is thus almost entirely due to the remarkable dedication of the small island nation of Sri Lanka in preserving the religious tradition that gave birth to the nation as such.

The fragmentation of the Sri Lankan state following the death of Devānampiya Tissa in about 207 BCE reflects the rapid degeneration of Aśoka's empire after the death of the great Indian monarch in about 230 BCE. Devānampiya Tissa was succeeded on the throne by three of his younger brothers, one after another. A fourth brother appears to have established a rival kingdom called Rohaṇa in the southeast of the island. Soon, another kingdom, Kalyāṇi in the southwest, appears in the *Mahāvaṃsa* account without explanation. Under the third of the successors to the Anurādhapura throne, in about 177 BCE, Anurādhapura was attacked and defeated by the Dravidian forces of the Chola empire of southern India. The Cholas controlled the northern half of the island for most of the next seventy-five years while two separate Buddhist kingdoms, Rohaṇa and Kalyāṇi, controlled the southern half. Though Sri Lanka was politically divided less than a century after it was founded, Theravāda Buddhism seems already to have been firmly established as the unifying ideology of the island. Even the Chola rulers of Sri Lanka, who were themselves followers of orthodox Brahmanism, appear to have ruled as Buddhist monarchs, observing the traditional Buddhist public ceremonies and fulfilling the traditional obligations to the Saṅgha and the maintenance of Buddhism as a whole.

It was a prince of the Kalyāṇi kingdom, Duṭṭhagāmaṇī, who eventually drove the Cholas out of Sri Lanka in 101 BCE and reunited the island under a true Buddhist monarch. Duṭṭhagāmaṇī's reign (r. 101-77 BCE), and that of his successor and brother Saddhātissa (r. 77-59 BCE), are remembered as a period of great prosperity and lavish patronage of Buddhism in Sri Lanka. It was probably during this period that the unification of the island under a Buddhist king — traditionally accomplished by Devānampiya Tissa — became an actual reality. During this period, most of the great structures which dominate the ruins of Anurādhapura were completed, and the capital from which Sri Lanka was ruled for the next millennium took on its definitive characteristics.

This period of prosperity in Sri Lanka, like that under Devānampiya Tissa, was short lived. There are some indications that friction between Saddhātissa and the increasingly powerful monks of the Mahāvihāra led the king to withdraw his favor from them. When Saddhātissa died in 59 BCE, it appears that the monks of the Mahāvihāra attempted to insure more favorable treatment by maneuvering to enthrone King Saddhātissa's second son, rather than his eldest son. The eldest son immediately asserted his rights militarily and took the throne by force, passing it on in the normal fashion to his next-oldest brother in 50 BCE. The earlier intrigue surrounding succession to the throne appears to have been either a symptom or a cause of deep political rivalries and religious jealousies, for within a few years the throne was usurped by a military coup d'état in 43 BCE. Saddhātissa's youngest son Vaṭṭagāmaṇī immediately crushed the usurper, only to be confronted by yet another rebellion, led by an influential Sri Lankan Brāhmaṇa named Tissa and supported by south Indian forces.

This rebellion succeeded in seizing power, and Sri Lanka was ruled for the next fifteen years by a succession of Brahmanic rulers from South India. This period is remembered as a dark time of persecution of Buddhism and oppression of the populace. This oppression was worsened by a severe, twelve-year famine known as the "Brāhmaṇatissa Famine," named after the leader of the rebellion which in the popular imagination seemed to have brought it on. During this period, the monks and nuns fled from the capital en masse and sought shelter in southern Sri Lanka or in India. Many died, and the community was depleted and dispersed. Particularly among the Saṅgha who stayed in Sri Lanka, it became obvious that parts of the Pāli canon — which was still preserved only in the memories of monks and nuns — were in danger of passing into oblivion.

Vaṭṭagāmaṇī was finally able to reassert his rule in 29 BCE, and the Saṅgha began to return to Anurādhapura from their fifteen-year exile. The monks of the Mahāvihāra soon found fresh cause for alarm, however, when Vaṭṭagāmaṇī established in Anurādhapura a second grand monastery, named Abhayagiri, as a reward for the monk Mahātissa, who had been instrumental in maintaining the loyalty of Vaṭṭagāmaṇī's generals during his military campaigns. This posed a direct threat to the authority of the monks of the Mahāvihāra, who evidently had alienated themselves from the royal family. The Mahāvihāra reacted forcefully to Vaṭṭagāmaṇī's apparent intention to dilute their power. They expelled Mahātissa, the abbot of Abhayagiri, from the Saṅgha, thereby precipitating a schism. For his part, Vaṭṭagāmaṇī neglected the Mahāvihāra and bestowed lavish patronage upon Abhayagiri, apparently having accomplished exactly what he wanted — a divided, weakened Saṅgha. Soon, the Abhayagiri monks came to be associated with scriptural and doctrinal innovations originating in India, thus forming a more liberal, eventually quasi-Mahāyāna branch of the Sri Lankan Saṅgha.

The sectarian threat posed by the Abhayagiri Saṅgha, combined with the near loss of parts of their orally transmitted tradition during the Brāhmaṇatissa Famine, induced the monks of the Mahāvihāra to commit to writing for the first time a Buddhist canon. It is likely that individual texts had been written down before this time, but this was the first systematic, written recording of the Buddhist oral tradition in history. It was probably the first written record of any extensive corpus of an Indian sacred tradition. This momentous task was undertaken at Alu Vihāra, a monastery in a central province remote from Anurādhapura, with the support of a local chieftain. Presumably the task was completed during the reign of Vaṭṭagāmaṇī, which ended with his death in 17 BCE.

From the early years of the common era there is evidence of disputes between the Mahāvihāra and Abhayagiri concerning the nature and content of scriptures. Such disputes had become sufficiently serious by the third century to prompt the King Vohārika Tissa (r. 263-285 CE) to order the burning of variant texts preserved by the Abhayagiri monks. Presumably these variant texts contained Mahāyāna influences which had begun to filter into Sri Lanka soon after the Mahāyāna began to consolidate as a separate branch of Buddhism in India. The beginning of this consolidation in India was marked by the career of the great systematist Nāgārjuna in the second century. At any rate, the Mahāvihāra monks appear to have been correct in anticipating textual innovations by the Abhayagiri monks.

During the fourth century, royal favor shifted predominantly to the Abhayagiri, to the extent that Mahāvihāra buildings were destroyed and its monks suppressed by King Mahāsena (r. 334-61), who issued a royal proclamation forbidding any subject of the realm to give alms to a Mahāvihāra monk. This ban forced the monks to take refuge once again in the southern part of Sri Lanka, which appears to have maintained some degree of autonomy vis-à-vis Anurādhapura. Mahāsena then appropriated temple lands of the Mahāvihāra and set up a third monastic establishment, the Jetavana, which seems to have occupied a middle doctrinal position between the liberal Abhayagiri and the conservative Mahāvihāra.

The actual suppression of the Mahāvihāra was apparently only intermittent, as the Chinese pilgrim Fa Xian (Fa Hsien), who visited Sri Lanka early in the fifth century, reports both the Mahāvihāra and Abhayagiri flourishing. From his account, however, it is clear that the Abhayagiri monastery was the larger and more influential of the two.[19] In the seventh century, the Chinese pilgrim Xuan Zang (Hsüan Tsang) reports both establishments still flourishing, and notes that the Mahāvihāra was Theravādin, while the Abhayagiri promulgated both Mahāyāna and Nikāya Buddhism.[20] Both pilgrims also mention what had become the most important holy relic in Sri Lanka, a supposed tooth of the Buddha that had been brought to the island during the reign of King Meghavaṇṇa (r. 352-379). Almost immediately, this apparently well-authenticated relic became the chief emblem of religious and political authority in Sri Lanka. It resided in the custodianship of the Abhayagiri, indicating that things were bad indeed for the Mahāvihāra during the fourth century.

At this critical juncture in the fortunes of Theravāda Buddhism in Sri Lanka, the great Theravādin systematist Buddhaghosa arrived from South India during the reign of King Mahānāma (r. 409-431). Residing and working at the Mahāvihāra, Buddhaghosa almost single-handedly accomplished the systematization of Theravāda doctrine by editing and translating into Pāli the numerous scriptural commentaries that existed in the native Sinhalese language of Sri Lanka. He also composed in Sri Lanka his famous treatise on Theravāda doctrine known as the *Visuddhimagga,* or "Path of Purity." From this point on, with a systematic account of its doctrines, the Theravāda was in a much better position to hold its own against the Abhayagiri monks, who had enjoyed heretofore the advantage of access to systematic formulations of Mahāyāna doctrine originating in India.

The tide of the struggle did not turn decisively at once, and over the second half of the first millennium, successive kings favored the Mahāvihāra and the Abhayagiri alternately, usually on the basis of political rather than religious considerations. During this period, Sri Lanka as a whole went through several more tumultuous periods of internal strife and domination by south Indian powers, interspersed with periods of recovery and prosperity. These alternate periods of hardship and prosperity, while affecting Buddhism as a whole, did not have a decisive effect on the rivalry between Theravāda and Mahāyāna Buddhism in Sri Lanka.

Toward the end of the first millennium, however, Buddhism in India began to decline as a result of competition from Hinduism. Finally, Buddhism vanished from India in the wake of the Muslim invasion, which began in earnest at the start of the second millennium. For many centuries Indian Buddhism had been the primary source of intellectual inspiration for the Abhayagiri Saṅgha, and as Mahāyāna Buddhism declined in India, so did the Abhayagiri decline in Sri Lanka. In some ways this was a sad development, but if only one form of Buddhism was destined to survive in Sri Lanka, it is fortunate for Buddhism that the Theravāda emerged victorious from this thousand-year struggle. Mahāyāna scriptures and practice had by this time been transplanted and preserved extensively in Tibet and China. Theravāda Buddhism, having been swallowed up elsewhere by the appealing exuberance of Mahāyāna Buddhism, survived intact only in Sri Lanka. From this precarious island haven, it was to spread on a massive scale to the states of Southeast Asia, which were only just beginning to emerge as political entities in the first half of the second millennium.

By the beginning of the second millennium, there was a sizable and permanent population of south Indian Tamils on the northern portion of the island. This Tamil population was constantly involved in overseas political intrigues between the dominant south Indian powers on the mainland, the Paṇḍu and Chola kingdoms. While often nominally allied with one or the other of these south Indian powers, northern Sri Lanka also provided a haven for dissidents and rebels against whichever faction was in power in southern India at any given time. This situation had a destabilizing effect upon Sri Lanka, and invited invasion by whichever south Indian power was dominant. Due to internal disturbances resulting in a revolt by his own troops, King Mahinda V (r. 982-1029) had to abandon Anurādhapura and set up a capital in the southern province of Rohaṇa. Hearing of this state of affairs, the Cholas invaded Sri Lanka decisively in 1017, captured the king and established a new capital at Polonnaruwa. From this base, they systematically looted the island and its monasteries, pursuing a vigorous persecution of Buddhism.

In about 1070 King Vijaya Bāhu I (r. 1055-1110), with substantial assistance from King Anuruddha of Burma, managed to throw off Chola domination, recapturing the island at least as far north as Anurādhapura. He made his own capital at Polonnaruwa, the site of the Chola capital, and set about restoring Buddhism in Sri Lanka. The Chola persecution had apparently been severe, for the *Cūlavaṃsa* records that Vijaya Bāhu found it necessary to invite a contingent of monks from Burma in order to hold a proper ordination ceremony and to transact business in the Saṅgha.[21] It appears that the Saṅgha of nuns had lapsed entirely by this time, but no efforts were made to revive it. To this day, it remains impossible to gain full ordination as a Theravāda nun, though orders of women do keep the vows and live in convents.

The alliance between Sri Lanka and Burma arising from the cooperation of Vijaya Bāhu and Anuruddha eventually resulted in the ascendancy of Theravāda Buddhism on the Southeast Asian mainland. Anuruddha himself was a Mahāyānist, and during his time Mahāyāna Buddhism was dominant throughout Southeast Asia. Theravāda Buddhism was practiced only by the Mon people of lower Burma, who were subjects of Anuruddha and must have been the source of the delegation of monks he sent to Sri Lanka. At this time there was no copy of the Pāli Tipiṭaka in Southeast Asia. The contingent of Burmese monks sent to Sri Lanka by Anuruddha stayed on for several years working with their Sri Lankan counterparts on a project of restoring and copying the Pāli Tipiṭaka. When they returned to Burma they brought with them a complete copy of the Pāli canon, probably the first such copy ever to leave Sri Lanka. Vijaya Bāhu is also supposed to have sent a miraculously produced copy of the tooth relic of the Buddha to Anuruddha, who supposedly built the great Shwezigon Stūpa in Pagan in order to house it. In actual fact, this monument is probably the work of a later king, and the tooth was probably a fake. The important point is the establishment of close ties between Sri Lanka and Burma during the reigns of Vijaya Bāhu in Sri Lanka and Anuruddha in Burma.

After the death of Vijaya Bāhu, Sri Lanka degenerated once again into a period of disunity until the rise of King Parākrama Bāhu I (r. 1153-86), who reunited the island and ascended the throne of Polonnaruwa in 1153. Parākrama Bāhu I was an enthusiastic patron of Buddhism. Not only did he decree many Buddhist construction projects in the capital Polonnaruwa, he also carried out extensive restoration work in Anurādhapura. The impressive ruins of Polonnaruwa, comparable to those of Anurādhapura, survive to the present day as a testimony to the reign of Parākrama Bāhu I. Parākrama Bāhu's most notable building achievements, however, were in the area of hydro-engineering. Pursuant of his motto that not a drop of water should return to the ocean without having served a human purpose, he masterminded the draining of malaria-infested swamps and the creation of an extensive series of reservoirs for irrigation and drinking water. Periodically up to the present time, there have been unsuccessful but probably well-advised moves to restore the irrigation system devised under Parākrama Bāhu I.

Parākrama Bāhu I also carried out during his reign a "purification of the Saṅgha," in an obvious attempt to emulate the great Indian monarch Aśoka. In actual fact, Parākrama Bāhu I abolished the Abhayagiri and Jetavana monasteries and decreed that their monks would have to return to the laity or seek reordination under the auspices of the Mahāvihāra. The issuance of this royal decree represented the final victory of Theravāda Buddhism in Sri Lanka. It also represented the establishment of a unified Saṅgha regulated by the state. It was during Parākrama Bāhu's reign that Sri Lanka's ties with Burma reached fruition when a Burmese monastic contingent came to Sri Lanka in order to be reordained in the Mahāvihāra lineage. The return of this contingent to Burma marked a complete transplantation of Sri Lankan Theravāda Buddhism into Southeast Asia. In subsequent centuries, after the Sri Lankan Theravāda tradition had spread through Burma and beyond, other Southeast Asian states would also send delegations to Sri Lanka in order to establish their own autonomous ordination lineages. Still later, during the period of European colonization, Sri Lanka in turn would have to reimport its own ordination lineages from Burma and Thailand.

After the death of Parākrama Bāhu I in 1186, Sri Lanka again descended into a period of disunity and domination by south India. In 1244 Parākrama Bāhu II (r. 1236-70) was able to muster sufficient support to recapture Polonnaruwa from the Tamils, but the north of the island had become a quasi-independent Tamil kingdom which continued to survive through alliances with various south Indian kingdoms until the arrival of the Portuguese in the fifteenth century. Following the reign of Parākrama Bāhu II, the history of Sri Lanka and of Buddhism in Sri Lanka is a sad story of foreign domination and decline. Visitors to the island — including Marco Polo in the thirteenth century and the Muslim geographer Ibn Baṭṭūtah in the fourteenth — wrote favorably of the living conditions on the island paradise, apparently failing to notice the decline of its ancient culture. Regardless of the fact that Sri Lanka was often dominated by the Tamils of southern India, it had become famous throughout the world as a haven of Buddhism and as the home of Buddhism's most sacred relic, the tooth of the Buddha.

Amusingly, Kublai Khan, founder of the Mongol dynasty in China, sent an envoy to the island requesting — or given that it was Kublai Khan, demanding — that the tooth relic of the Buddha be sent to him. The reigning king obliged by sending not one but two teeth, which Kublai received with great pomp and ceremony. Having become famous throughout the Eastern world as the possessors of a tooth of the Buddha, Sri Lanka's Buddhist kings appear to have exploited this reputation diplomatically by trading freely in dubious relics of the Buddha. The real tooth relic was jealously guarded and constantly spirited from one refuge to another during Sri Lanka's political upheavals, until finally the inevitable happened and it was captured and taken to the Paṇḍu kingdom of south India. It is not clear exactly when this momentous loss occurred, but it was toward the end of the thirteenth century.

By this time a firmly established tradition dictated that the legitimate ruler of Sri Lanka must have possession of the tooth relic in order to validate the reign. Until the tooth was regained by diplomatic persuasion, around the beginning of the fourteenth century, there was strictly speaking no legitimate ruler of the island. No Sri Lankan king after Parākrama Bāhu I ever actually regained control of the entire island, but the tooth continued to accompany the recognized king to various strongholds and refuges. Finally, at the beginning of the seventeenth century, it was enshrined in the famed Dalada Maligawa or "Temple of the Tooth" in the mountain capital of Kandy. At least twice more the tooth relic was spirited into the mountainous jungles around Kandy in order to preserve it from capture by foreign powers, this time the Portuguese and the Dutch. Finally the British succeeded in taking possession of the relic, which they surrendered voluntarily to its monastic custodians in Kandy after having subdued the island. The tooth relic resides in Kandy to the present day, the symbol par excellence of Sri Lankan independence and nationhood.

The tradition identifying the tooth relic as the palladium of the nation is easy to understand, for the fate of the tooth relic has seemed to mirror the fate of Sri Lanka. By and large, during periods in which the tooth has been safely enshrined and honored with regular, public ceremonial, Sri Lanka has enjoyed periods of relative strength and prosperity. When the tooth was taken into hiding or was in foreign hands, the island itself has suffered periods of instability and hardship. Even in modern Sri Lanka, as a token of the legitimacy of the elected government, the prime minister holds one of the three keys to the enclosure in which the tooth relic is kept.

Soon after the first circumnavigation of the globe by Vasco da Gama in 1498, a Portuguese fleet anchored at Colombo, by this time the capital of Buddhist Sri Lanka. At first the Sinhalese court welcomed the appearance of these powerful foreigners, hoping no doubt that they might aid them in their struggles against the Tamils on the northern part of the island. Soon, however, it became obvious to everyone, even some Portuguese chroniclers, that one of the ugliest chapters of European colonial history had opened. "We could have been masters of India," wrote Fr. Fernão de Queroz, "if we had been masters of ourselves."[22] With mind-numbing hypocrisy, the Portuguese attempted to convert the island to Christianity while themselves plundering Buddhist temples, looting the countryside, abducting women for use in brothels, and pressing children into slavery. One must wonder whether Fr. de Queroz realized that his assessment of the Portuguese failure in the East is a paraphrase of a well-known verse from the Buddhist *Dhammapada:* "One may conquer a million in battle, but the best of conquerors conquers himself" (verse 103).

A vigorous Sinhalese resistance movement centered in the mountain capital of Kandy managed to maintain control of the rugged interior of the island while the Portuguese dominated the coastal areas for a century and a half. Finally, in 1597, the last king of Sri Lanka died, having been forced to cede his kingdom to King Phillip of Portugal. The often troubled but nonetheless two-thousand-year-old lineage of kings of Sri Lanka had come to an end. Also in 1597, however, the Dutch established a trading outpost on Java and began to compete vigorously with Portugal in the Indian Ocean. Changing fortunes in Europe resulted eventually in the ascendancy of the Dutch in Sri Lanka. Sometimes helped and sometimes hindered by the Kandyan resistance, the Dutch gradually gained control of the island until the last Portuguese stronghold at Colombo fell in 1655.

The nominal sovereignty of the Portuguese king lapsed, and Rājasiṅgha II, the leader of the Sinhalese resistance, was recognized as king of Kandy, ruler of the mountainous interior of the island, while the Dutch controlled the coastal areas. On the whole, the Dutch administration in Sri Lanka was a great deal more civilized than the Portuguese had been. The Dutch, in fact, must be given credit for intervening to ameliorate the cruel tyranny of Rājasiṅgha II over his people. With the death of Rājasiṅgha II in 1687, inland Sri Lanka finally began a full-scale recovery. The mountainous interior of the island, with its capital at Kandy, remained autonomous and even at times defiant of the Dutch overlords of coastal Sri Lanka.

During the Dutch period in Sri Lanka, a movement began to revive the Buddhist Saṅgha on the island. In 1741 a delegation was sent to Thailand to explore the possibility of renewing the Sri Lankan Saṅgha from Thai sources. These contacts bore fruit in 1753, when a delegation of Thai monks came to Sri Lanka and conducted an ordination ceremony which resulted in the foundation of the "Siam Nikāya," Siam being an old name for Thailand. Sri Lankan tradition has it that prior to this time the Saṅgha had degenerated so drastically that even a group of five fully ordained monks — the number necessary to carry out higher ordination — was impossible to assemble in the island. Henceforward, the only ordination officially recognized by the Kandyan king was that of the Siam Nikāya, which lineage had been bequeathed earlier from Sri Lanka to Thailand.

Kandy, however, was not Sri Lanka, and after centuries of partition, the kingdom of Kandy had become isolated from other parts of the island. This situation would soon result in divisions in the Saṅgha.

At the beginning of the nineteenth century, Dutch dominance of coastal Sri Lanka gave way to British dominance, again due both to changed political fortunes in Europe and to the restiveness of the Sri Lankans under the Dutch. The Dutch, having started out benignly, had degenerated into tyrants like the Portuguese before them. For some years, Sri Lankan restiveness continued under the British, but the Kandyan monarchs who ruled during this period were so tyrannical themselves that finally in 1815, the British marched into Kandy welcomed by much of the populace as liberators. For the first time since Parākrama Bāhu I, the entire island was united under one government, albeit a foreign government. The British acted decently by establishing a treaty with Kandy whereby the hated king was deposed, torture outlawed, the death penalty curtailed, and Buddhism declared inviolable. The existing mechanism of government was to continue under the overriding control of the British. This egalitarian colonialism — at least egalitarian on the face of it — was no doubt welcomed after three centuries of oppressive, high-handed European domination. The British remained in control of Sri Lanka until voluntarily granting independence to the island in 1947.

In the end, British domination came to be as much resented as Portuguese or Dutch domination had been. Nonetheless, the British left an indelible stamp on all of their Eastern colonies that has no parallel among the other European powers which exerted power in the East. British forms of government still hold sway in India and Sri Lanka. Universally, the British left behind them in their Eastern colonies the dubious legacy of their cumbersome but on the whole impartial style of bureaucracy. The influence of Britain on the East, however, goes deeper than this. One still finds in Sri Lanka, Burma and India the phenomenon of people proudly claiming to be "more British than the British." One does not find a parallel phenomenon in the former Portuguese, Dutch or French colonies in Asia. The reasons for this are not entirely clear. Though British colonial rule in Asia was often despotic and cruel, perhaps it would be fair to say that underneath it all there shone a sense of decency and fair play that appealed in Asia.

After the advent of British rule, Buddhism in Sri Lanka embarked upon a marked if subtle transformation. The first obvious indication of a new trend in Buddhism was the formation of new lineages of monastic ordination initiated by and for the lower castes of Sri Lanka. The caste system, widely reviled as the most insidious aspect of Hinduism, has also been one of Hinduism's most contagious features. It infected even the Islam of

India, despite the rigorous egalitarianism of Islam as a whole. Sri Lanka's continual contact with the Hindu states of south India, including frequent periods of domination by these states, eventually resulted in the adoption of a caste system by the island's Buddhists, even though Buddhism explicitly repudiates the caste system.

The Siam Nikāya, established in Kandy in 1753, initiated into its ranks only members of the higher castes, which predominate in Sri Lanka's hill country. In 1799, a group of Buddhists from the lower castes, which predominate in the coastal regions of Sri Lanka, embarked on a mission to Burma in order to secure a separate lineage of monastic ordination for members of the lower castes of Sri Lankan society. This delegation was received by the king of Burma himself in the capital Amarapura, were duly ordained, and returned to Sri Lanka in 1803. In 1807 three more delegations, representing other castes, also journeyed to Burma and received ordination. Together, these lineages form the Amarapura Nikāya. In 1863, another delegation from yet lower castes journeyed to Burma for ordination and formed the Ramana Nikāya, named after the Burmese city in which their ordinations took place. To this day these three separate lineages of ordination survive in Sri Lanka in blatant contradiction of, and with little apparent concern for, the historical Buddha's repudiation of the caste system. At the present time, not only is ordination restricted by caste, but even responsibilities to the laity are divided among the three Nikāyas according to caste divisions. The Siam Nikāya services the upper castes, and the Amarapura and Ramana Nikāyas service the middle and lower castes. While there are obviously objectionable aspects of this arrangement, it does have the advantage of guaranteeing all levels of society direct and intimate access to the Saṅgha. Previously, the lower classes often had very limited access to the "official" tradition maintained and propagated by the nobility.

In addition to involving the laity more directly, the second major characteristic of the reformed Buddhism of modern Sri Lanka is the rationalistic face it turns to the West. In the nineteenth century, as in Burma and Thailand, Theravāda Buddhism in Sri Lanka began to take cognizance of the rational, scientific Western worldview. This has resulted in a form of de-mythologized Buddhism which has proved to have considerable appeal in the West, as will be discussed further in Chapter XIII. The non-rational beliefs and practices of traditional Sri Lankan Buddhism persist, but these are now widely regarded as nonessential trappings of the rational, canonical core of the religion. This reformed, rationalistic interpretation of the Theravāda eventually facilitated compromise between Buddhism and Marxism in Sri Lanka, Burma, Cambodia, and Laos. It has also proved to have great appeal in the secularized world of the capitalist West.

The development of this rationalistic interpretation of Buddhism is due largely to British influence in Sri Lanka, though the basis for such an interpretation clearly exists in the Pāli canon itself. On the one hand, British missionary groups supported by the Crown made vigorous and mostly unsuccessful attempts to gain converts among Sri Lanka's Buddhists. On the other hand, the nineteenth century saw the development in Britain of a strong tradition of anti-religious, rationalistic secularism. Many British were disenchanted with Christianity and were genuinely impressed by the practical, rational religion promulgated in the Pāli canon itself. While British missionaries railed against "paganism" in their colonies, other British — with the collaboration of some notable continental Europeans and even some Americans — began to study Buddhism seriously and mount anti-missionary campaigns to preserve and promote Buddhism in the East and to import it to the West. Most notable in this regard were the eminently scholarly Pāli Text Society and the somewhat eccentric Theosophical Society.

Both the pro- and anti-Buddhist campaigns initiated by the British had a profound and abiding effect upon Sri Lankan Buddhism. In many ways, this effect represented a genuine revival of the essentially rational character of the Buddhism of the Pāli canon. Clearly, the historical Buddha was not privy to the methods of empiricism or its philosophical expression in the scientific humanism of nineteenth century Britain. Nonetheless, Theravāda Buddhism was compatible with modern, scientific humanism, and it opened the way for a spiritual life that did not overtly contradict rational thought. The most notable example of British enthusiasm for Buddhism is the Pāli Text Society, founded in 1881 and still active. This organization published a scholarly journal dedicated to Theravāda Buddhism and initiated an ongoing project to publish the original Pāli texts in Roman script and translate the entire corpus into English. Much to their credit, they recognized that the scriptural tradition of Sri Lanka was of major historical and literary significance.

Many notable Sri Lankan monks and laypeople reacted enthusiastically to the appreciation of Buddhism shown by a significant number of the colonial overlords of Sri Lanka. This resulted in the development of a living Buddhist tradition that emphasized the rational aspects of the religion and de-emphasized its nonrational aspects. Many Sri Lankans discovered that by adhering to a purified version of their own religion they could be well and truly "more British than the British." The essential doctrines of canonical Theravāda Buddhism were more acceptable on prevailing British intellectual criteria than was British Christianity, and a significant number of British intellectuals were prepared to acknowledge this. It would be difficult to overestimate the gratification such recognition inspired in a Buddhist people who had been dominated, exploited and humiliated for centuries by European colonial powers that seemed to have nothing to recommend themselves other than brute force.

This is not to suggest that the British too were not guilty of high-handedness, repression and exploitation during their period of colonialism in Sri Lanka. The negative aspects of British rule, however, were balanced by positive developments, including the development of a reformed Buddhism that has great appeal in the modern, largely secularized world. Insofar as the spread of Buddhism beyond the Eastern world is concerned, the British discovery of Sri Lankan Buddhism can be compared to the Tibetan diaspora discussed below in Chapter XI. As Tibet in its hardship is now doing for Mahāyāna Buddhism, so Sri Lanka and the British did a century ago for Theravāda Buddhism. Both Theravāda and Mahāyāna Buddhism have now been thoroughly, albeit unobtrusively, infused into the intellectual traditions of the Western world. As a result, the survival of the full range of Buddhist scriptures and traditions, which has often been tenuous, is now all but guaranteed.

CHAPTER VII

The Development of
Buddhism in Southeast Asia

By virtue of sharing Theravāda Buddhism, the histories of Sri Lanka and several countries of Southeast Asia are interconnected at crucial points. The Theravāda countries of Southeast Asia proper include Burma, Cambodia, Laos and Thailand. Vietnam, lying along the coast of the South China Sea, was open to Chinese influence throughout its history, and thus embraces Mahāyāna Buddhism and a civilization based largely on Chinese precedents. Malaysia and the Indonesian islands of Sumatra and Java are inhabited by racial stock similar to that of Southeast Asia and are also heirs to Indian civilization, but are no longer significant homelands to Buddhism. Instead, Malaysia, Sumatra and Java are primarily Muslim, representing the easternmost extent of the Muslim conquest of India. Only eastern Java and the small island of Bali retain remnants of the Indian influence that once existed throughout Indonesia.

Racially, the present inhabitants of Southeast Asia derive primarily from ethnic stock who migrated periodically from southwest China starting in the first millennium BCE. These migrations continued through the thirteenth century CE. These periodic migrations from China were funneled into four north-south routes by the great rivers of the Southeast Asian peninsula — the Irrawaddy, the Salween, the Chao Phraya and the Mekong. A fifth route ran along the coast of Vietnam. Roughly speaking, these migration routes account for the historical and present political divisions of Southeast Asia. Migrants down the Irrawaddy and the Salween Rivers established Burma. The tribes that migrated along and dominated the Chao Phraya in relatively recent times became the modern Thais. Those who followed the Mekong to its delta became the Khmers of Cambodia. The latecomers along this route became the Laos, blocked from access to the sea by the Khmers and the Vietnamese. The Vietnamese migrated down the fifth route along the coast of the South China Sea. A more ancient migration, probably along the Chao Phraya and Salween rivers, accounts for the Malays and Indonesians.

Though these migrating tribes originated in territory dominated by China, they were not participants in the advanced civilization of classical China. Until the north-south partition of China in the fourth century, imperial China regarded its southern provinces as a barbarian hinterland.

Southwestern China in particular was inhabited in ancient times as today by numerous tribal societies with only marginal cultural ties to the Chinese. Until the Song (Sung) dynasty in the tenth century, the Chinese were not notably a seafaring people, and the lively maritime trade route between China and India was plied primarily by Indian ships. For this reason, with the exception of Vietnam, the cultural influences upon early Southeast Asia were primarily Indian and occurred during a period in which Buddhism and Hinduism were both influential in India.

According to Buddhist tradition, the Indian emperor Aśoka sent a Buddhist mission to Southeast Asia in the third century BCE. Aśoka's historically confirmed mission to Sri Lanka appears to have been Theravādin, so presumably the Southeast Asian mission, if it occurred, was Theravādin as well. There is some indication that the Mon peoples of ancient Burma may have received Aśoka's mission and been Theravādin from that time onward. The existing traditions of Theravāda Buddhism in Southeast Asia, however, were established in the second millennium as imports from Sri Lanka. Prior to these developments, Southeast Asian Buddhism was primarily Mahāyāna with a heavy admixture of Hinduism. This Hindu admixture is lacking in Vietnam, where Chinese forms of Buddhism predominated. Outside Vietnam, Mahāyāna influences are now minimal, except in Thailand where Mahāyāna Buddhism mixed with Daoism and Confucianism is practiced by a sizeable Chinese population of relatively recent origins.

Because of the numerous ethnic groups in Southeast Asia, their migratory origins, and their seemingly interminable conflicts, the history of the region is extremely complex. The following account examines the development of Buddhism from the points of view of the modern countries of Southeast Asia. These modern countries, however, are of relatively recent origin and have superseded older states which also must be considered in a history of Buddhism in the region. Because of the number of states and ethnic groups involved, and because of the constant conflicts among them, considering them separately entails some repetition. This approach has the advantage, however, of recognizing the role of Buddhism in shaping the national identities of the existing countries of Southeast Asia.

The Ancient Kingdoms: Funan, Champa, and Śri Vijaya

The earliest of the historically verified states to appear in Southeast Asia is known to historians by the Chinese name Funan, since Chinese records are the most important source of information concerning the early history of the region. Funan, comprising territory surrounding the

Mekong River delta, appears to have emerged as a political entity in the first century of the common era, at about the time Indian civilization began to exert a sustained influence on the region. No examples of the vernacular language of Funan survive, but it is generally supposed that the Funanese were racially and linguistically related to the Khmer. A rival state known as Champa — comprised of Malayo-Polynesian racial and linguistic stock — existed along the southeastern coast of present-day Vietnam. Champa was powerful in its day, but is not survived by any modern state. Also in the early centuries of the common era, the ancestors of the modern-day Indonesians and Malays were beginning to form a political conglomerate along the Malay peninsula and through to Sumatra and Java. In the seventh century, these people emerged as the kingdom of Śri Vijaya.

By the third century, only Funan had established diplomatic contacts with China, probably indicating that Funan was recognized as the supreme power in Southeast Asia at this time. In the fourth century the kingdom was taken over by an Indian ruler, possibly a displaced member of the Kushan dynasty, which had collapsed in India. Relationships between Funan and China continued through to the sixth century. Chinese records of these relationships establish that the state religion was Śaivite Hinduism, but that Buddhism, probably Mahāyāna, was also common. The greatest of the kings of Funan was its last powerful ruler, Jaya-varman I. When he died in 514, a conflict over succession to the throne appears to have resulted in the demise of Funan. By the seventh century, Funan had been superseded by its former vassal, the inland Khmer kingdom referred to by the Chinese as Chenla, the royal line of which appears to have had ties to the royal line of Funan. Chenla, however, remained weak and divided until the foundation of the Khmer kingdom of Angkor in the ninth century.

By the fifth century, the primarily Śaivite kingdom of Champa, with its capital near present-day Hué, Vietnam, had begun to assert itself in the region. By this time China had suffered its north-south partition, and the southern dynastic histories record conflict with Champa in the region of the Gulf of Tonkin. The Chinese chronicles record severe attacks on Champa by both China and Vietnam. These attacks — combined with pressure from the Khmer tribes pushing down the Mekong from their homeland in southwest China — diminished Cham power in Southeast Asia, though a separate Cham state held on until the fifteenth century. The ancient mainland kingdoms of Funan and Champa were eventually superseded by the Khmer (the ancestors of present-day Cambodia) and by the Vietnamese. In the meantime, from about 600 to 800 CE, the primarily Buddhist kingdom of Śri Vijaya was dominant in Southeast Asia.

Śri Vijaya is a blanket term for several states that developed on the Malay Peninsula and the islands of Sumatra and Java. The coasts controlled by Śri Vijaya were an important link in the sea trade between India and China, and diplomatic relations between China and Śri Vijaya are recorded from the fifth century. Otherwise, little is known of Śri Vijaya before the arrival of the Chinese pilgrim Yi Jing (I Ching). In 671, Yi Jing stopped over in Sumatra for six months on his way to India. After spending some thirteen years in India, primarily at the great Buddhist university of Nālandā, Yi Jing returned to Sumatra in 685 and stayed near the modern site of Palembang until 695, working on his translations. The fact that this important Chinese pilgrim and translator chose to spend such a long time in Sumatra indicates the importance of the area as a center of Buddhist learning. According to Yi Jing, both Theravāda and Mahāyāna Buddhism flourished there during his stay. Other than this, Yi Jing's diary contains little information about Śri Vijaya or the Buddhism practiced there.

On Java, Śaivite Hindus vied with Buddhists for supremacy. In the eighth century, the Buddhist Śailendra dynasty gained supremacy in Java and immortalized itself with the construction of Borobudur, one of the largest religious monuments ever built. Borobudur is actually a series of carved stone terraces built on a naturally occurring hill and culminating in a giant stūpa (dome-shaped Buddhist monument) that originally stood over sixty feet tall and, atop its terraces, rose nearly 150 feet above the surrounding plain. To traverse the entire length of the four galleries spiraling up to the the stūpa involves a walk of about a mile, past some 400 Buddha images (originally 504) and thousands of bas-reliefs depicting events from Mahāyāna sūtras. In the ninth century, the Śaivite Sanjaya dynasty gained the upper hand on Java and constructed equally magnificent, though smaller, Hindu shrines, while maintaining the Buddhist shrine of Borobudur. These Javanese shrines, both Hindu and Buddhist, reveal both the enormous wealth of these ancient kingdoms and a strong native influence upon Indian architectural and artistic forms.

After being ousted from Java, the Śailendra dynasty appears to have established itself on Sumatra. However, no archaeological remains comparable to the Śailendra's Javanese shrines survive on Sumatra. Chinese records show that hostilities between Sumatra and Java continued until Sumatra, under the name Śri Vijaya, emerged victorious in the eleventh century. In the same century, however, the south Indian Chola empire began to expand into the region and mounted a devastating attack upon Śri Vijaya. Little more is recorded of the kingdom until the Thais asserted control over the Malay peninsula in the thirteenth century, thus depriving Śri Vijaya of its mainland base. Also in the thirteenth century, the Mongols attacked Śri Vijaya and withdrew after causing great disruption. Finally, in the fourteenth century, the Thais invaded island Śri Vijaya and destroyed the kingdom forever. Through all of this, Śri Vijaya remains little more than a name occasionally mentioned in some other nation's historical records. Archaeological evidence from Java indicates, however, that the religion of Śri Vijaya developed into a unique mixture of Tantric Buddhism and Śaivite Hinduism with a distinctly Indonesian flavor.

In 1292, Marco Polo visited Sumatra and noted there the presence of Muslim traders and native converts to Islam. The Muslims, who were already dominant in northern India, were determined to control the maritime trade route eastward from India to the South China Sea. After gaining an initial stronghold on the Malay peninsula, during the fifteenth and sixteenth centuries the Muslims extended their control over Malaya, Sumatra, Java, and even northern Borneo, thus gaining control of the coveted trade route and establishing the primary religious orientation of Indonesia to the present day.

Remarkably, the small island of Bali managed to stave off the advance of Islam, surviving even a holy war declared by a Javanese sultan in the seventeenth century. Today, only Bali and eastern Java retain any living trace of the Buddhist and Hindu culture that once thrived in Indonesia. As a result of a twentieth-century Buddhist revival, there are now approximately three million Buddhists in Indonesia. Most of these, however, practice Theravāda Buddhism recently imported from Sri Lanka and Southeast Asia. The ancient Buddhist-Hindu civilization of Indonesia, which left some of the most impressive religious monuments ever constructed, has all but vanished. Today, only the majestic ruins rising from the jungles of Java testify to the ancient glory of Buddhism's southernmost advance in Asia.

Cambodia

Weakened by internal disarray and conflicts with Śri Vijaya, Funan eventually gave way to the Khmer tribes pushing down the Mekong River. The first step in this process was the annexation of Funan by Chenla in the seventh century. Chenla, however, was a weak and divided state, threatened by Champa and dominated by Śri Vijaya, until the succession to the throne of Jayavarman II, founder of the kingdom of Angkor, in about 800 CE. Early in his reign, Jayavarman II traveled to Java. Presumably this was a successful diplomatic mission to the Śailendra court, for in 802, Jayavarman II boldly declared the sovereignty of Angkor, successor of Chenla and Funan, and forerunner of modern-day Cambodia.

Jayavarman II appears to have been deeply impressed by the Śailendra court, for in order to consecrate his reign, he constructed a "temple mountain" — built like Borobudur on a naturally occurring hill but on a much smaller scale. Unlike Buddhist Borobudur, Jayavarman's monument was Hindu, enshrining the royal Śiva-liṅga, a phallic symbol representing the prosperity of the realm and the association of the king with the god Śiva. Following Jayavarman II, it became standard practice for his successors to construct their own temple mountains in order to consecrate their reigns. On the one hand, this practice resulted in the rich archaeological heritage of Angkor. On the other hand, the continual construction of these increasingly grandiose temples placed upon financial and human resources a strain that led ultimately to the demise of the kingdom.

The greatest of these temple mountains, the famous Angkor Wat, was built under Sūryavarman II (r. 1113-50), the most powerful yet of the Khmer kings, but also the most wasteful. Angkor Wat is truly grand by any standards. The entire temple complex covers almost a square mile. The central shrine rises 140 feet from a square, colonnaded platform measuring about 100 yards on each side. This, in turn, stands on another colonnaded platform about 200 yards square, which is surrounded by yet another enclosure measuring about half a mile on each side. All this is surrounded by a moat over 200 yards wide. From the grand western entrance to the central shrine is a half-mile walk along a broad causeway and up tier after tier of steep stairs. Angkor Wat is dedicated to Vishṇu rather than to Śiva, reflecting a change in the religious orientation of the dynasty. Apparently, Sūryavarman II adopted a new deity in order to distinguish his grand concept of an expansive Khmer empire in Southeast Asia from the more provincial reigns of his predecessors. His extravagance as a builder was matched by his extravagance as a military campaigner, though his military campaigns against neighboring Southeast Asian states appear to have failed as often as they succeeded. Not until the reign of Jayavarman VII, who ascended the throne in 1181, was the dream of a great Khmer empire in Southeast Asia realized.

For unknown reasons, Jayavarman VII (r. 1181-1218) was a fervent Mahāyāna Buddhist. In answer to Angkor Wat, he built the nearby but much smaller Buddhist temple mountain known as Bayon. Speculations as to why Jayavarman VII embraced Buddhism are numerous but inconclusive. According to his inscriptions, his father had converted to Buddhism before him. Perhaps these rulers wished to distinguish the Khmers sharply from their traditional enemies the Śaivite Cham, who were finally subdued during the reign of Jayavarman VII. Jayavarman VII's inscriptions indicate that he was anxious to win the approval of his subjects.

Perhaps he felt that the imagery of king as loving bodhisattva would be more appealing than the imagery of king as an exalted but distant god. The historical details of the Khmer conversion to Buddhism may never be understood, but at any rate, after Jayavarman VII, the kingdom was decisively Buddhist, although Hinduism continued to exert influence.

If Jayavarman VII was truly concerned about the welfare of his subjects, he did not act wisely. His ambitious program of mammoth construction projects and extensive military campaigns impoverished the realm. Many of his building projects were public-spirited constructions — including hospitals, travelers' rest houses, roads, bridges and reservoirs — and his inscriptions indicate that he undertook such projects out of the bodhisattva's concern for the welfare of his subjects. Nonetheless, these were a drain on Angkor's human and economic resources. In addition, he constructed a grand capital known as Angkor Thom surrounding the Bayon temple. These projects, following as they did upon the similarly extravagant projects of Sūryavarman II, appear to have destroyed the Khmer economy and alienated the peasantry, who ultimately had to carry and carve the stones for construction projects rivaling the pyramids.

After the reign of Jayavarman VII, which ended in about 1218, Angkor began to go the way of its Indianized neighbors to the west, the Thais and Burmese, and to follow Theravāda Buddhism. Even the broad outlines of the mechanism and chronology of this wholesale conversion remain unclear, but it seems to be linked to the demise of the old dynasty of Angkor. Jayavarman VIII, the last of the old dynasty, appears to have presided over a short-lived resurgence of Hinduism that resulted in the defacing of many of Jayavarman VII's Buddhist monuments. Jayavarman VIII abdicated in 1295 — whether willingly or unwillingly is not clear — in favor of a usurper, Indravarman III, who at some point, before or after the abdication, justified his claim to the throne by marrying the old king's daughter.

Indravarman III was the first Theravādin king of Angkor, though a son of Jayavarman VII is believed to have received Theravādin ordination in Sri Lanka.[23] After Indravarman III, the royal inscriptions of Cambodia were in Pāli rather than Sanskrit, and temple construction ceased abruptly, leaving some projects uncompleted. This dramatic cessation of the great architectural tradition of Angkor suggests that the ascendancy of Theravāda Buddhism in Cambodia, accompanied as it was by a change in dynasty, represented something of a populist rebellion against the burdens imposed by the mammoth construction projects of the Hindu and Mahāyāna dynasties. Another factor in the rapid conversion of the Khmer to Theravāda Buddhism must have been the increasing power of the Thais, who began to encroach upon Angkor in the early thirteenth century, shortly after the reign of Jayavarman VII. By this time the Thais, under the influence of the Burmese, were already firmly Theravādin.

Angkor remained powerful and prosperous as a Theravādin kingdom for several centuries, but continual Thai encroachments eventually forced removal of the capital to Phnom Penh in the fifteenth century. From this point, the alternatives "Cambodia" or "Kampuchea" supplant "Angkor" as the name of the country of the Khmer people. Traditionally, the Khmers trace the origins of their royal family to a mythical religious ascetic with the Sanskrit name Kambu Svayambhuva, "Self-existent Kambu," a name which implies a miraculous, self-generated birth. Both "Kampuchea" and "Cambodia" are mispronunciations of the Sanskrit "Kambuja," which means "born from Kambu."

Throughout the sixteenth century, the Thais remained the primary enemies of the Khmer, but in the seventeenth century, Vietnam's southward push resulted in the annexation of Cambodia's southeastern coastal territory all the way down to the Mekong delta. By the mid-eighteenth century, this sustained Vietnamese push had resulted in roughly the current border between Cambodia and Vietnam. At the same time, the Thais gradually assumed control of traditionally Cambodian territory in the northwest. In the seventeenth and eighteenth centuries, Cambodia became in effect the battleground for conflicts between Vietnam and Thailand, alternating helplessly between control by one and then another of these neighbors; sometimes by both.

The Thais justified their incursions into Cambodia as moves to protect Theravāda Buddhism from the Mahāyānist Vietnamese. Though self-serving, this claim was certainly true. Theravāda Buddhism and Khmer culture disappeared all but entirely in the Cambodian territory annexed by Vietnam. The Khmer regarded the Thais as enemies also, but the Vietnamese were particularly hated for their expulsion of Khmer people from coastal areas and their overall policy of colonization and imposition of Vietnamese ways. The Thais, by contrast, were Indianized relatives and co-religionists of the Khmer. This Khmer preference of the Thais over the Vietnamese became obvious when Vietnam appeared set to prevail decisively against Thailand for control of Cambodia. In 1842, rebellious peasants throughout occupied Cambodia surprised, isolated, and where possible massacred Vietnamese garrisons. The uprising had no known leader, but it appears to have been organized primarily by the Theravādin Saṅgha. This reversal against Vietnam drew Thai forces back into the struggle over Cambodia. An eventual Thai victory created just enough breathing space for the Cambodian monarch to negotiate a treaty with France in 1863-64. As a result, Cambodia avoided being annexed by either Thailand or Vietnam.

European colonial influence — both French and British — had the effect of freezing the heretofore fluid national boundaries of Southeast Asia into more or less their present configuration. It seems that everyone involved felt cheated once the map was drawn, but it is very possible that Cambodia would have ceased to exist without European intervention. A derivative, albeit inadvertent effect of this map-making was the introduction of nationalism and the desire for independence. Cambodian nationalism was closely associated with Buddhism throughout the period of French domination, which lasted from 1864 until 1953, when Cambodia's monarch, Prince Norodom Sihanouk, negotiated his country's independence from France.

From independence in 1953 until 1975, Buddhism enjoyed a limited resurgence in Cambodia, first under Prince Sihanouk, and then under General Lon Nol, who usurped power in 1970 by means of a military coup. This coup, which was backed by the United States, marked the end of a tradition of Cambodian monarchy going back at least to Jayavarman II in the ninth century. From 1970, America's infamous Vietnam War began to spill uncontrollably into Cambodia. In the ever widening struggle in Southeast Asia between American-backed regimes and communist revolutionary movements, Buddhism and Buddhist monks were courted by both sides for propaganda purposes. In Cambodia, Buddhism and its monks and monasteries appear to have suffered neither more nor less than the population at large.

In 1975, disaster befell Cambodia. The defeat of United States forces in Southeast Asia by Vietnamese communists left the way open for the most radical faction of the Khmer communist movement — known as the Khmer Rouge or "Red Khmers" under General Pol Pot — to seize power in Cambodia. The period of Khmer Rouge domination, from 1975 to 1979, represents one of the most debilitating persecutions that Buddhism — or any other religion for that matter — has ever undergone. It is still difficult, however, to determine the extent to which Buddhism was actually targeted by the Khmer Rouge as opposed to being dragged down in a general destruction of Cambodian civilization.

Under Pol Pot, the Khmer Rouge carried out a sustained program ostensibly designed to return Cambodia to "year zero." Theoretically, "year zero" referred to a point in time at which all foreign influence whatsoever would be eradicated from the lives and minds of the Khmer people. From this purified stock, Pol Pot vowed to mastermind the creation of the perfect communist society and restore the glory of ancient Angkor. In practice, Pol Pot's program resulted in the deaths of up to one fifth of Cambodia's seven million inhabitants. Estimates of the death toll vary widely and passionately, depending on their source, but at least a

half-million people died prematurely under the Khmer Rouge. Many of
these died incidentally of starvation, disease and overwork in the misera-
ble economic conditions under Pol Pot. Tens of thousands, however,
were methodically rounded up, tortured and brutally executed — often
clubbed or hacked to death so as not to waste bullets.

Buddhism, as a potential rival for the allegiance of the Cambodian
people, was one of Pol Pot's prime targets. Monks were first coerced
and then forced, on pain of death, to renounce their ordinations, so that
the Saṅgha vanished completely. Many monasteries and temples were
destroyed intentionally, while others succumbed to neglect or were used
as warehouses and barns. Mercifully, the ruins of the ancient capital of
Angkor, including Angkor Wat and Bayon, were spared as emblems of
the former greatness of the Khmer people, of which Pol Pot proclaimed
himself the restorer.

Ironically Vietnam, the traditional nemesis of Cambodia, intervened in
1979 to stop Pol Pot's lethal experiment. On the whole, the Vietnamese
were welcomed as liberators, and during the 1980s, under Vietnamese
protection, Cambodia was able to achieve a limited reconstruction of its
society and civilization. Guerrillas loyal to Pol Pot impeded this process,
however, operating from remote jungle hideouts. Although Buddhism
was not encouraged under the Vietnam-backed regime, on the whole it
was not discouraged either. Reconstruction work was at least begun on
most of the important temples and shrines, which the people were free to
attend. The few monks who had survived Pol Pot's "year zero" campaign
were allowed to resume their robes and work toward rebuilding the
Saṅgha. The first re-ordination ceremonies, however, required a
delegation of monks from Vietnam, since the Cambodian Saṅgha had
been eradicated under Pol Pot, and an ordination ceremony must be
conducted by at least five fully-ordained monks. As of 1980, about 800
former monks had been re-ordained. This represents a disappearance
of some 60,000 monks during the Pol Pot period.[24] During the 1980s,
Buddhist monks became once again a common sight in Cambodia,
though there were still restrictions upon the Saṅgha. Because of a scarcity
of manpower, men were prohibited from joining the Saṅgha until the
age of fifty, and the Saṅgha's funding and affairs remained under government control.

In 1990, after Vietnam had voluntarily withdrawn its troops from
Cambodia, Prime Minister Hun Sen declared Buddhism the state religion
and lifted most restrictions on Buddhism. This move was part of a bid
by the government to gain popular support vis-à-vis the various political
and military factions which claim legitimacy in Cambodia and continue to
wreak havoc in the beleaguered country. In 1992, the largest ever United

Nations peace-keeping force and budget was deployed in Cambodia in an effort to bring general elections, peace and stability after more than two decades of nightmarish chaos. The fate of Buddhism in the region rests in the balance alongside the fate of the Cambodian people and civilization.

Laos

Laos is a land-locked nation squeezed between Thailand to the west and Vietnam to the east, and sharing shorter borders with Burma in the northwest and Cambodia in the south. As its position on the map of Southeast Asia might suggest, Laos is the product of early contacts between the Khmers of Cambodia and the Thais who eventually established Thailand. As Thai tribes migrated into the Southeast Asian peninsula during the latter half of the first millennium, they came first down the Mekong River until they encountered the rear guard of the Khmer tribes who had followed that route before them. Some settled along the upper reaches of the Mekong, while others resorted to the relatively uninhabited Chao Phraya, which flows through the heart of present-day Thailand, reaching the sea at Bangkok. The Thai-related people who settled in the upper Mekong region became the ancestors of the modern-day Laos. Landlocked and surrounded by more powerful cultures, Laos remains the poorest country in Southeast Asia in every way except for the renowned Lao sense of humor and fun.

Lao history in fact begins in the fourteenth century with a risqué event, the seduction of one of the king's wives by his son Phi Fa, heir apparent to the throne. For his indiscretion, Phi Fa was banished. He and his son Fa Ngum journeyed south and took up residence in the Khmer royal court at Angkor. There, Fa Ngum studied under a Theravādin monk, gained the favor of the Khmer king, and eventually married one of his daughters. In about 1350, the king of Angkor provided Fa Ngum with an army so that he could reassert control over his father's lost inheritance.

By this time, Angkor was in a state of decline, and the political center of gravity in Thailand had shifted southward from Sukhothai to Ayutthaya. Angkor's weakness and this shift of power in Thailand left the way open for Fa Ngum to establish an independent kingdom, with ties to Angkor, along the upper reaches of the Mekong River. Fa Ngum's coronation at Luang Phrabang in 1353 marked the beginning of the historical Lao state. It also established the farthest northern extent of Khmer civilization, since Fa Ngum's kingdom was modeled on Angkoran precedents even though the Laos are racially related to the Thais. Furthermore,

Fa Ngum invited his Buddhist teacher at the Khmer court to act as his advisor and chief priest. Under his influence the new kingdom of Laos became firmly Theravādin, as it has remained to the present day. This Buddhist master brought with him from Angkor a Buddha image known as the "Phra Bang." This image accounts for the capital's name and, like the tooth relic of the Buddha in Sri Lanka, became the palladium of the kingdom.

From the very beginning, Laos seems to have been just barely strong enough to maintain a separate identity in the midst of its more powerful neighbors. This it was able to do only by means of a series of alliances, concessions, and submissions to the Thais, Burmese and finally the Vietnamese. As the Khmers too were finding at about this time, it was a question of being dominated by the related, Indianized cultures of Burma and Thailand or by the Vietnamese, who were especially hated because of their sacking of the Lao capital in 1479. Subservient alliances with Burma and Thailand were undesirable for Laos, but they had the effect of reinforcing Theravāda Buddhism, which became the country's primary symbol of continuity and identity in the face of its shifting political fortunes.

Because of the relatively weak central government of Laos, Theravāda Buddhism became the primary cement holding together the numerous ethnic groups and inaccessible villages scattered through the mountainous countryside. According to the Lao model of kingship, the king sat upon the throne not so much because of divine right as because of his obviously good karma in previous lives. He was expected to continue that good karma in this life by supporting the Saṅgha and promoting Buddhism through royal construction projects. Pursuing this role, King Visun (r. 1501-20) is remembered as the prime mover behind the splendor of Luang Phrabang, the first capital of Laos. Actually, Visun brought to fruition an ambitious Buddhist construction program which had been begun by his two older brothers in order to repair damage done by the Vietnamese in the previous century. Since they were made of wood, few examples of these early architectural works survive, but Luang Phrabang remains the site of some of the most attractive Buddhist monuments and ruins in Southeast Asia.

Visun's grandson Setthathirat (r. 1548-71) occupied the throne in 1548. Soon, Burmese expansionism forced Setthathirat to form an alliance with the Thais in 1560. The resulting treaty entailed shifting the capital from Luang Phrabang to Vien Chan (Vientiane), a site closer to the Thai capital at Ayutthaya and more conducive to trade with and supervision by the Thais. Setthathirat did for Vien Chan what King Visun had done for Luang Phrabang, carrying out a large-scale Buddhist construction program.

Remnants of Setthathirat's works still stand, the most notable being the hundred-yard square That Luang or "Great Shrine," a temple mountain built in the Khmer style. Setthathirat also built a second grand temple to house a precious jade Buddha known as the Phra Keo. This image was the second palladium of Laos until it was removed to Bangkok by a Thai invading force in 1778. It has remained in Bangkok ever since in the Wat Phra Keo as Thailand's most sacred image. This same image is also the primary symbol of Lao resentment against Thailand.

Twice during Setthathirat's reign, Burma attacked Laos unsuccessfully. In 1574 the Burmese finally conquered Vien Chan and took captive its new child-king, No Keo Kuman, holding him until 1591, when they voluntarily returned him to the throne. No Keo Kuman died in 1596 without producing an heir, and this plunged Laos into a forty year period of internal strife. Finally, Sūryavaṃsa ascended the throne in 1637 and re-established stability by forming a matrimonial alliance with the Vietnamese. Further strife following the death of Sūryavaṃsa in 1694 resulted in the partition of the country into a Lao-controlled state with its capital at Luang Phrabang and a Vietnamese-controlled state with its capital at Vien Chan. The Vietnamese-backed kingdom in the south was relatively stable, but the Lao kingdom in the north was weak and dominated by Burma and Thailand.

In 1778, Thailand conquered the southern kingdom of Vien Chan, asserted control over the northern kingdom of Luang Phrabang, and removed both the Phra Bang and Phra Keo Buddha images to Thailand. In 1782, the Thais restored the Vietnamese dynasty as a puppet regime in Vien Chan and returned the Phra Bang Buddha image. Despite continuing Thai domination of the entirety of Laos, the country remained divided into a northern and a southern kingdom until 1893, when the French blockaded Bangkok and forced Thailand to cede to France the upper reaches of the Mekong River. The French protectorate thus established over Laos had little to do with the distribution of the Lao people, many of whom still resided in Thai territory. The Thais, on the other hand, resented having been deprived of the most valuable portion of their Laotian holdings. Again, no one was happy with European map-making when Laos eventually became independent.

Briefly during World War II, Laos was nominally independent under Japanese control. After World War II, in 1946, reassertion of French control in Southeast Asia led directly to the formation of a communist independence movement known as the Pathet Lao, which had ties to the Vietnamese communist movement under Ho Chi Minh. The French collapse in Southeast Asia in 1954 led to a coalition government in which both Lao royalists and Lao communists were represented. This coalition quickly collapsed, and Laos, like Vietnam, entered the 1960s in the throes of a full-scale civil war between communist and pro-Western factions, which were now aided primarily by the United States. After the defeat of American forces in Vietnam in 1975, the communists quickly gained control in Laos, at about the same time as Pol Pot's Khmer Rouge gained control in Cambodia. In Laos, however, the transition to communism was not the nightmare that the Cambodians faced. Many of the intelligentsia and the more traditionally-minded Lao people sought refuge in Thailand to avoid "re-education" camps and the communist regime in general, but there was nothing like the "year zero" campaign to exterminate "class enemies" as witnessed in Cambodia.

In the course of this much more benign transition to communism in Laos, there is little evidence of significant suppression of Buddhism. Even during the revolution, one of the main propaganda tactics of the Pathet Lao was to promulgate the compatibility of Buddhism and communism and to enlist the support of monks for their revolution. While many monks worked against the communists, it is clear also that many worked actively for them. When the communists came to power, they forbade the giving of alms to monks, but announced provision of a state-controlled ration of rice for monks. This ration was to be supplemented by food produced or earned by the monks themselves. Since then, monks have been required to perform productive roles in the community, primarily their traditional roles as teachers and healers.

What they teach and the medicine they practice, however, are controlled by a Department of Religious Affairs, administered by the Ministry of Education. The Department of Religious Affairs has overseen a program designed to expunge "counter-revolutionary" and "exploitative" material from the traditional Buddhism of Laos. Under this program, in addition to teaching Buddhism, monks have a significant responsibility for teaching literacy and a patriotic, communist version of Lao history. Monks were traditionally consulted for the relief of illness, but prior to the communist takeover they administered primarily blessings and magical amulets. Now they administer traditional herbal medicine and where possible, Western medicine.

The communist reformation of Buddhism, implemented by a panel of respected Lao monks, has been criticized as repressive by some Thai and expatriate Lao Buddhists. Alternatively, it has been praised by Lao and Thai reformists as representing a return to a purer Buddhism unencumbered by superstitious accretions. There can be little doubt, from the standpoint of Theravāda doctrine, that traditional herbal and Western medicine are an improvement over the previous practices of performing exorcisms and selling blessings and magical amulets. It is also evident that the previous catering to traditional Lao spirit cults and ancestor worship had nothing to do with scriptural Buddhism.

It is not yet clear how extensive revisions of the Buddhist texts themselves may be, or how such revisions will affect Buddhism in Laos. On the surface, there does not appear to be much material in the Theravāda texts that conflicts with the moderate communism of the Lao regime. Some of the restrictions upon monks set forth in the Vinaya Piṭaka have been abandoned — most notably the prohibition upon working the soil — but the Vinaya rules are not strictly observed by all monks in any Buddhist country in the world. On the whole, most reports from Laos indicate that Buddhism there thrives in harmony with the communist regime. Clearly, there is much scope for a revival of the crippled Buddhism of Cambodia with recourse to the closely related and still healthy Buddhism of Laos. Laos and Cambodia have diplomatic relations going back to the fourteenth century, both espouse Theravāda Buddhism, and both have lived under communist regimes.

Burma

In Burma, as in Thailand, reliable history begins only in the second millennium CE. Prior to reliable historical records, the earliest known peoples to migrate down the Irrawaddy, Salween and Chao Phraya Rivers into present-day Burma and Thailand are referred to as the Mon. They were racially and linguistically related to the Khmer, who migrated down the Mekong river into present-day Cambodia at about the same time, the second half of the first millennium BCE. The Khmer had to contend with Funan and Champa for access to the sea. The Mon, by contrast, appear to have encountered only Stone Age cultures and to have established dominance easily in coastal Burma and much of present-day Thailand.

Traditional histories of Burma recount ancient dynasties going back to the third millennium BCE, but there is no archaeological evidence for any such ancient civilization. These accounts of very early Burmese history actually appear to recount legends borrowed from Indian sources. This legendary material does reflect the historical fact that the Mons looked directly to India for their pattern of civilization, while their cousins the Khmer derived their civilization from India via Funan. Burmese tradition has it that Aśoka sent a Theravāda Buddhist mission to ancient Burma in about 250 BCE, and some believe that ancient Burma may be identified with the land of Suvaṇṇabhūmi mentioned in the Sri Lankan chronicles as the destination of a Buddhist mission during the reign of Aśoka.[25] Be that as it may, it is clear that the Mons of ancient Burma and Thailand were largely responsible for the transmission into mainland Southeast Asia of Indian influences in general and of Theravāda Buddhism in particular.

Burmese history as such does not begin until about 650 CE, by which time a Tibetan people known as the Pyu had begun to encroach upon the Mon and had established the kingdom of Śrikshetra. Earlier, the Pyu appear to have established a foothold in northern Burma and pushed their way steadily toward the sea against Mon resistance. The details of the struggle between the Mon and the Pyu are unknown, but by about 850 CE the Pyu were attacked and annihilated by Thai peoples known to the Chinese as the kingdom of Nan Zhao (Nan Chao), which occupied territory in the present Chinese province of Yunnan. The Mon people further to the south appear to have resisted Nan Zhao successfully, if indeed they were attacked.

During the next two centuries, a second wave of Tibetan peoples assumed control of the territory formerly dominated by their cousins the Pyu. This second wave of Tibetan people are known as the Tibeto-Burmans, and were the primary ancestors of the present-day Burmese. (Since the Burmese are a multi-racial society comprised of Mons, Pyu and Tibeto-Burmans, the term "Burman" is used herein to indicate the Tibeto-Burmans in particular, while "Burmese" refers to the mixed population of Burma as a whole.) Presumably the Tibeto-Burmans intermarried with the remaining Pyu in their migration through upper Burma. By 1057 — when they overthrew the Mon state — they appear to have absorbed much in the way of cultural influence from the Mon.

The Burman king responsible for the overthrow of the Mon and the unification of Burma was Anuruddha (r. 1044-77). Anuruddha established his capital at Pagan in northern Burma, a site still famed for its magnificent Buddhist ruins. It was this same Anuruddha who came to the aid of Sri Lanka against the Tamils of south India in 1067, and who in 1073 is supposed to have sent a delegation of monks to Sri Lanka in order to participate in the coronation of King Vijaya Bāhu. This is all a bit surprising, for the Tibetans, to whom the Burmans are related, were by this time firmly Mahāyānist. Archaeological evidence indicates that even the Pyu, the advance guard of the Burmans, practiced Tantric Buddhism with an admixture of Vaishnavite Hinduism. On the basis of archaeological evidence, Anuruddha himself was very likely a Mahāyānist with Vaishnavite leanings.

According to Burmese tradition, Anuruddha was converted to Theravāda Buddhism by a Mon monk named Shin Arahan, and the king overthrew the Mon capital of Thaton in 1057 in order to obtain Theravāda scriptures. The attack on Thaton was real enough, and doubtless brought Anuruddha and the Burmans in closer contact with

Mon culture. Anuruddha's sympathy for Theravāda Buddhism, as well as Burma's reputation as a Theravādin country, are both attested by the dealings between Burma and Sri Lanka during his reign. Throughout the reign of Anuruddha, however, the Burmans probably remained primarily Mahāyānist. The wholesale conversion of the Burmans appears to have occurred instead as a result of a military resurgence of the Mons.

Although the Mons remain a shadowy civilization, the triumph of Theravāda Buddhism in Southeast Asia may be traced directly to their influence in the region. The nature and extent of Mon contacts with India are vague and mostly the stuff of legend. There is nothing inherently dubious in the traditional claim that Buddhism was introduced to the Mon under Aśoka, but there is no evidence to support it. Tradition has it too that the great Sri Lankan commentator Buddhaghosa introduced the Pāli scriptures to Burma in the fifth century. This is unlikely, but not impossible. Instead, it appears that the delegation of monks returning from Vijaya Bāhu's coronation in Sri Lanka brought with them the first complete set of the Pāli scriptures ever to exist in Burma or in Southeast Asia. This was in about 1080, at which time Burma was dominated by Mahāyānist Burmans rather than the Theravādin Mons.

The Burman flirtation with Theravāda Buddhism became an enduring marriage when the Mon sympathizer Kyanzittha usurped the throne in 1086. Kyanzittha had been a general under Anuruddha, but fell out of favor with the king and was banished. Kyanzittha then formed an alliance with the deposed Mon royal family of Thaton. When Anuruddha's son and successor was captured and killed in a Mon rebellion, Kyanzittha and his Mon allies succeeded in restoring order and unifying the state. To cement his alliance with the Mons, Kyanzittha's daughter married a prince of the Mon royal family. Subsequently, all of Kyanzittha's temples were built in the Mon style and were decorated with paintings and sculptures depicting events in the Pāli scriptures. Most of Kyanzittha's inscriptions were in the Mon language. These temples and inscriptions suggest that Theravāda Buddhism became widespread among the Burmese under Kyanzittha during a period of Mon political resurgence.

This Mon resurgence lasted only about a century, but by the time of the Burman cultural resurgence in the twelfth century, Theravāda Buddhism was firmly established. The importation of the Sri Lankan Mahāvihāra ordination lineage in 1190 may have been part of this Burman resurgence, as this would have served to establish a Saṅgha independent of the old Mon lineage. The Mon lineage continued to exist for about two more centuries, but the Mahāvihāra lineage enjoyed royal support and also proved to be the more successful among the people. This same Mahāvihāra tradition was eventually re-imported into Sri Lanka when the Sinhalese ordination lineage was itself in need of regeneration in the eighteenth and nineteenth centuries. Regardless of the possibility of a very early Mon lineage, all Theravāda Buddhism in Southeast Asia traces back to the Mahāvihāra lineage of Sri Lanka.

Having become established in Burma in the late twelfth century, Theravāda Buddhism of the Mahāvihāra lineage spread throughout Southeast Asia during the thirteenth and fourteenth centuries. Only Vietnam remained Mahāyānist. Incongruously, this expansion of Theravāda Buddhism occurred against a historical backdrop of almost incessant warfare. Such turbulence had become common in Southeast Asia, but it was worsened by the arrival of the dreaded Mongols, who wreaked disaster throughout the Eastern world during the thirteenth century. At this time, the Thais lived to the north of Southeast Asia in present-day Yunnan. During most of the first millennium, Thais had been gradually migrating south and establishing small settlements, mostly along the Chao Phraya River valley, in territory not controlled by the Khmer, the Mons, or the Burmans. The Mongol conquest of Yunnan in 1253 may have increased the southward migration of the Thai, though this widely accepted theory is questionable in the light of recent research.[26]

In 1287 Mongol forces sacked Pagan, the capital of Burmese territory in Southeast Asia. The Mongols made some attempt to organize and administer the Burmese empire, but after the death of Kublai Khan in 1294, Mongol influence in Southeast Asia declined sharply, leaving a power vacuum. By this time, Thais had settled all along the Chao Phraya River, and they also pressed upon the Burmese from Yunnan in the north. With the Mongols gone, the Thais moved swiftly to establish themselves in Southeast Asia. The Thais replaced the Burmese as the dominant power in the region until the middle of the sixteenth century, when the Burmese again asserted themselves. From this point until the advent of the Europeans, the history of Theravādin Southeast Asia is one of constant warfare and alternate domination by the Burmese and the Thais. The Mons were gradually swallowed up, though from time to time independent Mon kingdoms managed to exist for short periods. The Khmers and Laos, squeezed between the Thais and the Vietnamese, maintained national identities but suffered steady diminution of their traditional territories.

Beginning in the thirteenth century, the Thais adopted the Burmese Theravāda tradition, and in the fourteenth century helped pass it on to Laos and Cambodia, as discussed above. The Buddhism that developed in Southeast Asia during the thirteenth and fourteenth centuries was a somewhat different religious phenomenon than had been seen previously in the region. As the only enduring institution or ideology in Indianized Southeast Asia, it became a religion of the people rather than an appendage of one ruling dynasty or another. From the Mongol invasions to the advent of European powers, dynasties rose and fell, spheres of influence expanded and contracted, and alliances formed and broke with such confusing frequency that the only real continuity in the region was Theravāda Buddhism. The Buddhist Saṅghas of the various states of Indianized Southeast Asia provided spiritual stability where politically there was chaos. Prior to this time, it is doubtful that the state-sponsored Saṅghas associated closely with the common people or that Buddhism had a prominent place in their daily lives. During the unstable centuries following the Mongol invasions, the Theravāda Buddhism of Southeast Asia turned increasingly to the people for support while the people turned to Buddhism for solace, continuity and authority.

Following the Mongol invasion of the thirteenth century, the Thais were dominant in Southeast Asia during the fourteenth and fifteenth centuries. In the sixteenth century, however, the apparently insignificant Burman center at Toungoo, in the Sitting River valley, became the focus of a Burman revival. In 1550 the Toungoo leadership fell into the hands of the ruthless but capable military leader Bayinnaung. Under King Bayinnaung (r. 1551-81), Mon power was definitively crushed forever, the Burmese were united, and the Thai capital at Ayutthaya was conquered and sacked in 1569.

After the death of King Bayinnaung, the pendulum swung the other way, with a resurgent Thailand first driving out the Burmese and then invading and dominating Burma in the seventeenth century. The eighteenth century was a replay of the sixteenth. Burma again rallied, drove out the Thais, invaded Thailand and razed Ayutthaya once again in 1767, almost exactly two centuries after the first sack of Ayutthaya. This led the Thais to move their capital to its present location at Bangkok. From there the powerful Chakri dynasty of Thailand was able to drive the Burmese out of Thailand once again. This seesaw might have continued indefinitely but for the arrival of European powers and the consequent removal of Southeast Asia's right to self-determination.

The Burmese were the first in Southeast Asia to fall decisively under the influence of a European power. This came about largely as a result of the megalomaniac King Bodawpaya's (r. 1782-1819) ill-advised provoking of border disputes with the British in India. As an example of the true insanity of Bodawpaya, he dealt with an attempted coup early in his reign by ordering the destruction of all evidence of human habitation in the province where the plot was hatched: people, buildings, domesticated animals, cultivated trees and crops. Incongruously, he decreed the death penalty for violations of Buddhist precepts such as taking intoxicants or killing animals. His grandiose Buddhist construction projects and his demands for military service placed an unbearable burden on his subjects, many of whom took refuge in British-controlled territory in India. This led Bodawpaya to order repeated military incursions into British India in order to stamp out what he supposed were rebel movements. Bodawpaya's successor Bagyidaw ascended the throne in 1819 and demonstrated an equal level of recklessness. The British tried for many years to negotiate a diplomatic solution with these two tyrants before invading Burma in 1824. At a heavy cost in casualties, many from dysentery and malaria, the British secured the submission of Burma in 1826. The resulting treaty ceded to Britain the entire western section of Burma.

Independent eastern Burma, under a series of inept rulers, proved to be unable to come to terms with the reality of British power in the region. Soon, the British moved again and in the second Burma War of 1852 annexed all of coastal Burma. This disaster resulted in the overthrow of the existing dynasty and the ascent of King Mindon (r. 1853-78) to the throne of independent, upper Burma. Mindon, an ex-Buddhist monk, proved to be a wise ruler, well loved by his people and well respected by the British. His proudest achievement was the convening of a fifth Buddhist Council in the tradition of the great Buddhist emperors of India, Aśoka and Kanishka, who are said to have convened the third and fourth Buddhist Councils. He invited monks from Sri Lanka, Thailand, Cambodia and Laos to create a revised edition of the Pāli Tipiṭaka. Mindon had the result engraved on 729 marble slabs and enshrined in the Kuthodaw Temple, which he built in Mandalay. Mindon's progressive reign thrust Burma into the forefront of a Buddhist modernization movement that remains prominent in Sri Lanka and Thailand. Mindon also founded the reformed Schwegon Nikāya of monks as an alternative to the long-established and much larger Sudhamma Nikāya. This reformation was not concerned with points of doctrine, but only the formation of a stricter group of monks who adhere more assiduously to the letter of the Vinaya.

While Mindon steadfastly refused to acknowledge by treaty the British annexation of coastal Burma, he also refused to attempt the military measures against the British advocated by some of his court. Thereby he was able to maintain the independence of at least part of Burma during his reign. The death of Mindon in 1878 precipitated a bloody struggle for dominance in the Burmese court. The resulting chaos in independent Burma provided the British with the excuse they needed to annex the entire country. This they did in 1886, attaching Burma to their Indian Empire. Treating Burma as a colony of the Indian Empire was a regrettable mistake. Whereas the British normally attempted to adapt existing systems of government to British goals, in Burma they attempted to impose a system that had been derived from Indian precedents, ignoring the traditional Burmese system of government and economy. As a result, the Burmese suffered particularly grave hardships under British rule, the entirety of which was plagued by indigenous uprisings, resistance and resentment.

The demise of the Burmese tradition of kingship left Buddhism as the only tangible symbol of national identity available to the Burmese. This, in turn, resulted in a politicization of some members of the Burmese Saṅgha, who came to be a core of the anti-imperialist movement in Burma. The entire situation was worsened by extraordinarily strident intolerance on the part of Christian missionaries in Burma and complicit suppression of Buddhism on the part of the British authorities. The Young Men's Buddhist Association (YMBA) — founded originally in Sri Lanka with sponsorship from the Theosophical Society — gained center stage in a growing Burmese independence movement by campaigning successfully to prohibit the British overlords of Burma from wearing shoes when visiting temples — the removal of footwear being a traditional gesture of respect when entering a Buddhist temple. This symbolic victory in 1919 made the YMBA the primary voice in the General Council of Burmese Associations (GCBA), which coordinated resistance to British rule throughout the country.

Independence was achieved nominally in 1942 when Burmese freedom-fighters aided Japanese forces in their defeat of British forces in Burma. Initially the Japanese were welcomed as co-religionists and liberators, particularly since retreating British-Indian forces had followed a scorched earth policy of destroying everything that might prove useful to the enemy. Once in control of this already devastated country, however, the Japanese showed no mercy in exploiting the citizenry in the service of their war effort, aimed at an attack upon British India. In addition to Allied prisoners of war, tens of thousands of Burmese were pressed into virtual slave labor on the infamous "railway of death" and other Japanese projects. The requisitioning of food supplies and transportation for the Japanese war effort resulted in severe famine and mass starvation in many parts of Burma.

Although the puppet government of Burma was officially allied to Japan, a Burmese resistance movement aided forces under Lord Mountbatten when the Allies invaded Burma in 1945. The leadership of this resistance movement, known as the Anti-Fascist People's Freedom League (AFPFL), had previously been student agitators against the British colonial presence in Burma, and were Marxist in orientation. In their minds, "fascist" labeled the British as accurately as the Japanese. After the

Japanese defeat, however, they were national heroes, and it was clear that these young leaders would dominate independent Burma, now an inevitability. Negotiations between the British and Aung San, the acknowledged leader of the AFPFL, concluded successfully in 1947. Later the same year, Aung San was assassinated by political rivals, but the British saw to the installation of his close associate U Nu as the first premier of Burma in 1948.

In addition to the material devastation of Burma during the war, U Nu faced the daunting task of establishing a compromise between Marxist elements in the new leadership of Burma and the traditionalist elements led by Buddhist monks. U Nu's policy of primary commitment to Buddhism and secondary commitment to Marxism — as compatible systems aiming for the welfare of all human beings — kept him democratically, albeit precariously, in power until 1962. U Nu attempted to demonstrate his dedication to Buddhism by hosting in 1954-56 a sixth Buddhist Council, in imitation of King Mindon's fifth Council, but U Nu was bitterly resented for attempts to enact state control of the Sangha. During U Nu's years in power, Burma remained a leading participant in Theravāda Buddhism's movement of modernization and outreach to the West. This promising movement is discussed more fully in Chapter XIII. In Burma, however, the movement never reached fruition.

Aside from the international prominence of its Buddhist heritage, Burma languished during U Nu's years in power. The country was crushingly poor, and the rivalry between traditionalist Buddhist factions and modernist factions of various persuasions remained unresolved. These rivalries eventually led to chaos, and in 1962, to a coup under General Ne Win. Ne Win's solution, epitomized by the slogan "the Burmese road to socialism," was certainly not an improvement. Since 1962, Burma has deteriorated under a xenophobic military dictatorship with policies so unrealistic that it is universally recognized that the Burmese economy could not function without smuggling and the black market. Nonetheless, Ne Win's promotion of Buddhism minimized popular opposition to his regime until the late 1980s.

In 1988, widespread rioting in Burma and finally the massacre of some three thousand demonstrators by soldiers forced the retirement of the ageing Ne Win. He was replaced by a military junta but continued to exert influence from behind the scenes. Shortly thereafter, the Burmese people's movement gained a focus and a leader in Aung San Suu Kyi, daughter of Aung San, the architect of Burmese independence. Herself a Buddhist scholar, and the wife of Buddhist scholar Michael Aris of Oxford University, Aung San Suu Kyi was placed under house arrest by Burmese authorities in 1989. In 1990, her National League for Democracy won eighty percent of the parliamentary seats in an election staged and then suppressed by the military authorities. In 1991, while still imprisoned, she was awarded the Nobel Peace Prize, which focused the world's attention on Burma's plight, but has done little to ease it.

Since the demise of Burma's flawed but traditional system of kingship, Buddhism has been the foundation of the Burmese people's identity and repeatedly thwarted aspirations as a nation. Burma has become a headless country sustained by its heart. That heart, the perennial focus of Burmese political aspirations, is Theravāda Buddhism. Moreover, throughout the nineteenth and twentieth centuries — under British domination and inept indigenous regimes — Burma's primary source of international self-esteem has been its Buddhist heritage and the Burmese reputation for enthusiastic dedication to Buddhism, particularly in the realm of meditation. Several modern Burmese meditation masters are discussed in Chapter XIII because of their influence in spreading Buddhism to the Western world.

Thailand

In contrast to Burma, and indeed to all the other Buddhist nations of Southeast Asia, Thailand has avoided Western rule and thereby retained its traditional monarchy. As a result, the monarchy rather than Buddhism provides Thailand's primary symbol of national identity. Since 1932, Thailand has been ostensibly a democratic monarchy, but with its welter of coups and counter-coups Thailand appears less than democratic by Western standards. Nonetheless, the Thais are justifiably proud of their freedom and their centuries-old tradition of government. Ironically, though never ruled by a Western nation, Thailand is one of the most westernized countries in Southeast Asia. In spite of the unabashed materialism and commercialism evident in Thai cities, the people's dedication to Buddhism continues undiminished. Most Thai men still find time to enter the Saṅgha for at least a few weeks or months at some-time during their lives. This practice of "temporary ordination" is unique to Thailand and gives the Thai laity an especially strong relationship with the Saṅgha.

As in Burma, the earliest historical inhabitants of Thailand were the Mons, who by the seventh century had established the kingdom of Dvaravati in the Chao Phraya river valley of Central Thailand. Very little is known about Dvaravati, which survived until it was conquered by the Khmer in the eleventh century. Archaeological evidence indicates that the early Mon Buddhism of Dvaravati may have been a purer form of the

Theravāda than that practiced by the Mons of Burma. Mon architecture in Thailand seems to have Sri Lankan influences, while Mon architecture in Burma appears to have north Indian, Mahāyānist influences. This has led some to speculate that Thailand is the geographical center from which Theravāda Buddhism spread throughout Southeast Asia. A certain amount of national pride is at stake in such historical speculations, but it was the Mons, not the Burmese or the Thais, who were ultimately responsible for the introduction and spread of Theravāda Buddhism in the region. In both Burma and Thailand, the Mons are now a small minority of the population.

The Thais themselves did not begin to become a notable presence in Southeast Asia until the second millennium. During the first millennium, Thais had migrated in small groups and established themselves among the Mons, Burmans and Khmers already living there. The first known Thai state was founded in 1096. Throughout the twelfth century more and more of these small Thai states appeared. The weakening of the Cambodian empire after the death of Jayavarman VII in about 1218 gave the Thais more scope for asserting themselves in the region, and by 1238 they had become sufficiently well organized to wrest Sukhothai from the Khmer empire. As noted earlier, the Mongol conquest of Yunnan, the original home of the Thais, may have increased their rate of southern migration. Finally, the Mongol sacking of Pagan in 1287 created a power vacuum that allowed the Thais to become the dominant power in Southeast Asia. In this same year, 1287, the three principal kingdoms of the Thais — Chiang Mai, Sukhothai and Phayao — formed an alliance over which the ruler of Sukhothai, Rāma Khamhaeng, was recognized as king. Under Rāma Khamhaeng the Thais extended their power over most of the area of present-day Thailand, wresting territory from the Khmer, the Mons and the Burmese. At this time, the majority of the population under Thai control was still Mon and Khmer. From the Khmer, the Thais derived their systems of writing and government. From the Mons and Burmans they adopted Theravāda Buddhism in the tradition of the Mahāvihāra of Sri Lanka. Earlier contacts with the Chinese while in Yunnan may explain some aspects of Thai astrology, divination and spirit cults that are not shared by the Cambodians, Laos or Burmese. The Thais were the great assimilators of Southeast Asia, which may explain their talent for diplomacy, a talent which is largely responsible for keeping Thailand free of European colonialism.

Rāma Khamhaeng not only established Theravāda Buddhism as the state religion of the Thais, he also initiated what was to remain a notable feature of Thai Buddhism: its subservience to the throne. Rāma Khamhaeng set up a branching administrative hierarchy in the Saṅgha exactly analogous to the hierarchy of civil administrators who governed the principalities, provinces and villages of the kingdom. Both of these hierarchies culminated in the office of the king, who was both head of government and supreme patron of the Saṅgha. The Theravādin kings of Burma did not exercise this degree of control over the Saṅgha. Sukhothai had once been part of the Khmer empire, however, and throughout the Sukhothai period, the ancient Khmer tradition of divine kingship was strong.

After Rāma Khamhaeng, Sukhothai began to decline in power. By 1350 Ayutthaya emerged under King Rāmādipati as the center of Thai strength, though Sukhothai retained a measure of independence for another hundred years. The full name of the new Thai capital was Dvaravati Śri Ayutthaya, referring to the ancient Mon kingdom of Dvaravati and emphasizing the Theravādin orientation of the new Thai kingdom. Nonetheless, during the Ayutthaya period — approximately 1350-1781 — the Khmer model of kingship became even more pronounced than during the Sukhothai period. According to the Khmer model, which was based on a Mahāyāna-Hindu syncretism, the king was in some sense divine. Throughout the Ayutthaya period, Thai Buddhism remained staunchly Theravādin, but the king — cast as a bodhisattva incarnate or alternately as a *cakravartin* or "wheel turning monarch" — assumed an even greater ascendancy over the Saṅgha.

Neither the bodhisattva concept nor the concept of *cakravartin* monarch are alien to Theravāda Buddhism. The concept of king as *cakravartin* in particular had been prominent in Theravāda Buddhism at least since the time of Aśoka. The Khmer admixture of the concept of king as *avatār* or "incarnation" of Śiva or Vishnu, however, imbued Buddhist kingship in Southeast Asia with an aura of divinity and preordination lacking in the Buddhist monarchies of India and Sri Lanka. This was particularly so among the Khmer and the Thais, who derived their model of kingship primarily from Khmer precedents. While remaining staunchly Theravādin in religious orientation, the Thai monarchs of both the Sukhothai and Ayutthaya periods maintained at court Hindu brahmin priests to perform the various rites and rituals associated with the throne. This practice explains the continuing prominence of Hindu elements — in the form of shrines and festivals — in the religious life of Thailand. The continuing high status of the king of Thailand — though theoretically stripped of real power in the coup of 1932 — probably derives ultimately from the longstanding tradition of Khmer-style kingship in the Sukhothai and Ayutthaya periods.

The influence of Theravādin Mon culture in the Sukhothai and Ayutthaya periods also should not be underestimated, particularly in the realm of religion. Throughout these periods, the Thai court maintained connections, direct or through Burma, with Sri Lanka, which was regarded as the ultimate source of orthodox Theravāda Buddhism. During the Sukhothai period, the only apparent division in the Saṅgha was between the "town dwellers," who ministered to the needs of the laity, and the "forest dwellers," who concentrated on the practice of meditation. These appear to have been similar to actual orders within the Saṅgha rather than mere designations according to dwelling place. The "forest dwellers" appear to have maintained particularly close contacts with Burma and Sri Lanka, and to have been rewarded with especially high status. King Lu Tai (r. 1347-74), the grandson of King Rāma Khamhaeng, was briefly ordained in this lineage during his reign. During the Ayutthaya period, in 1425, a delegation of Thai monks journeyed to Sri Lanka and returned with a direct Sri Lankan ordination lineage known as Vanaratna or "forest jewel." All of these orders traced back ultimately to the Mahāvihāra lineage of Sri Lanka and are today subsumed under the Mahānikāya lineage which constitutes the large majority of Thai Buddhist monks.

At about the same time as the founding of Ayutthaya, the Lao relatives of the Thai formed the kingdom of Luang Phrabang. During the first two hundred years of its golden age, Ayutthaya dominated Laos and most of Burma. In 1431, Thailand was able to capture the Khmer capital of Angkor and thus precipitate removal of the Khmer capital to Phnom Penh. The centers of Thai power at Sukhothai and Chiang Mai remained resistant to control by Ayutthaya until King Naresuan the Great united Thailand following the sack of Ayutthaya by resurgent Burmese in 1569. From about 1600 Thailand was united and free of Burmese dominance until the second Burmese invasion and sack of Ayutthaya in 1767. In response to this second invasion by Burma, the Thai capital was moved to its present location, Bangkok, and the still existing Chakri dynasty was established there in 1781. Burma's conflict with the British, in which Thailand cooperated with the British, finally neutralized any further threat from Burma.

Through the skillful diplomacy of the Chakri kings, Thailand managed to avoid the European colonialism that was to be the fate of the rest of Southeast Asia. The Chakri kings have also been influential in reforming Thai Buddhism by diminishing its Mahāyānist and Hindu accretions. Rāma I (r. 1782-1809), the first king of the dynasty, following the example of Aśoka, undertook a purification of the Saṅgha by enacting regulations to curb laxity among monks. He also ordered a collection and revision of the Theravāda scriptures. During the reign of Rāma III (r. 1824-51) delegations were sent to Sri Lanka in 1840 and 1843. These delegations returned with authoritative versions of the Pāli canon upon which to base continuing efforts to rectify the Thai canon, which was judged to be inaccurate and incomplete.

With regard to the reformation of Buddhism, the most notable of the Chakri kings was Rāma IV, also known as Mongkut (r. 1851-68), who ascended the throne two years before his contemporary Mindon (r. 1853-78) became king of Burma. Mongkut was in a much stronger position than Mindon, whose country was already largely under British control, but otherwise they are comparable as reformers of Buddhism who led their nations into the modern world. Mongkut spent twenty-five years as a monk while his elder brother occupied the throne until his death. During this time, Mongkut became recognized as a serious Buddhist scholar and reformer. He also became fluent in English and familiar with Western culture. Mongkut is familiar to Western readers as the central character in "The King and I," although the film and stage play are still banned in Thailand because of the undignified light in which they portray one of the most beloved monarchs of Thai history.

Upon ascending the throne, Mongkut intensified the reformist efforts of his elder brother Rāma III by further tightening the procedures and standards of monastic examinations. In addition, he oversaw the completion of the thorough revision of the Thai Buddhist canon that had been in progress since Rāma I. As a whole, Mongkut's wide-ranging reform program came to be known as the *dhammayuttika* or "adherence to dharma" movement. Ultimately, this movement involved formation of the strict Dhammayut sect, which became the second major branch of Thai Buddhism in addition to the ancient Mahānikāya.

Both in revising the canon and founding a new order of monks, King Mongkut is directly comparable to his Burmese contemporary King Mindon, who also initiated a reformist group within the old lineage of monks. Moreover, Mongkut, again like Mindon, presided over a wide-ranging Buddhist modernization movement to cleanse Thai Buddhism of non-canonical accretions and to reinterpret non-rational elements of the scriptures themselves in the light of Western rationalism. As in contemporary Sri Lanka and Burma, these Thai reforms were inspired by annoyance at Christian missionary rhetoric as much as by admiration of Western rationalism. Virtually simultaneously, Theravāda Buddhists in Sri Lanka, Burma and Thailand recognized that their "heathen" religion, in its canonical roots, was more compatible with a rational, scientific worldview than was the Christianity of the missionaries.

Mongkut was instrumental in ushering Thailand into the modern world in the political and diplomatic spheres as well as in the religious sphere. His diplomatic efforts, which resulted in treaties with both Britain and France, probably preserved Thailand from European colonialism. These treaties were highly unfavorable to Thailand in terms of territorial and trade concessions, but they established Thailand's international status as an independent nation. Mongkut also made wide-ranging reforms in the Thai economy and society with the aid of Western advisors. During his own lifetime, the effects of these reforms were confined mainly to Bangkok, but today Thailand overall is one of the wealthiest and most modernized nations in Southeast Asia, largely as a result of the forces Mongkut put into motion.

Mongkut's son Chulalongkorn, King Rāma V (1868-1910) continued with his father's program of diplomatically playing the French off against the British and maintaining independence at the price of disadvantageous treaties with Western powers. He also continued Mongkut's policy of modernization and gradual Westernization. In Thailand, as opposed to the rest of Southeast Asia, this modernization process occurred under the auspices of the traditional form of government rather than under the compulsion of a foreign regime. As a result, Buddhism in Thailand remained a cooperative force in government rather than a focus of dissent. Chulalongkorn's major contribution to Buddhism in Thailand was his foundation of higher education facilities for monks. These eventually became Buddhist universities. The monks educated therein, mostly from the Dhammayut sect, served as the moving force behind Chulalongkorn's ambitious and successful policy of using Thailand's pervasive system of monasteries to spread primary education among the masses.

Chulalongkorn died in 1910, having produced thirty-four sons and forty-three daughters. Two of his sons reigned as Kings Rāma VI and VII. Both were educated at Cambridge and appear to have been sincerely progressive monarchs. Neither, however, was able to maintain the poise between traditional and modern values that their predecessors in the Chakri dynasty had negotiated so skillfully. During their reigns, the momentum behind modernization in Thailand shifted to the educated middle class, which was largely a product of Chulalongkorn's reforms. In 1932 this modernization movement resulted in a bloodless coup which Rāma VII accepted without complaint. The result was in theory a constitutional monarchy in which the king would play a purely ceremonial role as the figurehead of government. Thailand's constitutional governments have proved to be unstable, however, so that the king still wields considerable real power. The office of the king of Thailand retains the intense loyalty of the people and remains the primary symbol of national unity and pride. In addition, the king remains the titular head of the Thai Saṅgha.

This situation differs markedly from that in Burma and Cambodia, the ultimate sources of traditional Thai government. In these countries, European domination and its tragic aftermath have destroyed traditional systems of government without leaving behind viable replacements. Paradoxically, Thailand has managed to avoid being ruled by a Western power, but it has become one of the the most Westernized states in Southeast Asia. The talent of the Thais for skillful diplomatic compromise with foreign powers and assimilation of foreign ideas has maintained their independence, but at a price. That price is a contradictory society, on the one hand intensely loyal to Buddhism and its ancient royal tradition, but on the other hand deeply corrupted by Western influence.

During World War II, as an ally of Japan, Thailand was in fact an exploited colony. After the war, the United States granted generous economic aid to Thailand and backed Thailand in the re-negotiation of unfavorable treaties signed earlier with Britain and France. Eager to gain a trading partner in Southeast Asia, traditionally a European market, America invested heavily in Thailand, pursuing its own brand of colonialism. Later, during the Vietnam war, The United States used Thailand as a staging area and a "rest and relaxation" center for its troops. This pumped yet more American dollars into the Thai economy.

This American investment helped to make Thailand one of the most prosperous nations in the Eastern hemisphere, but it had a negative side. American furloughs to Thailand during the Vietnam war resulted in rampant prostitution. Today, many tourists visit Thailand for its sex trade alone. At the same time, an observant visitor will notice that every bar and brothel has a small Buddhist shrine at which the prostitutes pray without fail before going on duty. Thailand is infamous for its role in the manufacture and trade of illicit drugs, and organized crime is pervasive. The serious level of corruption in Thailand is recognized and deplored by many Thais, but it is a source of livelihood for many others.

It is remarkable that the decline of the moral fiber of Thai society under Western influence has not resulted in a similar decline of Buddhism. Thailand remains, along with Japan and Sri Lanka, one of the primary Buddhist voices in the modern world. Although some Westerners go to Thailand on "sex tours" or in order to purchase drugs or counterfeit merchandise, others go to see Thailand's magnificent temples or to gain instruction in Buddhist philosophy and meditation under modern masters. One has to marvel at the power of a religious tradition that can accommodate all of these contradictions and thrive. In the face of similar though usually less severe contradictions, the religious traditions of the Western world are suffering large-scale rejection by disillusioned societies.

Vietnam

Vietnam snakes down the entire length of the eastern coast of the
Southeast Asian peninsula. According to Western convention developed
during the French protectorate, it is divided into three zones: Tonkin or
Tonking in the north, Annam in the middle, and Cochin China in the
south. For the first thousand years of its history (111 BCE-939 CE), Tonkin
was a province of the Chinese empire. Annam and northern Cochin
China were part of Champa, and the far south was part of ancient Funan,
which was eventually superseded in the region by the Khmer kingdom of
Angkor. In 939, in the wake of the disintegration of the Tang dynasty, the
Vietnamese of Tonkin became independent and began to expand southward at the expense of Champa. In 1471, Champa finally succumbed to
the Vietnamese. Also in the fifteenth century, the Vietnamese wrested the
Mekong delta region from the Khmers, thus establishing the full territorial
extent of Vietnam. Due to Vietnam's aggressive settlement policy in conquered territories, the Cham people had virtually disappeared by the end
of the seventeenth century. By the mid-eighteenth century, the ruthless
policy of expelling conquered peoples and replacing them with Vietnamese settlers had thoroughly integrated this new territory into a relatively
homogeneous racial and cultural entity.

Throughout this period of expansion, Vietnam maintained close cultural ties with China, and absorbed virtually nothing from its Indianized
neighbors and adversaries on the Southeast Asian peninsula. For this
reason, the development of Buddhism in Vietnam is an offshoot of the
development of Buddhism in China. (Readers unfamiliar with Chinese
Buddhism may need to refer to "The Schools of Chinese Buddhism"
section of Chapter VIII.) All of the schools of classical Chinese Buddhism
reached Vietnam at one time or another, but differentiation among
them was minimal. The Chinese syncretism of Buddhism, Daoism and
Confucianism has always been more prominent in Vietnam than in China.
One form of Chinese Buddhism, however, has distinguished itself consistently in Vietnam. That form of Buddhism is the Chan or "meditation"
school, better known by its Japanese name: Zen.

Buddhism may have been introduced to Vietnam by sea as early as the
first century. By the second century, Chinese sources record a flourishing
Buddhist community in Tonkin or northern Vietnam. The history of Vietnamese Buddhism as such, however, begins in 580, with the arrival of
Vinītaruci, an Indian monk who had studied with the third patriarch of
Chinese Chan Buddhism, before its split into northern and southern
schools. This first lineage of Vietnamese Zen masters ended with the
death of its twenty-eighth patriarch in 1216, though the Vinītaruci sect

continues to be prominent, primarily in the north. The second Zen lineage in Vietnam was initiated by the Chinese monk Wu Yan Tong (Wu Yen T'ung, d. 826), who studied in China with Hui Neng, the sixth patriarch and founder of the southern school of Chan. This lineage of meditation masters also died out in the thirteenth century, though again the sect itself survives.

Although these first two lineages of Chan Buddhism did not survive as lineages of meditation masters, they did lay the foundations for a thorough integration of Buddhism and Vietnamese nationalism which began in the Dinh dynasty (969-81). King Dinh Bo Linh established a state-sponsored Vietnamese Saṅgha and initiated the practice of appointing eminent monks to advisory positions at court, offices formerly filled exclusively by Confucian scholars. In the Le dynasty (981-1009), the first complete Chinese Tripiṭaka was imported, establishing the scriptural basis of Vietnamese Buddhism. The Ly dynasty (1010-1225) spanned the golden age of Vietnamese independence and prosperity. Before this period, Vietnam, still confined to Tonkin in the north, was dominated by China. After this period, Vietnam, though expanding in territory, was harassed by the Mongols, coveted by the Yuan, Ming, and Qing dynasties of China, and finally dominated by France.

In 1069 the Ly dynasty's campaign of southward expansion against Champa reached its farthest extent, the seventeenth parallel, which forms the border between modern-day North and South Vietnam. In the course of this campaign, a very significant prisoner of war was brought to Tonkin from captured Cham territory. This prisoner was the Chinese monk Cao Dang (Ts'ao Tang), a proponent of the Chan–Pure Land synthesis, which was prominent at the time in Song dynasty China. With the avid support of King Ly Thanh Ton (r. 1054-72), the Chan–Pure Land synthesis gained a dominant position among the Vietnamese that it maintains to the present day. From this period onward, Buddhists became more prominent in high official posts, eventually displacing Confucianists in the majority of positions.

After an initial Mongol incursion in 1257, Kublai Khan, the Mongol emperor of China, began in 1284 a series of invasions of Vietnam, then ruled by the Tran dynasty (1225-1400). Faced with the mightiest military machine of the time, the Vietnamese responded as they did to France and the United States in the twentieth century. They resorted to guerrilla warfare, a tactic which undercut the military advantage of their adversaries and made territorial gains too costly to consolidate. Kublai Khan soon withdrew his beleaguered forces and agreed to accept tribute from the Tran dynasty in exchange for the unimpeded independence of Vietnam, which at this point comprised roughly the territory of modern-day North

Vietnam. By way of encouraging Vietnamese unity against the Mongol invaders, King Tran Nhan Ton (1258-1308) himself founded the Truc Lam school of Buddhism, which intentionally fused Chan–Pure Land Buddhism with Confucianism and Daoism. From this point, Buddhism became an essential element in Vietnamese nationalism, which was then focused against Champa and Angkor, the two powers that barred Vietnam's march to the south.

Following a brief resurgence of Champa — which resulted in the sacking of Hanoi in 1371 and contributed to the collapse of the Tran dynasty in 1400 — Vietnam was briefly but indeterminately ruled by Ming China from about 1407 to 1427. In 1428, the Latter Le dynasty established itself as sovereign in Vietnam until the end of the eighteenth century. The Latter Le rulers accomplished the final conquest of Champa in 1471, but from the mid-sixteenth century they ruled Vietnam in name only. In reality, northern Vietnam was ruled by the powerful Trinh family, while their rivals the Nguyen family ruled in the south and continued the southward expansion of the Vietnamese against the Khmer. Also in the sixteenth century, Catholic missionaries began to arrive in Vietnam in the wake of European adventurers and traders, first Portuguese and Spanish, then French.

As part of their own attempts to consolidate power, the Nguyen rulers were eager to foster new forms of Buddhism in the south. As a result, Chinese refugee monks from the Manchurian Qing (Ch'ing) dynasty (1644-1912) were particularly welcomed in the south. The most famous of these took the Vietnamese name Nguyen Thieu (d. 1712) and founded a lineage of Lin Ji (Lin Chi) Chan (Jap. Rinzai Zen). This Lin Ji tradition, known in Vietnamese as Lam Te, was consolidated and popularized under the third patriarch of the lineage, Lieu Quan (d. 1743).

Shortly after the consolidation of this last lineage of Vietnamese Buddhism, the thirty-year Tay Son rebellion (1772-1802) was initiated by a faction of the Nguyen, the ruling family of southern Vietnam. This so-called rebellion was actually a military campaign to reunify Vietnam and was inspired largely by Buddhist nationalism. Though Ming China attempted to quash the Tay Son rebellion, the movement was finally put down by French forces with the help of Vietnamese Catholics. Vietnam remained nominally independent from 1802 until 1883, when France imposed over the entire country a protectorate that endured until partition in 1954.

Until the French protectorate, Vietnamese history and culture had developed always under the influence of China. Nonetheless, from the tenth to the nineteenth centuries Vietnam was able to maintain political independence from its mentor civilization. As a result of its tenacious maintenance of independence, Vietnam has played a major role in the development of Southeast Asia. Until now, this role has been political more than religious, but Vietnam is now in a position to exert a major influence in the development of Buddhism in Southeast Asia. Buddhism has played a supportive role in Southeast Asia's communist movements, and as a result Southeast Asian communism has not been particularly anti-religious. In Vietnam as elsewhere in the peninsula, Buddhism was a part of the identity which communist independence movements were trying to reassert, and was often an ally in the struggle. Despite the existence of communist independence movements in Cambodia and Laos, Vietnam's communists were almost single-handedly responsible for ousting first the French in 1954 and then the United States in 1975. This gave Vietnam great prestige as the only country in Southeast Asia to forcibly eject Western powers. Since the American withdrawal from Southeast Asia, the communist regime of Vietnam has taken on primary responsibility for maintaining order in the eastern sector of the Southeast Asian peninsula.

As a part of Vietnam's struggle for independence, a movement began in 1932 at the Tu Dam Temple in Hué to consolidate Vietnamese Buddhism. This movement resulted first in the foundation of the Central Vietnamese Buddhist Association in 1932, and then, in 1952, the General Association of Buddhism in Vietnam. Under the communist regime, this movement culminated in the formation of the government-controlled Buddhist Saṅgha of Vietnam. This final development entailed government regulation of the Saṅgha, but does not seem to have resulted in excessive government manipulation of the Saṅgha. Significantly, this united Saṅgha in Vietnam includes a small number of Theravāda monks of Khmer extraction. Vietnam is thus the only country in the world with a Saṅgha in which both Theravāda and Mahāyāna Buddhism are represented. This made it possible in 1979 for Vietnam to provide a delegation of Theravāda monks to revive Cambodia's Saṅgha, which the Khmer Rouge communists had eradicated. Ever since, Cambodian Buddhism, though remaining staunchly Theravādin, has looked to Vietnam for revitalization. This situation renders possible a historic rapprochement between Theravāda and Mahāyāna Buddhism.

Most intriguing specifically is the possibility of a renewal of the Saṅgha of nuns in the Theravāda tradition. As noted in Chapter VI, the nuns' Saṅgha in Theravāda Buddhism died out during the tumultuous period in Sri Lanka before the Mahāvihāra ordination lineage was transmitted to Burma, and from Burma throughout Southeast Asia. As a result, there are no Theravādin nuns anywhere in the world who could conduct an ordination to revive the lineage. By contrast, the nun ordination lineage in Mahāyāna Buddhism remains intact. Since Mahāyāna and Theravāda Buddhists recognize virtually the same Vinaya, there is no technical reason why it would not be possible to revive the Theravāda nuns' Saṅgha in Cambodia from Mahāyāna sources in Vietnam. Such a revival is all the more feasible given the small Theravāda faction in the Buddhist Saṅgha of Vietnam. Discussions along these lines are under way among the hierarchy of the Buddhist Saṅgha of Vietnam, and while it is too early to predict the outcome, it would be difficult to overstate the good will that such a move would create between Cambodia and Vietnam. Like all of the world's major religions, all forms of Buddhism have been reluctant to recognize the spiritual equality of women, and therefore it is also difficult to overstate the positive impression that such a move would create throughout the modern world.

CHAPTER VIII

The Development of
Buddhism in China

Having considered the development of Buddhism in those countries primarily influenced by Theravāda Buddhism, this chapter begins an examination of the development of Buddhism in those lands influenced primarily by the Mahāyāna. Although China can no longer be characterized as a Buddhist country, China was crucially important in the spread of Buddhism, not only as a significant home of Mahāyāna Buddhism for many centuries, but also as the primary source from which this branch of Buddhism spread to Korea, Japan and Vietnam. As a result, China's influence upon Buddhism had a profound effect upon the religion as it developed in countries that do remain significantly Buddhist.

Normally, China's ancient historical records are remarkably thorough. During the early centuries of Buddhism's spread to China, however, the compilers of these historical records were conservative Chinese scholars who tended to be hostile toward the new religion. Primarily for this reason, the early history of Buddhism in China is somewhat obscure. According to Chinese tradition, Buddhism spread directly from India to China in the first century CE. In fact, Buddhism probably entered China initially from Central Asia in the first century BCE. As Chapter V notes in its section on Central Asia, Buddhism was known in Central Asia by the third century BCE, and was probably well known there by the second century BCE.

Because of the formidable barrier posed by the Himalayan Mountains, India and China existed for many centuries as near neighbors almost entirely unfamiliar with one another. The first significant contact between these two civilizations appears to have come about as a result of the spread of Buddhism to China. However, when contact was established between India and China, it was via a circuitous route through Central Asia, where Buddhism was already well known. From India, this route went westward across present-day Pakistan and through the rugged Khyber Pass into the Central Asian region now known as Afghanistan. The route then doubled back to the northeast across the Pamir Mountains to Kashgar on the Silk Road. Today Kashgar lies on the far western edge of the People's Republic of China. In ancient times, it lay in the center of the territory now known as Central Asia. The mountainous route described thus far was difficult and dangerous, as it is in fact today, but at Kashgar the truly difficult portion of the journey to China began.

The area to the east of Kashgar, in the modern Chinese Autonomous Region of Xinjiang (Hsin-chiang), is dominated geographically by the impassable Takla Makan desert in its center. In ancient times as today, the traveler had to skirt the Takla Makan desert to the north or to the south in order to continue an overland journey from China to the west or in order to enter China from the west. At the eastern end of the Takla Makan, the northern and southern branches of the Silk Road meet at Dunhuang (Tun-huang — see Pronunciation Guide), the eastern extremity of Central Asia and the gateway to imperial China. The first traveler to leave a record of this desert crossing, the fifth-century Chinese monk Fa Xian (Fa Hsien), described its perils as follows:

> [In the desert] there are many evil demons and hot winds. Travelers who encounter them perish all to a man. There is not a bird to be seen in the air above, nor an animal on the ground below. Though you look around most earnestly to find where you can cross, you know not where to make your choice, the only mark and indication being the dry bones of the dead.

The trade routes skirting the Takla Makan lay west of the Great Wall of China, beyond the traditional Chinese heartland. While imperial China was determined to maintain ultimate control of the Silk Road in order to keep it open for trade, it was content to allow the route to be serviced and administered by several mercantile city-states which had developed around the oases that established the course of the trade route. Though small in extent, these city-states became extremely wealthy and highly sophisticated as a result of the great financial and cultural wealth that flowed along the Silk Road. The spread of Buddhism along the Indian tributary of the Silk Road to these strategically placed Central Asian city-states was the first step in the spread of Buddhism to China.

Confucianism and Daoism: The Indigenous Religions of China

When Buddhism finally reached China, it encountered a civilization as ancient and advanced as that of India, and a civilization fully confident of its superiority over all others in the world. Confucianism and Daoism (Taoism), the two indigenous religions of China, were as old as Buddhism and were firmly established as the complementary ideologies of China. Both religions resisted Buddhism in China, Confucianism more than Daoism, but in the end both absorbed much of Buddhism, as Hinduism did in India.

Buddhism encountered Confucian opposition from the beginning of its spread to China. Confucianism played the role of the state religion of China, though in many ways Confucianism is more a political ideology than a religion. Its founder, Kong Fu Zi (K'ung Fu Tsu — 551-479 BCE), "Master Kong" or "Confucius" as mispronounced in the West, was a contemporary of the historical Buddha. Confucius was born in the declining years of the ancient and venerable Zhou (Chou) dynasty (1025-453 BCE), as China descended into a period of disunity and strife known as the "Warring States period" (453-221 BCE). Attempting to forestall the demise of law and order in China, Confucius formulated an integrated religious, political and moral philosophy that encouraged centralized, dynastic monarchy. At the time, Confucius' efforts failed to stabilize the empire, but following the reunification of China under the Qin (Ch'in) dynasty (221-206 BCE), his system was to serve as the ideological basis of a succession of dynasties that ruled in China until the twentieth century.

Confucius derived the elements of his system from traditional Chinese wisdom and social conventions. For Confucius, the source of political harmony on earth is *tian (t'ien),* the sky or heaven, an impersonal force that stands over the affairs of humankind as the celestial vault stands over the earth. A ruler who governs justly and wisely in accordance with the principles of *tian* gains thereby the "mandate of heaven," which will insure stability in the realm. Ideally, the ruler who gains the mandate of heaven should rule over the entire earth. Practically, such a mandated ruler should be the emperor of all China, known in Chinese as Zhong Guo (Chung Kuo) or the "Central Kingdom," which Confucius regarded as being the center of the world, surrounded by various insignificant, barbarian lands and peoples. The emperor's function was to serve as a conduit to earth of heavenly harmony. His duty was to insure the prosperity of his subjects, and to pass the mandate of heaven on to one of his offspring, thus establishing a just and enduring dynasty.

In turn, the subjects of such a mandated emperor were obliged to revere the emperor, obey his agents and live orderly, humble lives according to the virtuous traditions of Chinese society. For Confucius, the most important of these traditions were veneration of ancestors living or dead, deference to elders and those of superior rank or status. On the other hand, unhappiness, hardship and discord among the subjects of the empire were an indication that the ruling dynasty had lost the mandate of heaven. In such circumstances, the people were justified in rising up to overthrow the emperor and make way for a freshly mandated emperor to establish a new dynasty. Confucianism was thus a potent force for maintaining stability in the empire, but it could also be an impetus for rebellion against a mismanaged empire.

Like Confucianism, Daoism as a system of philosophy is a product of the Warring States period of Chinese history. Again like Confucianism, Daoism draws upon pre-existing, traditional Chinese concepts, ideals, and practices and synthesizes them into a systematic expression of the traditional Chinese mentality. In many ways, Confucianism embodies the practical, political side of the Chinese mentality, concerned with enjoying peace and prosperity here and now, while Daoism embodies the more individualistic, mystical side of the traditional Chinese mind-set. Whereas Confucianism is concerned with corporate welfare and harmony within the state, Daoism ignores politics and concentrates upon bringing the individual into harmony with nature.

"Nature" in the broadest sense of the term — including human nature, natural law and moral law — is a reasonable translation of the Chinese word *dao (tao)*, from which Daoism takes its name. Literally *dao* means "way," both in the sense of "a path or road" and in the sense of a process, as in "the *way* things work." According to Daoism, it is the responsibility of each individual to bring one's life into harmony with the *way* of nature, the all-pervasive *dao*. To accomplish such harmony requires a pure, simple life of introspection and meditation upon the workings of the world. Such meditation will reveal that all reality is a function of the interplay of two diametrically opposed forces, *yin* and *yang*. *Yin*, the female principle, is soft, gentle and yielding, whereas the male principle *yang* is rigid, strong and dynamic. All people and all phenomena are in essence combinations in varying proportions of these two principles.

Though all things contain both principles, the feminine *yin* is to be cultivated by a follower of the Way, for to yield to the Way of nature is the only source of true harmony and well-being. Water yields to a stone in the stream, but it is the stone that is worn away. Bamboo yields to the storm by bending, whereas the rigid tree stands firm and is broken off. A true follower of the Way goes through life effortlessly like a fish through water or a bird through the air. This is the Daoist ideal of *wu wei* or "non-action," not in the sense of inactivity, but in the sense of effortless action in harmony with the Way.

The sage who mastered the art of effortless harmony with the Way was supposed to be rewarded with everlasting life among the Immortals. The early Daoist concept of immortality envisaged imprecisely a quasi-mundane state of deathlessness, attained through meditation, techniques of breath control, and a simple, healthy diet. By the time of the intro-duction of Buddhism to China, the Daoist ideal of immortality had degenerated into the practice of a sort of dietary alchemy designed to stave off physical death. This practice is very likely responsible for the remarkable variety of Chinese cuisine, which in its traditional form offers such delicacies as monkey brains, turtle eggs, and shark fin soup.

Traditionally, Daoism was founded by one Lao Zi (Lao Tzu), who is supposed to have been a contemporary of Confucius. Actually, the historical existence of a single founder of Daoism is doubtful. Lao Zi is an honorific term of veneration for any wise old man and is also an alternative title for the foundational text of Daoism, the *Dao De Jing (Tao Te Ching)*. This short volume is a collection of traditional Chinese wisdom literature which was probably only compiled by Lao Zi. It is supposed to have been written at the request of the Keeper of the Pass, i.e. the border guard, when Lao Zi departed China, headed west on a water buffalo, never to be seen again. The legend of Lao Zi's mysterious departure from China eventually gave rise to the Chinese tradition that Lao Zi journeyed to India and there became known as the Buddha. This legend seeks to account for the obvious similarities between Daoism and Buddhism and to excuse the acceptance in China of a foreign religion, for in ancient China, all things foreign were considered barbarian.

Regardless of the accuracy of these stories, it is clear that around 500 BCE, roughly the time of the historical Buddha, Confucius and Lao Zi (or perhaps several people called Lao Zi) mirrored the activity of the Buddha in India by systematizing traditional Chinese ideals and aspirations into classical expressions of Chinese thought. Though fallen from official favor in communist China, Daoism and Confucianism remain embedded in the fabric of Chinese behavior, values and society. They remain to the present day the classical expressions of the essence of what it means to be Chinese.

The Introduction of Buddhism in the Han Dynasty (206 BCE- 220 CE)

Until the advent of communist China, the Han dynasty remained the unequaled ideal of Chinese territory, prosperity and power. Geographically, it included virtually the entire center and underbelly of present-day China, as well as Gansu (Kansu) province and parts of Xinjiang (Hsinchiang) in the far west. Han China did not include Tibet, Qinghai (Ch'inghai), Inner Mongolia, or the northeastern provinces of Heilongjiang (Heilung-chiang) and Jilin (Chi-lin), which together constitute approximately one fifth of the area of the modern People's Republic of China. The Han capital alternated between the central Chinese cities of Luoyang and

Xi'an (Hsi-an) — pronounced "She-an" and known in ancient times as Chang An (Ch'ang An) — which were thus regarded as the eastern termini of the Silk Road.

According to legend, Buddhism was introduced to China as the result of a portentous dream of the Han Emperor Ming, who ruled in Luoyang from 58 to 75 CE. One night in the year 64 CE, Emperor Ming is said to have dreamed of a flying golden deity. Ming was so impressed by the dream that when one of his ministers ventured that the deity was the Buddha, he immediately dispatched a delegation to India to discover the nature of this wondrous sage and his teachings. According to Chinese tradition, the delegation returned from India with a Buddhist text entitled *Sūtra in Forty-two Sections,* which was thus the first Buddhist sūtra in China. Emperor Ming may indeed have dispatched a delegation abroad to gain information about Buddhism, but it is doubtful that it went all the way to India, and the emperor was certainly not entirely ignorant of Buddhism before this time. As early as 65 CE, Emperor Ming mentioned Buddhism favorably, albeit offhandedly, in correspondence with a prince of his realm. Apparently impressed by the emperor's favor toward Buddhism, the prince in his reply promised to provide a vegetarian feast for the Buddhist monks and laymen in his domain.

The presence and imperial recognition of both monks and laymen in 65 CE indicates that Buddhism was already relatively well established in China by the middle of the first century. A later, third century source, the *Wei Lüe (Wei Lüeh),* a history of the Wei dynasty, mentions the oral transmission of Buddhist scriptures into China as early as the year 2 BCE.[27] Other quasi-historical sources push the earliest introduction of Buddhism back to the second and even the third century BCE, as is quite possible given Aśoka's enthusiasm for Buddhist missions and the volume of traffic on the Silk Road. It is in fact likely that the first Buddhists to reach China were merchants rather than missionaries.

On the whole, it is probable that Buddhism had been introduced to China by the middle of the first century BCE and that it was well known, if not widely practiced, by the middle of the first century CE. By this time the Kushans, former allies of China against the Huns, were well on the way to establishing a Buddhist dynasty in northern India and Central Asia. There are few early Chinese records concerning Buddhism, but it is notable that the majority of the early Buddhist monks known to have worked in China were Central Asian in origin. Most notable among these was An Shi Gao (An Shih-kao), the first great translator of Buddhist scriptures into Chinese. An Shi Gao arrived in China around 150 CE and formed a translation team that produced a large, though uncertain number of rough translations of Mahāyāna and Nikāya Buddhist texts concerned primarily with meditation. The practice of translating in teams, initiated by An Shi Gao, set the pattern for virtually all subsequent Buddhist translation work in China. About twenty years after An Shi Gao's arrival, a Kushan named Lokakshema formed a similar translation team, which concentrated specifically upon Mahāyāna texts. Lokakshema is thus traditionally regarded as the founder of Mahāyāna Buddhism in China.

In addition to these translations by Central Asian monks, one Buddhist treatise, written in Chinese by a Chinese author, survives from the Han dynasty. This text is known as the *Mou Zi (Mou Tzu)*, named after its author Mou Zi. The *Mou Zi* appears to be a defence of Buddhism against Confucian critics. Among other things, it addresses Confucian concerns regarding filial piety to one's ancestors as opposed to the Buddhist monastic ideal of renunciation of home and family, and Confucian accusations regarding the non-Chinese origins of Buddhism. Most surprising is its defence of the Buddhist doctrine of rebirth, for Mou Zi asserts that according to Buddhism, when one dies one's immortal soul lives on to be reborn again and again, a position that is the Buddhist equivalent of heresy. Mou Zi's preoccupation with Confucian criticisms of Buddhism, and his misunderstanding of basic Buddhist doctrine, indicate how tenuous was Buddhism's foothold in Han dynasty China. Nevertheless, from this foothold, Buddhism was to develop into the dominant religion of the empire.

The Ascendancy of Buddhism During the Partition of China
Fall of the Han (220) to the Rise of the Sui Dynasty (589)

The Han dynasty collapsed in 220 as a result of both internal decay and continual warfare with nomadic hordes on its frontiers. Three rival kingdoms arose out of the debris of the Han dynasty and descended into a sixty-year series of wars known as the Three Kingdoms period of Chinese history. The Jin (Chin) dynasty finally emerged victorious in 280, but traditional China had been weakened to its core by sixty years of warfare. Soon the unthinkable disaster occurred: non-Chinese, tribal peoples known to the Chinese as the Xiong Nu (Hsiung Nu) seized both of the traditional capitals of imperial China, first Luoyang in 311 and then Xi'an in 316. In disarray, the Chinese gentry and intelligentsia fled to southern China, taking with them what they could of their wealth. Thus began almost three centuries of a divided China ruled by "barbarians" in the north and by a series of weak, ethnic Chinese dynasties in the south. As it turned out, China's loss was Buddhism's gain, for the radically altered political and intellectual atmospheres in both north and south China proved to be advantageous for the new religion.

From the viewpoint of the Chinese aristocracy, it would be difficult to overstate the crushing demoralization of surrendering the heartland of China to non-Chinese overlords. The aristocratic northern Chinese regarded even southern China, their new home, as a provincial, quasi-barbarian backwater. From their point of view, the very heart of the Middle Kingdom, the veritable center of the world, had been wrested from its rightful rulers by savage, uncivilized hordes. A large aristocratic population, educated to govern and administer the elaborate bureaucracy of an empire, found themselves superfluous and idle in the much reduced and largely symbolic court of the southern dynasties. Over-educated and under-employed, they reacted primarily in one of two ways determined largely by their financial means.

Those who were so inclined and could afford it entered a life of idle socializing in which sumptuous food, wine, poetry and stimulating philosophical conversation were the primary requisites. Those who could not afford high society or became disenchanted with its futility fell back on the Daoist ideal of the simple life of contemplation and harmony with nature. In both contexts Buddhism fared exceptionally well. In the politically enervated south, Confucian opposition to Buddhism became a theoretical philosophical issue rather than a practical issue of political influence. Buddhists were much better prepared to challenge Confucianism over a bottle of wine than in the corridors of power in imperial China, where Confucianism had held undisputed sway. The sophisticated philosophy of Buddhism soon gained a large following in the polite society of the southern court. On the other hand, the advanced meditational techniques of Buddhism gained increased popularity among Daoist contemplatives leading simple, humble lives out of necessity if not out of choice.

In either circle, Daoist philosophy, resigned to the inevitable succession of *yin* and *yang* in the Way of nature, was better suited to the needs of a people in humiliating exile than was the dynamic, optimistic political philosophy of Confucianism. Increasingly, the aristocrats and contemplatives in southern China turned to the Daoist ideal of *wu wei*, non-action, and from it extrapolated the theory that all reality is grounded in the single metaphysical principle of *wu*, or non-being. The Buddhist doctrine of *śūnyatā* (emptiness) is of course remarkably similar to this "neo-Daoist" position and is at least partly responsible for its development.

Before the southern exile, few ethnic Chinese had become Buddhist monks or even lay converts. After the exile the number of Chinese Buddhists grew rapidly. As the size and influence of the Saṅgha increased, the question of the relationship between the Saṅgha and the emperor grew more contentious. As subjects, were the Buddhist monks subordinate to the emperor, or should the Saṅgha be an independent law unto itself as it was in India? Confucianism was adamant in its insistence that Buddhist monks must abide by the conventions of Chinese society. As the Saṅgha gained power, Confucianists became increasingly hostile in their attacks upon Buddhist doctrine, which they regarded as un-Chinese in its origins, unproductive in its practices, and irrational in its doctrine of rebirth. Though vehement, these Confucian attacks carried little practical weight among the politically enervated aristocracy of southern China. Buddhism continued to gain in popularity and power in the south, and the Saṅgha did eventually become virtually a state within the state.

The situation in northern China was altogether different during this period, but nonetheless favorable to Buddhism. Whereas one of Buddhism's greatest initial disadvantages in China had been its "barbarian," non-Chinese origin, northern China was now ruled by a succession of "barbarian" dynasties representing various non-Chinese peoples from homelands beyond China. These foreign dynasties understandably embraced the foreign religion Buddhism as the most appropriate religion to legitimize their rule in China. For this reason, Buddhism was both promoted and controlled by the imperial court in the north. In order to get around the dilemma of whether or not monks should pay homage to the emperor, a remarkable doctrine developed. The reigning emperor came to be regarded as a living incarnation of the Buddha himself.

An office of chief of monks was set up in the imperial bureaucracy, thereby establishing a firm liaison between the government and Buddhism and preventing the development of a Buddhist state within the state. Buddhist monasteries were supported lavishly by the government, and in return they became administrative centers for the collection of taxes and depots for the storage of grain to be distributed to the peasantry during famine. Monasteries even served as low-security work farms for convict labor. Although the taxes and grain collected by monasteries in theory remained the property of the emperor, in practice Buddhist temples became the equivalent of feudal estates, administering large tracts of land and large pools of labor.

These arrangements made the common people directly dependent upon the local Buddhist monastery as their landlord and as their source of relief during periods of hardship and famine. For the first time in China, Buddhism became a religion of the masses. For this reason, and because Buddhism in the north provided the ideological cement of the empire, the Buddhism that flourished was popular, devotional Buddhism as opposed to the intellectual Buddhism that gained acceptance in the south. In order to hold the attention and allegiance of the masses, the northern rulers embarked on lavish Buddhist construction projects. The stunning visual impact of the Buddhism of this period may still be glimpsed in the enormous complexes of man-made grotto sculpture at Datong (Ta-t'ung) and Luoyang. These great panoramas carved in living stone depict the legend of the Buddha and the mythology of Buddhism in gigantic proportions designed to impress the simple, illiterate devotee. Unfortunately, the Datong and Luoyang sites were severely plundered by Western treasure seekers in the nineteenth century, and many of the finest carvings may now be seen only in the museums of Europe and the United States.

Many eminent Buddhist monks operated in both Chinas during the period of partition. In the south, there were the meditation masters Hui Yuan (Hui Yüan), his disciple Dao Sheng (Tao Sheng), and the Indian Buddhabhadra, all of whom were influential in the dialogue with neo-Daoism. The great Indian translator Paramārtha (c. 498-569), who was primarily responsible for the introduction of Vijñānavāda (Consciousness school) ideas into China, also worked in the south. None of these scholar-monks, however, could compete with the efforts of the Central Asian Kumārajīva (344-413) and his team of translators in the northern capital of Xi'an.

Kumārajīva was a child prodigy who, through the efforts of a doting mother, became renowned from a very young age as a scholar of Buddhism. The emperor of northern China heard of Kumārajīva and summoned him to Xi'an, the capital. Unfortunately, en route to Xi'an, Kumārajīva was seized by a renegade warlord in northwestern China and detained for seventeen years. During this tragic period of detention, which rendered inactive one of the greatest scholars and translators in history, Kumārajīva at least learned excellent Chinese. Finally, the ruler in Xi'an sent an army to liberate him, and he arrived in the capital in 401. Building upon the foundations laid there by another great translator Dao An (Tao An), Kumārajīva organized a translation team on a grand scale, with hundreds of editors, subeditors, proofreaders and scribes. Under the guidance of Kumārajīva, the language of Chinese Buddhism attained its maturity, finally liberated from the Daoist terminology that had distorted earlier translations.

Another prominent figure of northern Chinese Buddhism was Fa Xian (Fa Hsien), the first notable Chinese pilgrim to make the journey to India and return to China. He left in 399, only two years before Kumārajīva's arrival, and returned in 414, a year after Kumārajīva died, to devote the rest of his life to translating the sūtras he had collected. One wonders if Fa Xian would have braved the hardships of the journey to India and back in order to collect texts if he had known that Kumārajīva would work in Xi'an during his absence. At any rate, Fa Xian's great contribution was his courage and endurance in completing an epic journey that was the first in a series of similar pilgrimages by Chinese Buddhists who would contribute so much to the maturing of Chinese Buddhism.

Despite the leadership of people such as Kumārajīva and Fa Xian, the wealth and power of Buddhism in the north eventually attracted ambitious and unscrupulous elements into the Saṅgha, and from time to time abuses of the system became widespread. Because of the tax exempt status of the property and lands administered by temples, they became havens for tax-avoidance schemes. Some monks illegally lent money and grain at high interest rates to wealthy customers, causing shortfalls in periods of famine. During times of war, temples became refuges for those seeking to avoid military conscription. Criminals sometimes sought to avoid capture and punishment by joining a temple's work force, and there is even evidence that some Buddhist temples may have been centers of political intrigue intended to overthrow the government.

One such incident led to the first of two suppressions of Buddhism under the northern dynasties. Alerted of a potential rebellion in Xi'an, the emperor Tai Wu Di (T'ai Wu Ti) of the Northern Wei dynasty set out in 446 to crush it and discovered there a large arms cache in a monastery storeroom. His anger inflamed by Daoist and Confucian advisers, the emperor concluded that this deception implicated Buddhism as a whole in a plot to overthrow the throne and decreed that all Buddhist monks were to be executed and all Buddhist temples, images and sūtras destroyed. Due to widespread resistance, this sweeping persecution was not fully accomplished, though many monks were put to death and many temples, images and scriptures destroyed. After a few years, restrictions were gradually eased and Buddhism could once again be practiced and taught in the privacy of one's home, but the religion remained in official disfavor. Emperor Wu died in 454, and his successor, Wen Cheng Di (Wen Ch'eng Ti), quickly moved to appease the masses by reinstating Buddhism into full imperial favor.

The second suppression of Buddhism by the northern dynasties, the suppression of 574, was also of short duration, was also perpetrated by an emperor named Wu (of the Northern Zhou or Chou dynasty), and was also reversed by his successor. By this time, foreign dynasties had controlled northern China for over two centuries, and the "barbarian" conquerors had become largely Chinese through intermarriage and acculturation. The ambition of a unified China reinstating the glory and territory of the Han empire had been revived, and with it the ancient ideal of a Confucian Chinese state. In this atmosphere, the conflicts among

Buddhism, Confucianism and Daoism became increasingly heated and urgent as each religion vied for influence at court. The three-way debate came to a head over the question of which religion was older, and finally degenerated into a quarrel between Daoists and Buddhists over the question of whether or not Lao Zi had actually gone to India to become the Buddha. Both sides produced extravagant forgeries in order to establish their cases, and finally Emperor Wu decreed that Confucianism was to be the religion of the state and that both Buddhism and Daoism were to be suppressed. Again, temples, images and sūtras were destroyed and monks and nuns forced to return to lay life. This unpopular suppression was partly responsible for the fall of the Northern Zhou (Chou) dynasty and its replacement in 581 by the Sui dynasty (581-618).

Emperor Wen, first ruler of the Sui dynasty (r. 581-604), was a shrewd and tolerant monarch. Himself a Buddhist, he recognized the place of Confucianism in bolstering the government and the traditional morality of the Chinese people. Northern China prospered under his rule, and in 589, with a strong economic base and popular support, he was able to conquer the reigning Chen (Ch'en) dynasty in the south, uniting China once again under a single dynasty after over two centuries of partition. Apparently, Emperor Wen regarded the independent southern Saṅgha as a potential focus for discontent and rebellion, and he instituted a brief suppression designed to bring the southern Saṅgha to heel. In 590, however, Emperor Wen himself dispatched a request to the monk Zhi Yi (Chih I) — the most eminent monk in southern China — asking his help in reviving Buddhism and establishing it as the ideology of united China. It is with Zhi Yi and Emperor Wen that Buddhism in China made the crucial transition to becoming Chinese Buddhism. Emperor Wen played his part in this transition by emulating the deeds of the Indian emperor Aśoka. He supported Buddhist scholarship lavishly. He issued edicts proclaiming his support of Buddhism and encouraging his subjects to follow suit. He built shrines and established monasteries throughout China and dispatched missionaries to spread Buddhism in his realm and beyond. The spread of Buddhism to Japan was largely a result of Emperor Wen's activities.

While Emperor Wen promoted the popular acceptance of Buddhism, the scholar monk Zhi Yi was busy formulating the intellectual principles that would shape Chinese and Japanese Buddhism to the present day. By Zhi Yi's time, in the late sixth century, large numbers of Buddhist scriptures had made the arduous journey along the Silk Road from India to China. Some represented Nikāya Buddhism, some Mahāyāna; some were devotional, some philosophical, some early, some late. Indian Buddhists of the time identified their various and often contradictory scriptures with more or less distinct schools and sects, but the Chinese had little basis for favoring one segment of the purported teaching of the Buddha over another. Moreover, the wide discrepancies in the Buddhist scriptures were alien to the native Chinese love of order and harmony and inimical to the imperial desire for an ideology to unify the realm.

For all of these reasons, Zhi Yi founded Tian Tai (T'ien T'ai) Buddhism, the first truly Chinese school of Buddhism, by constructing a hierarchical scheme of classification (discussed below) that would integrate and harmonize the vast array of Buddhist scriptures and doctrines. At the top of this hierarchy was Mahāyāna devotionalism as expressed in the *Lotus Sūtra*. Zhi Yi's personal convictions aside, it appears likely that imperial desire for a unifying ideology was a motivating force behind the devotional orientation of his teachings. In the first place, devotionalism is a simple form of Buddhism readily accessible to the masses. In the second place, Buddhism under the northern dynasties had developed the convention of identifying the emperor with the Buddha. Given this convention, devotional Buddhism reinforced traditional Chinese reverence for the emperor and alleviated the problem of whether or not the Saṅgha was subordinate to the state. Drawing upon the intellectual tradition of the south, Zhi Yi provided the doctrinal basis for the propagation of northern style, devotional Buddhism throughout China.

Despite its brilliant beginning, the Sui dynasty was not to last long. In addition to his many achievements, Emperor Wen suffered one great failure, his son Yang Di (Yang Ti). Yang Di, who was entrusted with the governorship of southern China, was a vigorous promoter of Buddhism, and like his father cultivated the assistance of the venerable Zhi Yi to forge Buddhism into the unifying ideology of China. He was, however, inordinately ambitious, so much so that in 604 he murdered his father the emperor in order to rule China himself. As the second and last emperor of the Sui dynasty, Yang Di ruled briefly and badly. His ambitious program of constructing palaces, temples, fortifications and canals, combined with ill-conceived military campaigns in Korea and Central Asia, exhausted the funds of the empire and the loyalty of its subjects. Rebellions broke out within the empire and finally a disastrous defeat in Central Asia forced Yang Di to flee to the south where he was assassinated in 618.

Tai Zong (T'ai Tsung), a general in Yang Di's army, emerged victorious from the havoc following the collapse of the Sui dynasty and established the glorious Tang (T'ang) dynasty. Where Yang Di had failed, Tai Zong succeeded in subjugating not only Central Asia, but Tibet as well. His successor re-established influence in Korea, and thereby the Tang dynasty had achieved the dream of every Chinese emperor since partition: recovery of the territory and power of the Han dynasty, which had been lost for almost five hundred years.

By the end of the Han dynasty, Buddhism was little more than a strange foreign novelty, comparable perhaps to the Hari Krishnas in the United States or Europe. When the Han ideal of China was again realized by the Tang dynasty, Buddhism had become the dominant religion of the empire.

Classical Chinese Buddhism: The Tang Dynasty (618-907)

Tai Zong (r. 618-26), the first Tang emperor, legitimized his rule by claiming descent from Lao Zi. He and his Tang heirs thus naturally favored Daoism. Indicative of the ambivalent yet generally supportive attitude of the Tang rulers to Buddhism was the relationship between Tai Zong and the great Buddhist pilgrim, scholar and translator Xuan Zang (Hsüan Tsang — 602-64). When the emperor refused to grant permission for a journey to India, Xuan Zang defied him and left China secretly in 629. On his journey to India, he survived a murder attempt and near starvation in the Takla Makan desert. Then he was imprisoned on the Silk Road and released only after a hunger strike. When he finally did reach India, he narrowly escaped being used as a human sacrifice by bandits. Xuan Zang's real life exploits were fantastically embellished and immortalized in the Chinese novel *Journey to the West,* widely known in the West as *Monkey,* the title of a popular translation by Arthur Waley.

Once in India, Xuan Zang traveled to Buddhist holy sites far and wide, studied at Nālandā in a direct line of transmission from the masters Asaṅga and Vasubandhu, and quickly gained fame throughout the land, even to the extent of being reverenced and entertained by Emperor Harsha himself. Xuan Zang returned to China sixteen years later in 645, bearing 520 cases of manuscripts. His fame had preceded him, and he received a hero's welcome from the repentant Emperor Tai Zong in the capital, an ironic response considering that Xuan Zang had to sneak out of China like a fugitive. The emperor established a translation bureau in Xi'an under the direction of Xuan Zang, and toward the end of his reign counted the monk among his closest friends.

For most of its duration, the Tang dynasty followed Emperor Tai Zong's tolerant example. Exotic minorities such as Christians, Muslims and Zoroastrians practiced freely in their midst. Daoism and Confucianism were reinstated as the religions of the court, and Buddhism was recognized and honored by the empire as the religion of the Chinese people. It was this tension between the popular influence of Buddhism and the courtly influence of Daoism and Confucianism that eventually led to the irreversible decline of Buddhism in China. In essence, Buddhism under the Tang dynasty succeeded too well for its own good.

As had become customary in the northern dynasties, Buddhist monasteries ministered to the physical as well as the spiritual well-being of the people by serving as centers for the storage and distribution of grain. In addition, the labor force and produce of temple lands remained tax exempt. In the economic prosperity of the Tang dynasty, both of these traditions resulted in excesses. Monasteries not only stored grain, they milled it, pressed oil from it, and sold the produce. Their profits, combined with the donations of the faithful, both royal and common, made them enormously wealthy. Tax avoidance schemes were rife. For example, wealthy landowners would claim to donate land to a temple but in reality give only a portion of the taxes thus saved.

In prosperous times, such excesses were tolerable, but when the Tang dynasty became drained by internal rebellion and external conflict, they were drastically curtailed. Buddhist monasteries had accumulated so much wealth, and siphoned off so much of the taxable land and peasant labor, that drastic steps were deemed necessary. Daoist and Confucian bureaucrats in the court naturally regarded the welfare of the state as paramount, and they resented the opulence of Buddhism. The result was a third suppression of Buddhism under the ardently Daoist Emperor Wu Zong (Wu Tsung — r. 840-46), a blow from which Chinese Buddhism never fully recovered. Thousands of Buddhist monasteries and tens of thousands of shrines were destroyed. Temple lands and treasure were confiscated, and a quarter of a million monks and nuns forced to return to the laity.

Buddhism had proved resilient to imperial suppression in a divided China. When suppressed by northern dynasties it had always been able to refuel its resources from the south. Lacking such a source of renewal, Buddhism never fully recovered from the Tang suppression. This was partly because the suppression itself was so widespread and thorough, blanketing all of China, and partly because of the development of neo-Daoism and neo-Confucianism. Neo-Daoism, which incorporated aspects of Buddhist philosophy such as *śūnyatā* (emptiness), had begun to develop as a result of the close ties between Buddhists and Daoists in the southern dynasties during the north-south partition of China. Neo-Confucianism, while retaining a distinctly Chinese flavor, incorporated the concept of a metaphysical principle similar to Dharma-kāya Buddha, the metaphysical absolute of Mahāyāna Buddhism. These developments began to blur the distinctions among Buddhism, Daoism and Confucianism.

Like the two prior suppressions of Buddhism, the Tang suppression also ended with the death of the emperor who initiated it. When Emperor Wu Zong died in 846, his successor immediately reinstated Buddhism into imperial favor. He did not, however, restore many of Wu Zong's economic reclamations from the Buddhist Saṅgha. Buddhists were allowed once again to practice freely, but without its economic base, Buddhism gradually melted into an increasingly homogeneous syncretism with Daoism and Confucianism. By this time, Indian Buddhism had also begun to decline and was being absorbed into Hinduism. Whereas Buddhism was completely absorbed in India, it maintained a separate identity in China until the twentieth century. Nonetheless, Buddhism in China survived primarily as an integral constituent of a syncretistic religious worldview that prevailed through most of the second millennium.

The Schools of Chinese Buddhism

As Buddhism developed in China from the Han dynasty to the Tang dynasty, several schools came to be recognized as the classic expressions of Chinese Buddhism. Usually these schools are reckoned to be ten in number. Very generally, schools of Buddhism in India represented doctrinal differences, whereas Chinese schools of Buddhism tended to arise from emphasis upon particular scriptures. This difference is understandable. Until the Muslim conquest of India, Indian Buddhism had easy access to virtually all of the Buddhist scriptures in existence. The Chinese, by contrast, had access only to those scriptures which reached China, and even these scriptures could have no widespread influence until they had been translated. It was natural that Chinese Buddhists tended to gravitate around available, translated scriptures and the few masters qualified to teach them.

While some of the classical Chinese schools have roots going all the way back to the Han dynasty, most of them developed their specific identities during the Tang dynasty. Of the ten commonly recognized schools of classical Chinese Buddhism, two represent Nikāya Buddhism and eight represent Mahāyāna. Of the latter, three were more or less direct imports of the existing divisions of Mahāyāna Buddhism in India, and five developed in China in the course of the adaptation of Buddhism to the Chinese mentality. Most of these schools developed counterparts in Vietnam, Korea and Japan when Buddhism spread to these countries from China.

Schools of Nikāya Buddhism

1. THE LÜ OR VINAYA SCHOOL was based on the Vinaya (rules for monks and nuns) of one of the seventeen schools of Nikāya Buddhism, the Dharmagupta school. The Vinaya never developed a specifically Mahāyāna version, and all forms of Buddhism recognize the validity and importance of the Vinaya rules. The Lü school was not particularly Nikāya Buddhist in philosophical outlook, it merely emphasized monastic discipline over doctrine. Vinaya literature had been well known in China since the work of Kumārajīva in the early fifth century, but the Vinaya school as a separate entity was established only in the seventh century by the eminent monk Dao Xuan (Tao Hsüan — 596-667). Dao Xuan founded the school in order to counteract a tendency in China to regard Buddhism as primarily a set of doctrinal alternatives to Daoism and Confucianism. He wished to emphasize instead that the most important teaching of Buddhism was the spiritual discipline to be followed by monks. Because it was confined to the concerns of monks and nuns, the Lü school never developed a large following in China. Eventually, however, a descendant of the Lü school would exert considerable influence in Japan, where it came to control entry into the Saṅgha nation-wide.

2. THE JU SHE (CHÜ SHE) SCHOOL was based on the *Abhidharma Kośa* of Vasubandhu. The name Ju She derives from the Chinese pronunciation of the Sanskrit word *Kośa,* which means "treasure house." In effect the school was established when Paramārtha translated the *Abhidharma Kośa* in 563-67. Abhidharma philosophy is usually, though somewhat erroneously, regarded as a form of philosophical realism because of its postulation of a set of irreducible principles (dharmas) which combine to make up reality. Nonetheless, when the Ju She school ceased to have any exclusive adherents, its teachings were maintained in the immaterialist Wei Shi school (discussed below) because of its association with Vasubandhu — author of the *Abhidharma Kośa,* but also a founder of Buddhist immaterialism in India.

Mahāyāna Schools Imported from India

1. THE SAN LUN OR MADHYAMAKA SCHOOL may be traced back to the Han translator Lokakshema, generally regarded as the founder of Mahāyāna Buddhism in China. The school began in earnest, however, with the translation activities of Kumārajīva in the early fifth century. The name San Lun means "three treatises" and refers to

three works translated by Kumārajīva: Nāgārjuna's *Madhyamaka Kārikā* and two works of uncertain authorship. This school attained its greatest influence in southern China during the north-south partition of the fourth, fifth and sixth centuries, when a close association developed between Buddhists and Daoists on the basis of the similarity of their doctrines of *śūnyatā* (emptiness) and *wu* (non-being). Madhyamaka philosophy influenced most forms of Chinese Buddhism, but the San Lun school itself arguably exerted its greatest effect in China by stimulating the development of neo-Daoism.

2. THE WEI SHI (WEI SHIH) OR VIJÑĀNAVĀDA SCHOOL, also known as the Fa Xiang (Fa Hsiang) school, was established in 563, with Paramārtha's translation of Asaṅga's *Mahāyāna Saṃgraha*. The school received a significant boost when the pilgrim Xuan Zang returned from India having studied with teachers who could claim a direct line of transmission back to Vasubandhu and Asaṅga, the founders of Vijñānavāda Buddhism. Vijñānavāda works naturally figured prominently in the crate-loads of texts that Xuan Zang brought back from India, and the vigorous work of his translation team in Xi'an soon made these texts accessible to the Chinese. Like the San Lun school, the Wei Shi school had a large general effect upon Chinese Buddhism without enjoying lasting success as a separate school.

3. THE ZHEN YAN (CHEN YEN) OR TANTRIC SCHOOL, as opposed to the San Lun and Wei Shi schools, had its first successes in the "barbarian" dynasties of northern China. In addition to the natural appeal that a foreign religion had to foreign conquerors, Buddhist monks of the time reportedly impressed the new and somewhat unsophisticated rulers of northern China with feats of magic and prognostication. Similar talents, an integral feature of Tantric Buddhism, would also lead to the establishment of Buddhism among similar peoples in Tibet and Mongolia. Tantrism did not come into its own in China, however, until the Tang dynasty and the advent of the "Three Masters" in the eighth century. The three masters, all of Indian descent, were Śubhākarasiṃha, Vajrabodhi and Amoghavajra. Each of the Three Masters gained the recognition and favor of the Tang throne, and Tantrism flourished briefly in Xi'an and Luoyang during the eighth century. In the end, however, these Tantric masters had less influence in China than in Japan. So many Japanese monks studied Tantrism in China that the head temple of Chinese Tantrism, the Qing Long (Ch'ing Lung) Temple in Xi'an, was regarded by many Japanese as the Nālandā of China, in

recognition of the great Buddhist university in India where so many Chinese pilgrims studied.

Mahāyāna Schools Developed in China

1. THE SAN JIE JIAO (SAN CHIEH CHIAO) OR THREE AGES SCHOOL was the only important school of Buddhism developed in China that failed to take root in Japan. Founded by Xin Xing (Hsin Hsing) in the late sixth century, it was the first of the Buddhist schools to attract the disfavor of the Tang dynasty and to suffer from their suppression. It is easy to understand why. The "three ages" refer to the common Indian notion, prominent in both Hinduism and Buddhism, that after a great teacher establishes dharma or truth on earth, there follows a succession of ages in which the dharma deteriorates progressively. Xin Xing and his followers felt that they lived in the third, degenerate age of dharma, in which people were so blinded by greed, hatred and delusion that they were capable only of simple virtues such as strict austerity and merit making through generosity. They held, of course, that the most appropriate beneficiary of such generosity was the Buddhist Saṅgha, and as a result of their unabashed solicitation of donations from their followers, accumulated vast reserves of wealth. Such hoarded wealth naturally drew the early attention of Tang economic reformers, but the school's real undoing was its doctrine that in the third, degenerate age of the dharma, no government could administer justice and prosperity, and therefore no government was worthy of allegiance or respect. As a result of this teaching, the empress Wu Ze Tian (Wu Tse T'ien) declared the sect heretical, and in 713 the wealth of the head temple of the San Jie Jiao school was confiscated by the empire. The sect as a whole was suppressed thereafter and declined steadily until it disappeared entirely in the Tang suppression of Buddhism as a whole.

2. THE TIAN TAI (T'IEN T'AI) SCHOOL is named after the mountain on which its founder Zhi Yi (538-97) habitually resided. It will be remembered that Zhi Yi came into prominence following the Sui dynasty's reunification of China in 589. Tian Tai Buddhism, the first truly Chinese school of Buddhism, is based on a scheme of classification intended to integrate and harmonize the vast array of Buddhist scriptures and doctrines. This scheme of classification, in turn, is based on the Buddhist doctrine of *upāya* or "skillful means," which asserts that the Buddha taught different levels of doctrine to cater to the different abilities of his audiences. The origins of

this school too may be traced back to the translation activities of Kumārajīva, who first rendered the *Daśabhūmika Sūtra* or *Sūtra of Ten Stages* into Chinese. On the basis of this sūtra, known as the *Di Lun (Ti Lun)* in Chinese, two fifth-century monks of northern China, Hui Guan (Hui Kuan) and Liu Qiu (Liu Ch'iu), had already formulated theories dividing the teachings of Buddhism into several levels of doctrine delivered during different periods of history.

Zhi Yi synthesized these earlier teachings of the *Di Lun* masters by dividing the Buddhist scriptures into "five periods" and "eight teachings." In the first period, lasting three weeks, the Buddha taught the mammoth Mahāyāna text known as the *Avataṃsaka Sūtra,* but his audience was perplexed by the subtlety and complexity of the doctrines therein. Realizing that this full-blown Mahāyāna doctrine was beyond the understanding of humankind, the Buddha entered for twelve years the second period of teaching the basic doctrines of Nikāya Buddhism: the Four Noble Truths and the Eightfold Path. In the third period, lasting eight years, the Buddha taught rudimentary Mahāyāna doctrines regarding the sameness *(samatā)* of all phenomena and the presence of Buddha-nature in all things. He then moved into the fourth period, teaching for twenty-two years the Madhyamaka doctrine of emptiness *(śūnyatā)* as contained in the several *Prajñā Pāramitā* sūtras. Finally, in the fifth period he taught the devotionalism of the *Lotus Sūtra,* the supreme culmination of the Buddhist path to salvation. Zhi Yi's further division of Buddhist doctrine into "eight teachings" attempts to explain the fact that some individual sūtras contain contradictory material appropriate to several different periods.

Note that for Zhi Yi, the ultimate form of Buddhism is Mahāyāna devotionalism as taught in the *Lotus Sūtra.* As noted above, it appears that imperial desire for a hierarchical ideology was a motivating force behind this orientation. In addition to recognizing the exigencies of empire and popular religion, however, Zhi Yi attempted to formulate doctrinal underpinnings to justify his system intellectually. For these, he turned to Vijñānavāda Buddhism, the Consciousness school, in a manner that is best explained in conjunction with the similar doctrines of the Hua Yan school.

3. THE HUA YAN (HUA YEN) OR AVATAṂSAKA SCHOOL takes its name from the mammoth *Avataṃsaka Sūtra,* of which the *Daśabhūmika* forms a portion. The *Avataṃsaka Sūtra* was first translated in its entirety by Buddhabhadra in 420. The Hua Yan school as such, however, is generally regarded as having been initiated over a

century later by Fa Shun (557-640) and finally systematized by Fa Zang (Fa Tsang — 643-712). Hua Yan Buddhism posits a classification of sūtras and doctrines similar to the five periods and eight teachings of the Tian Tai school, but of course regards the *Avataṃsaka* rather than the *Lotus Sūtra* as supreme.

Though no Indian counterpart of either the Hua Yan or Tian Tai schools existed, both Chinese schools are basically Vijñānavāda in orientation, with an absolutist metaphysical twist. Both Tian Tai and Hua Yan doctrines assert that mundane phenomena are impure aspects of the one, all-encompassing, absolute mind, of which Dharma-kāya Buddha is the pure aspect. All phenomena thus originate from and resolve into the Buddha as the ultimate metaphysical principle, just as all thoughts originate from and resolve into the mind. To illustrate the basic concept of Tian Tai and Hua Yan: just as the fish in my mind and the tree in my mind are not really different — in that both are merely manifestations of my mind in thought — so a "real" fish and a "real" tree are but manifestations of the absolute mind, and are therefore fundamentally nondifferent.

Beyond this basic concept, Hua Yan Buddhism takes the further step of identifying the fish and the tree *as phenomena*. The tree is present in the fish and the fish is present in the tree, as are all phenomena present in their entirety in every other phenomenon. Because of their metaphysical grounding in the absolute mind, all phenomena "interpenetrate" one another. As a well-known English phrase has it, one can literally encounter "the universe in a grain of sand." The grain of sand nonetheless remains unique, for it is *that particular* manifestation of the entire universe. The reader who fails to understand this doctrine may take solace in the fact that the Empress Wu Ze Tian did not understand either. To illustrate the doctrine, Fa Zang surrounded a Buddha statue with mirrors above and below and at the eight points of the compass. Each mirror reflected not only the Buddha statue, but also the images in the other mirrors, and images of images multiplied infinitely.

Even more than Tian Tai, Hua Yan Buddhism had a strong appeal for the Chinese emperors. By asserting the unity of all phenomena in the Buddha, it implied the unity of all subjects in the emperor. Moreover, by identifying all phenomena with one another, it implied the identity of all subjects of the empire with all others. Thereby it provided an admirable ideological basis for harmony in the empire as well as allegiance to the emperor. During the Tang dynasty, the other philosophical schools of Chinese

Buddhism — schools imported from Central Asia and India — gradually disappeared or were absorbed into the Tian Tai and Hua Yan schools. These two home-grown schools thus came to embody virtually the entirety of Chinese Buddhist philosophy. Chinese Buddhist practice, on the other hand, came to be embodied in the Pure Land and Meditation schools, which had roots in India but developed into specific schools in China.

4. THE JING TU (CHING T'U) OR PURE LAND SCHOOL is based on the *Sukhāvatī Vyūha* or *Pure Land Sūtra*. The sūtra was translated, and the first Chinese adherents of the school recorded, in the third century. Nonetheless, Hui Yuan, who founded the Pure Land Society in 402, is regarded as the first patriarch of the school. Despite its early origins, however, the Pure Land school, like the other popular schools of Chinese Buddhism, did not coalesce until the Tang dynasty. For the Pure Land school, the opportunity for rapid growth came with the suppression of the Three Ages school in 713.

Like the Three Ages school, the Pure Land school held that the spiritual quality of the world had been in decline since its zenith at the time of the Buddha, and that the current age was the utterly degenerate third age. Rather than emphasizing discipline and simple virtues, as the Three Ages school did, the Pure Land school encouraged its followers to cultivate through prayer and devotion a sincere intent to be reborn after death in the heavenly paradise of the Buddha Amitābha, the Buddha of Infinite Radiance. Though negative concerning the quality of life on earth during the contemporary age, the Pure Land school was not explicitly critical of governments and thus did not incur the disfavor of China's rulers.

Imperial disfavor toward the Three Ages school and the vigorous leadership of the Pure Land masters Dao Zhuo (Tao Cho, 562-645) and his disciple Shan Dao (Shan Tao, 613-681) paved the way for rapid expansion of the school after the Tang suppression of the Three Ages school in 713. Dao Zhuo encouraged single-minded dedication to chanting the name of Amitābha Buddha as a sufficient means of gaining rebirth in the Pure Land. In addition to this primary practice, Shan Dao encouraged chanting of sūtras, worship of Buddha images and meditation upon the Buddha. This difference in emphasis is paralleled in the division of Japanese Pure Land Buddhism into two sects, Jōdo (like Shan Dao) and Jōdo Shinshū (like Dao Zhuo).

The simple doctrines of the Pure Land school, easily understood and practiced by the masses — combined with imperial support against the Three Ages school — resulted in an enormous popular following for Pure Land Buddhism in China. Their vivid descriptions of the paradise awaiting the faithful and the hells awaiting the wicked became common themes in the visual arts of the Tang dynasty, a development which resulted from and simultaneously enhanced the popularity of this simple form of Buddhism.

5. THE CHAN (CH'AN) OR MEDITATIONAL SCHOOL, better known by its Japanese name Zen, also came into prominence during the Tang dynasty. The names Chan and Zen are both derived from the Sanskrit term *dhyāna,* which means "meditation." As this suggests, the Chan school emphasized meditation as the only means to a spiritual awakening beyond words or thought, dispensing almost entirely with the doctrines and other practices of Buddhism. Of all the schools of Chinese Buddhism, Chan arguably has the most ancient roots in China and certainly the most colorful story.

Meditation, of course, was a prominent feature of most forms of Buddhism since its inception, but there was no specifically meditational school of Buddhism in India. Traditionally, nonetheless, Chan Buddhism was brought to China by the mysterious Indian monk Bodhidharma, who actually was probably a from Central Asia. He arrived in China around 500 CE, though the precise date is unclear. Long before this, however, the first preëminent Buddhist monk in China, An Shi Gao, who came from Central Asia in about 150 CE, concentrated his translation activities on meditational texts. Several Chinese monks, most notably Dao An, Hui Yuan and Buddhabhadra in the fourth and fifth centuries, are recorded as having emphasized meditation and gained proficiency in its practice long before the arrival of Bodhidharma.

Nonetheless, the colorful Bodhidharma is universally credited as the first patriarch of Chan Buddhism and of Japanese Zen Buddhism as well. According to the legend, he appeared first in southern China, before the Sui unification of China in 589, and was summoned for an interview by the reigning emperor Liang Wu Di (Liang Wu Ti). The emperor asked Bodhidharma to estimate how much merit he, the emperor, had gained through all of his lavish Buddhist construction projects. Bodhidharma answered that he had gained none at all, and promptly departed as abruptly as he had appeared, bound for the Wei kingdom of northern China.

While in the north, Bodhidharma is said to have sat motionless before a wall for nine years in order to perfect his meditational practice. In order to stave off sleep, he is supposed to have cut off his eyelids, a legend which accounts for the bulging eyes in most representations of the first patriarch. He is said to have agreed to accept his first pupil, Hui Ke (Hui K'e) only after the latter cut off his arm to demonstrate his sincerity. The second patriarch was indeed one-armed, but it is doubtful that this condition was self-inflicted.

All sources agree upon the identities of the first five patriarchs, but the intrigue surrounding the sixth will probably never be unraveled. This intrigue appears to have resulted from an instance of the rivalry between northern and southern styles of Buddhism, which persisted even after the Sui unification and Tang consolidation of China in the sixth and seventh centuries. In the case of Chan, the northern school generally emphasized gradual enlightenment as the cumulative result of years of meditational practice and scriptural study. The southern school, by contrast, developed the doctrine that enlightenment is not a cumulative achievement, but a spontaneous event that may occur with or without scriptural study or prolonged meditational practice, and may be brought on spontaneously by the most mundane of events. Originally, the northern school, founded by Bodhidharma, was probably the more faithful to the Indian *dhyāna* tradition. The southern school, influenced by its close interaction with neo-Daoism, was probably somewhat questionable from the standpoint of Indian Buddhism.

The southern school appears to have gained ascendancy by means of a clever historical ruse fabricated by the southern Chan master Shen Hui (670-762). The northern school died out, however, and so the southern story is now universally accepted among Chan and Zen Buddhists. This story is recounted in the eleventh-century *Record of the Transmission of the Lamp,* the standard history of Chan Buddhism. According to this narrative, the fifth Chan patriarch Hong Ren (Hung Jen, 602-75), near death, announced that he would choose his successor on the basis of a poetry competition. As everyone expected, the most promising poem was posted by Shen Xiu (Shen Hsiu — 600-706), who was admired for his great learning.

The body is the Bodhi tree, the mind a mirror bright.
Take care to keep them always clean. Let not the dust alight.

An insignificant kitchen hand from the south of China, Hui Neng (638-713), is then supposed to have posted overnight a rival stanza.

Enlightenment is not a tree, nor mind a mirror bright
Since there is nothing from the first, where can the dust alight?

This impudence outraged the monks, but the master Hong Ren immediately recognized that Hui Neng was his rightful successor. Hong Ren is then supposed to have summoned Hui Neng secretly into his chambers, handed over to him the patriarchal robe of succession, and bade him flee lest he be harmed by the jealous monks. Hui Neng fled to the south and there set up a Chan training center where Shen Hui became his foremost disciple.

If Shen Hui's account were true, there should have been no northern school after the death of the fifth patriarch. Instead, the learned Shen Xiu was widely recognized as the sixth patriarch. The identity of the northern school's seventh patriarch, however, is doubtful. Different sources identify two of Shen Xiu's disciples as his successor. This indicates that there may have been a split in the northern lineage. Shen Hui appears to have taken advantage of this or some such confusion in the northern lineage to advance the southern school's claim to be the only legitimate Zen tradition in China. At any rate, for unknown reasons the northern school of Chan eventually died out, and the southern school prevailed. As a result, Hui Neng is now universally regarded as the sixth patriarch.

By the ninth century, the triumphant southern school itself had split into five "houses" or branches. Of these, only two survived: the Lin Ji (Lin Chi) and the Cao Dong (Ts'ao Tung). These two lineages were eventually established in Japan as the Rinzai and Sōtō branches of Zen Buddhism. Briefly, Lin Ji (Jap. Rinzai) focuses meditation upon an insoluble riddle such as "What is the sound of one hand clapping?" These riddles are known as *gong an (kung an)* in Chinese and as *kōan* in Japanese. Cao Dong (Jap. Sōtō) encourages the meditator to "just sit" with a focused mind empty of conceptual thought.

Because of its de-emphasis of scriptures and the external paraphernalia of religion, Chan Buddhism was better able than other forms of Buddhism to survive the Tang dynasty persecution. In addition, its monastic ethic of "no work, no food" made Chan less vulnerable to the charge of being a social parasite, a charge leveled effectively by Confucianists against Buddhism in general. Finally, during the prosperous period of Tang China, the spontaneous, aesthetic spirit of Chan Buddhism appealed to the elite, who had ample leisure time to pursue sudden enlightenment, not necessarily through the monk's strict regimen of meditation, but through creating or experiencing art and poetry, or merely communing with nature. The old bond between Buddhism and neo-Daoism served Chan Buddhism well during the Tang period. For these reasons

Chan Buddhism prospered in China more than one might have thought given the demands of its meditational discipline and the absence of doctrine upon which to hang one's hopes.

In conclusion, note that Chan and Pure Land Buddhism — which came to embody the practice as opposed to the philosophy of Chinese Buddhism — stand at diametrically opposite ends of the religious spectrum. Chan is a rigorously self-reliant path to salvation, whereas Pure Land places one's salvation in the hands of a supernatural savior figure. Chan eschews all beliefs, whereas Pure Land is based entirely upon faith. Nonetheless, these two schools proved to be the only ones adapted to survival during the long decline of Chinese culture that followed the collapse of the Tang dynasty. These two forms of Buddhism would also go on to become dominant in Korea and Japan.

The Decline of Chinese Buddhism

The Tang dynasty collapsed largely as a result of a bloody insurrection which, though not aimed at Buddhism in particular, completed the devastation begun in the Tang suppression. This insurrection began obscurely in about 875, but by 881, under the leadership of one Huang Zhao (Huang Chao), it had rampaged through most of China and overthrown the ancient capitals of Luoyang and Xi'an. The rebellion was finally crushed in 884, but its mindless destruction struck Buddhism during a vulnerable time before its economic base could be restored following the Tang suppression.

Following the final demise of the Tang dynasty in 907, China descended into a fifty-year period of turmoil that was somewhat stabilized but by no means rectified by the three-century rule of the Song (Sung) dynasty (960-1279). The Chinese Song dynasty did not rule alone, but competed with alien Manchurian and Mongol dynasties, which dominated northern China for most of this period. In effect, China entered a second period of north-south partition. Little is known of the fate of Buddhism under the Mongol Liao dynasty (907-1124) or the Manchurian Jin (Chin) dynasty (1115-1234), but it appears to have fared reasonably well. Significantly, a Liao edition of the Chinese Tripiṭaka, printed in 1031-64, served as the primary basis for the Korean Tripiṭaka, which is now widely regarded as the best existing edition of the scriptures of Chinese Buddhism. Nonetheless, developments within Chinese Buddhism during the Song period appear to have occurred primarily under the auspices of the Song dynasty itself rather than the competing Liao or Jin dynasties.

As noted above, during the Tang dynasty Tian Tai and Hua Yan came to constitute the bulk of Chinese Buddhist philosophy, whereas Pure Land and Chan came to constitute the bulk of Buddhist practice. Without disappearing entirely, the remaining schools were gradually absorbed into one or another of these major schools. Of these four primary schools, Tian Tai and Hua Yan, being dependant upon scriptures, were particularly hard hit by the material devastation of first the Tang suppression and then the Huang Zhao insurrection. Tian Tai and Hua Yan monks of the Song dynasty had to turn to Korea and Japan to try to retrieve copies of their lost scriptures, commentaries, and philosophical tracts.[28] Without ready availability these texts and without expensive institutions to educate monks, the doctrine-based schools of Chinese Buddhism declined throughout the Song period.

While radically different in theory, Chan and Pure Land were similar in that neither required elaborate material facilities for its propagation. Moreover, although neither Chan nor Pure Land required philosophical sophistication, both required discipline — either in meditation or in the recitation of prayers to Amitābha. During the Sung period, Chan monks in particular began to move toward harmonization of the various forms of Buddhism in China. They began to regard the recitation of Pure Land prayers as a form of meditation akin to the Chan concentration on the various *gong an* (Jap. *kōan)* or meditational riddles. They also began to take a greater interest in Buddhist literature, particularly in writings on the lives of Chan masters, but also in the scriptures and doctrines of the various schools.

As Buddhism itself became more homogeneous, it was in turn incorporated as a whole into a religious triumvirate composed of more or less equal parts of neo-Confucianism, neo-Daoism and Buddhism. All of the dynasties following the Tang officially embraced Buddhism, but each maintained a policy of encouraging the fusion of those elements of the three religions of China which were conducive to social order and harmony among the masses. Temples dedicated to the Three Teachers — Confucius, Lao Zi and the Buddha — became common, and distinctions among the various deities and sages of the three religions became blurred in the minds of the general population.

On an intellectual level, the neo-Confucian philosopher Zhang Zai (Chang Tsai — 1020-1077) began in earnest a program of systematizing this three-way syncretism. He devised a comprehensive metaphysics addressing the origin and nature of the universe and of the individual human being. According to this system, the "vital force" or *qi (ch'i)* in each individual person derives from and resolves into a single, universal source. On the one hand, this neo-Confucian thought was derived from

Mahāyāna Buddhist absolutism, which postulated that each person and thing is a manifestation of Dharma-kāya Buddha. On the other hand, the neo-Confucianists claimed to refute the alleged negativity and pessimism of the Buddhist doctrine of *śūnyatā* or "emptiness" with a countervailing teaching of interrelated fullness. The greatest neo-Confucian scholar of the Song dynasty Zhu Xi (Chu Hsi — 1130-1200), though anti-Buddhist, increased the movement's similarities to Buddhism by incorporating a neo-Confucian version of enlightenment. As Advaita Hinduism had absorbed the essence of Mahāyāna Buddhism in India, so neo-Confucianism did in China. Depending upon how one looks at it, these absorptions represent part of the triumph or part of the demise of Buddhism in both India and China.

While the religion of the lower classes became increasingly homogeneous, the middle and upper classes turned increasingly toward neo-Confucianism and the social mobility that a formal Confucian education afforded after the fall of the Tang dynasty. Such an education became imperative for employment in the Chinese equivalent of a civil service. Due to the progressive nature of neo-Confucianism, a formal Confucian education also afforded considerable intellectual, moral and aesthetic stimulation. It was therefore comparable to a modern Liberal Arts education in the West, in terms of both upward mobility and intellectual stimulation. None of the dynasties following the Song failed to see the advantages of such thoroughgoing state control of education and social mobility.

Like the first reunification of China, the second reunification — which united the territory of the Song, Liao, and Jin dynasties — was accomplished by a foreign power regarded as barbarian by ethnic Chinese. This power was the Mongols, who established the Yuan dynasty (1280-1368). Reputedly, the first contact these Mongols had with Buddhism was in the course of their conquest of China, and their cousins of the Liao dynasty had certainly been exposed to Chinese Buddhism. Nonetheless, soon after conquering China the Mongols formed an alliance with the racially related Tibetans and embraced the Tantric Buddhism of Tibet. This alliance established a thick crescent over the Chinese heartland, from the Himalayas to the Sea of Japan, in which Mongolia exercised political authority and Tibet exercised religious authority. The Mongol-Tibetan alliance remained in place even after the Mongols lost power in China proper. It was eventually formalized with the establishment by the Mongols in 1578 of the supreme religious office of the Dalai Lama of Tibet, a development which will be discussed in greater detail in Chapter XI.

The Mongols established their capital in Beijing, and ruled from there with little sensitivity or restraint. This, in conjunction with their non-Chinese, "barbarian" status led to unrest and finally widespread rebellion, fomented largely within quasi-Buddhist secret societies. Most notable of these were the Maitreya, White Cloud, and White Lotus Societies, which looked to the coming of Maitreya (the future Buddha) as a messianic incentive to rebellion. Finally in 1368, a rebellion led by the White Lotus Society overthrew the Mongols and established the Ming or "enlightened" dynasty (1368-1644), a name which sought to associate the rulers with the hoped for advent of an enlightened age under the future Buddha Maitreya.

Developments in Buddhism during the Ming dynasty are epitomized by the wide-ranging activities of the monk Zhu Hong (Chu Hung, 1535-1615). These included continuation of moves to harmonize the schools of Buddhism, attempts to find common ground with neo-Confucianism, increased emphasis upon lay Buddhism, and resistance to Christian missionary activities. Though the Ming emperors supported Buddhism, the brightest minds were attracted to the Confucian civil service, and the Saṅgha became a second-rate institution, albeit a large one. Still, the lower classes, for whom a Confucian education was out of reach, continued to have fervent spiritual aspirations. These were largely met through a combination of simple merit making and Pure Land devotion encouraged through extensive lay Buddhist societies like the White Cloud and White Lotus Societies. At the bottom end of the religious spectrum, a superstitious amalgam of increasingly indistinguishable elements of Buddhism, Daoism and folk religion prevailed.

The Ming dynasty gave way in 1644 to the Manchurian Qing (Ch'ing) dynasty (1644-1912), which continued with the same relatively stable government organization as their Ming predecessors. The Manchurians are racially related to Tibetans and Mongols, and therefore favored Tantric Buddhism. Nonetheless, Buddhism continued to decline, along with Chinese culture as a whole, throughout the Qing period. The Saṅgha had become corrupt and lethargic from almost a thousand years of nominal support combined with bureaucratic control by the succession of lackluster dynasties following the Tang. For good reasons, the Manchurian Qing dynasty, as aliens, feared the various lay Buddhist societies that had helped bring down the alien Yuan dynasty. Under Manchurian rule, these societies once again became clandestine organizations plotting revolution.

These quasi-Buddhist secret societies were an important organizational basis of the Tai Ping (T'ai P'ing) rebellion of 1851-64, a prolonged frenzy of destruction in which up to thirty million people perished. The Tai Ping rebellion and several other smaller, but still major, uprisings that it spawned accelerated the general decline of Chinese civilization during the nineteenth century. At about the same time, Western and Japanese imperialism began to contribute further to this general decline. Buddhism, of course, deteriorated along with Chinese culture as a whole.

Conventionally, the Manchurian Qing dynasty gave way in 1912 to the Republic of China, a modern nation-state. In reality, from about 1900 to 1928, China had a central government in name only. Real power was wielded by warlords in the provinces, by Japan, and by European governments and banks. Desperate poverty prevailed. Throughout this period Buddhism and Buddhist institutions suffered from neglect, from banditry and pilferage, and from confiscation of resources by provincial warlords and the central government. Confiscation of resources became particularly common after the collapse of the Qing dynasty removed even the appearance of imperial sanction of Buddhism. The ideology of Republican China was secularist and modernist. China was poor. Both the Republicans in the capital and the warlords in the provinces felt that Buddhist monasteries could be put to better use as schools, office-buildings, public housing, hospitals, barracks, or simply warehouses. The produce and income from monastery lands was needed to feed mouths, pay debts, finance government, and enrich the powerful.

In 1928, Chiang Kai-shek, a Chinese general trained in Japan and Russia, was able to assert at least the semblance of centralized government with the support of provincial warlords and Western powers, the Soviet Union in particular. Chiang Kai-shek's Guo Min Dang (Kuo Min Tang) or "Nationalist party" was Soviet communist in organization, capitalist in ideology, and Confucian in propaganda. As such, it was neither friend nor foe to Buddhism. In theory, Nationalist China was a single-party dictatorship. In reality, the Nationalists struggled incessantly to maintain power vis-à-vis provincial warlords, Japanese invaders, and increasingly, communist insurgents. In these unsettled conditions, Buddhism faced the same threats it had faced since the turn of the century and before: lack of government support, confiscation of resources, and a general decline in its economic base.

Throughout the Republican period (1912-1949), Chinese Buddhists attempted to adapt and respond to political and economic realities by organizing themselves into "Buddhist associations" aimed at forming closer ties to the laity and lobbying government. These modern Buddhist associations, the first of which was founded in 1900,[29] had precedents in the "Buddhist societies" that had existed since the fourteenth century and had helped overthrow the Mongol and Manchurian dynasties. The

Buddhist associations of the twentieth century, however, attempted to adapt Buddhism to modern realities and to negotiate with rather than overthrow governments. These associations worked to improve monastic education, enhance Buddhism's social relevance by establishing schools and orphanages, and make monasteries economically viable through fund-raising initiatives. It is difficult to say whether this Buddhist modernization movement in China would have succeeded in revitalizing Chinese Buddhism if communists under Mao Ze Dong (Mao Tse-tung, 1893-1976) had not seized power in 1949.

Chiang Kai-shek's Nationalist government, though Russian communist in inspiration and organization, was opposed from its inception by indigenous communist insurgents bent upon radical reform of the Chinese economy and society. The credibility of the Chinese communists was enhanced by Chiang Kai-shek's failure to revive the economy or to prevent Japanese territorial expansion into northeast China. This expansion culminated in 1937 when the Japanese bombed Shanghai and seized all of China's northeastern ports. Until 1945, the year of Japan's defeat in the Second World War, Nationalist and communist Chinese military forces were reluctant, mutually hostile allies against the Japanese invaders. Immediately after World War II, Nationalist and communist forces turned upon one another in a full-scale civil war. The communists under Mao emerged victorious in 1949 and proclaimed the People's Republic of China. Chiang Kai-shek's defeated government retreated to the island of Taiwan, which remains to the present day an independent nation claiming to represent the legitimate government of China.

Buddhism flourished on the small island of Taiwan, as did all aspects of traditional Chinese culture. One can only speculate whether this would have been the case in mainland China if the communists had not triumphed. As it is, the communists first tolerated and then actively suppressed Buddhism and other religions in China and in territory controlled by China, most notably Tibet. This repression escalated into a frenzy during the infamous Cultural Revolution instituted by Mao in 1966-69. This "revolution" was actually a sustained government campaign against all aspects of traditional Chinese culture. Religion in particular was targeted as being an anti-communist, reactionary fabric of superstition that was largely responsible for China's continuing economic failures. During this tragic period, which did little or nothing to alleviate poverty, the few remaining traces of China's Buddhist heritage were destroyed or damaged almost beyond recognition. For a decade, Buddhism virtually ceased to exist in China.

In 1976 Mao Ze Dong's death opened the way for social and economic reforms in communist China. The outcome of these reforms remains to be seen, but the 1980s witnessed a cautious resurgence of non-denominational, devotional Buddhism. A few of the major Buddhist temples were restored with government funds, mostly to encourage a foreign tourist trade. Monks were allowed to return to their robes, though few did, and people began hesitantly to practice Buddhism in public once again. Buddhist associations were revived, and particularly in China's remote areas the people themselves began to donate labor and money to the restoration of Buddhism.

This tentative resurgence of Buddhism came to an abrupt halt with the 1989 massacre in Beijing's Tiananmen (T'ien-an-men) Square of hundreds of protestors demanding more individual freedoms and an increase in the rate of governmental reform. This brutal crackdown marked the beginning of yet another communist suppression of traditional Chinese culture and religious freedom. At the same time, China has continued to move forward with economic reforms that ultimately would appear to entail a degree of personal freedom incompatible with religious suppression. Potentially, China contains the world's largest population of Buddhists, but their actual numbers will remain obscure until several continuous decades of religious freedom afford an opportunity for China's Buddhist heritage to re-assert itself. Optimistically, a resurgence of Buddhism in China, among a population comprising one fifth of the human race, could be the most significant religious phenomenon of the twenty-first century.

CHAPTER IX

The Development of
Buddhism in Korea

The miracle of Korea is that in spite of interminable internal strife and foreign interference, its people have maintained a strong national and ethnic identity and contributed significantly and distinctively to human history. This contribution is nowhere more evident than in the development and spread of Buddhism. Despite generally hostile relations with both China and Japan, Korea acted as an important intermediary in the spread of Buddhism from China to Japan, and developed its own distinctive form of Buddhism through intimate — though often unwanted — contact with its two powerful neighbors.

Surrounded by China to the west, Japan to the east and Manchuria and the Mongols to the north, it is surprising that Korea emerged with such a distinctive historical, ethnic and cultural identity. And yet Korea's roots extend deep into history. The Korean peninsula was inhabited by at least the fourth millennium BCE. The use of bronze in Korea began late in the second millennium BCE, and the local production of iron had begun by about 300 BCE, a technology imported by refugees from the turmoil of the Warring States period in China (453-221 BCE). From this period, Chinese influence in Korea grew steadily, through migration, military conflicts and diplomatic contacts.

In the second century BCE, the Han dynasty of China moved to subjugate the tribal peoples to the northeast of the Chinese heartland, including those of the Korean peninsula. By forming alliances and confederations, these various tribal peoples — including Mongols, Manchurians and Koreans — periodically threatened the security and integrity of imperial China, particularly in border areas. Chinese initiatives to subjugate these "barbarians" were largely successful by the second century BCE. This resulted in the establishment on the Korean peninsula of four Chinese administrative divisions, commonly known as "commanderies," which governed the peninsula.

These Chinese commanderies were intended to control the Korean peninsula and forestall the development of hostile powers in the region. Instead, the introduction of Chinese technology and statecraft had an opposite effect. Not only did the tribal peoples of Korea learn how to make better weapons, they learned by example the advantages of centralized government and diplomacy, particularly in the realm of military alliances. They soon began to employ this new knowledge in attempts to oust their Chinese overlords. By invading Korea, the Chinese initiated an indigenous movement toward unification, and thereby set in motion a process that centuries of inter-tribal warfare had failed to accomplish.

The first of the new Korean states to consolidate was Koguryŏ. Koguryŏ emerged in the early years of the first century CE, about the time Buddhism was being introduced into China from Central Asia. About 250 years later, a second, contending Korean state, Paekche, was established in the southwest of the peninsula. By 350, a third state, Silla had emerged in the southeast of the peninsula. This set the stage for the "Three Kingdoms" period of Korean history, a period of some 300 years of unremitting conflict between shifting alliances forged among the three contenders to Korean domination — Koguryŏ, Paekche and Silla. These conflicts were further complicated by smaller Korean tribal states and opportunistic Chinese and Japanese involvement on several different sides. It was during this tumultuous period that Buddhism was introduced from China into Korea and passed on from Korea to Japan. Out of this crucible, Korean national identity was forged.

The Introduction of Buddhism in the Three Kingdoms Period (c. 200-668)

The first of the Korean states to emerge was Koguryŏ. Recognizing that China was overextended in the region, in 12 CE the Koguryŏ clan refused to supply their supposed overlords with troops for the imperial army, in effect declaring independence. The Koguryŏ clan began to dominate and absorb neighboring clans as Chinese military influence in the region continued to decline throughout the remainder of the Han dynasty. By about 200 CE, Koguryŏ had become established as a stable political entity. Chinese influence in the area declined even further as the Han dynasty broke up into the Three Kingdoms of Chinese history. The Three Kingdoms period of Chinese history (220-265 CE) must not be confused with the overlapping but much longer Three Kingdoms period of Korean history (c. 200-668 CE). By the time of the north-south partition of China in 316, Koguryŏ had attained its full extent, covering the northern half of the peninsula.

As Koguryŏ grew in size and power, China attempted to stabilize the region through diplomacy rather than through military might. As part of this strategy, in 372 Emperor Fu Jian (Fu Chien — r. 357-84) of northern

China sent a diplomatic delegation to King Sosurim (r. 371-84) of Koguryŏ. A member of the delegation was a Buddhist monk named Sundo, a high-priest in the northern Chinese court, who presented the king of Koguryŏ with Buddhist images and scriptures. Thus, 372 is traditionally considered the year in which Buddhism was introduced into Korea. Traditional histories record that King Sosurim ceremoniously received the Buddhist monk at the gates of the capital rather than awaiting his arrival in the palace, as protocol would have dictated. This extravagant greeting set a precedent for royal receptions of Buddhist envoys that would be repeated several times in Korean history. According to tradition, King Sosurim built the Hŭnguk Monastery (originally Sŏngmun), supposedly the first Buddhist structure on the peninsula, to house Sundo, supposedly the first monk.

This traditional account probably dates the arrival of Buddhism later than it actually occurred. Also during the reign of Sosurim, in 383, the monk Ado is said to have arrived in Koguryŏ from northern China. According to tradition, Ado was a native of Korguryŏ who became a Buddhist monk at age five, having been inspired by his mother's piety. At the age of sixteen, he is said to have traveled to China to study Buddhism. He is said to have returned three years later, and King Sosurim is said to have built for him the Hŭngbok Monastery (originally Ibullan), the second Buddhist structure on the peninsula. If Ado's mother was a Buddhist, she must have been been exposed to Buddhism well before the arrival of Sundo in 372. Also, it is doubtful that the king would have welcomed Buddhist monks so lavishly if the religion had been entirely unknown. More to the point, another traditional Korean history, the *Haedong Kosŭng Chŏn* ("Biographies of Eminent Korean Monks"), records that the well-known southern Chinese monk Zhi Dun (Chih Tun), who died around 366, carried on a correspondence with the Koguryŏ monk Mangmyŏng. This too suggests that Buddhism was established on the Korean peninsula well before the traditional date of 372.

Concrete evidence of an earlier introduction of Buddhism than tradition supposes is provided by a mid-fourth century tomb, unearthed near P'yŏngyang, which incorporates Buddhist motifs in its ceiling decoration.[31] Some Korean scholars argue for a yet earlier date. They propose, with perhaps a tinge of nationalism, that Buddhism initially bypassed China en route to Korea and was introduced directly from Central Asia. Although doubtful, this is possible, since the Korean people are racially and culturally related to the ancient nomads of Central Asia. The Koreans may well have maintained some contacts with Central Asia through these nomads. The actual date of Buddhism's first entry into Korea will probably remain unresolved. What sparse evidence there is suggests that it was relatively well established by the middle of the fourth century. This evidence also suggests, as one would expect, that Buddhism was known first in the northern kingdom of Koguryŏ, which borders on outer China, and that it spread from there through the rest of the peninsula.

Traditionally, however, Buddhism was introduced independently to Paekche, the second of the Three Kingdoms of ancient Korea. Paekche emerged as a political entity hostile to Koguryŏ in about 350 CE. Shortly thereafter, in 384, the Indian monk Mālānanda (Korean Maranant'a) is said to have come from southern China. Like the king of Koguryŏ, the king of Paekche is said to have met the monk and his entourage at the city gates with great reverence. In 385, the king is said to have ordered the construction of a temple for him and ordained ten monks in his honor. Once again, such extravagance suggests that Buddhism was already well known in Paekche before the traditional date of introduction.

Interestingly, the traditional story of the advent of Buddhism in Silla is altogether different from the joyous welcomes the religion is said to have received in Koguryŏ and Paekche. Silla was the last of the Three Kingdoms to emerge, its first ruler being King Naemul (r. 356-402). Because Silla eventually prevailed over Koguryŏ and Paekche, the historical records of early Silla, though sparse, are relatively more detailed than those of its vanquished rivals. These records indicate that Buddhism received a hostile initial reception in Silla when monks began to arrive from Koguryŏ in the fifth century. The first of these early monks, Mukhoja, is said to have taken shelter, apparently in some danger, in the house of a clandestine Buddhist layman known as Morye. In the traditional account, Morye mentions ominously two earlier missionaries from Koguryŏ who had been martyred in Silla. Mukhoja, at any rate, eventually gained royal favor by curing the daughter of King Nulchi (r. 417-458) of a persistent disease. Mukhoja succeeded, it is said, by means of a ceremony involving a mysterious substance recently brought from China: incense.

After Nulchi, there begins a notable tendency to assign Buddhist-oriented reign titles to Silla kings. These ceremonial titles, by which Korean kings are conventionally known, often indicate respect for if not conversion to Buddhism by Nulchi's successors. Such reign titles are an important consideration, because Buddhism did not begin to be widely or enthusiastically accepted in Silla until about a century after King Nulchi, i.e. in the early sixth century. This indicates that Buddhism was accepted by the rulers of Silla before it was widely accepted by the people. Traditional history attributes the shift in popular attitudes toward Buddhism to the martyrdom of one Ich'adon in 529. Ich'adon was a court official who served under King Pŏphŭng (r. 514-540), whose reign title means "Flourishing of Dharma." According to traditional sources,

Ich'adon conspired with the king to dupe the anti-Buddhist court aristocracy by surreptitiously approving the construction of a Buddhist monastery. When officials at court discovered the ruse, the king was either powerless or disinclined to protect Ich'adon, and he was beheaded. At the public execution, Ich'adon's blood flowed as white as milk, and his head flew through the air and alighted on a mountain peak. No doubt these events would have moved the assembly to reconsider their opposition toward Buddhism.

A more reliable indication of wider acceptance of Buddhism in Silla is that in 534 King Pŏphŭng himself ordered the construction of the Taewang Hŭngnyun Monastery. It is said that the foundations of a previous monastery were discovered during excavation work for the new one. This tradition is doubtful, but if true would of course indicate a much earlier acceptance of Buddhism in Silla. In 540 King Pŏphŭng abdicated the throne to become a Buddhist monk resident in the new monastery. The queen also is said to have retired as a nun to a second monastery. This record is the first indication of Buddhist nuns in the Korean peninsula. Pŏphŭng's successor, his nephew Chinhŭng ("Advance of Dharma" — r. 540-76), who ascended the throne when only seven, was an ardent promoter of both Buddhism and the territorial expansion of Silla. King Chinhŭng initiated a military and diplomatic push that within a century resulted in the unification of the greater part of the Korean peninsula under the kingdom of Silla.

There is virtually no available evidence indicating precisely which school or schools of Buddhism were introduced into the Korean peninsula during the Three Kingdoms period. Presumably the early schools were among those already established in China. What evidence there is indicates that the magical aspects of Buddhism — primarily protection from disease and misfortune — were promoted and gradually accepted in early Korea rather than any particular doctrines. Buddhism, in other words, was presented and practiced as a new and perhaps more powerful form of shamanism.

The paucity of evidence notwithstanding, it is possible to draw several tentative conclusions regarding the introduction of Buddhism to Korea. It appears that as in China, Buddhism was accepted first by the rulers of Korea. Again as in China, there appears to have been considerable initial resistance from the aristocracy, who had much to lose from the demise of existing forms of religion. In China, however, the pre-Buddhist forms of religion were sophisticated, systematic, traditions thoroughly integrated into a centralized government. In Korea, by contrast, the pre-Buddhist religions were loosely organized, non-literate worldviews based primarily upon shamanism. In Korea, moreover, the hierarchy separating rulers from the masses was far less developed than in China. The court elite surrounding the ruler was much closer and more accountable to the governed. Even as the Chinese form of centralized government began to take root in Korea, the ministers of the Korean kings remained little more than chieftains of a restive welter of clans that had no real sense of national boundaries or loyalties. The office of clan chief itself was a largely religious position akin to chief shaman, and so for a king to embrace Buddhism required considerable tact and courage. The more perceptive rulers and their closest advisors, however, recognized the advantages of adopting the more stable Chinese form of government and the religion and culture that went with it.

The north-south partition of China had occurred in 316, so the Chinese with whom Korea was most intimately involved, whether in conflict or negotiation, were those of the northern "barbarian" dynasties. In the northern dynasties, Buddhism had been adopted early on as the ideological cement of the state. It is not surprising, therefore, that progressive Korean rulers saw Buddhism, rather than Confucianism or Daoism, as the essential religious component of sophisticated government and diplomacy. Diplomatic delegations exchanged between the Korean kingdoms and China usually included Buddhist monks. No doubt, Buddhist missions from China were often covers for diplomatic contacts. For all of these reasons, there was considerable incentive for Korean rulers to be sympathetic toward Buddhism, and to embrace it — at least superficially — even against the wishes of the clan chieftains.

Each of the three Korean kingdoms assimilated Chinese culture and modes of government. It was Silla, however, under a succession of strong monarchs following Chinhŭng, which proved most successful in the realms of diplomacy and warfare. In both realms, Buddhism played an important role. Toward the end of his reign, in 572, King Chinhŭng instituted the P'algwanhoe, a great Buddhist ceremony to bless the departed spirits of soldiers who died in the campaigns that had extended Silla's borders at the expense of Koguryŏ and Paekche. Performance of the P'algwanhoe, as well as another elaborate ceremony, the Paekchwa kanghoe, was also supposed to bless the king and protect Silla. In particular, the construction of pagodas was believed to be of direct, supernatural benefit to the king and the country, although any public construction project for the benefit of Buddhism was believed to convey blessings and protection upon the kingdom.

Interestingly, the famous seventh-century monk Chajang is said to have argued that the construction of a pagoda at the Hwangyong Monastery would insure the defence of Silla and promote unification of the Three Kingdoms. This Buddhist prophesy is the earliest explicit reference to the ideal of Korean unification and nationhood. The Hwangyong or "Yellow Dragon" Monastery itself was built, according to tradition, because King Chinhŭng ordered a halt to construction of a new royal palace when a yellow dragon was seen on the building site. Plans were modified, and instead of a new palace, the great Yellow Dragon Monastery was built.

The role of Buddhism in defining and solidifying the nation is clear in these public ceremonies and construction projects. Constructions and ceremonies that glorified Buddhism were thought to benefit the kingdom of Silla, which increasingly was seen to encompass the entire Korean peninsula. In such an atmosphere, one could not be un-Buddhist without appearing unpatriotic, nor could one be fully patriotic without being at least partly Buddhist. Regardless of one's true religious beliefs, one could hardly oppose a construction project or boycott a public ceremony intended to secure the success of the nation's troops in time of war. The mutual enhancement of religious fervor and nationalism is a common phenomenon across the spectrum of world religions. In Korea, most notably in Silla, this phenomenon served as the basis upon which Buddhism was accepted by the people. Koreans were used to the concept of magical, shamanistic practices enhancing the prosperity of clan groups. In its early period in Korea, particularly in Silla, Buddhism was portrayed as a sort of national shamanism. Its promotion and practice encouraged transcendence of the tribal concept of group identity in favor of participation in a much larger social group owing allegiance to a king instead of a tribal chief. Like traditional Korean clans, this nation was seen to be championed by supernatural forces, namely those of Buddhism. Thus Buddhism came to be seen as a source of protection different from and greater than the supernatural, shamanistic benefactors of the ancient clans.

In all these ways, Buddhism in Silla was associated with national identity and the military success of the state. Silla's military successes in this period were numerous indeed, so Buddhism must have seemed to be powerful magic. Of course, nothing succeeds like success in promoting a sense of national identity, and so it is understandable how Buddhism began to earn the loyalty of the Silla populace well before its doctrinal and moral teachings were widely disseminated.

Silla's success in the peninsula, however, was won not only on the battlefield, but also through diplomacy. According to traditional records, Chinhŭng received with great ceremony at least two diplomatic delegations from China. The first brought Buddhist relics, and the second brought some seven hundred volumes of Buddhist scriptures, a priceless treasure at the time. Both of these delegations were accompanied by Buddhist monks from Silla, who themselves presumably had gone to

China for diplomatic as well as religious purposes. In addition to military superiority, such diplomatic relations with China helped set the stage for Silla's triumph over Koguryŏ and Paekche.

King Chinhŭng's immediate successor ruled Silla for only three years, after which the great King Chinp'yŏng (r. 579-632) ascended the throne. Chinp'yŏng's long reign witnessed both the reunification of China under the Sui dynasty (589-618) and the rise of the glorious Tang dynasty (618-907). During the reign of King Chinp'yŏng, the monk Wŏn'gwang set out for China in 589. This journey initiated a new phase in the history of Buddhism in Korea. Before Wŏn'gwang, other Korean monks had already traveled and studied in China, even India. In 554, the monk Ŭisin returned from a tour of India, and in 565, Hyŏn'gwang returned to Paekche from China, having studied under Hui Si (Hui Ssu — 515-77), teacher of Zhi Yi who founded the Tian Tai school of Buddhism. No doubt the efforts of these monks fostered in Korea a more sophisticated understanding of Buddhist doctrine. Of the early Korean pilgrims, however, Wŏn'gwang was by far the most influential.

Wŏn'gwang's departure for China in 589 coincided with the reunification of China under the Sui dynasty. While in China, Wŏn'gwang specialized in the study of the *Nirvāṇa* and *Prajñā Pāramitā Sūtras,* texts of particular importance in the Tian Tai school, which Zhi Yi was formulating at the time. After he returned to Silla in 599, he exerted enormous influence at court, and in 608 he returned to China as an envoy to the Sui dynasty. An indication of Wŏn'gwang's stature is that he was personally tended on his death-bed in 631 by King Chinp'yŏng, who himself died a year later in 632. Wŏn'gwang's prestige and his close association with China initiated a flood of Korean monks to and from both China and India. These arduous journeys are all the more remarkable considering that the Korean peninsula was embroiled in interminable warfare during most of the seventh century.

After the death of Wŏn'gwang in 631, and the death of King Chinp'yŏng in 632, the development of Buddhism in Silla was dominated by three monks: Chajang (608-686), Wŏnhyo (617-687) and Ŭisang (625-702). The lives of these three contemporaries spanned the momentous period during which Silla emerged as the dominant power on the Korean peninsula and established its independence from China.

Chajang is notable for his determined renunciation of worldly affairs and his dedication to the intellectual doctrines and moral discipline of Buddhism. He was born into the royal clan, the very highest rank in Silla society, and yet became a recluse early in his life, reputedly during childhood. He is said to have defied even a royal threat of execution rather than leave his meditation to serve at court. Chajang traveled to China in 636, where he is said to have had a vision of Mañjuśrī on the sacred mountain Wu Tai Shan (Wu T'ai Shan). Emperor Tai Zong, founder of the Tang dynasty, invited Chajang to reside in one of the capital's grand monasteries, but Chajang chose to live in a simple, secluded hut in the mountains. Still, many students sought him out for instruction, until in 643 Queen Sŏndŏk requested that Emperor Tai Zong send the famous monk back to Silla. There he was made Kuksa, or "National Preceptor," in effect the head of all monks in Silla. Chajang used his influence to reform the Buddhism of Silla by instituting a four point program: 1) increased scriptural study by monks, 2) monastic examinations on doctrine every six months, 3) establishment of a single ordination center at the T'ongdo Monastery to administer entry into and dismissal from the Saṅgha, and 4) creation of a government bureau to oversee and maintain Buddhist temples and their lands and contents. Because of the third point in his program, Chajang is associated with the Vinaya school, which developed in China and was concerned with monastic discipline and its enforcement.

Ŭisang is remembered as a Master of Hua Yan (Kor. Hwaŏm) Buddhism and a great promoter of monastery and temple building. He failed to reach China on his first attempt in 648-49 — which he made with his friend Wŏnhyo — but he was successful in 650. Once in China, he studied with the second and third patriarchs of the Hua Yan school, Zhi Yan (Chih Yen) and Fa Zang (Fa Tsang). Fa Zang remained a close friend of Ŭisang and corresponded with him after his return to Silla. One famous letter of their correspondence still survives. Ŭisang's dramatic return to Silla occurred in 670 when the monk got wind of a Tang plot to attack Silla and hastened home to warn his king. No doubt partly as a result of this act of loyalty and courage, as well as on the basis of his eminent scholarship, Ŭisang was given permission to construct a total of ten monasteries, making him one of the greatest religious building contractors in history.

The immense importance of Chajang and Ŭisang notwithstanding, Wŏnhyo overshadows both of them in the power of his personality and the lasting influence he exerted upon Korean Buddhism. Wŏnhyo is said to have achieved enlightenment at age 32, while on an unsuccessful journey to China with his friend Ŭisang. One day on this journey, towards nightfall, a sudden storm forced the two monks to seek shelter in a cave. In the dead of night, Wŏnhyo woke up thirsty and, groping in the dark, was delighted to find a bowl of water. He drank eagerly, savoring the water's sweetness. In the morning, however, he discovered that they had actually slept in an opened tomb, and that he had drunk rain water from the partially decomposed crown of a human skull. This experience shocked Wŏnhyo into a vivid realization that all value and repugnance exist only in the mind. This realization Wŏnhyo construed as enlighten-ment, and he returned to Silla, seeing no profit in academic study abroad. The rest of Wŏnhyo's life, which is well attested, reveals a wayward, exuberant personality in keeping with the story of his enlightenment. Wŏnhyo spent a great deal of time wandering among the populace and teaching Buddhism to all and sundry. In his teaching, he performed songs of his own composition, accompanying himself on a lute or by drumming on a gourd. He frequented wine houses and brothels, and in later life had a sexual affair with a royal princess who bore him a son, Sŏl Ch'ong, one of the greatest intellectuals of the Silla period.

In addition to these exploits, Wŏnhyo was a prolific and influential writer of commentaries and treatises on Buddhist scriptures. Of the twen-ty or so extant works attributed to him, the five major works are commen-taries on the *Lotus, Nirvāṇa* and *Diamond Sūtras,* the *Awakening of Faith in the Mahāyāna* (attributed to Aśvaghosha) and a handbook of Bud-dhism for the laity. All of Wŏnhyo's works emphasized the similarities underlying the doctrinal divergences he perceived in Buddhism even before sectarian divisions became evident in Korea. Although Wŏnhyo's conciliatory doctrinal position was influential, the end of Wŏnhyo's life in 686 corresponds roughly with the beginning of the historical period in which distinct schools of Buddhism began to develop separate identities in Korea.

The Silla Period and the Solidification of Buddhist Schools (668-935)

In 589, toward the end of the Three Kingdoms period in Korea, the Sui dynasty accomplished the reunification of China. The Sui ruler imme-diately set about attempting to subdue threatening tribal peoples on Chi-na's northern frontier. These included Koguryŏ, which actually attacked China with considerable force in 598. The resulting warfare exhausted both Koguryŏ and the Sui dynasty, contributing significantly to the rise of the Tang dynasty in 618. Where the Sui dynasty had failed, the Tang succeeded, first by subduing the marauding hordes on China's northern frontier. Tang China then turned its attention to Koguryŏ, finding a will-ing ally in Silla, whose Buddhist-oriented diplomatic efforts began to pay off. Whereas Tang China's greatest enemy in the region was Koguryŏ, Silla's primary enemy was Paekche. A Tang-Silla alliance achieved the fall of Paekche in 660 and the surrender of Koguryŏ in 668.

The fall of Koguryŏ represented to Tang historians the definitive achievement of the perennial ideal of restoring to China the territory controlled at the height of the Han dynasty. In reality, however, Silla absorbed Paekche and retained its independence. In spite of Tang attempts to dominate the entire region, Silla remained in control of the peninsula south of the 39th parallel. Silla thus encompassed roughly the area of present-day South Korea. Meanwhile, the defeated remnant of Koguryŏ eventually joined with subjugated Manchurian tribes and formed the state of Parhae, which endured from 698 until 926. Parhae languished as a buffer state, subservient to the Tang dynasty, between China and independent Silla. It was in Silla that the history of Korea and the history of Buddhism in Korea continued to move forward. The Silla period saw the assimilation of Buddhism in Korea and the foundation of the classical schools of Korean Buddhism.

Traditionally, the first identifiable school of Buddhism in Korea was the Chinese Tian Tai, founded in Paekche by Hyŏn'gwang upon his return from China in 565. This traditional identification is dubious in that Hyŏn'gwang actually studied in China under the teacher of Zhi Yi. Zhi Yi himself later established classical Tian Tai in China after reunification in 589. Nevertheless, this early, eclectic school of Buddhism related to Tian Tai survived Paekche's absorption into Silla and facilitated the establishment of classical Korean Tian Tai in the eighth century. Its early credentials notwithstanding, Tian Tai Buddhism did not attain significant influence in Korea until it gained royal patronage under the Koryŏ dynasty in the tenth century. As in China, this royal favor toward Tian Tai was part of a political program to promote national unity by creating a unified Buddhism as the state ideology.

The second identifiable school of Chinese Buddhism to take root in Korea was Hua Yan, which is based on the mammoth *Avataṃsaka Sūtra*. The reader may recall that this Hua Yan Buddhism was introduced in 670 by Ŭisang, who spent twenty years in China studying with the second and third patriarchs of the school. Related to the Hua Yan school is the Haedong or Pŏpsŏng school, established by Ŭisang's friend Wŏnhyo. Though related to Hua Yan, this school is regarded as an indigenous Korean school because its founder Wŏnhyo did not study under Chinese teachers. Instead, as discussed above, he claimed to have realized enlightenment spontaneously in Korea.

Another school of Silla Buddhism without a Chinese counterpart was the Yŏlban or Nirvāṇa school. This school was named after and inspired by the *Nirvāṇa Sūtra,* a text imported from China by the Koguryŏ monk Podŏk in the seventh century. Podŏk had set out for China while Koguryŏ was still a viable state, but returned after 668 to a peninsula dominated by Silla, a situation to which the adaptable monk seems to have adjusted well. In all, eight monasteries were established for this school under the auspices of Silla. The *Nirvāṇa Sūtra* itself was influential in the thought of both Wŏnhyo and Ŭisang, but the Nirvāṇa school had little lasting influence.

The esoteric Zhen Yan (Chen Yen) or Tantric school — better known by the Japanese name Shingon — was also influential during the Silla period in the form of two sub-schools known in Korean as Shinin and Chinŏn. Traditional records indicate that these schools were associated primarily with the performance of miracles and the curing of disease, which highlights their similarity to Korea's indigenous shamanism. The best known of the Korean promulgators of Tantric Buddhism was the famous traveler Hyech'o. His diary of long years of travel and study in China, India, and Central Asia was rediscovered only in the twentieth century and is now available in English translation.[32]

As noted above, the miraculous, shamanistic elements of Buddhism played an important role in the religion's acceptance in Korea, as did Buddhism's function as the ideological cement of national unity. If the Tantric schools epitomize the shamanistic tendencies of Korean Buddhism, the Vinaya school epitomizes its nationalistic flavor. The monk Chimyŏng, who returned from China in 602, is credited with founding the Vinaya school in Silla, but the eminent Chajang, who returned from China in 643, consolidated the power and influence of the school. As noted above, Chajang was named National Preceptor by the queen and put in charge of an ordination center at the T'ongdo Monastery, which became the only place in the kingdom where one could enter the Saṅgha officially. This arrangement gave the throne at least the appearance of regulating entry into the Saṅgha and sponsoring its activities. The Saṅgha became, in appearance if not in reality, a privileged branch of the civil service. This royal strategy for controling the Saṅgha would be repeated a century later in Japan.

All of these "official" schools, most derived from Chinese precedents, exerted influence primarily among the aristocracy. Meanwhile, the charismatic Wŏnhyo's eclectic brand of Buddhism exerted influence among the masses. Particularly in his later years, Wŏnhyo became passionately concerned with encouraging "Unified Buddhism" (T'ong pulgyo), which he preached enthusiastically among the common people. Wŏnhyo himself epitomizes this unitarian movement. His spontaneous enlightenment experience has a Zen flavor, and his extravagant personal behavior invites comparison with Tantric masters. He is recognized as an intellectual of the Hua Yan school, but is also remembered as a Pure Land evangelist. The fact that Wŏnhyo eschewed study in China makes his eclecticism seem a uniquely Korean product. This personal and nationalistic appeal, combined with his prolific written output, secured for

Wŏnhyo an enduring place among the shapers of Korean Buddhism, as distinct from Buddhism in Korea.

The importation of Chinese schools of Buddhism continued after Wŏnhyo's death in 686, but so did his characteristically Korean, grass-roots movement toward Unified Buddhism. After the reunification of China in 589, the Chinese emperor attempted to unify Buddhism by decree, granting royal favor to the eclectic Tian Tai school. In Korea, by contrast, particularly after Wŏnhyo's career, the various schools of Buddhism developed within the context of a pervasive conviction that associated Buddhism with Korean national identity. Buddhism was unified by definition rather than by decree. This situation tended to blur the doctrinal and scriptural distinctions among the various classical schools of Buddhism as they developed in Korea. Though the machinery of state was organized on largely Confucian principles, by the zenith of Silla in the mid-eighth century, Buddhism was firmly established at the heart of Korean national identity.

Silla reached its zenith under King Kyŏngdŏk (r. 742-65). Immediately afterward, under King Hyegong (r. 765-80), Silla began a decline into oblivion. This decline began with a reassertion of ancient, traditional clan power when a confederation of ninety-six chieftains rebelled against the central government. King Hyegong was eventually murdered and a compromise king installed upon the throne, a move that resulted in con-flicting royal lines of succession and divisions among the aristocracy. The consequent weakness of the central government of Silla provided oppor-tunities for greater, often conflicting assertions of autonomy by clan chief-tains, disaffected aristocrats, wealthy merchants, and notably, Buddhist monasteries. The competing claims of these groups, in turn, placed intol-erable demands upon peasants and led to widespread banditry and peas-ant revolts. This chaos resulted in a brief re-emergence of the old states of Paekche (in 892) and Koguryŏ (in 901). In 918, the unpopular despot of Latter Koguryŏ was ousted by a group of his generals, and the new ruler Wang Kŏn renamed the kingdom Koryŏ, a name derived from Koguryŏ, to evoke continuity with, as well as change from, the old kingdom. With the final collapse of Silla in 935, and the defeat of Latter Paekche in 936, Koryŏ emerged victorious, in name and territory the direct ancestor of modern Korea.

During the declining years of Silla, Chan Buddhism, better known by the Japanese name Zen, gained widespread acceptance in the Korean peninsula. Traditionally, Sŏn Buddhism, as Zen is known in Korean, was introduced to Silla in the mid-seventh century by the monk Pŏmnang, who studied in China under the third successor to Bodhidharma himself. This introduction, then, occurred before the split of Chinese Chan into its northern and southern branches. Neither Pŏmnang nor his immediate disciples gained widespread influence at the time, but one of the nine lineages of Korean Sŏn traces its origins to this initial contact with very early Chan in China. The next seven Sŏn lineages were established in rapid succession during the first half of the ninth century. All seven were founded by Koreans who studied with one or another of the disciples of Ma Zu (Ma Tsu), the second successor of Hui Neng, the founder of the southern school of Chinese Chan. The ninth and last school of Korean Sŏn, known as Sumisan or "Sumi Mountain," was founded in 911 when Iŏm returned from China claiming to represent the northern school of Chan, which died out in China soon thereafter. Together, these Korean lineages are known as the "Nine Mountain" schools because of the location of their principal monasteries on nine sacred mountains in Korea.

The intentional association of these schools of Sŏn Buddhism with sacred mountains emphasizes the importance of incorporating elements of indigenous shamanism into Korean forms of Buddhism. Some have argued that the rapid success of so many schools of Sŏn Buddhism indicates a widespread desire to escape the tumultuous decline of Silla in favor of the quiet, contemplative life of a meditating monk. Equally important was the resemblance of the meditative regimen to the self-imposed ordeals of the traditional shaman. Also, the recurrent theme of Buddhism's association with Korean national identity resurfaces in the close and deliberate association between the founders of Koryŏ and the Sumisan lineage of Sŏn. For these and perhaps other reasons as well, Sŏn Buddhism accomplished a dramatic rise to prominence in the closing years of the Silla monarchy.

The Koryŏ period (918-1392)

King T'aejo, the first ruler of Koryŏ, though associated with the Sumisan school of Korean Sŏn, was careful not to precipitate jealousy and strife by aligning himself too closely with the Sumisan or any other school of Buddhism. As a final measure against favoritism, he issued from his deathbed a ten-point proclamation directing his successors to insure that the property and ceremonies of all forms of Buddhism be maintained at existing levels. T'aejo's successor King Kwangjong, however, openly advocated the Tian Tai school, known in Korean as the Ch'ŏnt'ae school. King Kwangjong looked upon the Ch'ŏnt'ae school as a means of encouraging harmony between Sŏn — which tended to disparage doctrine — and the various doctrinal schools of the realm. Despite its credentials as the earliest identifiable school of Buddhism taught in Korea, Tian Tai or Ch'ŏnt'ae had not to this point achieved in Korea the status or influence of the other doctrinal schools. This very lack of an established power base must have made the school seem an ideal vehicle for reconciliation among the competing power bases of Buddhism. In retrospect it seems predictable that this attempt to impose reconciliation eventually had the effect of creating a three-way power struggle among Sŏn, Ch'ŏnt'ae and the various doctrinal schools.

This power struggle dominated the history of Buddhism in Korea through the tenth and eleventh centuries and most of the twelfth. Throughout this period, the throne remained aligned with the Ch'ŏnt'ae school, while accommodating the still powerful Sŏn lineages on the one hand and the several doctrinal schools on the other. Monks of all schools enjoyed exemption from taxation, military service and conscripted labor. Membership in the Saṅgha afforded the prospect of amassing wealth and political power by gaining entry into the upper echelons of the monastic hierarchy. The lower echelons of the Saṅgha were composed of monk laborers, who specialized in temple construction and the production of Buddhist books and artifacts, and monk warriors who guarded temples and served the nation in time of war. Monasteries presided over large tracts of land, lucrative commercial enterprises and armies of laborers. Once again in its history, Buddhism in eleventh-century Korea had become a state within the state. The inevitably resulting power struggles and intrigues led to a degeneration of the spiritual and moral fiber of Korean Buddhism even while a golden age of Buddhism appeared to have dawned.

Arguably foremost of the many achievements in this golden age of Buddhism was the carving and woodblock printing of the first Korean canon — a forty-year project in some 6,000 volumes, completed in the reign of King Munjong (r. 1046-83). This canon was accompanied by an almost equally voluminous supplement. The monk responsible for compiling this supplement was Ŭich'ŏn (1055-1101), who was also the foremost protagonist in the on-going attempt to harmonize Korean Buddhism under the Ch'ŏnt'ae school. It is illustrative of the close ties between Buddhism and royalty that Ŭich'ŏn was the fourth son of King Munjong and that he lived to see each of his older brothers occupy the throne. Despite his well-deserved prestige and formidable political connections, Ŭich'ŏn too was unable to bring about the unification of Korean Buddhism, which had been an ideal since the time of Wŏnhyo and was a specific objective of the Koryŏ dynasty from its outset.

Ironically, the figure given credit for most effectively unifying Korean Buddhism was not a royal, not a proponent of the Ch'ŏnt'ae school, and apparently was not politically motivated. This figure was the Sŏn monk Chinul (1158-1210), widely regarded as the most influential Buddhist in the history of Korea. The sickly child of a minor official, Chinul entered the Sŏn order as a novice at age seven. After almost twenty years of scriptural study and meditation — mostly undertaken in solitude and without the benefit of a permanent teacher — Chinul proceeded to the capital and passed the monastic examinations. This opened the way to the upper echelons of the Saṅgha and political and economic success. Instead, Chinul and several other young monks became disillusioned, opted out of the ecclesiastical system, and formed an independent Buddhist society. This society, modeled on similar societies popular in Song China at the time, was open to both lay and ordained members. Chinul's was probably the first such society in Korea. Its name, the Samādhi and Prajñā (Meditation and Wisdom) Society, reveals Chinul's conviction that true Buddhist practice involves equal measures of meditation and doctrinal study.

Eight years passed before the small group of monks, which had dwindled to three or four, was able to find in 1190 a monastery in which to undertake their practice. During the intervening period of wandering, Chinul underwent two enlightenment experiences. From these he concluded that the key to an ideal Buddhism lay in harmonization of Sŏn meditational practice with Hwaŏm doctrine. It will be remembered that the Hwaŏm school (Chi. Hua Yan) is distinct from but doctrinally similar to the Ch'ŏnt'ae (Chi. Tian Tai) school, which was the focus of unsuccessful royal attempts to unify Buddhism in Koryŏ. By 1197, Chinul's following had grown to such an extent that it was necessary to move the society's headquarters. In the course of this move, Chinul went into a three-year retreat during which he achieved his third and final experience of enlightenment. By the time the new and very extensive society complex was completed in 1205, Chinul had attracted royal favor, and King Hŭijong (r. 1204-1211) declared 120 days of national celebration in honor of the opening of the complex, known as the Susŏn or "Sŏn Cultivation" Monastery. Throughout the Koryŏ dynasty, and indeed to the present day, the Susŏn Monastery, later known as the Songwang Monastery, remained a major center of Korean Buddhism.

The first three centuries of the Koryŏ dynasty saw the construction of many other grand monasteries and a flourishing of Buddhist art. Literature of all sorts — Buddhist, Confucian, artistic and academic — proliferated and was widely disseminated. This was possible largely because of the development of metal type, a Korean invention that is arguably the ancestor of the fifteenth century European development of movable type by Johannes Gutenberg. All this apparent prosperity, however, masked a deep unrest within an exploited populace and divisive ambitions among the monks, military and aristocracy. During this golden age, Kim Pu-sik (1075-1151), wrote his *Samguk Sagi* or *History of the Three Kingdoms,* one of the foremost sources of traditional Korean history. Kim Pu-sik is also a national hero credited with saving the dynasty from a rebellion. This rebellion was the second in the reign of King Injong, whose successor, King Ŭijong (r. 1122-46), was deposed by a military coup in favor of his brother, a move which obliterated all but the appearance of centralized government. Part of early Koryŏ's problems were external in origin, as the Mongol Liao dynasty of northeastern China invaded the peninsula three times — in 993, 1010 and 1018. As a result, Koryŏ's leaders became obsessed with the threat of invasion. Actual invasions and constant preparations for possible invasions placed further burdens on the general population in the form of taxation, military service and forced labor. Such labor was conscripted not only to build actual fortifications, but also for Buddhist construction projects intended to protect the nation super-naturally.

None of these preparations — supernatural or military — could save the divided country from a devastating series of six Mongol invasions between 1231 and 1258. These rampages were so thoroughly destructive that most of the few surviving artifacts representing Korean culture before the Mongol invasions are artifacts that were exported to Japan and are now housed in Japanese museums. Koryŏ finally surrendered formally to the Mongols in 1258, and became the staging point for two unsuccessful Mongol assaults on Japan in 1274 and 1281. The Koryŏ dynasty remained nominally in power as a puppet government representing the Yuan emperor in Beijing, but the peninsula was a lawless and exploited, frontier province of China until the fall of the Yuan dynasty in 1368 and its replacement by the Ming dynasty. Shortly thereafter, in 1392, the general Yi Sŏng-gye led a rebellion which deposed the last of the Koryŏ kings and placed himself on the throne as founder of the Chosŏn dynasty, which would endure until the twentieth century.

After the Mongol invasions, the one shining achievement of Koryŏ was the creation of the Restored Koryŏ Tripiṭaka to replace the first Korean canon and supplement that had been destroyed by the Mongols. This restored canon was based on the Liao and Northern Song dynasty Chinese editions. Now known simply as the Korean Tripiṭaka, it is the most complete and accurate of the several extant block print editions of the Buddhist scriptures in Chinese characters. In the twentieth century it was chosen by Japanese scholars as the basis of the authoritative Taishō

Tripiṭaka, which is in turn the basis of virtually all modern scholarship on Chinese Buddhist scriptures.

The Chosŏn Period (1392-1910)

Partly out of conviction, partly out of a desire to emphasize a break with the past, and partly to curb the divisive influence of the Saṅgha, General Yi Sŏng-gye, who was enthroned as King T'aejo (r. 1392-1398), declared himself and the new dynasty Confucian. Until the Mongol period, Confucianism and Buddhism in Korea had coexisted in relative harmony — Buddhism being recognized as the state ideology and Confucianism as the organizational basis of government. As such, the two religions occasionally came into conflict, but Buddhism had the upper hand so long as the peninsula remained free of foreign domination. The Mongol subjugation and humiliation of the peninsula, however, represented the failure of Buddhism as a supernatural protector of the nation. Moreover, the chaotic conditions under Mongol domination resulted in interminable power struggles and intrigues in which the Buddhist clergy played a mostly self-serving role that alienated the sincerely patriotic and reform-minded. In the meantime, Confucianism had been revitalized by the neo-Confucian movement in China, represented in Korea by a series of talented, radical young scholars.

The establishment of a Confucian dynasty associated with national liberation marked the beginning of a long period of decline in the influence of Buddhism in Korea. The first Chosŏn monarch, King T'aejo, was respectful of Buddhism, but the fifteenth century saw the closure of temples on a massive scale — under Kings T'aejong (r. 1400-18) and Sejong (r. 1418-50) — until only thirty-six significant temples remained. King Sejong also decreed the merger of all the doctrine-oriented schools into a conglomeration known as the Kyo or "Doctrinal" school. Half of the thirty-six remaining temples were assigned to this artificially created Kyo school, and the other half to a forcibly unified Sŏn school. This act of suppression marks the beginning of the uniquely Korean division of Buddhism into Kyo and Sŏn — "Doctrine" and "Meditation." In an ironic way, these repressive consolidations represent the culmination of a centuries-long campaign to harmonize Korean Buddhism.

Following this suppression of Buddhism, there were a few brief periods of revival, most notably under King Myŏngjong (r. 1545-67), the only Buddhist monarch of the Chosŏn dynasty. On the whole, however, Buddhism declined steadily while Korean Confucianism entered its golden age. This golden age began to tarnish at the end of the sixteenth century, when the Japanese invaded the peninsula twice — in 1592 and 1597. Both invasions were wantonly destructive of Korea's cultural treasures and left the kingdom economically devastated and culturally demoralized. To make matters worse, the coup-ridden country was soon drawn into a conflict between Ming China and Manchuria and was invaded twice by Manchurian forces in 1627 and 1637.

Also at the end of the sixteenth century, Western thought began to penetrate Korea through the work of Jesuit missionaries active in China. This Christian thought, which in true Jesuit fashion contained a large admixture of scientific and historical scholarship, came to be known in Korea as Sirhak or "Practical Knowledge." This "Practical Knowledge," particularly in the realms of agriculture, technology and economics, seemed to many Koreans to hold the key to revitalization of the ailing nation, beset by an extraordinary series of epidemics and famines as well as riots, rebellions, widespread banditry and mass starvation.

By the end of the nineteenth century, the Western-inspired modernization movement, in conjunction with the apparent failure of Confucianism, resulted in a royal suppression of Confucianism as thorough as the fifteenth-century suppression of Buddhism. Like the Buddhist temples before them, in 1871 all but forty-seven of the nation's Confucian academies were closed by royal decree. At the dawn of the twentieth century, both of Korea's traditional ideologies — Buddhism and Confucianism — had reached their nadir. The year 1871 also marked the conclusion of a five-year repression of Christianity, known as the Great Persecution, during which nine Catholic priests and some 8,000 lay followers were executed — fully half of the Christians in Korea. This was the last of a series of six major and innumerable minor repressions of Catholicism in the nineteenth century, all of which were portrayed as measures to prevent foreign infiltration, in keeping with the Chosŏn dynasty's overall policy of radical isolationism.

These persecutions of Christianity, however, served to excuse rather than to prevent foreign interference. In 1866 French warships briefly entered Korean waters to avenge their missionaries, and in 1871 the United States sent a flotilla in response to the sinking of an American merchant vessel. Both incursions were in part attempts to force Korea into trade and diplomatic relations. The real power struggle for the peninsula, however, was a three-way contest among China, Russia and Japan. Japan emerged victorious after defeating the Chinese in 1895 and the Russians in 1905. In 1910, Korea was annexed to Japan, and the five-hundred-year-old Chosŏn dynasty came to a close forever, as did an almost two thousand year tradition of dynastic kingship in Korea.

The Modern Period (1910-Present)

The Japanese overlords of Korea embarked on a hated policy of "Japanization" of the peninsula. Koreans of all religious persuasions resisted Japan's "cultural genocide" in the peninsula. As a result, all religions suffered under the Japanese. Buddhism, however, found itself in a particularly delicate position. The Japanese, being themselves Buddhists, attempted to impose a revival of Buddhism in Korea. At the same time, the Buddhist Saṅgha, being a focus of Korean resistance, was actually a target of suppression, and many monks were forced out. While Buddhism suffered as much as other religions in Korea, the Japanese show of support for Buddhism tended to associate Buddhism with the hated foreign overlords. In all, Japanese attempts to "revive" Buddhism in Korea were more a curse than a blessing for the religion.

At the conclusion of World War II in 1945, Japan surrendered northern Korea to the Soviet Union and southern Korea to the United States, the two Koreas being divided at the 38th parallel of latitude. This division, though ostensibly temporary, has in fact remained absolute until the present day. There are few promising signs of a reunification of North and South Korea, though unity remains the perennial ideal of virtually all Koreans. Under an extraordinarily repressive communist regime in North Korea, Buddhism and indeed all religions appear to have entered a state of oblivion. The Korean War of 1950-53, in which the United States backed South Korea, saw the replacement of Soviet by Chinese communists as the primary sponsors of North Korea, but no relief of the religious black-out in the North. Given the resurgent state of religion immediately prior to 1945, it seems certain that pent-up religious aspirations still exist in the north. For the time being, however, reliable information on the condition of religion in North Korea is unobtainable.

The religious exuberance of South Korea, by contrast, is renowned. According to the 1989 census of the Ministry of Cultural Information, about sixty percent of South Koreans do not identify themselves with any organized religion. Of course many of these do participate regularly in the shamanistic folk practices which have always pervaded Korean life. Of the forty percent of South Koreans who claim to follow an organized religion, roughly half are Buddhist and half Christian. In addition, about two percent of the population listed Confucianism as their religion, and a further two percent listed another of the world's established religions — including Greek Orthodoxy, Islam, Baha'i, and Mormonism — or one of Korea's "new religions." Of Korea's new religions, the large majority are new forms of Buddhism. Eighteen sects of Buddhism are recognized in Korea's census. Of these, twelve originated in the twentieth century. Of these twelve, eight are post–World War II phenomena. The number of new forms of Buddhism increases dramatically when forms of Buddhism not recognized in the census are counted.

By the end of the Chosŏn dynasty in 1910, Buddhism in Korea was at a low ebb, and most of the twentieth century has offered little relief. Today, Korea cannot accurately be termed a Buddhist country — particularly if North Korea is included in the assessment. Buddhism in South Korea, however, appears to be enjoying a modest revival at the close of the twentieth century. In conclusion, it appears that Buddhism has survived its worst times in Korea and will continue as a major element in the self-understanding and self-definition of the Korean people and a major inspiration in their continued quest for autonomy and unity.

CHAPTER X

The Development of
Buddhism in Japan

This narrative now returns to the time of Emperor Wen (r. 581-604), who reunited China and founded the Sui dynasty. While Emperor Wen ruled in China, Japan entered an era of enthusiastic assimilation of Chinese culture initiated by Prince Shōtoku (573-621), who came to power in 593. Shōtoku's first act as prince regent was to proclaim Buddhism the official religion of Japan. This proclamation definitively ended a period of some fifty years of strife in Japan between between pro- and anti-Chinese factions. The Japanese, of course, had long been aware of the existence of their much larger neighbor to the west. Being an island people, however, they had remained relatively isolated from Chinese influence, much more so than the Koreans, who are racially and linguistically related to the Japanese. The strait dividing the Korean peninsula from Japan is only about one hundred miles wide, and for several centuries before Shōtoku there had been steady contact between the two peoples. As a result of this contact with Korea, and through Korea with the advanced civilization of Han China, Japan developed rapidly during the early centuries of the common era.

Buddhism was formally introduced to Japan in about 550 by a delegation from the Korean kingdom of Paekche, Japan's ally against the Korean kingdom of Silla. The delegation included Buddhist monks bearing scriptures and works of art. This dramatic revelation of the attainments of Japan's continental neighbors split the existing political powers into two camps: those who favored the importation of foreign culture, and those who opposed it. Symbolically, the dispute was expressed in terms of allegiance to Buddhism versus allegiance to Shintō, the indigenous religion of Japan. As one would expect, the military and the priesthood opposed foreign incursion and foreign religion and thus became allies. The statesmen and intelligentsia, on the other hand, saw assimilation of Chinese culture as inevitable and desirable. In the end, the supporters of assimilation prevailed, though Japanese culture remained distinct, and Shintō remains to the present day a ubiquitous feature of that culture.

The twentieth-century Western world has witnessed first-hand the remarkable capacity of the Japanese to switch dramatically from rejecting to embracing foreign ideas and yet maintain a separate cultural identity. Having fought the United States fiercely during the second World War, the Japanese in two decades became economically more American than the Americans. Nonetheless, they remain unmistakably Japanese. Shōtoku's embracing of Buddhism heralded the beginning of a similarly remarkable period of Japanese assimilation of foreign influence. Buddhism was the banner under which Chinese culture and civilization became established in Japan, while Japan remained distinctively Japanese.

Shintō and Indigenous Japanese Culture

Little is known of the origins of the Japanese people. Racially, they are primarily Mongoloid. The Japanese language belongs to the Altaic family, of which Korean and Mongolian are also members. The Stone Age did not end in Japan until the first century CE. Japan more or less skipped the Bronze Age, however, importing from Korea the Iron Age technology of Han dynasty China. It is noteworthy that China had entered the Bronze Age by approximately 1500 BCE. This situation illustrates both the isolation of Japan from the mainland and the importance of Korea as a conduit for the transmission of Chinese civilization to Japan. Like their racial and linguistic relatives the Koreans, the Japanese also have strived to maintain a separate cultural identity in the face of the sheer mass of Chinese civilization.

Japan enters history via the Chinese chronicles, with the mention of a Japanese delegation to the Han court in 57 CE. This delegation, the members of which were heavily tattooed and carried bone-tipped arrows, must have amused their Chinese hosts, but their mission was deadly serious. At this time, Japan was a relatively primitive tribal culture, but some of the southwestern tribes, those in closest contact with the Koreans, had begun to develop the concept of empire and were seeking the techniques and technology of their more advanced neighbors in order to pursue it.

Each of the various Japanese clans, known as *uji,* was associated with a primary deity, or *kami,* which served to identify the clan. The chief of each tribe was simultaneously the high priest of the clan *kami.* As the southwestern tribes began to dominate the others, largely as a result of their contacts with the mainland, the resulting political hierarchy was symbolically represented by a similar hierarchy of deities. By the fifth century, the Yamato clan had gained sufficient supremacy to establish their own tribal deity, Amaterasu the goddess of the sun, as the supreme deity of Japan. The deities of other clans were ranked below Amaterasu according to the status of the tribes they represented. Similarly, the clan chieftains were ranked below the Yamato ruler — in theory if not always in political reality. Widespread acceptance of this state of affairs, combined with traditional recognition of the clan chieftain as the high priest of the clan deity, eventually resulted in the mythical identification of the Yamato clan chieftains as descendants of the sun goddess. As a result, to the present day the emperor of Japan is a descendant of the ancient Yamato chieftains, is regarded by many as a descendant of the sun, and is thereby considered divine.

The indigenous religion of Japan was a conglomeration of tribal cults without any central doctrine. Nonetheless, these cults had enough cohesiveness and general similarity to rouse widespread resistance to the introduction of Buddhism. It was only in the course of this resistance that the term Shintō, meaning "Way of the Gods," was coined to differentiate indigenous Japanese religion from its perceived rival, Buddhism. Shintō may be generally described as a deification of Japan and the Japanese way of life, reflected in observance of Japanese traditions, patriotic allegiance to Japan, and a nature-based polytheism expressing appreciation of the natural beauty of Japan.

The central concept unifying Shintō is that of *kami,* often translated as "spirit" or "deity," but probably better translated with an adjective as "powerful." Deities, to be sure, are *kami,* but impressive natural features such as mountains, trees and rock formations may also be *kami.* Useful items such as a tool, a weapon or a cooking pot may be regarded as *kami.* People too may be *kami,* especially dead people. Impressive living people as well may be *kami,* most notably an emperor or the high priest of a clan, but also a class of people known as *miko* or "shaman." The *miko* were thought to be able to communicate with and influence the supernatural world of the *kami,* and thus bring prosperity and avert catastrophe in this world. These two Shintō concepts — *kami* and *miko* — eventually had considerable influence upon the development of specifically Japanese Buddhism as opposed to the Buddhism that was imported from China and Korea.

The *miko* developed her powers — and most if not all spirit mediums in ancient Japan were women — through techniques typical of shamans everywhere. These included ordeals of fasting, isolation and physical pain — particularly ordeals of cold, like standing under a waterfall in winter — as well as arduous sacred journeys to places of power, and incessant repetition of magical spells. These exercises were thought to develop the *miko's* ability to influence the realm of *kami,* particularly the spirits of the dead. The *miko* were highly respected, if somewhat dreaded members of ancient Japanese society. Their lasting impression on the Japanese psyche is evident in the specifically Japanese forms of Buddhism that developed out of the religion as introduced from China and Korea.

The Introduction of Chinese Buddhism to Japan:

Shōtoku through the Nara Period (593-784)

Prince Shōtoku's embracing of Buddhism was not altogether a religious affair, though there is little doubt that he was a sincere Buddhist. His conversion also marked the beginning of a continuing movement toward the Chinese system of government and bureaucracy. As centralized government became established in Japan under Shōtoku's successors, the need for a permanent capital arose. The first such capital was established at Nara in 710. Historians commonly refer to the period between the ascendancy of Shōtoku in 593 and the abandoning of Nara as capital in 794 as the Nara period, even though the capital was actually at Nara during only the latter half of this period. The reason for this convention is that in 607 Shōtoku established in Nara an important Buddhist center of worship and learning known as the Hōryū-ji, so that Nara was an important center of Buddhism and culture in Japan long before it was the capital. The Hōryū-ji and other nearby Buddhist temples served as centers not only for the propagation of Buddhist learning, but also for the propagation of Chinese civilization and culture in general, the art of writing in particular. By the end of the Nara period, six schools of Buddhism derived from the classical Chinese schools had been established in Japan.

1. THE SANRON SCHOOL, equivalent to the Chinese San Lun or Madhyamaka school, is generally regarded as the first real school of Buddhism to be introduced into Japan. It was established in 625 by a Korean monk known in Japanese as Ekan. Ekan studied in China the three treatises by Nāgārjuna and Āryadeva from which the school derives its name. According to tradition, another, earlier Korean monk known in Japanese as Eji, who was Shōtoku's teacher, brought Sanron teachings to Japan as early as 595.

2. THE JŌJITSU SCHOOL, a branch of the Chinese Ju She or Abhidharma school of Nikāya Buddhism, was also founded in 625 by the Korean monk Ekan. Though the Abhidharma and the Madhyamaka schools were arch-rivals in India, in Japan they were

scarcely distinguished, probably because they shared a founder in Ekan. Neither the Sanron nor the Jōjitsu school survived through the Nara period in Japan. Nāgārjuna, however, is still widely studied and venerated in Japan as a Buddhist saint and scholar.

3. THE KUSHA SCHOOL was founded in 658 by the Japanese monks Chitsu and Chitatsu, who had studied its doctrines in China. It corresponds to the main-line Ju She school of Chinese Buddhism, and it is thus related to the Jōjitsu school mentioned above. Like its Chinese counterpart, the Kusha school is named after and based upon the *Abhidharma Kośa* of Vasubandhu. As in China, this Japanese Abhidharma school was absorbed into the Mahāyānist Vijñānavāda or "Consciousness school" because of Vasubandhu's authorship of the primary texts of both schools.

4. THE HOSSŌ SCHOOL of Japanese Buddhism corresponds to the Chinese Wei Shi or Consciousness school. It was established in Japan in approximately 653 by the Japanese monk Dōshō (628-700), who studied in China with the great pilgrim and translator Xuan Zang, who in turn had studied in India with teachers in a direct line of transmission from Vasubandhu himself. Dōshō was the most influential monk in seventh-century Japan, largely because his teachings were so up to date with the vogue in China. Following Dōshō as patriarch of the Hossō school was another remarkable Japanese monk, Gyōgi (670-749). It was Gyōgi who initiated the Ryōbu or "Double Aspect" Shintō movement which sought to identify Buddhist and Shintō deities and thus to dovetail the two religions. Largely through the efforts of these two monks, the Hossō school eclipsed all of the schools previously introduced into Japan and dominated the Buddhism of the Nara period until the ascendancy of the Kegon school in the eighth century.

5. THE KEGON SCHOOL, equivalent to the Hua Yan or Avataṃsaka school in China, was the first Japanese school of Buddhism founded by a Chinese missionary. Known to the Japanese as Dōsen (702-60), this missionary brought extensive commentaries on the *Avataṃsaka Sūtra* to Japan in 736. A few years later, the Kegon school was consolidated by the Korean monk Jinjō (d. 742), who gave a three-year series of lectures on the *Avataṃsaka Sūtra*. This lecture series was the premier intellectual event of the time and was attended by most of the Buddhist priesthood of Nara.

Unlike the Chinese Avataṃsaka school, the Japanese school emphasized the mythological aspects of the teaching over the philosophical. Supposedly the *Avataṃsaka Sūtra* was originally delivered by the celestial Buddha Vairocana, whose name means

"Radiant Buddha" and who is associated with the sun in Buddhist mythology. According to the Kegon school, Vairocana represents the supreme, omnipresent principle of Buddhahood, of which all other Buddhas, bodhisattvas and deities are but manifestations. This doctrine is the mythological counterpart of the Hua Yan philosophical doctrine of "interpenetration" whereby all phenomena are manifest in every individual phenomenon. Images of Vairocana typically portray him as sitting on a great lotus flower, each petal of which represents an entire universe encompassing myriad world systems presided over by innumerable Buddhas. Such symbolism was potent in Japan, especially considering the impetus given by Gyōgi to the identification of Buddhist and Shintō deities. Naturally, Vairocana was identified with Amaterasu, the Shintō sun goddess, and in turn with the emperor. The many universes and worlds represented by the petals of Vairocana's lotus throne were associated with the Japanese clans and the many Shintō deities.

6. THE RITSU SCHOOL, equivalent to the Chinese Lü or Vinaya school, was established in Japan in 753 by an astoundingly devoted and persistent Chinese monk known in Japan as Ganjin (688-763). Like the Vinaya school in China, the Ritsu school in Japan eschewed the subtleties of Buddhist doctrine and ignored sectarian divisions in Buddhism. The school concentrated instead on promoting strict monastic discipline and proper ordination procedures. Nonetheless, it should be noted that Ganjin is given credit for introducing the scriptures of Tian Tai Buddhism into Japan. Though Ganjin himself did not attempt to promote these teachings, their presence in Japan was to have momentous effects in the following century.

It was Japanese concern with proper ordination procedures in particular that resulted in the establishment of the Vinaya school in Japan. Having been pressed by Japanese monks on pilgrimage in China, Ganjin agreed to travel to Japan in order to institute formally legitimate ordination procedures. He set out in 742 on what was to be the first of five ill-fated attempts to reach Japan. On this first journey, his ship was confiscated by pirates. The next two sailings were beaten back by storms. The fourth attempt was prohibited by Chinese authorities reluctant to part with such an eminent monk. On Ganjin's fifth attempt to reach Japan, his ship was wrecked and many on board died of drowning or exposure. Finally, in 753, Ganjin landed safely in Japan. By this time he was sixty-six years old and blind.

Ganjin was received in Nara with great fanfare and given complete control over the ordination of Buddhist monks in Japan.

The Empress Kōken organized and presided over a grand ordination ceremony in which some 400 aspirants were simultaneously
inducted into the Saṅgha. Thereafter, she decreed, monks could be
ordained only at one of three Ritsu ordination centers, regardless of
the school to which they belonged. This arrangement had the effect
of establishing Buddhism as the state religion of Japan, with admission to the Saṅgha controlled by the throne. This policy remained
in effect until the end of the Nara period, making the Ritsu school
an influential Buddhist institution in Japan, even though it
professed no particular doctrines of its own.

Under the patronage of the emperor Shōmu (r. 724-49), the Kegon
school became the most influential form of Buddhism in the Nara period.
In 741, Shōmu ordered the establishment of an imperially sanctioned
Kegon monastery in each of the sixty-six provinces of Japan. These
branch monasteries were to be coordinated by the magnificent Tōdai
Temple in Nara, the greatest temple yet built in Japan. In its original
grandeur, it is thought to be the largest wooden structure ever built. The
focus of the Tōdai Temple was a statue of Vairocana that was fifty-three
feet high, still one of the largest bronze images ever cast.

Work on the great Buddha image began in 744, but the initial attempt
had to be abandoned due to lack of sufficient expertise in Japan to overcome the technical difficulties inherent in such a mammoth casting
project. After several more failures, the casting was finally completed
under the direction of a Korean expert in 749. The finished image, cast in
forty segments, contained over a million pounds of metal. Upon completion of the image, Shōmu ordered a lavish ceremony of thanksgiving in
which he and the entire court processed in state to the Tōdai Temple and
ranged themselves before the great Buddha image in the position of subjects at an audience with their sovereign. Shōmu then had a minister read
out a declaration proclaiming the emperor to be the servant of the Triple
Gem of Buddhism — the Buddha, the Dharma and the Saṅgha. Such a
declaration by the emperor of Japan, himself supposed to be the high
priest of the Shintō goddess Amaterasu, was indeed remarkable.

Shortly after making this momentous proclamation, Emperor Shōmu
abdicated in order to become a Buddhist monk and was succeeded by his
daughter the Empress Kōken, who presided over the actual consecration
of the Tōdai Temple and the great Buddha image in 752. This extravagant
ceremony, the grandest of its type ever seen in Japan, involved some
10,000 monks in the capital and was accompanied by coordinated ceremonies at the sixty-six provincial monasteries of the Kegon school. The
political symbolism of these events is clear. The great bronze Vairocana,

associated with the imperial throne, sat in Nara atop a sixty-six-petaled lotus representing the provinces of Japan. In 754, just over a year after the great consecration in Nara, Empress Kōken presided over the establishment of centralized, imperially sanctioned ordination procedures under the Ritsu school — a further integration of Buddhism into the imperial system of Japan.

From the time of Emperor Shōmu onward, the identification of Shintō gods as lesser aspects of Buddhist deities continued. Buddhist monks began to take part regularly in Shintō ceremonies and even to act as caretakers for Shintō shrines. This process of assimilation continued over the years, furthered by subsequently established forms of Japanese Buddhism, until there were relatively few purely Shintō shrines remaining in Japan, and hardly a Buddhist temple that did not shelter at least one Shintō shrine in its precincts. This remarkably successful absorption of Shintō by Buddhism, counterbalanced by the continuing distinct identity of Shintō embedded in Buddhism, remains a notable feature of modern Japanese religion.

The Heian Period (794-1185)

Despite Empress Kōken's politically astute leadership and her obvious dedication to Buddhism, her indiscretion eventually brought to a head conditions that resulted in the removal of the Japanese capital from Nara to Kyōto. As was expected of her, the empress abdicated as soon as there was a suitably mature male heir to the throne. The ceremonial transference of power occurred in 758, but in actuality Empress Kōken continued to rule Japan from behind the scenes. In this enterprise, her chief advisor was a Buddhist monk named Dōkyo, who also became her lover. The ever-increasing influence of the Buddhist Saṅgha at court, at the expense of the influence of the powerful clans, had piqued many chieftains. The ominous and scandalous alliance between the empress and a monk provided the spark that ignited rebellion in 765. The rebellion was crushed, and when Kōken died in 770 Dōkyo was banished. Still, an indelible impression had been made at court: Buddhism was too influential in Nara for the good of the Japanese state and its secular supporters, the various powerful clans.

One more emperor served out his reign in Nara before the capital was moved in 784, first temporarily to Nagaoka and then in 794 to Kyōto, auspiciously known at the time as Heian Kyō, the "Capital of Peace and Tranquillity," hence the term "Heian period." Kyōto remained the official capital of Japan until 1868, when the capital was moved to Tōkyō. Long before this, however, the emperor in Kyōto had ceased to govern Japan directly. The term "Heian period" refers only to the four centuries from 794 to 1185, when Kyōto was the actual center of Japanese government. In general, the Heian period was the period in which the Japanese turned their efforts to digesting and consolidating what they had learned from the Chinese in the Nara period. Written Japanese, heretofore a cumbersome adaptation of monosyllabic Chinese characters to the poly-syllabic Japanese language, was augmented with a quasi-alphabetic script that made writing Japanese much easier. As a result, a Japanese style of literature began to develop independently of Chinese prototypes. In the visual arts, both religious and secular, the ornate extravagance typical of Chinese art and architecture gave way to the elegant simplicity still associated with Japan. The typical Japanese love of nature surfaced in the art of landscape gardening, at which the Japanese remain the acknowledged world masters. Religiously, two new schools of Buddhism emerged and became dominant in Japan during the Heian period, the Tendai and Shingon schools. These schools, like the six Nara schools, were derived from Chinese prototypes and founded on the basis of contacts with the mainland. Unlike their Nara forebears, they began to develop specifically Japanese characteristics in doctrine and practice. As a result, they eclipsed the Nara schools entirely. Virtually all subsequent Japanese Buddhism derived from the Tendai and Shingon schools of the Heian period.

1. THE TENDAI SCHOOL derived from the Chinese Tian Tai school of Zhi Yi, which sought to harmonize Buddhist doctrine by means of the "five periods" and the "eight teachings." The founder of the Japanese school, Saichō (766-822), was born the son of a Chinese immigrant in a remote village at the base of Mt. Hiei, near present-day Kyōto. From this unlikely beginning, he became the first Japanese monk in history to be granted the title Daishi, "Great Teacher," by the emperor. As a result he is better known by his posthumous title Dengyō Daishi.

After studying Sanron, Hossō and Kegon Buddhism from an early age, Saichō was ordained in Nara in 785 at the age of nineteen, even though he had already become disenchanted with the political ambition and intrigue of the great monasteries in the capital. Perhaps emboldened by the fact that Emperor Kammu (r. 781-806) had already abandoned Nara in 784, Saichō did not take up residence in a Nara temple, but retired to a hut on Mt. Hiei, overlooking his birthplace. After three years, he and a small band of followers built a humble monastery on the site of his hut.

The solitude and simplicity of their lives did not last long, for in 794, the capital of Japan was moved to the foot of his mountain retreat and Saichō came into immediate prominence as the favored monk of Emperor Kammu. Saichō objected to precisely the same characteristics of Nara Buddhism which had necessitated removal of the throne, namely corruption, rivalry and political ambition among the Saṅgha. Moreover, the emperor's geomancers (diviners thought to be able to read portents in the landscape) determined that Mt. Hiei marked one of the "demon gates" through which malevolent forces could enter the new capital. Such magical weak spots, it was thought, had to be guarded by supernatural means, and it was thought that Saichō's monastery on Mt. Hiei was an auspicious sign.

Emperor Kammu paid an official visit to Saichō during the first year of his reign in Kyōto and immediately began to bestow upon him lavish support for the development of his monastery. Saichō's humble monastery quickly developed into a grand complex of temples, monastic colleges and monks' quarters and was officially proclaimed "Chief Seat of Religion for Insuring the Security of the Country."

In order to encourage harmony among the schools of Buddhism in Japan, Saichō began to develop a strategy based on the Chinese Tian Tai system. Tian Tai scriptures had been brought to Japan 150 years earlier by Ganjin, the Chinese founder of the Ritsu or Vinaya school in Japan. Eager to promote harmony among the Buddhist schools of Japan, the emperor sent Saichō to China with a political delegation in 804 so that he might study with Chinese masters of the Tian Tai school. His return in 805 marks the official founding in Japan of the Tendai school, the name of which is a Japanese pronunciation of Tian Tai.

The basic doctrines of the Chinese and Japanese Tendai are the same, as is their reverence for the *Lotus Sūtra,* but Saichō emphasized the mystical and esoteric aspects of Buddhism more than was common in Chinese Tian Tai. Saichō's primary goal was to harmonize the various schools of Buddhism in Japan. For this reason, Saichō's own distinctive elaboration of Tendai Buddhism included in addition to the "five periods" of doctrine, a fourfold classification of practice intended to be exhaustive of Buddhism as practiced in Japan. The four categories were: 1) morality, 2) monastic discipline, 3) esoteric practices, and 4) meditation. The last two categories encompass the preponderance of Buddhist practice as it developed in Japan and reveal Saichō's distinctly Japanese orientation.

Much of the esoterism of Tendai Buddhism was doubtless absorbed from the truly esoteric Shingon school, but Saichō himself was deeply committed to the primary hallmark of esoteric or Tantric Buddhism, namely the mystery of initiation. In Tantric Buddhism, the content of religious knowledge is no more important, perhaps even less important, than the mode of transmission of knowledge, i.e. the initiation process. For Saichō, ordination into the Saṅgha was in fact an initiation into the mystery of complete identity with the omnipresent Dharma-kāya Buddha, and thereby identity with the entire universe. This doctrine brought him into radical conflict with the Nara priesthood when in 818 Saichō petitioned the throne to allow him to establish a fourth ordination center, in addition to the three centers established by Empress Kōken under the control of the Ritsu school. All of the Nara schools banded together to prevent Saichō's ordination center, and Saichō spent the last years of his life in an acrimonious and unsuccessful struggle with his opponents in Nara. Saichō was held in such high official and popular esteem, however, that when he died in 822, permission for the Tendai ordination center was granted in his memory within a week of his death.

2. THE SHINGON SCHOOL, derived from the Chinese Zhen Yan or Tantric school, was founded in Japan by Saichō's younger contemporary Kūkai (773-835), who also received the title Daishi from the emperor and is thus often referred to as Kōbō Daishi. In contrast to Saichō, Kūkai was born into one of the great aristocratic families of Japan. Initially he was trained to enter government service. His family's political intrigues, which implicated them in the murder of a high-ranking opponent, may have influenced his decision to enter the Saṅgha. As a monk, he became a renowned calligrapher and a brilliant scholar of Confucianism and Daoism as well as Buddhism. As a result, Kūkai was sent to China in 804 with the same imperial delegation that hosted Saichō, though he traveled on a different ship. His diary records the hazardous nature of such voyages at this early date and reminds one of the courage and dedication of these early Japanese pilgrims in search of true Buddhism. Kūkai returned to Japan in 806, a year after Saichō.

While in China, Kūkai studied Zhen Yan or Chinese Tantric Buddhism at the renowned Qing Long Temple in Xi'an with Hui Guo (Hui Kuo), the direct disciple of Amoghavajra, the third great Chinese Tantric Master. He also studied the Sanskrit language with Indian monks in China, an important consideration in Tantric

Buddhism because most of the magical incantations (*mantras*) occur in Sanskrit. These incantations cannot be effectively translated, because the very sounds of a *mantra* are supposed to contain the true power inherent in the incantation. As a result of this training in Sanskrit, Kūkai is said to have invented a phonetic script for Japanese, a development which greatly facilitated the flowering of Japanese literature in the Heian period.

Kūkai returned from China in 806 just after the death of Emperor Kammu, Saichō's benefactor. This situation left the way open for the establishment of a second great school of Buddhism in the capital. Emperor Saga (r. 806-24), Kammu's successor, may have promoted Kūkai in part as a counterbalance to the influence of Saichō's Tendai school, but there is little doubt that Saga and Kūkai were genuinely close. The emperor was an aficionado of literature and calligraphy, and Kūkai was a prime mover in both fields. Saga and Kūkai are supposed to have received together Shintō initiation rites, and Kūkai himself initiated the emperor into the Shingon school. The receipt of Shintō initiation by Kūkai is particularly significant in that it was he and his followers who pursued most vigorously and effectively the integration of Shintō and Buddhism by encouraging Ryōbu or "Double Aspect" Shintō.

As a result of his close ties with the emperor, in 816 Kūkai was allowed to establish a great Shingon temple complex on Mt. Kōya, about fifty miles from Kyōto. This Shingon complex came to rival the Tendai complex on Mt. Hiei. After the death of Saichō in 822, Kūkai became the most influential monk in Japan. Under his able and charismatic leadership, Shingon grew to rival the Tendai school in wealth, popular following and political influence. Kūkai is said to have ended his career by choosing to be entombed alive, while in a meditational trance, in 835. Some, of course, regard this as a hoax perpetrated by his followers. Be that as it may, his unique passing secured for Kūkai an enduring status as one of the saints of Japan. Many believe that he did not die at all, but still sits in a deep meditation from which he will arise at the coming of the future Buddha Maitreya. Kūkai's tomb on Mt. Kōya remains one of the most venerated pilgrimage sites in Japan.

Kūkai was without doubt the most illustrious Buddhist of Heian Japan. His Shingon school is still popular and powerful in Japan. Saichō's Tendai school is now less influential in its own right than Shingon. However, Tendai exerted more influence than Shingon upon the development of Buddhism in Japan. With the exception of Shingon, all of the major forms of popular Japanese Buddhism developed out of the Tendai tradition of Mt. Hiei. These developments, however, occurred only after the Heian period of Japanese history had come to a dramatic close brought about largely by the Tendai and Shingon monks of Kyōto.

Toward the end of the Heian period, there were over three thousand Tendai temples and monasteries on Mt. Hiei. There were nearly as many Shingon institutions on Mt. Kōya. By virtue of generous tax exemption and land grant schemes, both schools had become enormously wealthy and powerful. The exercise and pursuit of wealth and power embroiled the Shingon and Tendai schools in increasingly hostile conflicts with one another and with the aristocratic clans in the region of Kyōto. Eventually, either school could field an army of several thousand men led by trained soldier-monks. Both schools did so frequently, for aggression as well as defence against one another and against rival clans in and around the capital.

The monks and their armies of mercenaries became increasingly bold in the eleventh and twelfth centuries, fighting not only among themselves, but from time to time attacking opponents in the capital and intimidating even the imperial guard. Early in the twelfth century, the Tendai and Shingon monasteries came to the brink of staging a full-scale battle in Kyōto itself, with some twenty thousand men on either side. Such a conflict never occurred, but amid such turmoil and uncertainty, Kyōto could not survive long as the nation's capital. A bit of black humor from the time notes that the Emperor Kammu's geomancers were certainly accurate in locating Kyōto's "demon gates," which marked the directions from which the capital was threatened. Ironically, however, the Buddhist monasteries built at these points to ward off encroaching evil themselves turned out to be the forecast nemesis of Kyōto.

The military might of the Buddhist monasteries forced the emperor and the aristocratic clans of Kyōto to rely increasingly upon warrior clans living beyond the precincts of the capital. This reliance eventually transferred the actual rulership of Japan into the hands of powerful provincial warlords, who vied among themselves for absolute supremacy. Eventually this rivalry came down to a prolonged and bloody struggle between the Taira and Minamoto clans. This conflict plunged the whole of Japan into a civil war that raged intermittently for some thirty years. The Minamoto triumphed decisively in 1185 and established their military headquarters at Kamakura, an all but impregnable stronghold surrounded by mountains on three sides and the ocean on the fourth. Until 1333 the Minamoto stronghold was the real center of political power in Japan. While the emperor continued to reside in Kyōto and continued to be the figurehead of government, in reality the shōgun in Kamakura controlled the state.

The Kamakura period (1185-1333)

In general, the Kamakura shōguns ruled harshly but justly. Much to the consternation of the heretofore privileged aristocracy, a more equal distribution of wealth was enforced through a complex feudal system overseen by warlords loyal to the Minamoto clan. Disputes were generally settled through warfare, but the Kamakura period may be characterized as a period of stable instability, during which almost constant military strife was overseen and largely controlled by the Kamakura shogunate.

Thus far, this account of the development of Buddhism in Japan has been dominated by three social groups: the aristocracy, the military and the monastic communities. During the Kamakura period, a fourth group, an emerging middle class, assumed a central role and became a focus of proselytization and controversy in Buddhism. The Nara period was an era of acquisition of Chinese culture in general and Buddhism in particular. The Heian was a period of selective digestion according to the needs and inclinations of the Japanese aristocracy. The Kamakura period witnessed a promulgation of distinctly Japanese forms of Buddhism among the middle and lower classes. In broad terms, with the advent of the Kamakura period, Japan had come full-circle back to a reaffirmation of the age-old clan system of military government that had been superseded by the aristocratic imperial government of the Nara and Heian periods. Though the Kamakura period was a perilous age of considerable hardship for most of Japan, it was also a period of reaffirmation of traditional Japanese virtues including egalitarianism, thrift and endurance, personal valor, and in general a simple, earthy pragmatism. In this atmosphere, the great popular sects of Japanese Buddhism emerged to dominate the Japanese mentality until the present day.

The four forms of Buddhism that emerged during the Kamakura period — Jōdo, Jōdo Shinshū, Nichiren, and Zen — are properly termed "sects" rather than "schools" because they are distinguished not by doctrinal subtleties among intellectuals, but by distinctive modes of belief and practice that identify their rank and file adherents. Each of the popular sects of the Kamakura period developed out of the Tendai tradition of Mt. Hiei, the great melting pot of Buddhism in Japan.

1. THE JŌDO OR PURE LAND SECT, corresponding to the Jing Tu school of Chinese Buddhism, is generally reckoned to have been established in Japan with the publication in 1175 of the treatise *Senchaku-shū* by Hōnen (1133-1212). Actually, forms of Pure Land thought and practice had already begun to gain prominence during

the Heian period, most notably within the fold of the Tendai school, for whom the devotional Buddhism of the *Lotus Sūtra* is the pinnacle of the religion. In Japan as in China, however, the central scripture of Pure Land Buddhism is the *Sukhāvatī Vyūha* or *Pure Land Sūtra,* which prescribes loving devotion to the Buddha Amitābha as the means to be reborn in the Pure Land or paradise over which he presides.

The ninth century Tendai monk Ennin (794-864) is credited with having brought from China to Japan the practice of devotion to Amitābha Buddha (known as Amida in Japan), who presides over the "Western Paradise" of Pure Land Buddhism. In the following century, the great Genshin (942-1017) wrote a popular Pure Land tract, entitled *The Essentials of Salvation,* which later influenced Hōnen profoundly. Genshin incorporated the visual arts into his attempts to popularize the cult, becoming arguably the greatest religious artist of Japan as a result of his revolutionary depictions of the joys of paradise and the torments of hell. Other Tendai monks, notably Kūya (903-972) and Ryōnin (1072-1132), specifically set out to popularize Pure Land devotion among the masses, by their own examples encouraging the people of Kyōto to sing praises of Amida while dancing for joy in the streets.

This joyous exterior, however, masked a deep-seated pessimism in Pure Land Buddhism. A recurrent phenomenon in Buddhism, and in fact in many religions, is the emergence of a widespread conviction that the end of the world is at hand. In Buddhism, this belief invariably has been associated with the doctrine of progressive decay of the dharma during successive ages, a doctrine noted already in the "Three Ages" and Pure Land schools in China. Given the tumultuous history of Japan, there was often ample reason to conclude that the end of the world was at hand and that expedient religious measures to suit a degenerate age were in order. The measures taken normally involved ardent and single-minded prayers to be reborn in the age of renewal of dharma to be initiated by the coming Buddha Maitreya, or to be reborn in the Pure Land paradise of Amida Buddha. Such convictions led to the formation of Pure Land cliques in both Tendai and Shingon Buddhism during the Heian period. These cliques existed unobtrusively within the existing structures of the great schools, but were usually composed of pious monks banding together in reaction to the worldliness and corruption they perceived in Heian Buddhism.

Such elements within the established schools of the Heian period were paralleled by a tradition of quasi-monastic holy persons operating beyond the pale of the great monasteries. These religious personalities were known variously as *ubasoku* (derived from the Sanskrit *upāsaka,* meaning pious Buddhist layman), *hijiri* or *shamon* (holy persons of unspecified affiliation, *shamon* deriving from Skt. *śramaṇa*) and *yamabushi* (mountain dwellers). Such figures had operated among the people since the Nara period, performing the traditional functions of the shamans of Shintō: magical healing, exorcism and blessing. Naturally, these religious figures tended to gravitate toward the more popularly accessible aspects of Buddhism, most notably the great savior deities like Maitreya and Amida. With the appearance of Hōnen in the Kamakura period, this fringe dwelling, twilight form of religion began to enter the mainstream with a specifically Buddhist identity.

Hōnen was born in 1133, the only son of a minor clan chieftain who, in the turbulent times toward the end of the Heian period, was slain in a raid upon his home. On his deathbed, Hōnen's father instructed his young son to forsake revenge, which would only beget further violence, and instead to enter the Buddhist Saṅgha. Such advice was uncharacteristic of the tribal militarism of the time and indicates that Hōnen's childhood environment was uncommonly enlightened for the age, a consideration that may account for his piety and sincerity in later life. Hōnen was ordained at the age of thirteen and trained for nearly thirty years in the Tendai tradition on Mt. Hiei. In the eclectic Tendai school, he gained a thorough knowledge of all known forms of Buddhism and a wide reputation for scholarship and integrity that would have put him in line for an influential position within the existing hierarchy. At about forty years of age, however, Hōnen broke decisively with the Tendai school. Following in the footsteps of the shamanistic holy persons of his day, he took up solitary dwelling in a humble mountain hermitage, where he began to attract a following and wrote the founding tract of Pure Land Buddhism in Japan, the *Senchaku-shū.*

After the completion of this work in 1175, Hōnen began actively to preach the simple faith of the Pure Land among the people of Kyōto. Following the precedent set by Kūya and Ryōnin, Hōnen encouraged his followers to dedicate themselves to prayer to Amida Buddha, but Hōnen simplified this practice even further by confining it exclusively to the repetitive incantation of a single, short formula *"Namu Amida Butsu"* which is known as the *nembutsu* and means "Homage to Amida Buddha." Hōnen's predecessors as preachers to the masses, Kūya and Ryōnin, had been little more than eccentric characters in the capital. Hōnen, by

contrast, became enormously popular, partly because of his genuine holiness and personal appeal, and partly because the perilous
times were conducive to a simple religion of hope for a better lot in
the next life. It is doubtful that the pious and humble Hōnen actually intended to inspire controversy and political unrest. Nonetheless, his single-minded dedication to repetition of the *nembutsu*
made it clear that he regarded the other doctrines and practices of
Buddhism as all but worthless. Moreover, his emphasis upon the
doctrine of the degenerate age of dharma, in a period of constant
strife and hardship, cut close to the bone of the political leadership.
Eventually Hōnen's popularity became so great that this single,
unaffiliated monk came to be regarded as a threat to the established
schools of Buddhism and to the shogunate itself. As a result, he was
expelled from the Sangha and banished from Kyōto in 1207. He
was allowed to return to Kyōto as a layman in 1211, and died in
the following year, his popularity undiminished, possibly even
enhanced by the persecution of the authorities.

Hōnen's followers were a new breed of Buddhist in Japan —
simple, everyday people passionately committed to a faith that was
of direct relevance in their own daily lives. Before Hōnen, the
Japanese people had been little more than spectators of the official
Buddhism that sheltered behind temple walls and was paraded
before the masses on special occasions. Due to the enthusiasm and
dedication of Hōnen's disciples, the Jōdo sect continued to grow in
numbers and continued to attract and thrive on persecution until
well after the fall of the Kamakura regime. Hōnen's chief disciple
Shinran carried on so enthusiastically with his master's work that he
came to be regarded as the founder of the second and largest of the
Pure Land Sects, the Jōdo Shinshū.

2. THE JŌDO SHINSHŪ OR TRUE PURE LAND SECT invites a comparison
between the two forms of Japanese Pure Land Buddhism and the
two forms of Pure Land Buddhism that developed earlier in China.
In China, the first Pure Land master Dao Zhou taught a simple faith
of chanting the name of Amitābha, while his disciple Shan Dao
encouraged a more complex practice. In Japan, precisely the opposite process of evolution occurred. Hōnen's disciple Shinran (1173-
1262) actually simplified the faith through his dedication to his
master and his eagerness to draw out the full implications of
Hōnen's teaching. Shinran entered the Sangha in the Tendai sect at
the age of eight and was trained on Mt. Hiei. At the age of twenty-
nine he became a follower of Hōnen, only six years before Hōnen
was expelled from the Sangha and banished in 1207. Probably

included in the exile order, Shinran also left the capital to teach in the countryside. He gave up the monk's robe, and even took a wife with whom he had several children. The actual circumstances and timing of these actions remain in doubt, but regardless of their immediate motivations, they were clearly part of a sustained and deliberate attempt on the part of Shinran to actualize in his life and teaching the full implications of Hōnen's thought.

Like the similar doctrine of grace in Christianity, Hōnen's doctrine of salvation through the grace of Amida Buddha raised questions concerning the role of morality and good works in gaining salvation. In Japan, this problem was expressed in terms of "self-power" — one's own ability to attain salvation through good works — and "other-power" — the saving power of Amida's grace. Hōnen's opponents leveled persistently and vehemently against Pure Land Buddhism the charge that in emphasizing salvation through grace it neglected morality and good works. Shinran reacted to this attack by defiantly affirming total reliance upon the saving grace of Amida Buddha and denying emphatically the relevance of morality and merit in gaining salvation. The robes and celibacy of the monk, rituals, morality, merit making, and in fact all aspects of traditional piety, were for Shinran only vanities that obscured one's utter reliance on the saving grace of Amida Buddha. He wished even to discard the distinction between teacher and pupil, and to de-emphasize repetitive chanting of the *nembutsu,* which was the chief hallmark of the Pure Land Sect. Instead, Shinran held that even one heartfelt thought of reliance upon Amida Buddha insured one's salvation and thereby obliterated any possibility of distinguishing one's own spiritual status from that of others who were similarly reliant upon the "other-power" of Amida's grace.

Aside from the enormous popularity that the Jōdo Shinshū sect eventually attained among the masses of Japan, Shinran's most influential innovation was his open, unabashed abandoning of celibacy. Before his time individual Buddhist monks of various schools and sects in Japan quietly and discreetly took de facto wives and raised families. Shinran's openness in doing so, however, paved the way for hereditary succession to the leadership of the sect. This proved to be a relatively stable system of passing on authority, and it has endured to the present day. The heads of both the Western and Eastern branches of the "Temple of the Original Vow" in Kyōto — the two major seats of Jōdo Shinshū Buddhism — are both descendants of Shinran. This stable leadership succession was of particular importance during the turbulent times in which the sect originated and consolidated its following.

The humble Shinran was hardly the sort of figure to found a major religious sect during such turbulent and violent times. Though his master Hōnen was allowed to return to Kyōto from exile in 1211, Shinran remained in the provinces as a missionary of the Pure Land faith. He eventually returned to Kyōto in approximately 1230, when he was almost sixty, and lived there quietly among his followers until his death at the age of ninety in 1262. Shinran's descendants and disciples, however, provided the initiative necessary to establish and maintain a powerful religious sect in feudal Japan. The Jōdo Shinshū sect, in fact, participated in the militant feudal society of Japan by becoming itself a militant, quasi-feudal institution. During times of strife and persecution, the followers of the sect showed unflinching loyalty to their hereditary leaders and a ferocious determination to withstand all onslaughts, whether religious, political or military.

In particular, Shinran's descendant Rennyo (1415-99) is credited with organizing the Jōdo Shinshū sect into an efficient religions and military organization that was able to withstand over a century of armed conflict with older schools of Buddhism and ambitious warlords. In addition to defending itself against attack, the Jōdo Shinshū became a feared source of militant uprisings in fifteenth- and sixteenth-century Japan. It is ironic that the unobtrusive, egalitarian Shinran founded what turned out to be one of the most hierarchical, authoritarian and assertive institutions in Japan.

3. THE NICHIREN SECT is named after its founder Nichiren (1222-82), who was born the son of a humble, lower-class fisherman. Nichiren was anything but humble, styling himself "the pillar of Japan, the eye of the nation."[33] Early in life he entered a monastery near his home and eventually found his way through the monastic establishment to the Tendai center at Mt. Hiei in 1243. After studying at Mt. Hiei for ten years, Nichiren became obsessed with discovering the original doctrine of Buddhism. Eventually, he decided that the *Lotus Sūtra*, the foundational text of Tendai Buddhism, was the essence of the religion. Obsessed too with what he believed to be the degenerate nature of the age, Nichiren concluded that human beings were no longer capable of any but the simplest of religious observances.

The *Lotus Sūtra* was of course venerated in most forms of Japanese Buddhism, and the doctrine of the degenerate present age was not uncommon, but the lengths to which Nichiren took the implications of these common elements of Japanese Buddhism were unprecedented. Though himself an accomplished philosopher and scholar, he concluded that for the present degenerate age mere recitation of the title of the *Lotus Sūtra* was the extent of religious practice within the grasp of human beings. In place of the *nembutsu* of Jōdo and Jōdo Shinshū, Nichiren proclaimed repetition of the "Holy Title" of the *Lotus Sūtra* to be the only practical means available for human salvation. In place of the phrase *Namu Amida Butsu* Nichiren substituted the invocation *Nam-myōhō-renge-kyō* — "Homage to the *Lotus Sūtra*" — as the be-all and end-all of Buddhist practice.

Though his doctrine and practice bore obvious similarities to Pure Land Buddhism, from the very beginning of his ministry in 1253 Nichiren mounted a vehement campaign against Pure Land Buddhism. He neglected to attack the Jōdo Shinshū sect, possibly because it was as yet little known, but he attacked all other forms of Buddhism in Japan. Nor did he spare the political leaders who supported the religious establishments he regarded as so corrupt. Publicly and repeatedly he referred to the religious and secular authorities of Japan as liars, traitors, demons, and hypocrites. Unless the Japanese people were to reject their false teachings and corrupt political leadership, he warned with the vigor of an Old Testament prophet, Japan would suffer calamity upon calamity. For his troubles, Nichiren was twice exiled by authorities to remote parts of Japan and narrowly escaped death on several occasions at the hands of an angry mob, assassins and government authorities. His memoirs claim that on one occasion he was saved from death when a miraculous light dazed and confused his would-be executioners. More sober accounts say that he was pardoned at the last minute.

On the one hand, Nichiren's lack of tact and diplomacy verged on the demented, particularly according to the polite conventions of Japanese etiquette. On the other hand, Nichiren showed a remarkable capacity to foretell large-scale events. Just four years after Nichiren began making public his dire prophesies, a great earthquake struck Japan in 1257, followed in subsequent years by floods, famine, plague and the dreaded appearance of a comet. Despite his apparent prophetic accuracy, the offensive and divisive character of his preaching caused him to be driven from his home village in 1260. He settled in Kamakura and began to prophesy in the capital that Japan's degenerate religious and political condition would cause the nation to suffer disaster at the hands of foreign invaders. Again, he proved to be correct, but for his efforts he was twice exiled to remote areas of Japan, in 1261 and 1271.

As a well-educated Buddhist monk, Nichiren was probably aware through Buddhist contacts in China that the warlike Mongols under Kublai Khan posed an almost inevitable threat to the independence of Japan. One way or another, Nichiren became thoroughly associated with the prophesy of foreign invasion. When it became clear that the Mongols actually did intend to attack Japan in 1274, Nichiren was released from exile and summoned back to Kamakura by government authorities seeking rallying points for resistance to the invasion. Nichiren obstinately rejected their conciliatory overtures and insisted that the only way to save the nation was to obliterate all other forms of religion, punish their leaders, and adopt his own faith as the national creed of Japan. This, of course, the authorities refused, and Nichiren left Kamakura forever, to live out the rest of his life surrounded by a small but dedicated band of followers on the slopes of Mt. Fuji.

The Mongol invasion of 1274 and a second much more devastating Mongol invasion in 1281, involving perhaps the largest armada the world had ever seen, were both repulsed without the benefit of Nichiren's program, albeit at a great cost in lives and resources. Nichiren died a year after the second Mongol invasion, convinced to the end that Japan was doomed without the reforms he advocated. While the preventive measures Nichiren proposed may have been unrealistic, he was certainly accurate in his prediction of the dark days ahead for Japan. Orderly government collapsed in the wake of the Mongol invasions, and Japan disintegrated into a three-hundred-year period of disunity and strife among political, military and religious interests, which resulted in unremitting suffering for the common people. Nichiren's correct prognosis of the fate of Japan increased the prestige and numbers of his zealous followers, who themselves contributed significantly to the strife and chaos that their founder had predicted.

4. ZEN BUDDHISM, the fourth important sect to develop during the Kamakura period, epitomizes for most Westerners the artistic and religious aspirations of Japan. The term "zen" is a Japanese pronunciation of the Chinese word *chan,* which in turn is a rendition of the Sanskrit term *dhyāna,* meaning "meditation." The practice of meditation is a prominent feature of most forms of Buddhism, but not until Bodhidharma gained prominence in China in the sixth century was a specific Meditation school of Buddhism identifiable. Already in the seventh century, Dōshō, founder of the Hossō

school, had established a Zen meditation hall in Nara. Several other Zen monks visited Japan during the Nara period, but Zen did not catch on immediately in Japan. As late as the ninth century, a Chinese Chan master known in Japan as Gikū left in Kyōto an inscription lamenting the futility of his efforts to establish the Meditation school in Japan.

These early failures of Zen in Japan are understandable. Zen Buddhism avoids intellectualism and de-emphasizes scriptures, doctrine and ceremonial. This rendered the religion inappropriate in the Nara and Heian periods of Japanese history, when the Japanese were striving to master the principles of stable, literate social organization. With the advent of the Kamakura period, however, came a backlash against the aristocratic sophistication of imported Chinese culture and a reassertion of more traditional Japanese values. The middle and lower classes turned largely to devotional forms of Buddhism, and the newly assertive military class found inspiration primarily in the practical, no-nonsense discipline of Zen.

The Japanese monk Eisai (1141-1215) is usually considered to be the first successful proponent of Zen in Japan. He began his monastic career at the Tendai center on Mt. Hiei, and like many others became disenchanted with the doctrinal rigidity and political intrigue of establishment Buddhism in Japan. As a result of his dissatisfaction, he made two trips to China, one in 1168 and the second in 1187. In 1191 Eisai returned to Japan from his second Chinese pilgrimage a full-fledged Chan master, and he set about attempting to establish Zen practice in Kyōto. Eisai appears to have had no desire to found a sect. Instead, he urged that Zen meditation is the essence of all Buddhism and is therefore beneficial in all forms of Buddhism. Unlike the Chan schools of China, Eisai affirmed the authority of Buddhist scriptures. He never broke his Tendai affiliation, and he openly advocated Shingon esoterism. Nonetheless, he encountered stubborn resistance from the established schools of Kyōto. As a result, he took the bold step of relocating to Kamakura, the new center of political power in Japan. Eisai had already established credentials as a patriot with the publication of his essay "The Propagation of Zen for the Protection of the Nation." After his move to Kamakura, his association with the shōgun and his samurai warriors propelled Eisai into national prominence. In 1202 he was named abbot of his own temple and awarded the title of Dai Sōjō, the highest ecclesiastical rank in the land.

As noted in Chapter VIII, Chinese Chan developed two viable branches: the Lin Ji (Lin Chi) and the Cao Dong (Ts'ao Tung). Eisai practiced and taught the Lin Ji tradition, which came to be known as Rinzai in Japan. As in China, this branch of Zen is associated with meditation upon insoluble riddles, known in Japanese as *kōans,* and dramatic question-answer exchanges *(mondō)* between master and pupil. Eisai was not, however, merely a passive transmitter of Chinese Chan to Japan. He introduced into Zen Buddhism elements of nationalism that would have been alien if not antithetical to the Chinese tradition. His favorable attitude toward scriptures and the doctrines of other schools was also a departure from Chan precedents. As a result, Eisai came to be regarded as the founder of Rinzai Zen only after his death, when the second branch of Chinese Chan, the Cao Dong, had been introduced.

Dōgen (1200-1253), is given credit with introducing the Cao Dong branch of Chinese Chan into Japan, where it came to be known as Sōtō Zen. In many ways Dōgen is comparable to Eisai, but in personality he appears to have been less diplomatic than Eisai and more focused on sectarian preoccupations. Dōgen was of aristocratic birth, having an emperor and a prime minister in his ancestry. He showed great intellectual talent in his early life, so much so that the ruling Fujiwara family wished to adopt him and groom him for a high government post, possibly the prime ministership. The young Dōgen rejected this opportunity, however, and entered the Tendai Buddhist establishment on Mt. Hiei at the age of thirteen. Like many others, he was disappointed with what he found there. As a result, he took up Zen practice in Eisai's monastery in 1217. Following Eisai's example, Dōgen journeyed to China in 1223. He stayed almost five years, during which time he studied under several teachers in various monasteries. Toward the end of his stay, he met the aged Sōtō master Ru Jing (Ju Ching), who was known for the strenuous meditational discipline he imposed upon his students and himself. Under Ru Jing, Dōgen claimed to realize enlightenment. The venerable master confirmed this realization and bestowed upon Dōgen the seal of succession, naming him the next patriarch of the Cao Dong lineage. Shortly afterward, in 1227 or 1228, Dōgen returned to Japan.

Upon his return from China, Dōgen taught Zen meditation to a steadily growing following in the Kyōto area. By 1233 he presided over his own temple. Over the next ten years, he wrote most of his magnum opus, the *Shōbōgenzō,* and established himself as an important teacher in the capital. In 1243, Dōgen gathered the inner core of his disciples and relocated in a remote temple on the rugged northern coast of Japan. His reasons for doing so are not clear. Some sources indicate pressure from the Tendai establishment, even that his monastery may have been attacked by Tendai soldiers. Others cite competition from the Rinzai sect. Still others venture that he felt that seclusion would intensify meditational discipline.

Despite the inaccessibility of Dōgen's new monastery, a steady stream of serious practitioners of Zen, including many samurai warriors, sought him out in order to undergo the rigorous training for which he became renowned. His aversion to public attention notwithstanding, in the later years of his life, Dōgen had become one of the most eminent monks in Japan. At the request of the regent himself, Dōgen visited Kamakura briefly in 1247. To induce him to stay, the regent made an extravagant offer of lands and facilities, but Dōgen refused, returning to his remote sanctuary and vowing that even an imperial command would not induce him to leave again. In 1250, three years before Dōgen's death, the retired Emperor Go Saga conferred upon him the purple robe of honor. Characteristically, Dōgen is said to have rejected the honor twice, and when he finally accepted the robe, he never wore it.

Like Eisai, Dōgen came to be regarded as the founder of a school only after his death. Dōgen's writings dismiss the notion of "schools" or "sects" or "houses" or "branches" in Buddhism. Much like Eisai, he claimed that what is called Zen is actually the pure, unadulterated teaching of the historical Buddha. Again like Eisai, he maintained that the Buddhist scriptures were an important repository of these teachings, and himself contributed several important treatises to the canon of Japanese Zen. Paradoxically, in advancing these points of view, he was often critical of Rinzai Zen, aligning himself and his followers by default with the Sōtō branch of Zen. The issue at stake was the same issue that divided Chinese Chan: the question of meditational technique. Dōgen regarded the Rinzai form of Zen as suspiciously artificial and dramatic in its *kōan* and *mondō* practices. He advocated instead the Sōtō path to enlightenment — the austere practice of "just sitting" with a focused mind emptied of conceptual thought. The monk Enni Bennen (1201-1280), a contemporary of Dōgen, is generally given credit for consolidating the Rinzai tradition as an independent branch of Japanese Zen. Initially, the Rinzai form of Zen was the more successful in Japan. Today, however, the Sōtō branch has the larger following and is more unified than Rinzai Zen.

The establishment of Pure Land, Nichiren and Zen Buddhism in Japan during the Kamakura period marks the completion of Buddhism's transplantation to Japan and of the transition from Buddhism in Japan to Japanese Buddhism. To the present day, the Kamakura schools remain the dominant forms of Japanese Buddhism and indeed of Japanese spirituality, although the Shingon and Tendai schools survive with millions of adherents.

The dramatic close of the Kamakura period eerily validated the doomsday prophesies of Nichiren. Massive Mongol onslaughts in 1274 and 1281, though repulsed, devastated the Japanese economy. Japan descended into a prolonged period of recurrent turmoil from which it did not recover fully until after World War II. After the Kamakura period, developments in Buddhism during the Ashikaga, Tokugawa and Meiji periods were relatively minor, but since these periods form part of the traditional outline of Japanese history it is necessary to consider them briefly.

The Ashikaga Period (1336-1600)

Because the Ashikaga clan eventually emerged victorious from the chaos following the Mongol invasions, the "Ashikaga Period" of Japanese history is conventionally dated from 1336, the year the first of the line dubiously declared himself shōgun. The Ashikaga clan did not consolidate their rule, however, until 1392, and the last century of their rule was a period of constant strife and unclear leadership in Japan. The century in between the chaotic periods which opened and closed the Ashikaga period was scarcely less strife-ridden. During this tumultuous era, Zen Buddhism gained considerable ground in Japan.

Following the lead of Eisai, Zen monks, particularly Rinzai monks, of the Ashikaga period achieved influence by performing diplomatic and advisory roles for Japan's rulers. Amid the constantly shifting political and military alliances which characterized the Ashikaga period, however, such roles inevitably attract the charge of duplicity. The career of the Rinzai monk Musō Soseki (1275-1351) is a notable example of stunning ends achieved through ambiguous means. Musō's early life was dedicated to Zen practice under several masters. He became dissatisfied with his progress, however, and set out on his own solitary quest, wandering in remote mountains and forests. Finally, he is supposed to have realized enlightenment while gazing into the embers of a dying campfire.

Musō gained a reputation for shrewdness, and was invited by the last of the Kamakura regents to preside over a monastery there and act as mentor and advisor at court. Reading the signs of the times, however, Musō transferred his loyalty to Emperor Go Daigo when the latter began a push to reassert imperial power. Once the first Ashikaga shōgun Takauji had driven Go Daigo into hiding, Musō changed allegiance again and served the Ashikaga rulers. Despite his malleable loyalty, Musō proved to be effective in the roles of political advisor and spiritual mentor. He was instrumental in convincing first the Emperor Go Daigo and the shōgun Ashikaga Takauji to send diplomatic and trade missions to China, thus opening a new era of foreign commerce and diplomacy. In addition, Musō convinced the Ashikaga shōgun to do for Zen what Emperor Shōmu had done for Shingon in the eighth century — establish a Zen monastery in each of the sixty-six provinces of Japan. This in effect made Rinzai Zen the state religion of the Ashikaga period and increased immeasurably the status and influence of Zen throughout Japan. For his services to Buddhism and the rulers of Japan, Musō was awarded the title of Kokushi or "National Master" under seven successive emperors, three while he was alive and four after his death.

Building upon the broad base in the countryside resulting from the establishment of a Zen monastery in every province, the Rinzai sect set up a network of provincial schools throughout the land. Talented students from these provincial schools had a real opportunity to continue their studies at the celebrated Ashikaga college in Shimotsuke Province, or in the five great Zen monasteries in Kyōto. As a result of these arrangements, Zen Buddhism provided a large preponderance of the educated minds in Japan during the Ashikaga period. In addition, artists and scholars gravitated toward Zen for the protection the Saṅgha provided from the vagaries of the times as well as for the relative freedom of lifestyle and thought that Zen offered. Thus, in turbulent times when learning was scarce, Zen Buddhism provided a repository of education and literacy. This made the sect useful for the purposes of diplomacy and negotiation among the numerous warring factions in Japan, and also for such civil administration as existed from time to time. During the war-torn Ashikaga period, Zen was able to establish itself as the preëminent arbiter of Japanese moral, aesthetic and cultural values. In the eyes of many, Zen maintains this position to the present day.

The Tendai and Shingon schools of Buddhism had become militarized even during the Heian period, and so were in a sense prepared for the constant strife of the Ashikaga period. Both schools contributed notably to this strife, the Tendai school in particular. The Tendai stronghold on Mt. Hiei had been the spawning ground for all of the popular sects that sprang up in the Kamakura period. As a result Tendai also developed a considerable mass following. This support, combined with its longstanding tradition of militarism, propelled the Tendai school into the thick of the hostilities during the Ashikaga period. In 1465, alarmed by the increasing popularity and power of the Jōdo Shinshū sect, an army of Tendai monks descended upon Kyōto and sacked the head Shinshū temple, driving the Shinshū priests into desperate flight.

Though driven out of Kyōto, Jōdo Shinshū prospered in the provinces and had re-established its headquarters near Kyōto by 1480. In 1532, the Nichiren sect set upon and destroyed the new Shinshū headquarters. This resulted in an alliance between the Shinshū sect and their old enemies the Tendai. By 1537 this alliance included all of the Buddhists of Kyōto and the shōgun himself, all united against the Nichiren sect. One has to credit the courage of the followers of Nichiren for daring to confront such odds. Battle cries of *Nam-myōhō-renge-kyō* and *Namu Amida Butsu* filled Kyōto as armies of monks and their followers fought a pitched battle in the city streets. By all accounts, both sides fought bravely with the disregard for death that faith in a heavenly reward instills. The Nichiren sect suffered a crushing defeat, resulting in the deaths of over fifty thousand of its followers and the destruction of all of the twenty-one Nichiren temples in the capital. After this defeat, the Nichiren sect did not regain its former importance until its resurgence after the second World War.

Of all the Buddhist factions during the Ashikaga period, the Jōdo Shinshū plunged most enthusiastically and ferociously into the warlike spirit of the times. Since it was led by married priests rather than by monks, the Shinshū sect naturally had no monasteries, the traditional power bases of other sects. The sect established many fortified temples, however, in which its mass following gathered for worship and instruction. Organizationally, the Shinshū sect was particularly well prepared for the turbulence of the times. Following the example set by Shinran, the sect's founder, Shinshū priests were allowed to marry. The resulting hereditary descent of its acknowledged leaders rendered the sect similar in organization to the shogunate. The sect's large provincial temples, all owing allegiance to the hereditary leader of the sect, were roughly equivalent to the feudal estates of high-ranking clans swearing allegiance to the shōgun. From its bases in its fortified temples, the Jōdo Shinshū sect waged interminable wars with other sects and even with feudal warlords. In the sixteenth century alone, the Shinshū sect fought in some twenty major military conflicts. The Jōdo followers of Hōnen contented themselves with remaining quietly in the shadow of their much larger sister sect and consequently never attained the prominence of the Jōdo Shinshū sect in Japan.

The Ashikaga period ended as it began and as it had continued throughout, in violence and duplicity. In the latter half of the sixteenth century, three ruthless warlords formed an alliance bent upon dominating all Japan. These warlords were Oda Nobunaga (1534-1582), Toyotomi Hideyoshi (1536-99) and Tokugawa Ieyasu (1542-1616). As a result of its thorough involvement in the intrigues of the time, Buddhism suffered greatly at the hands of Nobunaga and Hideyoshi, who treated Buddhist establishments with the same ruthlessness they wreaked upon rival warlords. Indeed, many of the prominent Buddhist monasteries and temples were practically indistinguishable from feudal baronies. The resulting suppression of Buddhism in late sixteenth century Japan was therefore not really similar to the earlier suppressions witnessed in China. The religion itself was not targeted. Instead, Buddhist opposition was overcome temple by temple, sect by sect, in exactly the same way rival secular powers were reduced to submission fortress by fortress, clan by clan.

The Tendai establishment on Mt. Hiei was razed to ashes by Nobunaga in 1571 because of its participation in an unsuccessful military alliance against the strongman. Some three thousand temples and monasteries were destroyed, and practically all of their inhabitants perished in the conflagration or by the sword. Shortly thereafter, Nobunaga attacked the Jōdo Shinshū sect. He drove them from their provincial strongholds, but was unable to overthrow their fortified stronghold in Ōsaka. Finally, in 1580, after a ten-year siege, the Jōdo Shinshū forces surrendered in accordance with a settlement negotiated by the emperor himself.

After Nobunaga was assassinated in 1582, his ally Hideyoshi took charge of the campaign to unify Japan. Soon he came into conflict with Shingon Buddhism. In 1584, an army of fifteen thousand Shingon troops unwisely attacked Hideyoshi's stronghold in Ōsaka. Some four thousand of these soldier-monks perished at the hands of Hideyoshi's forces, and in the course of their retreat many more were hacked and clubbed to death by the peasantry of Ōsaka, an indication of the popular attitude toward militarized Buddhism.

The Tokugawa period (1601-1867)

Hideyoshi died of an illness in 1599, leaving Tokugawa Ieyasu to reap the benefits of the former three-way alliance. After achieving a decisive military victory over his remaining rivals in 1601, Ieyasu obtained imperial recognition as shōgun. He established the Tokugawa regency at the site of his own fortress in Yedo, now known as Tōkyō. Like most of the Tokugawa clan, Ieyasu was a follower of the Jōdo sect of Buddhism, the earlier form of Pure Land founded by Hōnen. By most accounts the new shōgun was a dedicated Jōdo practitioner. In his attempts to restore unity and peace to Japan, and thereby consolidate his own rule, Ieyasu consistently favored Jōdo Buddhism, thus lifting the sect from the relative obscurity in which it had existed during the Ashikaga period.

No doubt, Ieyasu's motives for promoting the Jōdo sect were in part an element of a strategy to insure that Buddhism would not threaten Tokugawa rule as it had threatened Ashikaga rule. The Jōdo sect had not become politicized or militarized like the other schools and sects of Buddhism, and therefore did not pose a threat to Tokugawa supremacy. To promote harmony, Ieyasu also recognized the other sects and helped them to recover — within limits — from the devastation of the Ashikaga period. He re-established the Tendai monastic complex on Mt. Hiei on a greatly reduced scale, and continued the practice of employing Zen monks as advisors. Partly to insure ties with Buddhism and partly to prevent a proliferation of rival families within the Tokugawa clan, Ieyasu also instituted the policy of requiring most of the princes and princesses of the clan to enter celibate Buddhist orders. Finally, he seized the opportunity provided by a succession dispute within the Jōdo Shinshū hierarchy to divide the sect into Eastern and Western branches, an administrative division that survives to the present day.

In part, Ieyasu's promotion of Buddhism was an element of the isolationism for which the Tokugawa period is renowned. During the latter part of the Ashikaga period, around 1550, Christian missionaries from Europe had begun to arrive in Japan. As a result of political maneuvering as much as evangelical activity, they had gained considerable influence by the dawn of the Tokugawa era. Ieyasu was aware of Europe's military might, its appetite for power, and the capacity of Christian missionaries for political intrigue. He became determined to discourage Christianity, which he regarded as a dangerous foreign interloper in Japan. Ieyasu's mistrust of Christianity escalated under his successors into full-scale persecution, involving torture and executions by 1620. Sporadic executions of Christians continued until 1640, when a systematic, nation-wide inquisition was initiated to eradicate the religion entirely.

As part of the Tokugawa policy of minimizing the scope for religious strife in Japan, all Japanese were required to register membership with the Buddhist temple of their parish, attend ceremonies on prescribed holy days, and conduct all funerals and ancestral rites according to the tradition of the parish school or sect. This had the effect of freezing the existing distribution of membership among the various Buddhist schools and sects in Japan. On the one hand, this policy resulted in the preservation of all existing forms of Buddhism in Japan, some of which might otherwise have died out. On the other hand, it stifled the dynamism and development of Buddhism as a whole.

The only noteworthy developments in Buddhism during the Tokugawa period occurred within Zen. In 1655, at the invitation of both the emperor and the shōgun, a Chinese Zen master whom the Japanese call Ingen (1592-1673) came to Japan and established the Ōbaku sect of Zen. This small sect still survives, with its headquarters at Uji, near Kyōto. It is distinguished from other forms of Japanese Zen primarily by the Chinese character of its architecture, accoutrements and ceremonies. Also in the fold of Zen, the Rinzai poet Bashō (1644-94), originally a civil servant with the Waterworks Department, introduced and popularized the *haiku,* a short, free-style poem for which the only restriction is that its three lines must contain five, seven, and five syllables respectively. For many Westerners, the *haiku* epitomizes Japanese literary expression, though the Japanese can point to stunning achievements in every genre of literary art. Another important Rinzai monk of the Tokugawa period was Hakuin (1685-1768), whose inspirational sermons are still widely read.

On the whole, though, Buddhism became stagnant under the stiflingly cozy religious policy of the Tokugawa regime. Since religious affiliations had been frozen by the government, there was no incentive to seek converts. Moreover, since every person in Japan had to register with a Buddhist temple, Buddhism assumed the unpopular role of census bureau and tax collector for the Tokugawa regime. As Buddhism stagnated, Shintō — which though not suppressed had been left out of the Tokugawa religious establishment — embarked upon an enthusiastic revival toward the end of the Tokugawa period. Shintō reformers developed a patriotic systematization of doctrine based on a dovetailing of Confucian political philosophy with the traditional Japanese political and religious values enshrined in Shintō. This reformed Shintō attracted a large following and eventually led to the reassertion of imperial rule in Japan after more than five centuries of a puppet throne controlled by a series of warlords.

The Meiji restoration (1868-1945)

Though the Tokugawa period was in general a period of stability, peace and prosperity, it harbored several fatal weaknesses. The apparent prosperity of the period did not really penetrate much below the ranks of the wealthy vassals of the shōgun and the pampered Buddhist establishments. The common people themselves were exploited by their overlords often to the point of desperation. While the emperor of Japan had been a puppet for some five hundred years, the average Japanese was not aware of this, as the shōguns had always been careful to give lip service to the overriding authority of the throne. This situation made resurgent Shintō a far more potent force than the Tokugawa regents recognized. Most significantly, however, the isolationism of the Tokugawa regime was completely out of step with the march of global history. Nonetheless, anti-foreign sentiments were strong among the Japanese, so that when finally the inevitable happened and the modern, outside world forced itself upon Japan, Tokugawa rule collapsed almost immediately.

The United States, in the course of increasing its trade interests in the Pacific, first broke the isolationism of Japan, though the Russians and the British had been exerting pressure since the turn of the nineteenth century. In 1837, 1845 and 1849, American ships entered Japanese waters with the ostensible purposes of gaining better treatment for shipwrecked American seamen — who were often maltreated and even imprisoned when washed ashore on Japan — and obtaining permission for American shipping to take on fuel and supplies in Japanese ports. All were turned away. In 1853, however, Commodore Perry arrived in Tōkyō Bay with four warships and delivered a letter to the emperor of Japan from the President of the United States to the effect that the United States insisted upon a trade treaty with Japan. Without making an overt threat, Perry announced that he would return in one year with an even more powerful fleet in order to receive the emperor's acceptance. Japan's rulers realized that they had no alternative but to agree, and they signed the American treaty when Perry returned in 1854. This agreement was followed in the next year by similar agreements with Britain, Russia and the Netherlands.

The forced influx of foreigners that followed highlighted dramatically the ineffectuality of the shōgun, whose full title was Sei-i Dai Shōgun, "Great General for Expelling Foreign Barbarians." Opponents of the shōgun, although not necessarily anti-foreign themselves, fanned Japan's smouldering xenophobia into an intense blaze of public protest. In the end, the emotional furor over the influx of foreigners boiled down to the more practical consideration of streamlining Japan's unwieldy political system so that the country could deal effectively with the outside world. Faced with this widespread sentiment, as well as peasant revolts and a large-scale defection of vassal clans, in 1867 the last Tokugawa shōgun retired after only one year in office and returned his commission to the throne. An interim government put down a brief civil war and restored full imperial authority in 1868. As was the ancient tradition, the new era of imperial rule was inaugurated with the adoption of a reign title, in this instance Mei-ji, "Enlightened Government."

At this crucial point in Japanese history, Buddhism was at a low ebb. Internally, it was decadent as a result of 250 years of complacent stagnation during the Tokugawa period. Externally, it faced low esteem in the eyes of the masses and outright hostility from the new political powers, who had come into office on a nationalistic, pro-Shintō platform. The emperor immediately declared Shintō to be the state religion. The imperial capital was relocated from Kyōto to Tōkyō, and the new palace declared off-limits to Buddhist images or ceremonies. Shintō shrines, having been administered by Buddhist monks for centuries, were handed back to Shintō priests and purged of Buddhist trappings. The land holdings of Buddhist temples reverted largely to the throne. The monks themselves were forbidden to go on alms rounds and required to resume their family names as opposed to their adopted Buddhist names. Many Buddhist monks became Shintō priests.

The initial frenzy of the Shintō revival had subsided by 1877 when the abolition of the state-controlled "Ecclesiastical Board" granted autonomy to Shintō and Buddhist institutions on an equal footing. At the time, vigorous Christian missions threatened to siphon off the following of both Buddhism and Shintō. By the turn of the twentieth century the Christian missions had fizzled out, due primarily to a recovery of Japan's sense of national pride, pride which had been shaken by the imposition of the modern world upon Japan by condescending Western powers. The short-lived success of Christianity and the abiding influence of Western ideas in general, however, helped to reduce the animosity among the various sects and schools of Buddhism and Shintō. This emergent solidarity among the traditional religions of Japan was vital in order to face the real threats posed by the influx of the outside world: secular ideologies, a capitalist global economy, and an industrial revolution.

In the course of reasserting its national pride, Japan fought successful wars against China in 1894-95 and against Russia in 1904-5. These victories resulted in the establishment of Japanese colonies on the Korean peninsula and Taiwan. In 1914 Japan entered World War I as an ally of Britain. The Japanese saw little fighting, but Japan's emerging industrial economy boomed as a result of wartime demand for industrial goods. By the end of the first World War, Japan was emerging as the foremost economic and military power in East Asia. In 1937 another victory against China, though tainted by Japanese atrocities, consolidated Japanese domination in East Asia.

Fearing American interference in China and Russian aggression against her colonial holdings in Korea — and hoping as well to pick up British and French colonies in Asia when these powers were defeated in Europe — in 1940 Japan signed an alliance with Hitler and Mussolini.

This, of course turned out to be a disastrous step, resulting in a crushing defeat at the hands of the United States in 1945. Reeling from the experience of being the first and as yet the only nation to be attacked with nuclear weapons, the Japanese were further traumatized by the humiliating terms of unconditional surrender exacted by the United States. The American occupation of Japan was the first time in history that the country had been occupied by a foreign power. In the solemn words of Emperor Hirohito, the Japanese had to accept that "the unendurable must be endured."

The Modern Period (1945-Present)

The American occupation of Japan from 1945 to 1952 was benign and in many ways constructive. In other ways it was highly disruptive. In the religious sphere, it was both simultaneously. One of the first actions of the occupying force was to issue a "Bill of Rights" based on the American model. This legislation, which was adopted in the new Japanese constitution of 1946, removed existing restrictions on political, civil and religious freedom. As a result, the twenty-eight recognized, state-controlled Buddhist denominations of 1945 — including the major schools and their subsects — had splintered into 260 Buddhist groups by 1950.[34] This number was cut back to 170 by legislation in 1951, but most of the established schools of Japanese Buddhism were weakened by this prolific splintering.

In addition to inviting schism, freedom of religion opened the way for a welter of over two hundred "new religions" in Japan. Most of these new religions are based upon Buddhism and Shintō, but some derive elements from Christianity and "new age" spiritualism, and even occasionally from Hinduism, Islam, and other religions of the world. In the context of Buddhism, the three most successful new religions are the Reiyūkai, the Risshō Kōseikai and the Sōka Gakkai, all of which derive from the Nichiren sect. Each of these movements began before World War II, but they became significant only after the war, increasing from hundreds to millions of adherents in the course of a decade.

Of these three major forms of new Buddhism, the Sōka Gakkai has become by far the largest and most controversial. In the first place, the Sōka Gakkai organization both is and is not a religion, and it both is and is not new. It characterizes itself as a lay organization of the Nichiren Shōshū sect. This sect was founded in the thirteenth century, shortly after Nichiren's death, by his disciple Nikkō. The Nichiren Shōshū sect differed from mainstream Nichiren by claiming that Nichiren himself was the

Buddha of the present age. Nichiren Shōshū remained insignificant until after World War II, when the Sōka Gakkai leadership began an aggressive recruitment drive in Japan and the world at large. This world-wide mission will be discussed further in Chapter XIII. In Japan, Nichiren Shōshū is now the largest single Buddhist denomination. Most adherents of Nichiren Shōshū are probably also members of the Sōka Gakkai, which makes it an extraordinarily powerful political and economic force in Japan. This in itself would make the organization controversial. In addition, however, the Sōka Gakkai is extremely hierarchical and authoritarian, almost military in its command structure. This, in conjunction with the Sōka Gakkai's stated intention to convert and govern the entire world, unnerves many observers, who fear demagoguery and a resurgence of expansionist militarism in Japan.

Because of the bewildering number of sects and subsects of Buddhism in Japan, and because individual Japanese tend to mix Shintō and Buddhist practice and participate in more than one form of Buddhism, it is difficult to provide an estimate of the number of followers of the various forms of Buddhism in Japan. Of Japan's total population of roughly 125,000,000, about eighty percent practice some form of Buddhism, usually mixed with some form of Shintō. Twenty percent practice other religions or none. About a third of the total population of Japan are adherents of the Nichiren sect, with half of these belonging to the newly popular Nichiren Shōshū, and half belonging to numerous other Nichiren subsects, primarily the Reiyūkai and the Risshō Kōseikai. About a fifth of the Japanese are Pure Land adherents, mostly Jōdo Shinshū. About a tenth of the population follow some form of Zen. The unified Sōtō sect accounts for about three quarters of Japan's Zen adherents, while the rest follow one of the numerous Rinzai subsects. Another tenth of the total population follow one of the many sects of Shingon. About five percent of the population follow Tendai, and only about two percent follow one or another of the old schools of the Nara period.

In Japan at the end of the twentieth century, Mahāyāna Buddhism has reached both its farthest departure from and its closest return to the teachings of the historical Buddha. Though ostensibly one of the most populous Buddhist nations, about half of Japan espouses devotional forms of the religion — i.e. Nichiren and Pure Land — which have less in common with the Buddha's original teachings than do some forms of Hinduism. At the same time, Japan is preëminently the home of Zen Buddhism, which arguably approaches the Buddha's original teachings more closely than any other form of Mahāyāna Buddhism. Between these two extremes, virtually every form of Mahāyāna Buddhism that has ever been practiced anywhere is now practiced somewhere in Japan.

CHAPTER XI

The Development of
Buddhism in Tibet

The development of Buddhism in Tibet bears several notable similarities to the development of Buddhism in Japan. Buddhism was introduced into Tibet in the seventh century, only slightly later than it was introduced into Japan. As in Japan, Buddhism encountered in Tibet a vigorous indigenous shamanism that exerted a marked and pervasive influence on the Buddhism that developed there. As in Japan, the introduction of Buddhism to Tibet involved also the introduction of a written language and organized civilization. As in Japan, Buddhism played a large role in the political development of Tibet. Tibetan Buddhism, writing and civilization, however, were developed almost entirely on the basis of Indian rather than Chinese models.

It is perhaps surprising that China did not play a larger role in the introduction of Buddhism, writing and civilization to Tibet. Racially and linguistically, Tibetans are closer to Chinese than to Indians. Geographically, access to China is easier than to India, which is separated from Tibet by the Himalayan Mountains. Historically, Tibetans were probably in contact with the Chinese since well before the dawn of the common era. Tibet lies immediately south of the southern branch of the Silk Road, and Tibetans, being inveterate traders, no doubt had business dealings with Chinese caravans from very early times. From the seventh to the tenth centuries, the period when Buddhism took root in Tibet, Tibet vied with China for control of the Silk Road, and from time to time extended its influence eastward even to Xi'an, often the capital of ancient China. Perhaps Tibet turned to India precisely because of the proximity of China and the consequent rivalry between the two powers. Because of the tragic domination of Tibet by communist China since 1950, it is easy to lose sight of the fact that Tibet and China existed as separate countries on a relatively equal footing until recent times. The influence that Tibet has wielded in its part of the world is all the more remarkable considering that the number of ethnic Tibetans has probably never exceeded five million.[35]

At any rate, in the middle of the seventh century, Tibet embarked upon a policy of voracious importation of Indian civilization and religion. The resulting mix of Indian Buddhism and Tibetan shamanism gave birth to a unique and vigorous form of Buddhism that later exerted influence throughout East Asia as a result of its adoption by the Mongols. Though Tibetan Buddhism developed several distinct sects, all of them are Tantric, and all share in common the elaborate ceremonial and strange regalia that characterize Tibetan Buddhism as a whole. Underneath its exotic surface, however, the Buddhism of Tibet is the purest surviving repository of the ancient Mahāyāna tradition of India.

The Bon Religion

The peculiar, even eerie character of Tibetan Buddhism, which is immediately apparent to an outside observer, no doubt derives from Tibet's indigenous shamanism, known as Bon. Little precise knowledge of the nature of the ancient Bon religion survives, but some idea of its broad outlines may be reconstructed on the basis of: 1) the surviving but heavily Buddhized Bon religion, 2) the peculiarities of Tibetan Buddhism, 3) Tibetan folklore, and 4) the religious practices of neighboring peoples less affected by Buddhism.

In general, the Bon religion appears to have been shaped by the overwhelming power of the Tibetan landscape and climate. The Tibetan Plateau, averaging some 14,500 feet above sea level, is the highest inhabited area in the world. Many Tibetans have never in their lives ventured below 12,000 feet. Vegetation is sparse or nonexistent except in a few surprisingly pleasant and fertile southern valleys, which have entered Western mythology as the location of the inaccessible paradise of Shangrila. Beyond these valleys, on Tibet's rugged mountain ranges and endless, barren plains, the climate is harsh. Violent hail storms can pommel unprotected people and animals to death and wreck nomadic tent dwellings. Some winds are so strong that they carry not only snow, dust and sand, but even gravel. In addition to physical dangers, there is the awesomeness of the vast, unbroken silence of the land and the austere crags jutting up from the plains. At that altitude, the light itself is stark and strange. On a bright day, one cannot see the flame on a match. On a clear, moonless night the stars alone light shapes. One feels watched by the landscape.

In keeping with Tibet's overwhelming terrain, the Bon religion was a dramatic shamanism that sought to placate and manipulate the capricious spirits which seem even to a modern visitor to pervade the very fabric of Tibet's climate and geography. The origin of the word "Bon" is uncertain, but its most probable original meaning is "to invoke." The beings invoked were the numerous gods *(Lha)* and demons *('Dre)* which still characterize the religion of Tibet, whether Buddhist or Bon. As the duality of gods and demons suggests, not all of these supernatural beings were regarded as malevolent, but all were considered capricious and dangerous, like the Tibetan environment itself, constantly requiring cautious attention.

The Bon shamans, known as *gShen* (see Pronunciation Guide), attempted to propitiate the gods and demons with material, animal and even human sacrifices. Like shamans elsewhere, they were believed to be able to communicate with and influence the spirit world through entering a trance or being possessed by a spirit. In this capacity, it was their duty to guide and pacify the spirits of the dead, who were regarded with considerable apprehension. The magical powers of the *gShen* were called upon to cure — or alternatively to inflict upon enemies — illnesses and misfortunes, which were almost invariably attributed to supernatural causes. Finally, as a result of their magical proficiency and connections with the spirit world, they were believed to be able to foretell the future through reading omens or communicating with the gods, demons, and departed ancestors. Most of these characteristics of Bon — with the exception of animal sacrifices and inflicting curses upon enemies — came to be prominent features of the Buddhism of Tibet. In addition, much of the distinctive regalia of Tibetan Buddhism — for example ceremonial horns made of human thigh bones and votive bowls made of human skulls — appears to have derived from the indigenous Bon religion.

Though the historical origins of Bon are lost forever, the Bon-po, as its adherents call themselves, attribute the religion to a founder, gShen Rab or "Great Shaman." Bon legends also record an imprecise period during which Bon was persecuted by the evil King Gri Gum ["Di Gum"]. No doubt this legend is in part a projection backward in time of an actual suppression of Bon under the Buddhist King Khri Srong lDe bTsan [Ti Song De Tsan] (742-97). These persecutions serve as the basis of the Bon claim that during times of persecution ancient scriptures were concealed so as to avoid their destruction. Much later, starting in the eleventh century, Bon priests claim to have rediscovered these concealed texts, which serve as the basis of the Bon canon.

These rediscovered *gTer-ma* or "treasure" texts, however, betray pervasive Buddhist influence. Western scholars normally assume therefore that the "discoverers" of the *gTer-ma* literature actually composed or edited the texts at a time when Buddhism was well known in Tibet. Supposedly, this ruse was intended to provide Bon with an ancient scriptural basis similar in authority to the canon that Buddhism had already developed in Tibet by the eleventh century, when the Bon texts began to be discovered. This assumption may not be altogether correct. It is possible that Bon and Buddhism had been in contact through Himalayan India long before Buddhism as such was introduced to Tibet. In this case, borrowings either way are possible. The similarities between Bon and Tantric Buddhism may be due partly to borrowings by Indian Tantrism from Himalayan shamanism. At any rate, if the Bon scriptures were not actually composed and edited with the express intent of emulating Tibetan Buddhist texts, they appear to have been at least selectively compiled from ancient traditions in light of the Buddhism existing in Tibet at the time of their discoveries. Despite the use of Bon rather than Buddhist terminology, the content of Bon texts is overtly similar to that of Buddhist texts. Like the Tibetan Buddhist canon, the Bon canon is divided into a Kanjur [bKa' 'Gyur], which is supposed to contain the teachings of the original founder of the religion, and a Tanjur [bsTan 'Gyur], which contains supplementary writings by the great teachers of the religion.

Bon survives to the present day in Tibet, but has so thoroughly assimilated Buddhist doctrines and practices as to be for all intents and purposes a somewhat renegade sect of Tibetan Buddhism. The most obvious feature that distinguishes Bon from Buddhism is Bon's intentional reversal of the clockwise orientation of Buddhist ceremonial. Buddhists always circumambulate a shrine or temple in a clockwise direction. The Bon-po circumambulate counter-clockwise. They do not hesitate to honor Buddhist shrines in this manner, and Buddhists do not seem to object. Buddhists rotate their prayer wheels clockwise, the Bon-po counter-clockwise. The Buddhist swastika — an Indo-European star symbol long before it acquired infamy as the Nazi emblem — is reversed in Bon iconography. The Bon-po typically place a greater emphasis upon magic and divination than the Buddhists of Tibet, and are widely recognized as the true experts in these areas. Tibetan Buddhists, however, also incorporate a great deal of magic and divination in their religious observances. Although magic and divination are not unknown in other forms of Buddhism, the unique form they take in Tibet indicates a pervasive influence of the archaic Bon religion in all forms of Tibetan Buddhism.

The First Introduction of Buddhism to Tibet (600-1000 CE)

Traditionally, Buddhism was introduced into Tibet under King Srong bTsan sGam-po [Song Tsan Gampo], who ascended the throne in 627 and died in approximately 650. Srong bTsan sGam-po was the grandson of the first proclaimed king of Tibet, who ascended the throne in about 600. Until perhaps a few centuries before this time, Tibet had been inhabited by warlike, nomadic clans wandering over the vast wilderness with herds of yaks and goats. Gradually, the more sedentary clans of the relatively fertile southeastern river valleys began to claim territorial holdings and vie for supremacy under increasingly powerful chieftains operating from fortified strongholds. Toward the end of the sixth century, several of these warlords united under the chieftain of the Yarlung district of central Tibet, thus initiating a convulsive transition into centralized power under a priest-king with the title Lha bTsan-po, "Divine Mighty One," which suggests that the dynasty was legitimized partly on the basis of religious authority.

Given the priestly aspect evident in the title of the early Tibetan kings, the traditional Tibetan portrayal of Srong bTsan sGam-po as a pious Buddhist is dubious. He did have two Buddhist wives, however, one a princess from China and the other a princess from Nepal, taken in the interests of solidifying political alliances with Tibet's neighbors. These wives were probably responsible for the formal introduction of Buddhism to Tibet. In the popular imagination, the wives of the king have been divinized as manifestations of the Buddhist goddess Tārā. In Tibet they are venerated as the White Dolma (Chinese) and the Green Dolma (Nepalese). Dolma [sGrol-ma] is the Tibetan equivalent for the Sanskrit Tārā, "Savioress," the consort of Avalokiteśvara, the bodhisattva of compassion. The White and Green Dolmas remain a common feature in Tibetan temples. Supposedly, in order to make his foreign wives comfortable in their new surroundings, the king built the Jo Khang Temple, the first Buddhist edifice in Tibet, which still stands, much modified, in the center of Lhasa.

As in Japan, the introduction of Buddhism to Tibet is inextricably associated with the acquisition of civilization from abroad. The same king under whom Buddhism was introduced, Srong bTsan sGam-po, is also believed to have dispatched a delegation to India in order to devise a script and grammar for the then unwritten Tibetan language. This delegation was headed by the great Tibetan linguist Thon-mi Sam-Bho-ta, who is given credit with the single-handed creation of the literary Tibetan language. There may have been some rudimentary attempts at writing Tibetan before Thon-mi, and he may not have accomplished himself the entire task of creating the grammar of classical Tibetan, but it is clear that these momentous developments occurred at about this time, i.e. the first half of the seventh century, and that they marked the beginning of what was to become the most enthusiastic and efficient importation of literacy and religion that the world has ever seen. By the eighth century, several

Tibetan translators were at work rendering Sanskrit Buddhist scriptures into their newly created written language.

In the five hundred years from 700 to about 1200 CE, Tibet was able to import virtually all significant Sanskrit Buddhist literature in existence and render it into a literary Tibetan language that had been tailor-made for the translation of Sanskrit. Over the centuries, the conventions of scriptural translation from Sanskrit became so consistent that today it is possible to recreate a virtually exact reconstruction of the Sanskrit original of any Buddhist text that was translated into Tibetan. This is of course immensely important given that the Sanskrit originals of most Buddhist scriptures have been lost. Chinese translations of Sanskrit texts give some idea of their original content, but Tibetan translations are practically as good as the Sanskrit originals themselves.

This immense translation achievement — arguably the most ambitious, successful and significant in history — took many centuries. Although their actual roles and piety may be exaggerated in traditional history, King Srong bTsan sGam-po and the linguist Thon-mi Sam-bho-ta deserve a great deal of credit for having initiated the importation of Buddhism and literacy into Tibet. In doing so, they initiated the preservation of an important corpus of literature that otherwise would have been lost. It is clear, however, that Buddhism was only marginally established in Tibet by the time of Srong bTsan sGam-po's death in about 650. His successors to the throne over the next century do not appear to have been particularly enthusiastic about Buddhism, and may even have suppressed the religion from time to time. Tibetan records from the period, preserved with caches of Chinese manuscripts recently discovered at Dunhuang (Tun-huang), in western China, scarcely mention Buddhism.[36]

Whether or not there was an actual suppression of Buddhism under the immediate successors of Srong bTsan sGam-po, Khri Srong lDe bTsan (742-98), the fifth successor to Srong bTsan sGam-po, is remembered as the great restorer of Buddhism in Tibet. In reality, he was probably the first Buddhist king of Tibet, and it appears that Buddhism was firmly established in Tibet only during his reign. Khri Srong lDe bTsan's patronage of Buddhism centered around his establishment of the first abiding Buddhist monastery in Tibet at Sam-ye [bSam-yas]. The design of this monastery, which combined Indian, Chinese and Tibetan motifs, is supposed to have been inspired by Śāntarakshita, an eminent Indian monk who reputedly was attracted to Tibet by the generous payment Tibetans were prepared to give for scriptures and teachings.

With the cooperation of Khri Srong lDe bTsan, Śāntarakshita appears to have masterminded foundational victories of Indian Buddhism over both Chinese Buddhism and indigenous Bon. Śāntarakshita summoned his disciple Kamalaśīla from India to argue in a great debate between Chinese and Indian Buddhism. This debate was held in about 792 at the Sam-ye Monastery. According to Tibetan records, the Chinese faction presented a minimalist doctrinal position based on Madhyamaka and Chan (Zen), both of which stressed spontaneous enlightenment and de-emphasized morality and scriptures. Kamalaśīla, by contrast, emphasized the bodhisattva path of gradually perfecting wisdom and compassion for the benefit of all sentient beings.

The verdict in favor of Kamalaśīla may have been influenced by the fact that Tibet was vying for territory with Tang China at the time. On the other hand, the outcome may have been predetermined on the basis of the foothold Indian culture and religion had already established in Tibet under Srong bTsan sGam-po. At any rate, this debate is regarded as the watershed after which Buddhism in Tibet developed almost exclusively along Indian rather than Chinese lines. The classical, scholarly Buddhism advocated by Kamalaśīla, however, was not to gain ascendancy in Tibet until over half a millennium had passed, by which time Tibet had put its own indelible stamp on the religion. Instead, it was the mysterious, flamboyant, somewhat renegade form of Buddhism known as Tantra which initially appealed to the Tibetan mentality sufficiently to prevail over the indigenous Bon shamanism.

Again, Śāntarakshita is given credit for masterminding the ascendancy of Indian Buddhism, this time over the indigenous Bon religion. Tibetan sources say that in spite of the victory over their Chinese rivals, Śāntarakshita realized that the conservative Buddhism he and Kamalaśīla represented would not in the end appeal sufficiently to the Tibetans, who were devoted to the magical rituals of their own Bon priests. To overcome this predilection among the Tibetans, it is said that Śāntarakshita summoned the Tantric master Padma-sambhava from the Himalayan kingdom of Swat in order to rival the magical powers of the Bon priests and overcome the hordes of demons in league with them. Khri Srong lDe bTsan is supposed to have arranged for a contest of magical prowess between Padma-sambhava and the most powerful Bon shamans in the land. According to traditional accounts, Padma-sambhava triumphed decisively over the Bon priests and their demon allies with spectacular feats of magic. This victory resulted in the foundation of the Nyingmapa [rNying-ma-pa], the first sect of Tibetan Buddhism.

The legend of Padma-sambhava's dramatic victory notwithstanding, it appears that in the century following the succession of Khri Srong lDe bTsan the influence of Buddhism in Tibet was relatively small and was mostly confined to court circles. Moreover, far from rivaling Bon shamans, figures such as Padma-sambhava during this period were eagerly exploiting the common ground that existed between Tantric Buddhism and Bon in order to gain acceptance for Buddhism in this new environment. Similarly, Bon shamans were appropriating what they could of the magic and metaphysics of Tantric Buddhism. Given that Indian Tantrism, both Buddhist and Hindu, developed significantly in the north and northwest of India — in Himalayan lands bordering upon Tibet — Buddhism and Bon may well have been exerting influence upon one another long before Buddhism as such was introduced into Tibet. It is undeniable, though, that during the first several centuries of their record-ed association in Tibet, Buddhism and Bon grew more and more similar due to apparently uninhibited borrowing on both sides.

Eventually, the term Nyingmapa or "Ancient Ones" came to designate the form of Buddhism that developed in close association with Bon under the early kings of Tibet. The Nyingmapa is now regarded as a sect of Tibetan Buddhism. It differs from other sects primarily in its emphasis upon Tantric rituals, veneration of special Tantric scriptures, and the non-celibate lifestyle of many of its monks. In all of these regards Nyingmapa Buddhism is similar to the Bon religion. Both Nyingmapa and Bon divide their syncretistic teachings into "Nine Ways," which differ in arrangement, but are similar in content. Both include in their distinctive religious literature *gTer-ma* or "treasure" scriptures which they claim had been concealed during periods of persecution under the early kings of Tibet. The implication of all this is that each party eventually became reluctant to acknowledge its borrowings from the other, and that both therefore tried to project the literary bases of their doctrines and practices back into a time before the borrowings had taken place. Though both Bon and Nyingmapa were eventually to be superseded by newer sects of Buddhism, the initial syncretism they worked out endures to the present day as the core of Tibetan Buddhism. Unlike in China and Japan, "Buddhism in Tibet" became "Tibetan Buddhism" almost from the point of its introduction.

It appears, then, that the tradition of intense rivalry between Bon and Buddhism under the early kings of Tibet is largely a historical fantasy propagated by later followers of the religions. On the whole, the two religions appear to have exchanged teachings and practices quite freely, taking only the most rudimentary measures to conceal their mutual borrowings. Instead of being primarily concerned with maintaining their respective identities, they seem to have been more concerned with making certain that they left nothing out in their syncretisms. Both, it must be remembered, even at court, were attempting to appeal to a highly superstitious clientele who were concerned with immediate magical results here and now rather than with lofty philosophical and moral ideals. Over the next two centuries, the relative backwardness of Tibet would undergo a remarkable transformation under turbulent circumstances. As the outside world pressed in on Tibet, Buddhism proved to be more adaptable than Bon, because Buddhism was a major constituent of this outside world.

Both Buddhism and Bon claim to have been persecuted by one or another of the kings of Tibet. Traditionally, the great enemy of Bon was Khri Srong lDe bTsan, who is said to have been forced to abandon his persecution of Bon only by a disease magically inflicted upon him by the Bon sorcerer Gyer sPungs. What actually appears to have transpired is a diplomatic alliance between Khri Srong lDe bTsan and a powerful chieftain in western Tibet who practiced and promoted Bon in his realm. Khri Srong lDe bTsan was obviously well disposed toward Buddhism, and he may have forced some concessions from the Bon priests in his realm. Nonetheless, he retained throughout his life the traditional Bon title of Tibetan kings, Lha bTsan-po, "Divine Mighty One," and was buried in the traditional Bon manner in the ancient burial ground at 'Phyong rGyas [Chong Gye].

Like Bon, Buddhism may have been suppressed from time to time. In particular, the last of the Tibetan kings, gLang Dar-ma (r. 836-42), is remembered as an actual demon because of his persecutions of Buddhism. After only about six years as king, gLang Dar-ma was assassinated in 842, leaving two potential heirs to the throne. Rival clans, loosely identified with Buddhism and Bon respectively, divided their loyalties between the two claimants to the throne. An uneasy truce held until 866, when all-out civil war drove the pro-Buddhist faction of the old royal line into exile in "Western Tibet," the conventional name of the kingdom they established centered upon present-day Ladakh, in far-north India. The development of Buddhism in Western Tibet at this time is examined in Chapter XII.

Buddhist histories portray the two-hundred-year period beginning with gLang Dar-ma as a dark age of Bon persecution of Buddhism. Actually, civilization as a whole in central Tibet suffered a setback during this period of disunity, but there is little indication that Buddhism was actively persecuted. In Western Tibet, the supporters of the old royal line found themselves in close contact with long-established Buddhist societies in the northern Indian regions of Kashmir and Gandhāra. In this environment, Buddhism began to sink deep roots into the Tibetan mentality. Meanwhile, Buddhism appears to have continued quietly to co-exist with Bon in central and eastern Tibet.

The Second Introduction of Buddhism and the Development of Sects (1000-1200)

What is traditionally regarded as the restoration of Buddhism in central Tibet was in effect a second introduction of Buddhism. The first introduction of Buddhism had resulted in the amalgamation of Buddhism and Bon that was to color all subsequent forms of Tibetan Buddhism. Each of these forms of Tibetan Buddhism may be described as Tantric, emphasizing the mystery of empowerment passed from guru to disciple. In Tantric Buddhism, magical spells and rituals always have a higher significance known only to the initiated. This convention allowed the grafting of more sophisticated aspects of Indian Buddhism onto the syncretism of Bon and Buddhism that had become established in Tibet.

The disintegration of centralized rule in Tibet, while often regarded as detrimental to the development of Buddhism, actually facilitated the formation of the classical sects of Tibetan Buddhism. The demise of the Tibetan kingship resulted in political control of Tibet by several powerful clans. Virtually all of these clans were eager to identify themselves with a lineage of recognized religious masters, Buddhist, Bon or both. In addition to what appears to have been sincere spiritual aspiration, such identification reassured the superstitious peasantry that they would not become victims of the magic of a rival clan's priests. The lineages of religious teachings that survived — and many must have died out — eventually became the recognized sects of Tibetan Buddhism.

The timing of these developments is crucial in the history of Buddhism. Already in the tenth century, Muslims were making incursions into western India and would soon sweep through the entirety of northern India, utterly destroying Buddhism in India by the thirteenth century. By the fourteenth century, Kashmir and most of the other Himalayan Buddhist kingdoms had also fallen to the Muslims. Buddhist monks and scriptures in particular were targeted for destruction by the Muslims in the course of their conquest of India. It is fortunate indeed that at precisely the right time, Tibet was eager to accommodate Buddhist refugees and to acquire as many Buddhist scriptures as possible.

The various sects of Buddhism that arose in Tibet in the course of these far-flung historical events are distinguished from one another not primarily upon the basis of doctrine or practice, nor even on the basis of scriptures, but rather on the basis of the lineage of masters upon whose teachings the sects are based. Their doctrines and practices in fact differ very little, and even though each sect maintains its own special scriptures, all sects regard as sacred the vast Buddhist canon of Tibet — the Kanjur and Tanjur. Each of the sects resulting from the resurgence of Buddhism in Tibet, however, is Tantric, and as noted above, in Tantric Buddhism the lineage of transmission is often more important than the teaching transmitted.

Nyingmapa and Bon

Though the Nyingmapa [rNying-ma-pa] has the most ancient roots of any sect of Tibetan Buddhism, the school itself did not begin to consolidate until the second period of Tibetan Buddhism. It was not until the other sects of Tibetan Buddhism began to form in the eleventh century that Nyingmapa monks began to claim to discover *gTer-ma* or "treasure" texts that supposedly had been concealed during the persecution under King gLang Dar-ma. Such discoveries proliferated in the fourteenth century and continued even into the nineteenth century. These texts provide the primary scriptural basis for the identification of the Nyingmapa as a separate sect of Tibetan Buddhism. In addition, the Nyingmapa preserves a large corpus of Tantric texts that are supposed to have been composed or translated in Tibet before the eleventh century, some of them by Padma-sambhava himself. These are known as the "Old Tantras" as opposed to the "New Tantras" which are recognized by the other sects of Tibetan Buddhism and contained in the Kanjur of the standard Tibetan canon. The Nyingmapa also venerate and study the standard Kanjur as well as the Tanjur, which contains religious treatises and commentaries recognized by Tibetan Buddhism as a whole.

The "Old Tantras" and the *gTer-ma* literature of the Nyingmapa probably contain a great deal of truly old material composed before the eleventh century. It is unrealistic to imagine a group of conspirators sitting down and making it all up. This corpus appears, however, to be an eclectic, almost haphazard amalgamation of disparate material rather than a record of a coherent tradition of knowledge. It is of course possible that some of the *gTer-ma* texts actually were hidden and discovered later, but the Nyingmapa inadvertently emphasize the generally non-historical nature of their claims by insisting that the lamas who eventually found these concealed texts, the *gTer sTon* or "Treasure Discoverers," were often reincarnations of the ancient lamas who hid them in the first place. The major *gTer sTon,* who are highly revered in the sect, began to appear in the twelfth century and continued to appear until as late as the nineteenth century.

The Nyingmapa claim as their founder Padma-sambhava, the great Tantric magician who triumphed over the Bon priests under King Khri

Srong lDe bTsan in the eighth century. Though universally venerated by all Tibetan Buddhists, Padma-sambhava is dubious as a historical figure. The Nyingmapa, however, preserves a corpus of legendary material, known as the "Padma Scrolls," purporting to relate the biography of their founder. As in the case of the "Old Tantras" and the *gTer-ma* literature, this material probably incorporates much truly ancient material. All sects of Tibetan Buddhism regard as authentic the Padma Scrolls and resort often to the legend of Padma-sambhava. Colorful figures like Padma-sambhava doubtless stand in the distant background of each of the sects of Buddhism that flourished in Tibet, and it is appropriate that they receive corporate recognition in the form of Padma-sambhava, Tibet's universally acknowledged "Guru Rinpoche" or "Precious Teacher." Like the Nyingmapa, the Bon-po preserve an equally fanciful biography of their supposed founder gShen Rab. Ironically, it is based on the life of the Buddha, whereas Padma-sambhava appears to be modeled upon an ancient Bon shaman.

In summary, the Nyingmapa sect appears to represent an amalgam of the forms of Buddhism that developed in association with Bon between the first and second introductions of Buddhism. As a result, Nyingmapa and Bon share many characteristics. Both were consolidated at about the same time and with similar recourse to *gTer-ma* literature, supposedly concealed when one or the other was in disfavor with one of the early Tibetan kings. As noted above, both the Bon and the Nyingmapa practices are divided into nine "ways" *(theg-pa,* Skt. *yāna).* Both divide these nine ways into "ways of cause," i.e. preliminary practices, and "ways of effect," the higher practices. The nine paths of Bon and Nyingmapa are similar, but do not correspond exactly. The lower three ways of the Nyingmapa encompass the beliefs and practices of Buddhism before the advent of Tantra. The lower four ways of Bon refer to the traditional magical practices of Bon before the advent of Buddhism. In both sects, the higher ways relate to the realization of enlightenment through Tantric practices involving the chanting of magical spells *(mantra),* making special hand gestures *(mudra),* mystical diagrams *(maṇḍala),* and ritualized sexual intercourse.

The sexual practices of Tantric Buddhism seem to fascinate Westerners whether their bias is for or against Buddhism. Tantric visual art depicting deities copulating with their consorts can be quite explicit and erotic, and the descriptions of the sexual escapades of the ancient Tantric masters are sometimes outright bawdy. Nonetheless, in every context, Tantric sexual symbolism serves a higher purpose than sensual gratification or titillation. It seeks in fact to focus the whole of one's physical and spiritual being on the consummation of all the aspirations that spiritual enlightenment represents. From time to time, the sexual side of Tantra has been abused, primarily by Western poseurs who know next to nothing of the rigors of legitimate Tantra. For the vast majority of the Nyingmapa lamas, their Tantric sexual partners are their wives alone, and the practice has the effect of sanctifying rather than debasing sexuality. Some Tibetan lay Buddhists also practice Tantric sex under the guidance of a master in addition to their normal sexual activities. In the other sects of Tibetan Buddhism, the monks and nuns are strictly celibate except in rare circumstances. Although there are bound to be lapses of discipline — as there are in celibate orders the world over — Tantric sexual practices in these other sects usually do not go beyond meditative visualization of copulating deities. Such visualizations generally represent the resolution of abstract, opposite principles such as good and evil or ignorance and enlightenment.

As discussed below, from time to time there have been reform movements intended to curb the exuberance of Tibetan Buddhism, but none of them has attempted to do away with the Tantric side of the religion as practiced in Tibet. The sects to be examined below follow an overall pattern of building upon Tantric foundations an increased emphasis of scholarship and monastic discipline.

Kadampa

The most austere of these new sects was the Kadampa [bKa' gDams-pa], founded by the Indian monk Atīśa (982-1054). Atīśa's wanderings in the interests of amassing Buddhist wisdom are legendary. He did not become a monk until the age of thirty, by which time he had traveled from his home in Bengal to Burma in the east and to Afghanistan in the west in his quest for knowledge. He came to Western Tibet in 1042, after repeated entreaties by the noble families in the region. He was already sixty at the time. Spurred on by tales of thousands of eager monks in Lhasa, Sam-ye and elsewhere, he moved on to central Tibet and taught there as well. Reputedly, he sent the vast sums of money he received back to his home monastery in India, the famous Vikramaśīlā in Bihar. He may well have done so, as Buddhism in India was in a state of decline by this time. In fact, this decline of Buddhism in India, rather than vast sums of money reputedly paid by the Tibetans, probably accounts for the presence of prominent Indian monks in Tibet at this time.

Tibetan sources pinpoint the beginning of the restoration of Buddhism in central Tibet in 978, when a contingent of monks from eastern Tibet returned to Lhasa and set up a monastery there. The primary impetus for this revival, however, came from the west with the arrival of Atīśa. Around this same time, the Indian monk Smriti in eastern Tibet and the great Rin Chen bZang-po (958-1055) in Western Tibet were busily collecting and translating Buddhist texts from India. Rin Chen bZang-po in particular had excellent access to Indian teachers and texts, living as he did on the borders of the old Buddhist kingdoms of northwestern India. He is supposed to have made two trips to Kashmir and one to India, spending a total of seventeen years abroad, collecting and translating authentic Indian Tantras and establishing thereby the core of the so-called "New Tantra" tradition.

It is Atīśa, however, who is remembered as the first great restorer of Buddhism in Tibet. This status derives principally from his reputation as the first great integrator of scholarly and Tantric Buddhism in Tibet. Atīśa concentrated on the *Prajñā Paramitā Sūtras* of Madhyamaka Buddhism, but he is also given credit for having introduced the important *Guhya Samāja Tantra* to Tibet with an important innovation. At the center of its hierarchy of deities, Atīśa located the bodhisattva of compassion, Avalokiteśvara, thus initiating the Tibetans' continuing recognition of him as the chief divinity of their pantheon. Atīśa also wrote a famous compendium of Buddhist doctrine known as the *Bodhi-patha Pradīpa* intended to harmonize the various versions of Buddhist doctrine current in Tibet at his time.

Atīśa is associated with strict monastic discipline and requiring devotion and obedience from his pupils. In the latter regard, his position was identical to that of the Tantric masters, but Atīśa wished to enforce monastic discipline in Tibet rather than add yet another Tantric lineage. Atīśa himself achieved little success, but his influence eventually prevailed under the leadership of the great Buddhist reformer Tsong Kha-pa, whose Gelugpa [dGe Lugs-pa] sect is referred to by its adherents as the "New Kadampa" because of its emphasis upon scholarship and orderly monastic discipline.

Traditionally, the reason for Atīśa's lack of immediate impact in Tibet was his austere chief disciple 'Brom sTon [Dom-ton — 1008-64]. Though highly respected, 'Brom sTon is blamed for having repressed Atīśa's desire to teach Tantric Buddhism in Tibet. Such resistance is unlikely, given Atīśa's authoritarian attitude toward disciples and 'Brom sTon's extreme devotion to his master. After Atīśa's death, 'Brom sTon continued his work by founding the first sectarian monastery in Tibet at Rva sGreng [Ra Dreng] in 1056. The name of the Kadampa sect means literally "bound by laws," i.e. the four rules of the Rva sGreng monastery: abstinence from sex, intoxicants, travel and possessions.

Before the advent of the Kadampa sect, Tibetan Buddhism was a
highly individual affair, with practitioners formulating their own spiritual
disciplines in consultation with their teacher or teachers. Tibet's first
monastery at Sam-ye continued to function at this time, but housed practitioners of many different teachings and methods, most of them no doubt
Tantric. It was from this center that the other sects of Tibetan Buddhism
began to coalesce in imitation of the model established by Atīśa and
'Brom sTon. Each of these sects derived from the combined influence of
Atīśa on the one hand and the great Tantric translator Rin Chen bZang-po
on the other.

Sakyapa

The first of the major sects of Tibetan Buddhism to form was the
Sakyapa [Sa-sKya-pa], which regards 'Brog-mi [Dog-mi — 992-1072] as its
founder. 'Brog-mi, a contemporary of Atīśa, journeyed to India and
studied at Vikramaśilā, Atīśa's home monastery, gaining a reputation as a
great scholar and translator as well as a powerful magician and miracle
worker. As a result of his experience in India, 'Brog-mi rejected the
"Old Tantras" followed by the Nyingmapa in favor of the "new teachings"
introduced to Tibet by Atīśa. Unlike 'Brom sTon, however, 'Brog-mi emphasized Tantric teachings and practices, especially the *Hevajra Tantra,*
which emphasizes sexual symbolism and practices.

Possibly as a result of this sexual emphasis, the Sakyapa sect did not
initially require celibacy of its monks, which resulted in the establishment
of an ecclesiastical dynasty similar to that of the Jōdo Shinshū in Japan.
Later, when celibacy did become mandatory for Sakyapa monks, the
hereditary leader of the sect took a special form of ordination that
allowed for the continued, hereditary propagation of the sect's leadership. The religious dynasty thus propagated survives to the present day.
As in the case of Jōdo Shinshū Buddhism in Japan, this stable succession
of leadership contributed to the political power of the sect, which at its
height was great indeed. During much of the the thirteenth and fourteenth centuries, the Sakyapa abbot was in effect the ruler of Tibet and
the head priest of the Mongol empire.

'Brog-mi's chief disciple was dKon mChog rGyal-po. Previously a lay
follower of the Nyingmapa, he founded in 1073 the monastery from
which the Sakyapa sect takes its name. Literally, *Sa sKya* means
"gray earth." The monastery was so named because of the color of the
ground upon which it was built. dKon mChog rGyal-po's son, Kun dGa'
sNying-po (1092-1158), is given credit for actually having systematized

the teachings brought back from India by 'Brog-mi, and may thus be regarded as the true founder of the sect. The hallmarks of the sect are its emphasis upon scholarship and its central doctrinal position, known as *Lam 'Bras* [Lam-de] or "path and fruit," which comprises classical Madhyamaka philosophy on the one hand and Tantric initiation and practice on the other.

As the chief Tantric text of the Sakyapa sect is the *Hevajra Tantra*, with its overt sexual content, these Tantric rites may sometimes involve sexual intercourse. The sexual symbolism of the Sakyapa sect, however, is primarily metaphorical, expressing the classical Madhyamaka position, first formulated by Nāgārjuna, of the union of saṃsāra and nirvāṇa. According to the Sakyapa teaching, the "path" *(Lam)* through saṃsāra and the fruit *('Bras)* of nirvāṇa are to be merged through wisdom, meditation and Tantric rituals. The full *Lam 'Bras* doctrine encompasses the philosophical and meditational resolution of a whole series of related but apparently distinct concepts corresponding to "path" and "fruit." These include among others the pairs saṃsāra and nirvāṇa, compassion and wisdom, object and subject — all intended to be merged into transcendent unities through the overriding sexual symbolism of the union of male and female.

Kagyudpa

Each of the great lamas discussed thus far is associated in legend and in the popular imagination with numerous highly fanciful and entertaining stories concerning the superhuman arduousness of their spiritual practices and the miraculous events punctuating their careers. The most colorful of these legends, however, surround the founding figures of the Kagyudpa [bKa' rGyud-pa] sect. The classical literary and doctrinal basis of the sect was formulated by the relatively staid scholar monk sGam-po-pa (1079-1153), but the story of the Tantric lineage leading up to this classical formulation abounds with some of the most colorful characters in Tibetan literature, or in any literature for that matter. At the same time, underneath the extravagant veneer of fantasy one can readily perceive genuine historical characters of delightful eccentricity and great charisma.

The first Tibetan master in the Tantric lineage that was to become known as the Kagyudpa or "Sect of Transmitted Law" was Marpa (1012-96). The name of the sect indicates the importance its followers place upon the Tantric chain of transmission from guru to disciple. Fantastic biographical accounts of the primary figures in this chain of transmission form the primary sacred literature of the sect.[37] Like the other Tibetan sects, the Kagyudpa reveres the standard Kanjur and Tanjur, but the biographies of the sect's founders are its own special treasure.

Marpa is said to have studied for a time under 'Brog-mi, the founder of the Sakyapa lineage, who had studied at the famous Vikramaśilā monastery in India. He regarded the fees demanded by 'Brog-mi to be exorbitant, however, and determined to go to India himself in search of religious instruction. It is said that even before he left Tibet Marpa was aware, through dreams and visions, that the guru he sought was the great Tantric master Nāropa. It is actually historically possible that Marpa did indeed set out specifically to find Nāropa. Nāropa, for all the legendary material that surrounds accounts of his life, was an eminent historical figure in India who lived from 1016 to 1100. From 1049 to 1057 he was the abbot of the famous Nālandā monastic university in India, but as a result of a vision of his own predestined guru Tilopa, Nāropa is said to have abandoned his exalted post to search for his spiritual master. This intriguing story may well have attracted a seeker such as Marpa.

At any rate, it is with Tilopa (988-1069) that the earthly Kagyudpa lineage begins. Only the earthly lineage begins here, however, for Tilopa is believed to have been initiated, through the medium of a sorceress, by none other than Nāgārjuna himself. Nāropa is said to have been inspired to abandon his post as abbot of Nālandā upon being ridiculed by "an old woman with thirty-seven ugly features" for being so deluded as to imagine that he understood the true meaning of the Buddhist scriptures. She urged him to seek out Tilopa, and then, to impress her point, she "disappeared like a rainbow in the sky."

This experience convinced Nāropa to set out on a quest for his predestined guru. Guided by a voice from the sky, he encountered eleven more disgusting visions in the course of his search, among them a leprous woman without hands or feet, a maggot-infested dog, a man disemboweling a human corpse with his bare hands, another disemboweling a living man, and yet another in the act of torturing his parents. In each case, when Nāropa showed his disgust, the vision vanished into a rainbow and in a disembodied voice rebuked him for having failed to rid himself of aversion by purifying his own vision of saṃsāra. Finally, despairing of ever finding his guru, Nāropa was on the verge of suicide when Tilopa appeared in person, "a dark man dressed in cotton trousers, with protruding, bloodshot eyes."

Nāropa was overjoyed, but this meeting with his guru marked the beginning of twelve years of discipleship entailing twelve superhuman tests of Nāropa's dedication to his master and determination to gain his secret Tantric teachings. These included leaping from a high tower, jumping into a blazing fire, chasing phantoms through the desert, and finally making a *maṇḍala* (sacred diagram) out of his own body by cutting off his legs, arms and head and arranging them on the ground. These twelve tests, like the previous twelve visions, represent the twelve levels of initiation in the Mahāmudra or "Great Gesture" tradition practiced by the Kagyudpa sect. The severity of the ordeals symbolize the unquestioning devotion that a Tantric aspirant must develop for the guru, and the dedication the aspirant must demonstrate before the secret teachings of the lineage will be passed on. At the conclusion of these symbolically depicted initiations, Tilopa enjoined Nāropa to set out on his own and to "act in a way which is beyond words or thoughts," signifying that Nāropa had gained enlightenment. According to tradition, Nāropa followed his master's advice enthusiastically, scandalizing the countryside by hunting deer with a pack of hounds while having sex with the local chieftain's daughter, apparently all at the same time. The chieftain had him burned at the stake, but found him the next morning dancing in the embers and still having sex with his daughter. Such episodes symbolize the enlightened mind's transcendence of conventional morality.

Tilopa's final instruction to Nāropa was to act for the benefit of all sentient beings, i.e. to perform the traditional bodhisattva role of Mahāyāna Buddhism, and to make his way to the monastery at Pullahari, there to meet his own predestined disciple Marpa from Tibet. Marpa, of course, was already in search of Nāropa. As had been foretold, the two met, and Nāropa passed on to Marpa the secret knowledge he had gained at such pains from Tilopa, apparently without requiring similar ordeals of Marpa.

Marpa was not so generous to his own disciple Milarepa [Mi-la Ras-pa — 1040-1123], whose initiatory trials under the tutelage of his master are recorded in an autobiographical account supposedly written by Milarepa himself. On the whole, Milarepa's account rings true, aside from the numerous feats of magic that he claims to have performed. Though possibly somewhat exaggerated, the ordeals to which Marpa is alleged to have subjected Milarepa are nonetheless humanly possible. Most notably, Milarepa was required to build, dismantle and rebuild several times a stone house for his guru. Tibetan tradition dubiously identifies the structure built by Milarepa as a striking nine-story tower that still stands at Sras ["Sray"]. Without the occasional kindness shown by Marpa's wife, it is doubtful that the pupil could have endured his master's ill-treatment and neglect, which involved drunkenness, violent outbursts of temper, beatings, scoldings and constant humiliations. Despite all this, which may be partly true, Milarepa persisted and was eventually rewarded by receiving the precious lineage of initiation passed on from Tilopa.

Milarepa himself justifies all of these hardships at the hands of his master as being necessary to neutralize the evil karma of his past. To the present day, such atonement is a theoretical aspect of the ordeals to which Tantric aspirants are subjected before gaining initiation. These "ordeals" now normally involve performing many thousand prostrations and repetitions of *mantras,* which are counted up on the ubiquitous prayer beads that pious Tibetans always carry. Thus the exaggerated trials of Nāropa and Milarepa illustrate two important purposes of the ordeals that invariably precede Tantric initiation: 1) to demonstrate one's sincere determination to receive the initiation, and 2) to cleanse oneself of bad karma and amass a sufficient store of merit to render the secret teaching effective. Such ordeals also serve a third, very practical purpose. They keep the teachings secret among the initiated. No one is likely to go to all that trouble out of mere curiosity or lightly pass on to others the teachings thus gained.

In contrast to Tilopa, Nāropa and Marpa, Milarepa is remembered as a strictly celibate, self-mortifying ascetic. After his training under Marpa, he retired for most of the rest of his life to a lonely mountain cave, where he subsisted clad in rags on a diet of boiled nettles. The biography of Milarepa appears to mark a transition period in the Kagyudpa lineage from a concern with fanciful magnification of its founders to a concern with an accurate historical record of its propagation. Evans-Wentz, the translator of Milarepa's biography into English, points out tellingly that the account is probably as accurate historically as the Christian *New Testament,* if not more so.[38]

Though Milarepa's painful apprenticeship and withdrawn ascetic life appear grim and joyless, he is most remembered for his songs of joy. These "songs" — which are actually inspirational poems expressing the euphoria of enlightenment — are collected in a scripture known as the *Hundred Thousand Songs of Milarepa.*[39] This collection of songs of joy, interspersed with stories explaining the occasion of each song, is one of the most popular Tibetan scriptures and is regarded by many as the greatest literary masterpiece in the Tibetan language.

Milarepa's life of isolated asceticism attracted few disciples, but one accomplished scholar of the Kadampa sect, sGam-po-pa (1079-1153), on hearing of Milarepa by chance from a beggar, is said to have realized immediately that this was his true master. Milarepa had been miraculously aware for a year that sGam-po-pa would come, and he sent out a disciple to meet him as he approached. To humble the pride of the stodgy scholar monk, Milarepa is said to have kept sGam-po-pa waiting for thirty days before agreeing to see him, and then to have greeted him with a human skull full of wine. This he insisted that sGam-po-pa drink, despite the prohibition of alcohol for monks, signifying his initiation onto the Tantric path. Thereafter, sGam-po-pa built a mud hut at the foot of a boulder near Milarepa's cave and received a rigorous initiation into the lineage of Tilopa, Nāropa and Marpa.

Though regarded as a great Tantric master capable of magic and miracles, sGam-po-pa's lasting achievement was his systematization of Kagyudpa doctrine and the formal organization of the sect itself. In effect, sGam-po-pa synthesized the scholarly tradition of the Kadampa sect with the Tantric tradition of the Kagyudpa sect. In so doing, sGam-po-pa actually did what Atīśa is supposed to have done — he accomplished a synthesis of scholarly and Tantric Buddhism. His best known work, *The Jewel Ornament of Liberation*,[40] is possibly the best general introduction to Mahāyāna Buddhism ever written. It is regarded as authoritative by all sects of Tibetan Buddhism. By attracting many disciples and exhibiting great organizational skills, sGam-po-pa also insured the preservation for posterity of the special Tantric practices handed down to Milarepa. These are known as the "Six Teachings of Nāropa," and in the end they had a profound influence upon the development of Tibetan Buddhism as a whole.

These Six Teachings (*Chos Drug,* lit. six dharmas) may be viewed as a systematic course of training designed to allow one to gain control over one's fate after death and in rebirth.[41] The first, "heat teaching," trains one in the physical discipline that allows yogic practitioners the world over to exhibit indifference to pain and to control normally involuntary bodily functions such as heartbeat and respiration. Tibetan yogins in particular are renowned for their ability to withstand extremes of cold by generating the "mystical heat" for which this first teaching of Nāropa is named. In the second, the "teaching of illusory body," one develops the capacity to view the material world, including one's own body, as insubstantial and illusory. Building upon this attainment, in the "teaching of dreaming" one learns to maintain awareness and control even during sleep and dreams. This continuity of practice allows the perfection of the "teaching of the clear light," representing uninterrupted awareness of the undefiled radiance of the true mind. This attainment is regarded as equivalent to the realization of *śūnyatā* or emptiness as propounded in Madhyamaka philosophy.

The fifth teaching, that of the *Bar Do,* or "intermediate state" between death and rebirth, allows one to retain control of one's destiny during the immediate post-mortem period, which Tibetans regard as a conscious though normally highly disoriented state wherein one's past karma takes over and determines one's fate in the afterlife. The well-known *Tibetan Book of the Dead*,[42] or *Bar-Do Tho-sGrol* [Bar-do To-dol], meaning literally something like "Crossing the Stages of the *Bar-Do*," is widely used by Tibetans of all sects as a guide to the departed. It is read over the corpse of one recently deceased in order to ameliorate the terrors of the intermediate state between death and rebirth, a state which can last for as long as forty-nine days.

The accomplished Tantric yogin is believed to be able to maintain complete control during this disembodied period. By practicing the sixth of the teachings of Nāropa, the "teaching of transference," one is believed to be able to determine the identity of the future being in which rebirth will occur. This remarkable teaching led to the equally remarkable convention of replacing deceased abbots by locating their supposed reincarnations. This practice, which became widespread in Tibetan Buddhism, began among the followers of the first Karmapa (1110-93), one of the chief disciples of sGam-po-pa. The reincarnating lineage of Karmapas continues to the present day. The sixteenth Karmapa — who was one of the foremost propagators of Tibetan Buddhism in the West — passed away in the United States in 1981. Soon afterward, his reincarnation was discovered in Tibet, but due to communist China's hostility toward Buddhism, the identity of the seventeenth Karmapa was kept secret until 1992. State recognition of the young lama's status represented the first official acceptance by communist China of a new, reincarnating lama.

Although the convention of leadership succession by reincarnation may seem odd to Westerners, it actually proved to be a practical and flexible system. In the first place, the reincarnations of deceased lamas have often been discovered among the children of wealthy or influential patrons of the sect, a situation perfectly in line with the theory that advanced lamas are able to determine the identity of their rebirths. This has had the effect of cementing relations between the sect and its patrons. In the second place, the reincarnation, known as a Tulku [*sPrul-sKu*, Skt. *nirmāṇa-kāya*], will be an infant, usually only a few years old by the time identity is established. Until the child attains maturity, the de facto control of the sect rests in the hands of senior members of the order, as does the upbringing and training of the young abbot. The system thus allows flexibility in the political and financial alliances formed by the sect and insures continuity in the orientation of its leadership. Pioneered by the Karmapa subsect of the Kagyudpa, this system of succession became common throughout Tibetan Buddhism. When adopted by the Gelugpa sect, it resulted in the institution of the Dalai Lama, whom most Tibetans regard as the legitimate ruler of Tibet.

At the time of the first Karmapa's death in 1193, the wide world at the feet of Tibet's mountainous refuge was awash with cataclysmic developments. In northern India, the Muslim eradication of Buddhism was almost complete. It is a remarkable coincidence, some would say a miracle, that Tibetan love of Buddhism had just barely outpaced Muslim hatred of the religion. By the time Vikramaśilā, the last of the great Buddhist universities, had been destroyed in 1203, zealous Tibetans had succeeded in transporting virtually the entire scriptural basis of Indian Buddhism to Tibet. This achievement laid new foundations for Buddhism in the only country in mainland East Asia not to be devastated by the second great cataclysm of the era, the Mongol hordes.

The Mongol Period (1200-1400)

Relations between Tibet and the Mongols under Genghis Khan (1162-1227), the first Mongol emperor, are unclear. It appears that Tibet submitted to Mongol overlordship without a struggle. There was no central government authority in Tibet at the time, but in about 1207 submission to Genghis Khan is said to have been negotiated by a descendant of the ancient kings of Tibet, whose dynasty had been defunct for 350 years, and by a high lama of the Kagyudpa sect. It was under Genghis' successor Ogodai (d. 1241), however, that the first definite Tibetan encounters with the Mongol empire occurred, and these were initially hostile.

In 1239, Ogodai's son Godan sent a raiding party into Tibet. This force looted several wealthy monasteries and almost reached Lhasa. This, it should be noted, was the first invasion of Tibet in history. The Mongol force did not stay to consolidate its victories, but withdrew with its booty. According to Tibetan sources the Mongols withdrew because their commander had been overawed by the personality of a Kagyudpa high lama. Be that as it may, in about 1245 Godan sent an envoy ordering a representative of Tibet to appear at his court to offer Tibet's submission to the Mongols. It is not clear how this representative was selected or even whether there was a formal selection procedure, but eventually the great Sakyapa scholar known as Sakya Paṇḍita presented himself at Godan's court. The move was a gamble, as no one could have known Godan's intentions or foreseen his reaction to the Tibetan envoy. As things turned out, the gamble paid off. In return for Sakya Paṇḍita's guarantee of Tibet's full submission to the Mongols, Godan appointed him viceroy of Tibet, an office he exercised from Godan's court through ministers in Tibet.

Both Godan and Sakya Paṇḍita died in 1251, the same year that Mongka Khan ascended the throne of the Mongols. Godan's territory went to Kublai (d. 1294), brother of the Grand Khan Mongka, and Sakya

Paṇḍita's office was inherited by his nephew 'Phags-pa (d. 1280), himself a great Buddhist scholar and the inventor of the Mongolian script. 'Phags-pa and Kublai appear to have become genuinely close while Kublai was still only a territorial governor under Mongka Khan. Not only did 'Phags-pa take over as viceroy of Tibet, he also became the chief priest and spiritual advisor of Kublai Khan in 1253. This status was further enhanced in 1260 when Kublai became the Grand Khan of the Mongols, and yet again in 1280 when Kublai completed the conquest of China and became the first emperor of the Yuan dynasty (1280-1368). From the middle of the thirteenth century until the Yuan dynasty began to decline in the early fourteenth century, the chief abbot of the Sakyapa sect was not only the de facto ruler of Tibet, he was also the foremost religious authority of Yuan China. Thus began the "patron-priest" relationship between Mongolia and Tibet. In theory the two countries formed an alliance over which the Mongol khan exerted political authority and the Sakyapa abbot exerted religious authority.

This situation, as might be expected, was not welcomed by everyone in Tibet. On the one hand, many of the powerful nobles of Tibet resented Mongol overlordship. On the other hand, the large monasteries of the Kagyudpa sect were envious of the wealth and power that the Sakyapa enjoyed as a result of Mongol patronage. This led to bitterness and intrigue on the religious front in Tibet as the various large monasteries scrambled to align themselves with powerful Mongol and Tibetan chieftains. These alliances in turn embroiled Tibetan Buddhism in the constant internal feuds of the Mongols and resulted from time to time in open warfare between powerful monasteries that fielded armies of monks reminiscent of the roughly contemporary Ashikaga period (1336-1600) in Japan.

While Kublai and his successor Timur ruled in China, the Sakyapa had the upper hand in these struggles, being supported by a standing army maintained by the Yuan dynasty. After Timur's death in 1307, however, the Yuan dynasty began to weaken and the tide began to turn in Tibet. The dissolute emperors of the waning Yuan dynasty no longer took an active interest in Tibet's internal affairs. In these unsettled conditions, a Tibetan noble named Byang-Chub rGyal-mTshan [Jang-chub Gyal-tsan] was able to play upon existing rivalries and forge an alliance which in 1354 attacked and occupied the Sakyapa headquarters and thus established his dominance over Tibet. Though he sought and received the Yuan dynasty's recognition of his rule in Tibet, he pursued vigorously and openly a nationalistic program intended to do away with foreign overlordship. He revived the ancient Tibetan tradition of monarchy by founding the Phag-mo Gru ["Phag-mo-du"] dynasty, named after the branch of the Kagyudpa sect with which this line of kings was aligned. This dynasty endured for over a century. It is important to note, in light of present Chinese claims upon Tibet, that Tibet threw off the Mongol yoke more than a decade before the Chinese themselves were able to do so. Tibet was not to be dominated by another foreign power for three and a half centuries, by which time the same foreign power, Manchuria, dominated China as well.

Although the Mongol period was turbulent for Tibet as a whole and for Buddhism in particular, it must not be imagined that Buddhism ceased to develop during this period. The years from 1200 to 1400, in fact, could just as accurately be called the "Period of Consolidation" of Tibetan Buddhism. By about 1200, Tibet no longer had Indian Buddhism to turn to for inspiration. Most of the scriptures brought back from India had by this time been translated in at least a preliminary form. At about this time, Tibetan Buddhism passed from an age of collectors and translators into an age of scholars, whose task it was to refine existing translations, organize the vast amount of material available, and compose treatises to explain this material in a systematic way.

The most significant figure in this period of consolidation was Bu sTon (1290-1364). A prolific author, Bu sTon wrote the first comprehensive history of Buddhism in Tibet. He is even more renowned as the scholar who was primarily responsible for organizing and editing the standard Tibetan canon (the Kanjur and Tanjur), which in all comprises over 4,500 separate works in over 300 large volumes. This enormous corpus represents the culmination of the labors of hundreds of dedicated scholars and travelers, many of whom lost their lives in the treacherous journey to India and back.

As Bu sTon was completing the mammoth task of compiling the standard Tibetan canon, the Nyingmapa lamas and the Bon priests were also compiling their own non-standard canons on the basis of the *gTer-ma* or "treasure" texts they claimed to have been discovering since the eleventh century. In the fourteenth century, when Byang-Chub rGyal-mTshan, the liberator of Tibet from Mongol overlordship, embarked upon his program of encouraging Tibetan nationalism, he resorted to this same tactic, claiming to discover a set of five scrolls that had been written in the ancient royal period and concealed for future generations. This move by the secular ruler of Tibet, combined no doubt with the consolidation efforts of the dominant religious sects, resulted in a spate of *gTer-ma* discoveries by Nyingmapa and Bon-po practitioners in the fourteenth century. Though these religious orders claim with some justification to be the oldest in Tibet, they also assumed their abiding, classical forms during the Mongol period.

Medieval Reform (1400-1700) and the Institution of the Dalai Lama

As Tibet was asserting its independence from the Mongols of the Yuan dynasty, Tsong Kha-pa (1357-1419), the great reformer of Tibetan Buddhism, was born at a place now called sKu 'Bum, near Xining (Hsi-ning) in the present-day Chinese province of Qinghai (Ch'ing-hai). The present fourteenth Dalai Lama, heir to Tsong Kha-pa's authority, was also born near sKu 'Bum, a situation that illustrates the extent of Tibet's territorial dispute with China. Until the twentieth century, not only the "Tibetan Autonomous Region," but most of Qinghai province as well constituted a distinct cultural unit known as Tibet.

Tsong Kha-pa traveled widely and studied with distinguished teachers from all of the existing Buddhist sects in Tibet. It is remarkable that the various sects were rivals sometimes to the point of open warfare, but when it came to transmitting the teachings of Buddhism, the boundaries between sects appear to have been minimal. By the age of twenty-five, Tsong Kha-pa had established himself as a scholar and teacher of wide-ranging knowledge and considerable repute. Eventually, by the age of forty, he gravitated to the strict Kadampa sect, which had been initiated by Atīśa, the first great reformer of Buddhism in Tibet. At about this time he began to compose his own comprehensive treatise on Buddhism, his famous *Lam Rim Chen-mo* or "Great Treatise on the Stages of the Path," which serves to the present day as the doctrinal basis of the Gelugpa [dGe Lugs-pa] sect, by far the largest sect of Tibetan Buddhism. The primary orientation of Tsong Kha-pa's *Lam Rim Chen-mo,* as well as the Gelugpa sect, is the Madhyamaka philosophy of Nāgārjuna.

By 1408, Tsong Kha-pa's prestige had grown to the degree that he was able to establish at the Jo Khang cathedral in Lhasa what came to be the primary annual celebration in the Tibetan calendar, the sMon-lam Chen-po or "Great Prayer" marking the Tibetan new year. Apparently disillusioned with the worldliness and political intrigue that characterized Tibetan Buddhism at the time, in 1409 he founded his own monastery, known as Ganden [dGa' lDan], on an isolated mountain top about twenty-five miles from Lhasa. There Tsong Kha-pa promoted serious scholarship, withdrawal from worldly affairs and strict monastic discipline. Soon Ganden became the center of a movement first known as "New Kadampa" in recognition of its adherence to the principles of strict monasticism advocated by Atīśa. Eventually the reform movement initiated by Tsong Kha-pa came to be called the Gelugpa or "Model of Virtue Sect," again emphasizing the strict monastic spirituality which characterized Tsong Kha-pa and his followers.

By the time of Tsong Kha-pa's death in 1419, his disciples had established two more Gelugpa monasteries near Lhasa. These monasteries, Sera and Drepung ['Bras sPungs], developed into enormous institutions, each housing some ten thousand monks at the height of their glory in the first half of the twentieth century. Though somewhat smaller, Ganden, the original monastery founded by Tsong Kha-pa, remained the seat of the sect by virtue of the fact that the founder's embalmed body was entombed there as the holiest treasure of the order. Viewing today the desolate ruins of Sera, Drepung and Ganden, one can scarcely imagine that until 1959 they were virtual monastic cities, the three largest monasteries in the world.

From the early 1400s until the Chinese invasion of Tibet in 1950, these monasteries continued to grow in prestige and splendor, even though Tsong Kha-pa's immediate successors, like the great reformer himself, showed little interest in gaining political power. Tsong Kha-pa clearly did not regard himself as the founder of a new sect. Apparently he made no specific arrangements regarding leadership succession. His first two successors as abbot of Ganden and head of the Gelugpa sect were his most accomplished disciples. Only after they had died did the abbacy devolve onto his nephew dGe 'Dun Grub [Ge-dun Dup — 1391-1475], who by an odd series of events eventually came to be regarded as the first Dalai Lama of Tibet.

dGe 'Dun Grub was an able organizer, though he too seems to have followed the pattern established by Tsong Kha-pa of avoiding involvement in political maneuvering. In 1445 he established the fourth great monastery of the Gelugpa sect, Tashilhunpo [bKra Shis Lhun-po] in Shigatse, the second largest city in Tibet, some 150 miles west of Lhasa. dGe 'Dun Grub's most significant move, however, was announcing that upon his death he would join the ranks of the reincarnating lamas already prominent in other sects of Tibetan Buddhism, most notably the powerful Karmapa sect. dGe 'Dun Grub's decision to reincarnate established the lineage of Gelugpa abbots known as the Dalai Lamas of Tibet.

After the death of dGe 'Dun Grub, his reincarnated successor was located, as an infant, of course. Eventually this successor, dGe 'Dun rGya mTsho (1475-1553), came to be regarded as the second Dalai Lama, though in his lifetime the title did not yet exist. During the second Dalai Lama's abbacy, resentment among the older sects of the growing popularity of the Gelugpa order reached a dangerous level. Resentment was particularly strong in the dominant Karmapa sect, whose system of succession by reincarnation the Gelugpa had copied, and whose territorial authority appeared to be threatened by the Tashilhunpo monastery.

Partly because of the danger resulting from the resentment of such powerful rivals, the "second Dalai Lama" spent most of his career traveling
throughout Tibet and teaching at far-flung monasteries, thereby further
increasing the sect's reputation for piety and missionary zeal. By the end
of his reign, Drepung was the largest monastery in Tibet, housing some
1,500 monks. Still, the Gelugpa sect remained aloof from involvement in
the political intrigue which preoccupied the more established sects. This
made them not only popular among many of the noble families, but also
useful. The non-aligned Gelugpa monks, with their reputation for sanctity
and humility, proved to be ideal mediators in the interminable disputes
among rival powers in Tibet at the time.

The aloof, non-political spirituality of the Gelugpa sect was dramatically transformed under the leadership of the third Dalai Lama,
bSod-Nams rGya-mTsho [Sonam Gyatso — 1543-88]. Following the political precedent established by the Sakyapa sect some three centuries
before, in 1576 bSod-Nams rGya-mTsho journeyed to Mongolia at the
invitation of Altan Khan (r. 1543-83), chief of the Tumed Mongols, the
most powerful of the several rival Mongol factions of the day. Both par-
ties at this historic meeting were well aware that they were symbolically
re-establishing a relationship that had been formed three centuries earlier, when in 1260 Kublai Khan conveyed the honorific title "Ti Shi" upon
the Sakyapa lama 'Phags-pa, in effect bestowing upon him the rulership
of Tibet. In this ceremonial re-establishment of that bond between Tibet
and the Mongols, Altan Khan bestowed upon the Gelugpa abbot the title
"Ta-le Lama." This half Mongolian, half Tibetan title is now normally rendered "Dalai Lama." As bSod-Nams rGya-mTsho was the third in a line of
reincarnating lamas, it became customary to refer to his predecessors as
the first and second Dalai Lamas, even though they were never known by
this designation during their lifetimes. *Ta-le* means "ocean" in Mongolian,
as does *rGya-mTsho* in Tibetan, so it was not a particularly imaginative
title. It did eventually become an extremely important title, however, des-
ignating the line of so-called "God-kings of Tibet." To the present day, the
vast majority of Tibetans regard the Dalai Lama as the legitimate religious
leader and political ruler of Tibet, Chinese domination of the country
notwithstanding.

This almost unanimous recognition of the Dalai Lama's supreme status
in Tibet did not begin immediately upon the bestowal of the title. At the
time, the Mongols under Altan Khan exercised only an indirect effect
upon Tibet's internal affairs. They performed the role of a very wealthy
patron of the Gelugpa sect, sending lavish gifts to their monasteries and
patrons in Tibet. Although this alliance with the Mongols eventually had
a profound political impact upon Tibet, it appears that the third Dalai

Lama was more interested in spreading Buddhism than gaining political power. He spent most of the last ten years of his life as a missionary among the Mongols. He was so successful in gaining the respect and allegiance of the many Mongol factions that the Ming emperor of China invited the third Dalai Lama to visit Beijing. Presumably the emperor wished to forestall the potential threat to China from a Mongolian nation reunited under Tibetan Buddhism. Again, this situation illustrates the relative equality of China and Tibet until recent times.

This meeting between the third Dalai Lama and the Chinese emperor never occurred, because bSod-Nams rGya-mTsho died in 1588, the year the invitation was issued, at the age of forty-five. Politically speaking, it is not surprising that his reincarnation, the fourth Dalai Lama, was discovered in a great-grandson of Altan Khan. This development, however, turned out to be unfortunate for Tibet. It set in motion a series of events that soon resulted in the reassertion of Mongol military authority in Tibet.

This intervention did not actually materialize until the fourth Dalai Lama died in 1616, reputedly from poisoning, at the age of twenty-five. His reincarnation, the fifth Dalai Lama (1617-1682), remembered by Tibetans as the "Great Fifth," was soon discovered in a prominent Tibetan family. Several Mongol chieftains arrived in Tibet with large, armed entourages to honor the new Dalai Lama and see to his safe installation in Lhasa. Thereafter, armed Mongol forces, ostensibly protecting the Dalai Lama, became a regular presence in Tibet. After the death of Altan Khan in 1583, however, the Mongols on Tibet's borders were without firm leadership, and these Mongol "protectors" of the Dalai Lama were often little more than relatively well-behaved brigands until the ascent of Gushi Khan in about 1636. Gushi molded the Mongols of the Kokonor region to Tibet's northeast into an orderly fighting force. In 1642, Gushi Khan was proclaimed king of Tibet, a title retained by his successors until 1720. With Gushi Khan's backing, the fifth Dalai Lama of the Gelugpa sect became the undisputed religious authority in Tibet and among the Mongols.

So long as the fifth Dalai Lama lived, the Mongol connection must have seemed advantageous to most Tibetans. Gushi Khan was genuinely devoted to the Dalai Lama, and allowed him full control in Tibet, even though Gushi was its titular king. Unlike the previous situation under Kublai Khan, this time the "patron-priest" relationship between the Mongols and Tibet was a relationship of true equals. Under Kublai Khan, the Sakyapa viceroy of Tibet had been confined to the Mongol court and constrained to exercise rule in Tibet through agents. The fifth Dalai Lama resided in Tibet and was able to call in or call off Mongol intervention at will. As a result of this arrangement, the fifth Dalai Lama exerted actual authority over virtually all of the Tibetan people, more control than had ever been exercised by any of the so-called "kings of Tibet."

Beyond Tibet, the fifth Dalai Lama's status as the recognized religious master of the Mongols gave him political power analogous to that of the Pope in Europe. The first emperor of the Manchurian Qing dynasty (1644-1912) in China ignored traditional imperial protocol and journeyed to the boundary of China to meet with the fifth Dalai Lama. Such deference to a foreign power by an emperor of China was unheard of, but the emperor recognized both the threat the Mongols posed to China and the influence the Dalai Lama exerted over these normally unruly hordes. The Manchurians, who originated in the easternmost end of the "Mongol crescent" over China, were culturally related to the Mongols and Tibetans. As a result, they proved to be more astute in dealing with their kinsmen than the ethnic Chinese had been.

On the whole, the fifth Dalai Lama used his autocratic power in Tibet temperately against the former rivals of the Gelugpa, though he lost no time in assuring that his own sect was paramount in Tibet. He confiscated much of the extreme wealth of the previously dominant Karmapa subsect of the Kagyudpa, but he allowed them to retain a viable religious establishment. He embarked on an extensive, personal tour of inspection of monasteries, and transformed many apparently derelict monasteries of other sects into well-supported Gelugpa establishments. He banned outright only one subsect, the Jo-Nang-pa branch of the Kagyudpa, and transformed all of their monasteries into Gelugpa establishments. Not averse to sharing power, the fifth Dalai Lama declared that his teacher, abbot of the Tashilhunpo monastery, would be reincarnated after his death. The abbots in this new line of reincarnating lamas were dubbed the "Panchen" Lamas, a shortened form of the half-Sanskrit, half-Tibetan phrase *Paṇḍita Chen-po,* meaning "great scholar."

Arguably, the fifth Dalai Lama's most enduring achievement was the establishment of the Potala Palace. This great cream and burgundy structure, seeming to grow organically out of a rocky ridge in central Lhasa, has come to symbolize Tibet and the rule of the Dalai Lama. In mythology, Potala is the residence of Avalokiteśvara, the bodhisattva of compassion. The fifth Dalai Lama's construction of this magnificent palace initiated a tradition of identifying the Dalai Lama as the earthly manifestation of Avalokiteśvara. This tradition continues among Tibetans to the present day, who regard the Dalai Lama with a sense of awe and devotion that is difficult for a Westerner to imagine without actually having been among Tibetans when the Dalai Lama is present.

The Manchu Period (1700-1900)

Gushi Khan, the fifth Dalai Lama's powerful Mongol patron, died in 1656. By this time the fifth Dalai Lama was the unchallenged religious and secular master of all Tibet. In theory, the secular side of Tibet's affairs was in the hands of a Tibetan regent jointly appointed by the Mongol khan, as titular king of Tibet, and the Dalai Lama. No effective successor rose to take Gushi's place, however, so that when the jointly appointed regent died, the Dalai Lama single-handedly appointed a close associate, who functioned more or less as the deputy of the Dalai Lama. The Dalai Lama himself became the only true figure of authority among both the Tibetans and the Mongols.

When the fifth Dalai Lama died in 1682, the regent of Tibet decided that in the unsettled conditions created by Mongol disunity, it would be best to conceal his death and rule in the name of the Dalai Lama until his reincarnating successor had gained maturity. In retrospect this decision was extremely unwise. It is often reviled as a grab for power by the regent, though in the circumstances it may well have seemed prudent. At any rate, it is clear that the regent could not have acted alone, given the complex scheme he carried out. He concealed the Dalai Lama's death by announcing that the aging monk had gone into an intensive meditational retreat, a credible ploy given the Great Fifth's reputation for sanctity. Apparently the regent then secretly had the search for the Dalai Lama's reincarnation carried out, located the infant, and had him secretly housed and trained near Lhasa. Meanwhile, the regent himself ruled for some thirteen years, until the secret was leaked and the sixth Dalai Lama had to be hastily enthroned in 1696.

According to traditional accounts, the sixth Dalai Lama (1682?-1707?) made his public debut wearing the blue silk robe of a noble, sporting flowing black hair, covered in jewelry and carrying a bow and arrows. He showed little interest in Buddhism, none in monastic discipline, and much in wine, women and song. His only literary output was a series of romantic love poems. The most remarkable thing of all is that apparently no attempt was made to conceal his true personality, even though this would have been a fairly simple exercise for one who could so easily have remained aloof from the public gaze. At any rate, the majority of Tibetans — who despite their preoccupation with religion are among the most fun-loving and tolerant people on earth — have always regarded the sixth Dalai Lama with great fondness, as something of an eruption of Tantric exuberance into an otherwise staid line of religious figures. Tibet's neighbors misjudged the Tibetans' allegiance to the sixth Dalai

Lama, and serious consequences followed when he was treated with disdain.

The political situation at the time was complex throughout east Asia. In 1700, the heretofore symbolic kingship of Tibet devolved upon the Mongol leader Lhabzang Khan, who decided actually to assert his titular authority. He may well have been annoyed by the Tibetan regent's deception concerning the death of the fifth Dalai Lama. Apparently aware of Lhabzang Khan's intentions, the regent of Tibet intensified ties with a rival Mongol faction under Galdan Khan, an open enemy of the Manchurian Qing dynasty in China. This alarmed both the Qing emperor and Lhabzang Khan, who thus became allies. In 1705-6, Lhabzang Khan marched on Lhasa with the Manchurian emperor's support, defeated the Tibetan forces and executed the Tibetan regent. The Qing emperor immediately appointed Lhabzang Khan Governor of Tibet. Apparently seeking to consolidate his power, Lhabzang Khan then arrested the sixth Dalai Lama, declared him to be a fake, and deported him under guard to Beijing. The Dalai Lama agreed to go along quietly, thus forestalling serious riots in his favor which threatened to break out in Lhasa. The sixth Dalai Lama died en route to Beijing — very likely by foul play — further intensifying Tibetan resentment.

Despite ample indications to the contrary, both Lhabzang Khan and the Qing emperor seem to have been unable to believe that the Tibetans were serious in venerating such a hedonistic character as the sixth Dalai Lama. Pushing ahead despite the obvious popularity of the sixth Dalai Lama in Tibet, Lhabzang Khan declared an obscure twenty-five-year-old monk, presumably a supporter, to be the real reincarnation of the fifth Dalai Lama. The Tibetans themselves ignored this replacement en masse and soon the sixth Dalai Lama's reincarnation was located in eastern Tibet. This seventh Dalai Lama was kept safely at the great monastery of sKu 'Bum in far eastern Tibet (near present-day Xining in the Qinghai province of China), while Lhabzang Khan ruled over a resentful and rebellious populace in central Tibet.

In secret, the monastic establishment in Lhasa pursued the alliance between the previous regent of Tibet and Galdan Khan. Finally, in 1717 a descendant of Galdan Khan invaded Tibet, ostensibly to restore the rightful Dalai Lama to power. Lhabzang Khan, the governor of Tibet, appealed to the Manchurian emperor for help. The emperor, who had been carefully monitoring the Tibetan situation, was unable to prevent the success of the invasion, but his forces did move swiftly to gain custody of the seventh Dalai Lama, who was only about ten years old at the time. The invaders conquered central Tibet, executed Lhabzang Khan and deposed the unpopular pseudo-sixth Dalai Lama he had appointed. At first, the

Tibetans welcomed the invading Mongols as liberators, but it soon became clear that their real intention was to plunder the country. They looted many of the great monasteries and even ransacked the tomb of the fifth Dalai Lama.

The Manchurian emperor had to mount two massive counter-attacks before the invading Mongols were dislodged in 1720. Having been pillaged for three years, the Tibetans naturally welcomed this intervention. The Manchurian emperor's trump card was the young seventh Dalai Lama — by now universally recognized as legitimate by the Tibetans. Having saved Tibet from its Mongol oppressors, the emperor was now able to return the Dalai Lama to Lhasa in a complete popular triumph. Thanks to his shrewd statesmanship, not to mention some good luck, the Manchurian emperor of China was now in a position to dictate his own terms to the grateful Tibetans. The Qing dynasty of China thus became the nominal overlords of Tibet until their fall from power in 1912.

In the early years of Manchurian overlordship, there was turbulence in Tibet amounting to civil war as rival Tibetan clans contended with one another for ascendancy. A capable Tibetan general named Pho Lha eventually emerged victorious. Tibet's Manchurian overlords quickly recognized Pho Lha, who ruled under the restored title "king of Tibet" until his death in 1747. Throughout his reign, the Mongols remained a potential threat to political stability in Tibet and to the Manchurian dynasty, which was justifiably anxious regarding the potential re-establishment of a "priest-patron" relationship between Tibet and one or several of the Mongol factions.

After Pho Lha died in 1747, his son took over as king and made moves to re-establish an alliance with the Mongols. As a result, in 1750 he was assassinated by agents of the Qing emperor, an act which brought Tibet to the verge of open rebellion. The seventh Dalai Lama himself managed to restore order before a Chinese military force arrived. The Qing emperor abolished the office of "king of Tibet" — which had been revived under Pho Lha and had proved to be a focus for rebellion — and restored titular supremacy to the Dalai Lama. The office of regent was revived and henceforth occupied by a monk whose theoretical role was to head the government during periods when the Dalai Lama was too young. In actual fact, this monk-regent exercised the real authority in Tibet from 1757, when the seventh Dalai Lama died, until 1895, when the thirteenth Dalai Lama assumed full power.

The eighth Dalai Lama (1756-1806) lived until middle age, but he showed little interest in exercising political power. During the balance of the nineteenth century, the Dalai Lamas remained perpetually under age due to their premature deaths. The ninth Dalai Lama died at the age of ten, the tenth at the age of twenty-one, the eleventh at the age of seventeen and the twelfth at the age of twenty. The tenth Dalai Lama is widely believed to have been assassinated at the behest of the regent, and the premature deaths of the others are somewhat suspicious as well. At any rate, during this period of monastic political intrigue, a series of monk-regents headed a stable government in Lhasa with only minimal influence from the Manchurian court in Beijing, which was separated from Lhasa by a journey of some eight months. During this century of child Dalai Lamas, the prestige and authority of the Panchen Lamas (the second reincarnating lineage of the Gelugpa) increased considerably, particularly under the very capable third Panchen Lama. Throughout, however, the Dalai Lama remained the supreme authority in the minds of the people.

Throughout the nineteenth century, the Manchurian dynasty in China was beset by internal strife and rebellion that culminated in the establishment of the Republic of China in 1912. Also during the nineteenth century, Britain from its base in India, and Russia sprawling to the north of Tibet, began to maneuver for political and economic influence in Central Asia. Governed in the name of the Dalai Lamas by a series of efficient if often unscrupulous monk-regents, nineteenth century Tibet attempted to remain aloof from the large-scale international events of the time by closing its borders to foreigners.

This policy, which mirrored the isolationism of Manchurian China during its declining years, was unwise in retrospect. It deprived Tibet of diplomatic contacts and experience with the rapidly developing outside world. Both would be needed when Tibet's independence was once again threatened by a resurgent, expansionist China. At the time, however, Tibet's isolationist policy must have seemed successful. Tibet was able to maintain virtual independence of foreign influence throughout the nineteenth century. It was only during the nineteenth century that the popular Western mythology of Tibet as the "Forbidden Kingdom" was justified. Previously, despite its geographical isolation, Tibet had been a cosmopolitan crossroads hosting — and sometimes suffering — influences from India, China, Mongolia, and Manchuria. During the eighteenth century even Europeans were not uncommon in Tibet. Several Christian missions, though spectacularly unsuccessful in gaining converts, were hospitably accommodated in Lhasa and left some interesting if biased accounts of eighteenth century Tibet through European eyes.[43] A more successful European transplant than Christianity was the potato, introduced by George Bogle in the course of attempting to improve trade relations between British India and Tibet. Bogle married the sister of the third Panchen Lama and is survived to the present day in Britain by descendants resulting from that alliance.

The Twentieth Century

In 1895, the thirteenth Dalai Lama, who managed to survive what appears to have become a customary assassination attempt by the regent, assumed full power and ruled over Tibet until his death in 1933. He was thus the only Dalai Lama other than the Great Fifth actually to exert in Tibet the theoretical authority of the office. The reign of the thirteenth Dalai Lama spanned a period of turmoil the world over, and soon after his assumption of power, Tibet's closed doors were forced open. Tibet's position at this time must be regarded with some sympathy.

Russia, having annexed a large Mongol population who accepted allegiance to the czar as their "tsagan khan," regarded Tibet as falling within its legitimate sphere of influence. The British in India looked upon Tibet as a traditional trading partner of their colony, and were extremely wary of Russian expansionism, particularly near the borders of the British colonial empire. After some two centuries of nominal overlordship, China began to attempt to exert real power in Tibet once again. The ruling powers in China during the thirteenth Dalai Lama's reign — first the fading Manchurian dynasty and then the Republic of China — claimed Tibet as their territory. The twentieth century was poised inevitably to break in upon the Forbidden Kingdom, and Tibet was not equipped to exercise the sophisticated diplomacy that would have been necessary to maintain independent neutrality in such a position.

The first intruders were the British. Concerned about increasing Russian influence in Central Asia, they sent an armed force to Lhasa in 1904 in order to negotiate a trade treaty with Tibet. The outnumbered but well-equipped British force easily defeated Tibetan defensive forces and moved inexorably upon Lhasa. The Dalai Lama fled to Mongolia, only to find that once the desired trade agreement was secured, the British withdrew peacefully. In 1907, the Manchurian Chinese moved into Tibet with an armed force, intending to assert actual authority instead of the nominal authority they had exercised for two centuries. In 1910, when the Chinese force reached Lhasa, the Dalai Lama again fled, this time to India, where he stayed as an honored guest of the British until the Manchurian dynasty fell in 1912. The Tibetans, now able to throw off Chinese interference, turned to the colonial masters of India as allies and concluded a second treaty with the British in 1914. This resulted in a flurry of contacts between Britain and Tibet and the beginnings of accurate Western knowledge of this isolated country and its centuries-old way of life.[44]

The death of the thirteenth Dalai Lama in 1933 returned Tibet to rule by regent and a reversal of the Dalai Lama's policy of modernization and outreach to the West. The major political events in East Asia following the second World War swiftly, drastically and disastrously altered Tibet's position in the region. First, in 1947 the British withdrew from India, thus depriving Tibet of its primary contact with the modern, "outside" world of international treaties, law and diplomacy. Shortly thereafter, in 1949, communists under Mao Ze Dong (Mao Tse-tung) rose spectacularly to power in China. Communist China invaded Tibet almost immediately, and established an overwhelming military presence around Lhasa by 1950. The maintenance of the large Chinese garrison placed a major strain upon Tibet's limited resources and caused severe hardship for the Tibetan people. Nonetheless, under the ominous and burdensome shadow of communist China's military presence, Tibet managed to carry on with its traditional way of life for almost a decade. This reprieve was largely due to the remarkable skill and intelligence of the fourteenth Dalai Lama, who was prematurely empowered with the full prerogatives of his office in 1950, at the age of sixteen, in an attempt to present a unified response to the Chinese threat.

Tensions increased steadily until March of 1959, when rumors that the Chinese intended to abduct the Dalai Lama induced a large crowd of crudely armed Tibetans to gather around the walls of the Dalai Lama's summer palace to protect him. After several days of increasingly ominous negotiations, the Chinese fired two artillery rounds near the palace — apparently warning shots or perhaps range-finding exercises. The Dalai Lama and his closest associates set in motion their last-ditch contingency plan, a daring escape from Lhasa in disguise. About forty-eight hours after the Dalai Lama and his entourage had fled the palace, the Chinese unleashed a full-scale artillery barrage upon the summer palace and central Lhasa, killing thousands of civilians, laying waste to many of the architectural treasures of Lhasa and apparently intending to kill the Dalai Lama as well.

This left the Dalai Lama no alternative but to seek asylum in India. About a hundred thousand Tibetans managed to follow their leader into exile, suffering first the hardships of the tortuous route to India, and then destitute poverty in a strange new world. The suffering of the Tibetans who remained behind was far worse. Executions, torture and imprisonment killed tens of thousands. Tens of thousands more died of starvation and over-work in the years of systematic exploitation of Tibet which followed the Chinese takeover.

Tibet's desperate plight worsened yet again during the infamous "Cultural Revolution" that swept through China at Mao's behest in 1966-69. This attack upon all things and people deemed to represent the "four olds" — old ideology, old thought, old habits and old customs — fell with extraordinary vengeance upon Tibet, which had steadfastly attempted to maintain its traditional lifestyle and religion since the Chinese takeover in 1959. Thousands more Tibetans were tortured, imprisoned and killed in the fanatical excesses of the Cultural Revolution. Impractical and irresponsible "re-location" and "re-education" schemes administered primarily by ignorant youths and peasants resulted in the deaths of many more thousands of Tibetans through over-work and starvation.

The three years of the Cultural Revolution also saw the systematic destruction of Tibetan temples and religious art, which heretofore had been only incidentally damaged in the Chinese occupation of Tibet, or had suffered repairable damage from maltreatment and neglect under the communist regime. As a result of the mindless destruction wreaked during the Cultural Revolution, Tibet's great monastic cities, which still functioned on a diminished scale before 1966, are today pitiful, bombed-out ghost towns. Ganden in particular — the world's third largest monastery and arguably its most beautiful in 1959 — today looks like a thousand-year-old ruin.

In Tibet as in China, the deaths of Mao Ze Dong and Zhou En Lai (Chou En-lai) in 1976 marked the beginning of relief from the excesses of the communist regime. This relief began to become apparent to the Tibetans themselves in approximately 1980, which Tibetans remember as the year in which the food shortage broke and limited religious freedom was once again allowed. A program of restoring and reconsecrating damaged and desecrated temples — funded by the Tibetans themselves with minimal Chinese support — began soon thereafter. Also in 1980, a relaxed Chinese tourism policy began to allow Western visitors limited access to Tibet. By 1987, however, increased contact with Tibetan communities and sympathizers abroad had rekindled aspirations for independence and resulted in anti-Chinese demonstrations and then riots in Lhasa. The Chinese authorities responded with renewed suppression of Buddhism and restrictions upon travel to Tibet. The Tibetan spirit of rebellion continues to the present day, though the Chinese military has been able to enforce at least the appearance of order in Tibet.

After their escape in 1959, the Dalai Lama and his fellow refugees established in northern India a Tibetan government in exile. From this headquarters, numerous Tibetan communities were established, first throughout India and then throughout the Western world. Wherever these communities have been established, they have attracted sympathizers, students and converts to Tibetan Buddhism. Several major Western universities now employ learned lamas on their faculties and offer a full range of courses on Tibetan language, history and religion. Building upon the success of these contacts throughout the world, the Dalai

Lama's government has enjoyed remarkable though as yet indeterminate success in drawing the world's attention to Tibet's grievances. Symbolically, the culmination of these efforts occurred in 1989, when the fourteenth Dalai Lama received the Nobel Peace Prize.

The Tibetan diaspora itself, tragic though it is, represents the culmination of Tibet's sustained effort to preserve and transmit Buddhist literature and traditions. In the first instance, the Tibetans narrowly managed to preserve Indian Mahāyāna Buddhism before it was wiped out in its homeland by the Muslim invasion of India. Now, as a direct result of the communist Chinese invasion of Tibet and its attempt to wipe out Buddhism there, Tibet's unique and invaluable fund of Buddhist scriptures and tradition has been so thoroughly dispersed throughout the world that nothing short of a third World War could eradicate it. Though a tragedy for the Tibetan people, the Tibetan diaspora has guaranteed the survival of the full range of Buddhist thought in a world which has often proved hostile toward this basically humane, positive and tolerant faith.

CHAPTER XII

Tibetan Buddhism Beyond Tibet

Given the precarious position of Buddhism in Tibet, it is particularly encouraging that Tibetan forms of Buddhism survive among peoples bordering upon the Tibetan plateau. Among these, the best known in the West are the Mongols, about half of whom live in so-called "Outer Mongolia" in territory recently relinquished by the defunct Soviet Union. Among these Mongols, there has been a predictable resurgence of Buddhism in response to the return of political self-determination. The fate of Buddhism in "Inner Mongolia," territory controlled by China, remains in doubt. Chronologically, the most ancient traditions of Tibetan-style Buddhism beyond Tibet belong to those peoples living on the southern slopes of the Himalayas, the northern verge of India. Nepal and Bhutan, in the southeastern Himalayas, are independent kingdoms. A third kingdom, Sikkim — sandwiched between Nepal and Bhutan — became the twenty-second state of India by referendum in 1975. Just south of Sikkim, around Darjeeling in the far northern districts of Bengal, Tibetan-style Buddhism is also practiced. Northwest of Nepal, Tibetan-style Buddhism is notable in Kinnaur and Lahaul Spiti — in the modern Indian state of Himachal Pradesh — and in the Ladakh district of the Indian state of Jammu and Kashmir.

Political and social instability in many of these regions make even rough estimates of numbers of Buddhists difficult to state. The Mongols at present number approximately four million total. Of these, perhaps half may be considered Buddhist in some sense. Religion has always sat lightly on the shoulders of the Mongols, however, and it is impossible at this point to assess the effects of the communist domination (both Russian and Chinese) of Mongolia during the twentieth century. Of Nepal's total population of some fourteen million, about half may be considered Buddhist in some sense. In the case of Nepal, an estimate is particularly difficult because of a pervasive syncretism of Buddhism with Hinduism. About half of Nepal's population is definitely Hindu, and most of the other half practice a Buddhist-Hindu synthesis rather than pure Buddhism. The one million inhabitants of Bhutan are virtually all Buddhist. The total of Tibetan-style Buddhists in the Himalayan regions of India is somewhat over 200,000, although again estimates are difficult because of Hindu syncretism and an alleged tendency of the Indian census bureau to undercount Buddhists.

Buddhism as a significant religion among the Mongols is relatively recent in its origins, dating from the thirteenth century. In the Himalayan regions mentioned, Buddhism is a much more ancient presence, in some cases dating back to the time of Aśoka (about 250 BCE) and even possibly to the Buddha himself. The traditional histories of Buddhism in most of these areas, however, indicate that the religion was introduced from Tibet. Most of the Himalayan areas where Tibetan-style Buddhism is practiced trace its origins to Padma-sambhava, the legendary founder of Tibetan Tantrism in the late eighth century. It is unlikely that Padma-sambhava himself founded Buddhist communities in all of these areas, but it is not unlikely that Tantric Buddhism began to flourish there in the ninth century. More ancient Buddhist roots are apparent in Nepal, which for this reason will be considered first in the following survey.

Nepal

The earliest known inhabitants of Nepal, the Newars of the Kathmandu Valley, today number only about half a million. Though the Newars are not and probably never were exclusively Buddhist, it is among these people of Tibetan descent that the continuous, though obscure, history of Buddhism in Nepal resides. The majority of Nepal's Buddhists and quasi-Buddhists are to be found among a welter of Tibetan tribal groups that reside in the mountainous north of the country. These tribal groups arrived in Nepal at undetermined times both ancient and recent. The dominant ethnic group of present-day Nepal, the Gurkhas, are and have always been primarily Hindu. Fleeing the Muslim conquest of India, they began to arrive in Nepal in about 1000 CE, but they did not become dominant in Nepal until the eighteenth century. Before the advent of the Gurkhas, Nepal had been ruled by the primarily Hindu Licchavi and Malla dynasties since the fourth or fifth century. Nonetheless, Nepal may lay claim, though not demonstrably, to harboring the world's longest continuous history of Buddhism.

Present-day Nepal includes the birthplace of the historical Buddha, which is marked by an Aśokan pillar inscription at the village of Lumbini, about a hundred miles west of Kathmandu. Kapilavastu, the sight of the Buddha's early life, is nearby in the modern Nepalese district of Lumbini. Buddhism as such did not originate until the preaching of the first sermon at Sarnath in India, but tradition has it that several of the Buddha's relatives and clanspeople were early converts. Of all modern nations, Nepal can thus boast the second earliest introduction to Buddhism (next to

India) and the longest association with its founder, who was born there. Until the consolidation of the present 750,000 square mile kingdom of Nepal by the Gurkhas in the eighteenth century, however, "Nepal" referred only to the 200 square miles of the Kathmandu Valley. The birthplace of the historical Buddha and surviving Aśokan monuments lie well beyond this valley and are thus technically not part of the history of ancient Nepal and the Newar people.

The history of Buddhism among the Newars of the Kathmandu Valley begins instead in ancient legends, which in some cases cannot be entirely discounted. This traditional history locates the origins of Buddhism in central Nepal long before the Buddha himself was born. According to the *Svayambhu Purāṇa,* which purports to record the history of the Svayam-bhu Stūpa, this monument was erected many eons ago to commemorate the miraculous draining of the Kathmandu Valley by the celestial bodhi-sattva Mañjuśrī. The historical Buddha himself is said to have visited the stūpa after returning to Kapilavastu to preach to his father. According to legend, this was not his first visit, for in seven previous lives, the Buddha is supposed to have paid homage at the ancient monument. In addition, Tibetan sources indicate that both Nāgārjuna and Vasubandhu — founders respectively of Madhyamaka and Vijñānavāda Buddhism — visited the stūpa. Accordingly, a nearby hill bears the name of Nāgārjuna and a stūpa in the area is associated with Vasubandhu. Near the Svayam-bhu Stūpa stands the ancient Buddhist city of Patan, defined by four great stūpas at the points of the compass and a fifth in the center. The dates of these stūpas are uncertain, but their initial construction — and the strikingly Buddhist layout of Patan — must have predated the Hindu dominance that began in the fourth century.

Several historical and quasi-historical considerations tend to verify these indications of an ancient presence of Buddhism in the Kathmandu Valley. An unverified tradition holds that a daughter of Aśoka married a Newar prince. The Nepalese wife of Tibetan King Srong bTsan sGam-po (r. 627-650) almost certainly came from the Kathmandu Valley. Because Srong bTsan sGam-po's wife is credited with having helped convert the king to Buddhism, Nepal is recognized as a source of the earliest introduction of Buddhism to Tibet. About a hundred years later, in the eighth century, Śāntarakshita, Padma-sambhava, and Kamalaśīla are all supposed to have stopped over in the Kathmandu Valley en route to Tibet. These visits by some of the earliest verifiable founders of Buddhism in Tibet are not unlikely. By the eighth century, the Kathmandu Valley had become the primary corridor for trade between India and an expansive Tibetan empire which dominated Nepal and the other Himalayan regions examined in this chapter.

In 704, King Śivadeva II of the Licchavi dynasty of Nepal decisively overcame Tibetan dominance to the north of the Kathmandu Valley and established diplomatic and matrimonial alliances with Hindu dynasties in India. Śivadeva II and his Licchavi successors, though themselves Hindu, were careful to maintain relations with Tibet in order to foster the thriving trade that flowed through the Kathmandu Valley. As a result, though central Nepal was ruled by Hindus, Buddhism flourished throughout the Licchavi period, which lasted until the eleventh century or thereabout. This situation in Nepal did not differ significantly from situations in many parts of India, where Buddhism and emergent Hinduism co-existed under rulers who espoused one religion or the other but tolerated both. As in Tibet, throughout the Licchavi period in Nepal the primary source of Buddhist inspiration and renewal was India. Because of its long contact with the Indian tradition, by about 1200 and the completion of the Muslim conquest of India, Nepal had become one of the last outposts of Indian-style Buddhism. Along with Tibet, Nepal received the last great exportation of Indian Buddhism in the form of Buddhist refugees fleeing Islam. This created a brief resurgence of Buddhism in Nepal, but without a continuing parent tradition in India, Buddhism's absorption of Hindu elements quickened.

The details of the replacement of the Licchavi dynasty by the Malla dynasty, the next Indian dynasty in the Kathmandu Valley, are obscure. Presumably this occurred in the course of northward migrations of high-caste Hindus who, like Buddhists, were fleeing from the Muslim conquest of India. At any rate, several lines of Malla kings ruled the Kathmandu Valley from about 1200 until 1768. In addition to the Malla rulers in the Kathmandu Valley, numerous other small Hindu kingdoms and principalities were established throughout the lower lying regions of present-day Nepal. The early Malla kings appear to have continued the Licchavi policy of encouraging Newar Buddhism and culture. King Jayasthiti Malla (r. 1382-95), however, introduced sweeping legislation aimed at the Hinduization of the Newars by incorporating them into the caste system. Similar policies were adopted in surrounding kingdoms and principalities, so that the separate identity of Indian-style Buddhism was eroded throughout the lower reaches of Nepal.

This loss of identity was exacerbated by an influx of high-caste Hindus throughout most of the Malla period. During this period, it must be remembered, Hinduism in India also suffered, first under Muslim and then under British rule. Nepal, free of foreign domination, became an attractive haven for the elite of Hindu society. The gradual Hinduization of Nepal, then, was not merely a matter of imposing Hinduism from above. The Hinduism of Nepal represented an attractive, even heroic resistance to foreign imperialism on the Indian sub-continent. The Newars in the Kathmandu Valley and beyond, though increasingly Hindu in outlook, remained culturally distinct, and they continued to practice Buddhism. In addition to absorbing elements of Hinduism, however, the Buddhism of the Newars also became increasingly Tibetan in style because the main source of inspiration for Buddhism became the mountainous north of Nepal, where Tibetan influence remained strong.

The next dramatic step in the decline of Indian-style Buddhism in Nepal occurred in 1768 when Śāh Pṛthivī Nārāyan conquered the Kathmandu Valley and established the Gurkha Śāh dynasty that rules Nepal to the present day. The warlike Gurkhas, who later served as a renowned fighting force in the British army, had begun to migrate into Nepal during the Muslim conquest of India. They first established themselves quietly beyond the Kathmandu Valley, but in the eighteenth century they began systematically to gain control over the trade routes north and south of the central valley. In 1767, the British launched a military campaign to halt Gurkha expansion in Nepal and protect the trade routes to Tibet, but to no avail. After capturing the Kathmandu Valley, Gurkha forces struck out in all directions and established within about two decades a unified kingdom covering most of modern-day Nepal.

Unlike the Hindu Licchavis and Mallas, the Gurkhas attempted to impose a homogeneous, Hindu culture upon Nepal. This included an attempt to impose their own Gurkhali language, now known as Nepali. These steps were motivated primarily by the political ambition to create a modern nation, but Newari culture and Buddhism were repressed and declined rapidly under Gurkha rule. Even among the mountain peoples of Tibetan descent, Buddhism survives in Nepal only with a heavy admixture of Hinduism. Newar religious life continues to revolve around the ancient Buddhist temples and monasteries of Nepal, but these have become communal family residences for Newars of the priestly caste of Hinduism. Although the ritual cycle of Newar life still involves many vestigial features of Buddhism — in the form of monastic titles, deities, and terminology — the ceremonies themselves have become the equivalent of the ritual caste obligations of Hinduism.

The traditional Buddhism that now exists in Nepal is wholly Tibetan in origin and largely the product of conscious attempts to re-introduce Buddhism into Nepal in the twentieth century. Starting in the nineteenth century, mostly as a result of Indian and British scholarship, Nepal was recognized as a rich repository of the Sanskrit Buddhist tradition of India. Many otherwise lost Sanskrit versions of Indian Buddhist texts were retrieved from Nepal and now form a large portion of the Mahāyāna scriptures that survive in Sanskrit. Unfortunately, these texts are primarily of academic significance and no longer serve as the sacred canon of any living Buddhist tradition. Nonetheless, a resurgent sense of Newar self-identity has initiated a limited revival of Buddhism in Nepal and a renewed sense of pride in the unique place of Nepal in the history of Buddhism.

Western Tibet: Ladakh, Lahaul Spiti and Kinnaur

During and after the reign of King gLang Dar-ma (r. 836-42), the great persecutor of Buddhism in Tibet, Buddhists fled to the south, east, and west of the central kingdom. In the course of these migrations, a segment of the Tibetan royal family established itself in exile in an area conventionally referred to as "Western Tibet." In addition to a significant western portion of modern Tibet, the area known as Western Tibet included and was governed from the mountainous crescent between Kashmir and Nepal, territory that is now within the borders of India. On the modern map, these Buddhist areas include the Ladakh district of Jammu and Kashmir state and the Lahaul Spiti and Kinnaur districts of Himachal state. In addition, Western Tibet included the ancient kingdom of Guge, which lay between modern Himachal state and Nepal.

Numerically, the 125,000 or so Buddhists living today in the Himalayan regions northwest of Nepal are insignificant. Historically, their continued presence is of great interest and importance. Because of their proximity to Kashmir, these regions very likely saw the introduction of Buddhism during the reign of Kanishka (78-123 CE), if not in Aśokan times (c. 250 BCE). The *Mahāvaṃsa* chronicle of Sri Lanka mentions several Aśokan missions to spread Buddhism beyond his domain. Among these is a mission to Kashmir and another to *Himavat* or "Himalayan region," which may refer to the area under examination. In any case, the colorful, cheerful and hardy Buddhists of the northwestern Himalayas represent one of the most ancient continuous traditions of Buddhism now in existence.

The Buddhism practiced in these regions today is derived from Tibet, and its truly ancient Indian heritage has been obliterated. Even so, the Tibetan Buddhism in these regions is particularly noteworthy because of the relatively large proportion of followers of the Nyingmapa and Drugpa ['Brug-pa] sects. The Nyingmapa is the oldest sect of Tibetan Buddhism, but is not now widely practiced among Tibetans. The Drugpa sect is actually a subsect of the Kagyudpa and is now found almost exclusively in the northwestern Himalayas and Bhutan. Bhutan is predominantly

Drugpa, whereas the northwestern Himalayan Buddhists are approximately evenly divided among Nyingmapa, Drugpa and Gelugpa, the sect of the Dalai Lama, which is overwhelmingly predominant among Tibetans. The preponderance of the Drugpa subsect in the northwestern Himalayas is something of a mystery, but the relatively large following of the Nyingmapa may be explained by the hypothesis that in these regions Tibetan Buddhism has remained chilled if not frozen since the time of its introduction. At the time of gLang Dar-ma's persecution, in the ninth century, only the Nyingmapa existed in Tibet, and so only the Nyingmapa could have been introduced into Western Tibet at this time. Although the Himalayan regions of Western Tibet clearly facilitated the re-introduction of Buddhism to central Tibet (in the eleventh century), these regions did not participate fully in the rapid development of Buddhism in Tibet following its re-introduction.

Despite the infamy of gLang Dar-ma, the kings of Western Tibet were anxious to legitimize their reigns by tracing their ancestry through him to the kings of ancient Tibet. For this reason, a "Chronicle of the Kings of Ladakh" *(La-Dvags rGyal-Rabs)* was compiled from early times.[45] According to this chronicle, which includes the several regions under examination in addition to Ladakh, the first noteworthy king of Western Tibet was the great-grandson of gLang Dar-ma, sKyid lDe Nyi-ma mGon, who consolidated the entire Himalayan region of Western Tibet sometime around 950. King Nyi-ma mGon divided this territory among his three sons. The eldest got Ladakh proper; the second got Guge, which probably included modern Kinnaur; and the youngest got Lahaul, Spiti and Zanskar, the southern verge of modern Ladakh. This ancient division of territory is the ultimate basis of the modern map of the region.

Because of its proximity to Kashmir, Ladakh has the most ancient verifiable history of Buddhism in this region. Until 1979, the Ladakh district of Jammu and Kashmir state was in area the largest district in India; in population one of the smallest. In 1979 it was split into two districts — Kargil and Leh — which correspond roughly to the Muslim and Buddhist areas of Ladakh. Islam is predominant in the modern district of Kargil, southwest of the Indus River's headwaters, though several pockets of Buddhism persist in the district. The most significant of these pockets is the Zanskar River valley region, which corresponds roughly to the ancient kingdom of Zanskar. The Leh district, which lies northwest of the Indus, is almost exclusively Buddhist.

The origins of Buddhism in Ladakh must go back at least to Kushan times (78-225 CE), although there is no direct evidence of this. The Kushan dynasty was clearly dominant in Kashmir, and must have exerted influence in its northernmost reaches, which now constitute Ladakh.

The influence of Aśoka may well have penetrated Ladakh as well, but again no direct evidence exists. Snellgrove and Skorupski feel that the earliest direct evidence of Buddhism in Ladakh are eighth-century bas-reliefs created under Kashmiri influence, but their dating of these reliefs is questionable.[46] Nonetheless, it is clear that the earliest Buddhism in Ladakh was Indian in origin and filtered through Kashmir. In Ladakh, the last wave of this influence occurred in the fourteenth century, following the Muslim conquest of Kashmir.

Well before this time, Ladakh was firmly in the orbit of Tibet, which as early as the eighth century had already begun to challenge the Kashmiri monarchs in this region. The ninth century saw the reign of King gLang Dar-ma and the dispersion of Buddhists from central Tibet. As noted in the chapter on Tibet, it was primarily among the western faction of Tibet-an refugees that Buddhism gathered momentum, fueled from Kashmir and India, for its second and definitive introduction into Tibet proper between 1000 and 1200.

The two major figures in this re-introduction — the Tibetan translator Rin Chen bZang-po (958-1055) and the Indian scholar-monk Atīśa (982-1054) — are both associated with the northwestern Himalayas. Both fig-ures were sponsored by rulers of Western Tibet, several of whom bore names suggesting that they may have been Buddhist monks. If so, West-ern Tibet — along with Bhutan as we shall see — may have originated the Tibetan custom of combining religious and secular authority in the persons of monks.[47] Supported by rulers of Western Tibet — most nota-bly prince Ye Shes 'od or "Light of Wisdom" — Rin Chen bZang-po trav-eled to Kashmir and India in search of authentic Buddhist scriptures and traditions. In addition to his prodigious translation activities, Rin Chen bZang-po founded monasteries all through Ladakh, Lahaul, Spiti and Kinnaur. Some of these institutions still function; others survive only as ruins. Atīśa is supposed to have spent two years (1042-44) in Guge before traveling on to central Tibet.

Throughout the northwestern Himalayas, traditions associate the intro-duction of Buddhism with Padma-sambhava, and portray the activities of Rin Chen bZang-po and Atīśa as a re-introduction of Buddhism parallel to that which occurred in Tibet proper. This is doubtful, as Padma-sambhava is more likely to have traveled to Tibet through Nepal. Given the relative prominence of the Nyingmapa sect in the northwestern Hima-layas, it is not surprising to encounter legends of visits by the founder of the sect. In addition, the legendary visits of Padma-sambhava probably represent an appropriation of the Tibetan historical pattern of introduc-tion, decline and re-introduction of Buddhism. Though little of the history of these remote Himalayan areas is clear, it appears that once Buddhism was introduced, whenever that was, it did not decline significantly. Instead, these areas served as a haven from which the decline of Buddhism in Tibet was overcome.

Once Buddhism was re-established in central Tibet, Buddhism in Western Tibet underwent what appears to have been a smooth transition from primarily Indian to primarily Tibetan influence and inspiration. The first recorded indication of this transition is in the reign of King Lha Chen dNgos Grub [La Chen Ngo Dub], sometime around 1200, when the tradition began of sending novice monks to central Tibet rather than to Kashmir for the completion of their training.[48] Lha Chen dNgos Grub also imported an entire Kanjur (Tibetan canon) from Tibet. His predecessor of uncertain date, King Lha rGyal, is credited with the first copying of Buddhist scriptures from Tibetan rather than Kashmiri or Indian sources.[49] These events represent a turning away from India, where Buddhism was dying out, and a turning toward Tibet, where Buddhism was resurgent. This Tibetan connection helped preserve the Buddhism of these Himalayan regions from the Hinduization of Nepalese Buddhism. Popular practice in these areas exhibits Hindu influence, but "official" Buddhism as such is a pure and respected variety of Tibetan Buddhism.

From the fourteenth century, when Kashmir became decidedly Muslim, the Buddhist kingdoms of the northwest Himalayas, particularly Ladakh, faced constant pressure from expansionist Islam. This pressure increased dependence upon Tibet, but never resulted in a complete political domination by Tibet of the Himalayan kingdoms skirting the Tibetan plateau. Ladakh's independence of Tibet was symbolically expressed by its rulers' encouragement of the Drugpa subsect of the Kagyudpa rather than the Gelugpa sect of the Dalai Lama. Tsong Kha-pa himself (1357-1419) sent an envoy to Ladakh in the reign of King Grags 'Bum lDe [Drag Bum De], and the first Gelugpa monastery was built at this time. Tsong Kha-pa's reformist influence may account for a rock edict, ordered by King Grags 'Bum lDe, prohibiting animal sacrifices.[50] Regardless of the apparently enthusiastic reception of the Gelugpa sect in Ladakh, the Drugpa sect retained a significant following in the region.

This allegiance to the Drugpa sect, which is also prominent in Bhutan, is partly responsible for Ladakh's ill-advised involvement in protracted hostilities between Tibet and Bhutan in the seventeenth century. As a result of this involvement, Tibet annexed the interior territory of Western Tibet, as formalized in the Ladakh-Tibet treaty of 1684. This treaty also extracted from Ladakh's rulers a pledge to encourage the Gelugpa. Even so, the Drugpa subsect remains surprisingly strong in Ladakh and indeed throughout the Himalayan fringes of Tibet. In addition, Tibet extracted from Ladakh a commitment not to allow any Indian army to pass through its territory en route to Tibet. In essence, this made Ladakh a buffer state between Tibet and Muslim Kashmir. In the end, however, Tibet's Ladakh card was played against an unexpected adversary.

Since the fourteenth century, Muslim Kashmir had been making inroads upon Ladakh, and it continued to do so after the treaty of 1684. When Ladakh finally ceased to exist as an independent state, however, it fell to the vigorous Sikh state of Jammu, which annexed both Kashmir (in 1819) and then Ladakh. Having overrun Ladakh, the Sikhs launched an unsuccessful invasion of Tibet, after which they retreated to Ladakh and signed with Lhasa the Treaty of Leh in 1842. In return for Ladakh, the Sikh ruler Gulab Singh renounced all ambitions in Tibet, and the present border between Ladakh and Tibet was ratified. Thus was formed the forerunner of the modern Indian state of Jammu and Kashmir.

Partly as a result of Ladakh's preoccupation with its struggles against Tibet in the seventeenth century, the Sikh kingdom of Kulu was able to annex Lahaul at this time. Spiti continued to be associated with Ladakh until 1846-49, when a series of Anglo-Sikh treaties granted Kulu, Lahaul and Spiti to the British. Kinnaur, apparently a remnant of the ancient kingdom of Guge, along with Lahaul and Spiti, makes up the Buddhist north of Himachal state in modern India. This is not to say that these regions are entirely Buddhist. It is probably fair to say that their populations are half Buddhist and half Hindu, with the purer Buddhists concentrated in the higher mountains in the north, the purer Hindus in the southern hills, and a syncretistic population in between.

The total number of Buddhists in all of these areas combined — Ladakh, Lahaul Spiti and Kinnaur — probably does not exceed 125,000, depending upon what one counts as "Buddhist." No matter how one counts, they are a miniscule statistic even compared to India's five million professed Buddhists,[51] not to mention India's total population of near a billion. Nonetheless, they are significant by virtue of preserving a centuries-old way of life, relatively rare forms of Tibetan Buddhism, and what is probably one of the world's most ancient continuous traditions of Buddhism.

Bhutan

Sikkim and Bhutan, at the southeastern extreme of the Himalayas, cannot lay supportable historical claim to have received Buddhism in the first instance from ancient India. Instead, the Buddhism of both regions appears to have been developed entirely from Tibetan precedents.

Bhutan possesses the more ancient recorded history of Buddhism, and therefore will be considered first.

Traditional sources indicate that two temples in Bhutan — the sKyer-chu and Byams-pa [Jam-pa] temples — were built during the reign of the Tibetan king Srong bTsan sGam-po (r. 627-50), who is credited with sponsoring the first introduction of Buddhism to Tibet. His Chinese wife is supposed to have brought with her from China a magical scheme of temple locations that would insure the conversion of Tibet to Buddhism. The sKyer-chu and Byams-pa temples are widely believed to have been two of the twelve crucial temples in this scheme. The architectural style of the temples in question is consistent with an early date, but the entire story of Srong bTsan sGam-po's temple building scheme is dubious, whether within or beyond the borders of Tibet proper. All things considered, it is more likely that these early Bhutanese temples were built during the reign of King Khri Srong lDe bTsan [Ti Song De Tsan] (742-98) and that Buddhism was introduced to Bhutan during his reign.[52]

This eighth-century date corresponds with traditions that Śāntarakshita and Padma-sambhava visited Bhutan. A persistent tradition credits Padma-sambhava with having resolved a dispute between a king of Bhutan and an Indian monarch known as sNa'u Che, meaning "Big Nose." The king of Bhutan in this legend is commonly known as Sindhu Rāja, meaning "Indian King," but Michael Aris has shown that this name is a corruption of a local Bhutanese name.[53] Nonetheless, this legend is the first indication of contacts between Bhutan and India, and once again the legendary time-frame for such contacts may be approximately correct even though the characters and events may be fictitious or distorted. As in other Himalayan regions, the appearance of Padma-sambhava serves to legitimize the Nyingmapa sect in Bhutan. Once again, however, in historical reality the relative prevalence of the Nyingmapa sect in Bhutan probably traces back to the dispersion of Tibetan Buddhism during and after the reign of King gLang Dar-ma (r. 836-42), a period when only the Nyingmapa existed in Tibet.

All of the foregoing material on Bhutan traces ultimately to *gTer-ma* or "treasure" texts discovered by the Bhutanese monk and famous *gTer sTon* or "treasure finder" Padma gLing-pa (1450-1521). As discussed above in Chapter XI, the entire genre of treasure texts — which were supposedly hidden in ancient times and discovered later — is inherently dubious from a historical point of view. Regardless of the sanctity of their discoverers, such material must be treated as legendary unless corroborated by other sources. As in the northwestern Himalayan regions examined above, corroborated history in Bhutan begins with the reign of King gLang Dar-ma.

Tibetan and Bhutanese sources agree that Prince gTsang-ma, the elder brother of gLang Dar-ma, took refuge in Bhutan after his anti-Buddhist brother usurped the throne of Tibet. Tradition holds that gTsang-ma was a Buddhist monk. This may be no more than an attempt to explain his name, which means "pure." On the other hand, this tradition calls to mind the parallel tradition that early kings and princes of Western Tibet were monks. If these traditions are true, it means that the practice of combining religious and secular authority in the person of a Buddhist monk originated in refugee communities on the borders of Tibet following gLang Dar-ma's persecution of Buddhism. In addition to sectarian affiliations, such parallels following upon the dispersion of Buddhism from central Tibet may also help explain the alliance noted above between Ladakh and Bhutan.

Once Buddhism was re-established in central Tibet, several of the sects and subsects that emerged there spread to Bhutan. Of these, the Drugpa ['Brug-pa] branch of the Kagyudpa sect became overwhelmingly dominant in the seventeenth century, providing even the Bhutanese name of the country — 'Brug-yul [Drug-yul] or "Thunder-dragon Land." Naturally, the Nyingmapa, probably established at roughly the time of Padma-sambhava in the eighth or ninth century, was the first to flourish. Other than the Drugpa sub-sect, the Nyingmapa is the only prominent form of Buddhism in present-day Bhutan. No doubt this survival is due largely to the fact that the Nyingmapa in Bhutan never organized itself into a political force.

Nonetheless, two of the most illustrious historical figures of the Nyingmapa sect are significantly associated with Bhutan. These are kLong Chen-pa (1308-63) and Padma gLing-pa (1450-1521). To the extent that Nyingmapa doctrines ever attained systematic expression, kLong Chen-pa was responsible. His best known work, the *Ngal gSo sKor gSum* is readily available in English translation.[54] He fled to Bhutan at an unknown date after the Phag-mo Gru [Phag-mo-du] branch of the Kagyudpa sect attained supremacy in Tibet under King Byang-Chub rGyal-mTshan in 1354. In Bhutan, kLong Chen-pa founded eight monasteries and wrote some of his most important treatises.

Padma gLing-pa, a native of Bhutan and the second of Bhutan's illustrious Nyingmapas, claimed to be the reincarnation of kLong Chen-pa, and more distantly of Padma gSal, consort of Padma-sambhava and daughter of King Khri Srong lDe bTsan. Needless to say, Padma gLing-pa was a colorful character. Though a monk, he had several children by several consorts and was the common ancestor of both the sixth Dalai Lama and the present royal family of Bhutan. He is best remembered, however, as one of the five "Treasure Finding Kings" *(gTer sTon rGyal-po)* of Tibetan Buddhism and the only non-Tibetan among them. His long autobiography — which recounts the miraculous circumstances surrounding his discoveries of hidden *gTer-ma* texts in a disarmingly matter-of-fact style — is the only indigenous textual source of Bhutanese history prior to the foundation of the modern kingdom in the seventeenth century. Obviously, this autobiography is not a work of history as such, but otherwise the early history of Bhutan has to be pieced together from Tibetan sources.

In addition to the Nyingmapa with its eighth or ninth century roots, several branches of the Kagyudpa existed in Bhutan from at least the thirteenth century, and the Sakyapa, Kadampa and Gelugpa sects appear to have gained influence starting in the fifteenth century. Tsong Kha-pa himself (1357-1419), the founder of the Gelugpa sect, is supposed to have visited Bhutan briefly. With the exception of the Nyingmapa, however, all of the Buddhist sects of Bhutan were either absorbed or eclipsed by the Drugpa branch of the Kagyudpa in the seventeenth century.

The Drugpa sect was established in Bhutan by the shadowy figure Pha-jo (c. 1208-76), who is supposed to have waged magical warfare against and been poisoned by Lha Nang-pa (1164-1224), founder of the first Kagyudpa subsect in Bhutan, the Lha-pa. The probable dates of the two lamas belie the tradition of their personal rivalry, but the Lha-pa subsect was indeed the principal adversary of the Drugpa subsect, though both groups were branches of the Kagyudpa and both were associated primarily with Bhutan rather than Tibet. The eventual victory of the Drugpa was so complete that little reliable history of the Lha-pa subsect survives.

The ascendancy of the Drugpa subsect in Bhutan began in 1616 with the arrival from Tibet of Ngag dBang rNam rGyal [Nga-wang Nam-gyal — 1594- c. 1651], commonly referred to by his title as the Zhabs Drung ["Zhab Drung"], meaning "Most Reverend." Born into a powerful noble family in Tibet, the Zhabs Drung was widely believed to be the reincarnation of Padma dKar-po (1527-92) the greatest scholar of the Drugpa subsect and one of the greatest in Tibet's entire history. At the age of thirteen, in 1606, the Zhabs Drung's enthronement in Tibet as head of the Drugpa subsect attracted eminent lamas and royalty from all over Tibet and beyond, including fortuitously Bhutan. Despite this widespread recognition, the ruler of Tibet seems to have sided with a rival clan's claim to possess the reincarnation of Padma dKar-po, so that in 1616, at the age of 23, the Zhabs Drung fled to Bhutan. The Drugpa subsect was already well-established in Bhutan, and the arrival of the head of the order and one of the highest lamas in all Tibet no doubt gave it a tremendous boost.

The status of both the Zhabs Drung and the Drugpa subsect was further increased by the repulsion of three invasions of Bhutan staged by the disgruntled ruler of Tibet. Each of these invasions appears to have been supported by rival Buddhist sects in Bhutan, so that the Zhabs Drung's victories over Tibet represented also victories over other forms of Buddhism in Bhutan. The third Tibetan invasion was repulsed in 1639, and the chief fortress of the rival Lha-pa subsect of Bhutan was overthrown in 1641. The Zhabs Drung's victory in Bhutan was followed immediately by the demise of his enemies in Tibet. In 1642, the fifth Dalai Lama of Tibet sealed an alliance with the Mongols under Gushi Khan. This alliance deposed the old rulers of Tibet and established the Gelugpa sect as paramount in Tibet.

The demise of the Zhabs Drung's enemies at home and abroad provided only brief respite for Bhutan, for in 1644 and 1649, combined Tibetan and Mongol forces mounted two further invasions of Bhutan. Both were driven back by the armies of the Zhabs Drung, who was now the undisputed religious and secular authority in Bhutan, just as the fifth Dalai Lama became the undisputed ruler of Tibet when Gushi Khan died in 1656. A third Tibetan-Mongol invasion was repulsed by Bhutanese forces loyal to the Zhabs Drung in 1657, although the Zhabs Drung himself was probably dead by this time.

The Zhabs Drung probably died in 1651, but the date is uncertain because his death was concealed from the public. For over fifty years, Bhutanese authorities maintained that the Zhabs Drung was in a meditation retreat. No doubt the concealment of his death was motivated by a desire to maintain the political stability of Bhutan during tumultuous times. This same strategy was employed by authorities in Tibet when the fifth Dalai Lama died in 1682. By this time, the Zhabs Drung had been dead for some thirty years, and would have been 88 years old, so that one must suspect that the Tibetan authorities knowingly copied a Bhutanese precedent in concealing the death of their most effective ruler. At any rate, it is indeed remarkable that in the closing decades of the seventeenth century, the acknowledged religious and secular heads of state in both Tibet and Bhutan were not only lamas, but dead lamas.

The Bhutanese were boldly consistent in maintaining that the Zhabs Drung really was in a meditational trance for some fifty-six years, until 1705. The Tibetans, it will be remembered, secretly located the reincarnation of the fifth Dalai Lama and enthroned him at the age of thirteen in 1696. The Bhutanese, by contrast, located the reincarnation of the Zhabs Drung as an infant born in 1708. In doing so, they affirmed a common belief in Tibetan-style Buddhism that advanced lamas can remain indefinitely in a state of suspended animation after their apparent vital functions have ceased. Accounts of high lamas remaining seated thus in a meditational posture for long periods of time are too numerous to be dismissed lightly, although the case of the Zhabs Drung of Bhutan is truly extraordinary. His "meditational retreat" outlasted the reigns of six regents and spanned a period of territorial expansion and consolidation that accounts for the present borders of the kingdom.

As if the foregoing did not sufficiently strain even the most generous credulity, subsequent disputes over the identity of the Zhabs Drung's reincarnation resulted in the official position that his body, speech and mind had reincarnated separately in Sikkim, Tibet and Bhutan. The Bhutanese line of "mental" incarnations enjoyed the greatest prestige, but two further Tibetan invasions in 1714 and 1730, and internal civil strife throughout the nineteenth century, divided the country to the extent that subsequent Zhabs Drungs and their regents ceased to exercise real authority in Bhutan. In the end, an alliance against Tibet between Britain and the most powerful regional ruler of Bhutan in 1904 accounts for the present monarchy, which was instituted in 1907 with the coronation of the first King of Bhutan. Under the dynasty established at that time, tiny Bhutan survives to the present day as the only independent nation still guided by the Tibetan religion and culture, a religion and culture that once dominated an enormous swath of territory including Mongolia, western China, northern India and much of Central Asia.

Sikkim

The Indian state of Sikkim — measuring only about seventy by forty miles — lies in high mountainous territory between Nepal and Bhutan. Its earliest inhabitants, tribal people known as Lepchas, were joined at unknown times by Tibetan and Nepali settlers to form the present racial mix of Sikkim. Under the influence of the British, in the late nineteenth century a large influx of Gurkhas from Nepal dramatically increased the Hindu population of Sikkim. Today, the Lepchas and Tibetans constitute the Buddhist third of Sikkim's total population of about 300,000. Of the Himalayan regions on India's northern frontier, Sikkim possesses the least ancient verifiable history of Buddhism. In Sikkim, as in most of the Himalayan regions examined, tradition holds that Padma-sambhava subdued local demons and introduced Buddhism in the eighth century. Once again, there is no evidence for a visit by Padma-sambhava himself, but there is little reason to discount the rough time-frame that traditional history proposes for the introduction of Buddhism to Sikkim.

History as such in Sikkim begins only in the seventeenth century with the arrival of three Nyingmapa lamas from Tibet. Presumably, they were refugees from the Mongol-Gelugpa alliance that had come to dominate Tibet, for they consecrated the first king of Bhutan in 1642, the same year in which the fifth Dalai Lama and Gushi Khan became the undisputed rulers of Tibet. Of these three lamas, Lha Tsun Chembo is recognized as the foremost and is regarded as the founder of Sikkim. According to tradition, lama Chembo informed the other two lamas that Padmasambhava had prophesied that four noble persons would meet in Sikkim and found a Buddhist kingdom there. He also proclaimed that the fourth person was a man named Phun Tshog, descended from a noble family of Tibet. Phun Tshog was duly located in Gantok, the capital of present-day Sikkim, and consecrated as the first Chogyal [Chos rGyal = "Dharma King"] of Sikkim (r. 1642-70). This consecration marked the beginning of the Namgyal dynasty in Sikkim, which ruled the kingdom until the twentieth century.

Traditionally, the ancestors of this first king of Sikkim migrated from Tibet and settled in Bhutan. From their base in Bhutan, they are said to have established cordial relations with and residence among the indigenous Lepchas of the Gantok area in Sikkim. Bhutanese sources confirm a Buddhist connection between eastern Tibet, Bhutan and Sikkim going back to the thirteenth century, and one of the "treasure texts" discovered by the Bhutanese *gTer sTon* Padma gLing-pa (1450-1521) is in part a guide to Buddhist sacred sites in Sikkim.[55] All of this suggests that during the reign of the fifth Dalai Lama, Nyingmapa refugees from Tibet established with a Tibetan ruling house in Gantok a sharing of religious and secular authority. This power-sharing arrangement was similar to the Gelugpa-Mongol alliance from which they were fleeing. As in Tibet, this arrangement seems to have worked admirably, for the first Chogyal of Sikkim and his Nyingmapa allies were able to convert or subdue the Lepchas and extend the kingdom well beyond the current borders of Sikkim into present-day Tibet, Nepal, Bhutan and India.

During the eighteenth century, several incursions and invasions by Bhutan and the Gurkhas of Nepal — as well as the paternal but opportunistic involvement of Tibet — chewed into Sikkim's borders and threatened to reduce the kingdom to a memory. In the reign of the seventh Chogyal (r. 1793-1864) — which lasted a full seventy years from his coronation at the age of eight — much of Sikkim's former territory was restored by the British in the course of their conflicts with Nepal. The present borders of Sikkim were formalized in the Treaty of Titalia in 1817, following the Anglo-Gurkha war of 1814-15.

During this period of strife in the eighteenth century, Sikkim often turned to Tibet for help. The third Chogyal had to seek refuge in Tibet, where he became close friends with and official astrologer to the sixth Dalai Lama. The fourth Chogyal established close relations with the head of the Karmapa subsect of the Kagyudpa, and during his reign the first Karmapa monastery was established in Sikkim in about 1730. In addition to the Nyingmapa, the Karmapa subsect remains today the only other prominent branch of Buddhism practiced in Sikkim. The status of the subsect in Sikkim was enhanced significantly in 1950 when the sixteenth Karmapa grand lama fled to Sikkim following the Chinese invasion of Tibet. Since that time, the Rumtek Monastery near Gantok has remained the world headquarters of the Karmapa subsect of Tibetan Buddhism and one of the most important centers for the propagation of Tibetan Buddhism to the Western world.

Buddhism Among the Mongols

Some discussion of the development of Buddhism among the Mongols has been presented already in the preceding chapter on Tibet. As noted there, the first clear indication of Buddhist influence among the Mongols was the conversion of Kublai Khan in approximately 1250 by the great Sakyapa scholar 'Phags-pa. Buddhist ruins at Khara Baishing, near Ulan Bator, indicate that the religion was known in Mongol territory, if not widely practiced by the Mongols themselves, at least two centuries before this time.[56] In 1280, Kublai Khan established in China the Yuan or Mongol dynasty, which survived almost a century until it was replaced in 1368 by the ethnic Chinese Ming dynasty. Throughout the Yuan dynasty, Tibetan-style Buddhism was not only the official religion of the Mongols; it was also the de facto state religion of China. Following the collapse of the Yuan dynasty, it appears that the Mongols of the steppes quickly reverted to their nomadic lifestyle and their traditional, shamanistic religion, if indeed they had ever departed far from it in large numbers.

Many Mongols remained behind in Ming dynasty China, however, and Mongolian-Tibetan Buddhism in China did not lapse until it was officially suppressed, beginning in the early sixteenth century. The Ming suppression drove Mongolian and Tibetan Buddhists out of China and back to their nomadic kinsmen. This exodus marked the beginning of a resurgence of Buddhism among the Mongols. Naturally, this resurgence began among the southern Mongols, who were closest to China and most susceptible to influences from China.

In the south, resurgent Buddhism gained official recognition when Altan Khan, the most powerful of the southern chieftains, invited to his court the abbot of the Gelugpa sect of Tibet. It was at this meeting in 1576 that Altan Khan conveyed upon the Gelugpa abbot the title of Dalai Lama, thus inaugurating the most famous institution of Tibetan Buddhism. Since the Gelugpa abbot was regarded as the reincarnation of two predecessors, he became known as the third Dalai Lama. Altan Khan's embracing of Buddhism resulted in an immediate prohibition of many of the more unsavory rituals of Mongolian shamanism, including human and animal sacrifices.

In 1577, a year after the conversion of Altan Khan, Abadai Khan, the most powerful ruler of the northern Mongols, also embraced the Gelugpa sect. The third Dalai Lama's second visit to Mongolia in 1586 included a triumphal tour of northern Mongolia. On this occasion, Abadai Khan announced restrictions upon shamanism similar to those already in force in the south, and embarked upon an extensive program of temple building to rival that already underway in the south.

Because of the dramatic ascendancy of Buddhism throughout Mongolia in the latter half of the sixteenth century, traditional Mongolian history — like the traditional history of Western Tibet — appropriates the Tibetan pattern of introduction, decline and reintroduction of Buddhism. The resurgence in the sixteenth century is usually credited to the spiritual prowess of the third Dalai Lama and depicted as a spontaneous conversion of the Mongols as a whole to Gelugpa Buddhism. In reality, much of the impetus for the resurgence came from China, and several sects of Tibetan Buddhism — including the Nyingmapa, Sakyapa and Karmapa sects — participated in this resurgence. The Gelugpa became dominant only toward the middle of the seventeenth century, when an influential line of reincarnating Gelugpa lamas was established among the Mongols.

It is curious that the unruly and warlike Mongols finally gravitated to the strictest and most conspicuously pacifist form of Tibetan Buddhism. In part, credit for the conversion of the Mongols must indeed go to the third Dalai Lama himself, who spent much of the last ten years of his life as a missionary among the Mongols. The discovery in 1588 of the fourth Dalai Lama in the person of a great-grandson of Altan Khan clearly helped to increase the prestige of the Gelugpa sect. Following the discovery of the fourth Dalai Lama in their midst, the institution of reincarnating lamas became widespread among the Mongols. In the early seventeenth century, under the patronage of Ligdan Khan (1603-34), the Kanjur — the enormous central core of Tibetan Buddhist scripture — was translated into Mongolian in 113 volumes.

Buddhism among the Mongols received a further boost when the Manchurian Qing dynasty (1644-1912) replaced the Ming dynasty in China. The Ming emperors had suppressed Tibetan-style Buddhism in China. The Manchus, however, were ethnically related to the Mongols and Tibetans. As a result, Tibetan-style Buddhism underwent a revival in China, and the Qing emperors vigorously promoted Buddhism among the Mongols. Historians of Mongolia commonly suppose that Manchu China promoted Buddhism among the Mongols in order to pacify them. No doubt this is partly true, but it is also clear that the Mongols had become fervently devoted to Buddhism and that they themselves played a large part in promoting and financing Buddhism in Mongolia.

The Manchu encouragement of Buddhism — as well as the Mongols' own enthusiasm — is particularly evident in the literary sphere. Under Manchu patronage, in 1718-20 Ligdan Khan's edition of the Mongolian Kanjur was block-printed and distributed throughout Mongolia. In 1742-49 the Tanjur, the secondary section of the Tibetan canon, was translated, printed and published in 226 volumes, again with the sponsorship of the Manchu emperor of China. The Manchu emperors also supported the Mongolian Saṅgha lavishly and financed the building of many temples and monasteries.

In addition to its religious role, Buddhism in northern Mongolia assumed a dominant political role. The northern khan Tushetu (1594-1655) apparently recognized the futility of attempting to unify the Mongol tribes under a single "Grand Khan" such as Genghis or Kublai had been. Pursuing an alternative strategy, he managed to gain from seven northern tribes recognition that his son was a reincarnating lama, in Mongolian a *khutuktu,* and would be the spiritual master of the northern Mongol tribes known as the Khalkha. This child was born in 1635, and in 1649 received from the Panchen Lama of Tibet the title Jebtsundamba Khutuktu. He died in 1723, having become enormously popular through-out southern and northern Mongolia because of his reputation for saintly conduct and supernatural powers. Recognizing the potential for political organization and rebellion under the Jebtsundamba Khutuktu, the Manchu emperor of China decreed in 1759 — after probably having arranged the murder of the second Jebtsundamba Khutuktu — that all future Jebtsundamba Khutuktus were to be discovered in Tibet. This practice continued until the eighth and last Jebtsundamba Khutuktu died in 1924. No replacement was sought due to Soviet influence in the increasingly secularized Mongolian state. Despite continuous foreign influence upon the office, during the 200 year period between 1723 and 1924 the Jebtsundamba Khutuktu remained the most powerful and respected religious and political figure among the Mongols.

Even as Mongol culture blossomed under the influence of Tibetan Buddhism, Mongol military might and territory declined dramatically throughout the seventeenth and eighteenth centuries. While promoting Buddhism among the Mongols, the Manchu emperors extended China's territory and influence at their expense. As it was to do in twentieth-century Tibet, China pursued in southern Mongolia a hated policy of colonization by ethnic Chinese, even though the Manchu rulers of China were themselves related to the Mongols. From the north, Russia also began to encroach upon Mongolian lands. The once feared Mongolian cavalry with its bows and arrows was no match for the modern firearms and artillery of the Manchus and the Russians. By the end of the nineteenth century, Manchu and Russian expansion had reduced the once expansive empire of the Mongols to roughly the present borders of Mongolia.

The futility of waging military campaigns against impossible odds encouraged the development of a more sedentary and stable lifestyle and economy. This, in turn, increased the attractiveness of Buddhist ordination for Mongolian males. In addition, the suppression of Mongolian shamanism resulted in an absorption by Buddhism of the traditional tribal shamans and their deities. The absorption and camouflage of shamanistic elements accounts for the unique liturgy and practices of Mongolian Buddhism. It also helps to explain the surprisingly large proportion of Mongolian males who joined the Saṅgha. Before the triumph of Buddhism, virtually every important family had at least one member proficient in shamanistic magic and ritual. After the ascendancy of Buddhism, virtually every family aspired to have at least one son in the Saṅgha. As a result, by the nineteenth century, up to half of Mongolian men were in some sense members of the Buddhist Saṅgha, although not always celibate or childless. As of 1900, there were almost 2,000 Buddhist monasteries and temples in Mongolia, and about 250 reincarnating lamas.[57]

Upon the collapse of the Manchu dynasty and its replacement by the Republic of China in 1912, Mongolia declared independence as a monarchy ruled by the eighth and last Jebtsundamba Khutuktu. Real independence was short-lived, as China was able to reassert sovereignty by 1914. Nonetheless, Mongolia survived as an autonomous state — though ruled by a Tibetan *khutuktu* and dominated by China — until 1924, when the last Jebtsundamba Khutuktu died. In 1920, the first communist party to be founded outside Russia had been organized in Mongolia through the efforts of Soviet agents. In the early days, the Mongolian communist party declared itself loyal to Buddhism. Nonetheless, when a Soviet-backed revolution against Chinese domination began in 1921, the Jebtsundamba Khutuktu declared allegiance to the Chinese overlords of Mongolia. By 1924 and the foundation of the Soviet-backed People's Republic of Mongolia, Moscow had gained sufficient influence among the northern

Mongols to establish an "official" consensus that the ninth Jebtsundamba Khutuktu would be born in a heavenly abode rather than on earth. This consensus was not resisted among the Chinese-dominated southern Mongols, and the primary symbol of Mongolian unity lapsed formally. However, a ninth Jebtsundamba Khutuktu was "unofficially" discovered in India, where he now lives with a wife and children in Dehra Dun. Rumors persist among the Mongols that he will return, re-establish the institution, and re-unite the Mongols.

For the time being, however, Mongolia remains divided. The Soviet-backed People's Republic in the north is commonly known as "Outer Mongolia." "Inner Mongolia" refers to the southern part of the country, which remains under Chinese control. In the Russian-dominated north, Buddhism was progressively suppressed until 1937-38, when the remaining monasteries were forcibly closed down. Those monks who had not been coerced into leaving voluntarily were forcibly evicted, often into the dead of the bitter Mongolian winter. Precious gold and silver images were melted into bullion, less valuable artifacts wantonly destroyed, and temple buildings converted into offices, communal residences, and warehouses. To all appearances, Buddhism had been eradicated in Outer Mongolia by 1939. Meanwhile, Buddhism languished in Chinese-dominated Inner Mongolia until the triumph of Chinese communism in 1949. Since that time, under the domination of Chinese communism, the fate of Buddhism and Mongolian culture as a whole in Inner Mongolia has followed the depressing pattern of Tibet. Like the current status of Buddhism in China and Tibet, the status of Buddhism in Inner Mongolia remains unclear, reviving and declining according to government policy. Since the collapse of the Soviet Union in the 1980s, however, Outer Mongolia, free of Russian political domination, has witnessed an enthusiastic revival of Buddhism, with prayer-houses springing up across the country-side and the beginning of restoration work on some ruined temples.

Conclusion

The survivals of Tibetan-style Buddhism beyond Tibet discussed in this chapter bear witness to the remarkable influence that Tibet exerted in its area of the world. The number of people who now bear traces of Tibetan influence is relatively small, but the territory involved is truly vast, stretching from Mongolia through to northern India. As a result of events in the twentieth century, the influence of Tibetan Buddhism has spread beyond East Asia into South Asia, Europe and the Americas. This account of Tibetan Buddhism beyond Tibet must therefore be completed in the following chapter on Buddhism in the West.

CHAPTER XIII

Buddhism in the West

Buddhism's encounter with the Western world has been both a blessing and a curse for the religion. As the careful reader will have noted, this ambiguity has characterized Buddhism's encounter with virtually every foreign culture beyond India. In its contacts with the West, Buddhism has suffered persecution and distortion — both malicious and benign — as it has suffered at the hands of alien cultures in the East. At the same time, contacts with the West have resulted in the religion's diversification and revitalization, as have contacts through history with various Eastern societies beyond its homeland. In general, the primary difference between Buddhism's development in the West and its development in the East has been that the West came to Buddhism rather than vice versa.

The West came to Buddhism first in the form of Muslim invasions of Central Asia and India toward the end of the first millennium. These invasions were uniformly and relentlessly disastrous for Buddhism and its followers, whom Muslims regarded as not only godless, but paradoxically idolatrous as well — denying God while worshipping countless gods. Next, beginning in the sixteenth century, the West came to Buddhism in the form of European colonialism, invariably accompanied by Christian missionary activity. Initially these contacts too were deleterious for Buddhism, but in the long run they proved to be the gateway through which Buddhism began to spread to the Western world. In the third instance, the West came to Buddhism in the form of communism. In China, Tibet, and Mongolia, the advent of communism was as disastrous for Buddhism as the advent of Islam in India and Central Asia. In other instances, notably Southeast Asia, communism appears to have been a mixed blessing. The advent of communism in Southeast Asia has diminished the wealth and influence of Buddhism in the region, sometimes forcing the Saṅgha to serve as propagandists for the regime. At the same time, communists in Southeast Asia have initiated reforms that have imposed upon an initially reluctant Saṅgha some of Buddhism's own ideals in addition to the ideals of communism. Buddhism's denial of God, precisely the characteristic that made the religion intolerable to Islam, seems to have made it the most tolerable of religions in the eyes of communists.

The preceding chapters have already touched upon the influences of Islam, colonialism and communism on the development of Buddhism in the East. This chapter will consider the influence of Buddhism upon the

Western world, an unexpected reversal of colonialist, communist and missionary efforts to dominate Asia. Of all the Asian religions encountered in the course of Western expansion, Buddhism has proved to be the most viable in the West. Interestingly, precisely those Western cultures that most successfully perpetrated colonialism and Christian proselytization in Asia are now those in which the influence of Buddhism is strongest. These are the cultures of Western Europe and North America, most notably the United States, Britain and France. All of the nations of Western Europe, however, now harbor Buddhist immigrants and converts, as do Canada, South America, Australia, New Zealand, South Africa and some East European countries. Although an accurate assessment of numbers is difficult, and estimates vary widely, there are probably some five million Buddhists in the West, about three million in North America, about a million in Western Europe (including Britain), and another million scattered through the other countries mentioned above.[58]

Early Contacts

Buddhism's influence in the West began well before any Western person had heard of Buddhism. From very early times, the ancient trade route known as the Silk Road, which ran between the Mediterranean world and imperial China, carried more than mercantile commodities. It carried lore as well, traded in idle hours by traveling merchants in the multilingual caravanserais across Asia with an alacrity almost equalling that of their financial transactions. In the fifth century BCE, Herodotus incorporated in his historical writings legendary material that is recorded also in the *Jātaka Tales* of Buddhism.[59]

The Indian campaigns of Alexander the Great in the fourth century BCE almost certainly resulted in increased knowledge of Buddhism in the Western world, though no specific evidence survives. The place-name Alasanda, found in several Pāli texts, may refer to the Greek city of Alexandria in northern Africa. One of these texts, the *Milinda Pañha* or *Questions of King Milinda*, records an extensive dialogue between a Buddhist monk and the Greek king Milinda (Menandros) of northwestern India in the second century BCE. This degree of contact in India could hardly have escaped the attention of Mediterranean Greeks entirely. Already in the first century, the Greek biographer Plutarch apparently confuses the life of Menandros with the life of the Buddha, establishing at least an indirect acquaintance with Buddhism.[60] The first explicit Western reference to Buddhism occurs in the writings of Clement of Alexandria in about 200 CE. Another explicit reference is not found, however, until

Hieronymus in the fourth century.[61] Soon thereafter, in the fifth century, the Dark Ages engulfed Europe, yet even during this extended cultural doldrum there is evidence of Buddhist influence in the West. Most of the tales traded along the Silk Road were pure fantasy, but some bore a kernel of historical truth. Among these was the story of Barlaam and Josaphat, confirmed in Greek manuscript as dating back to at least the tenth century, and in Persian to the sixth century. The Greek version describes Barlaam and Josaphat as early Christian missionaries in the East. On the basis of this account, Josaphat has been a Catholic saint since 1583. It is now clear, however, that the name "Josaphat" is a corruption of the Sanskrit term bodhisattva, and that his biography is based on the life of the Buddha. In effect, the Buddha has been recognized as a Catholic saint since the sixteenth century, and his feast day is still celebrated on November 27.

Starting in the thirteenth century, explicit although unreliable accounts of Buddhism began to appear as a result of Pope Innocent IV's envoys to the Mongol court in China. Marco Polo's popular thirteenth-century travelogue also mentions Buddhism. Beginning in the sixteenth century, Jesuit missionary activity began to produce the first creditable Western descriptions of Buddhism. The most important of these were the accounts of St. Francis Xavier's travels in India and Japan, and Fr. Matteo Ricci's work in China. In the eighteenth century, Fr. Ippolito Desideri's account of his journey to Tibet contained the first reliable, if incomplete, Western description of Buddhism.

Leibnitz, the seventeenth-century German philosopher and mathematician, was influenced by neo-Confucianism, which in turn was strongly influenced by Buddhism. By the nineteenth century, fragmentary accounts of Buddhism were sufficiently numerous in the West to allow the influential German philosopher Schopenhauer to declare Buddhism the best of all religions, on the basis that it dispensed with dubious doctrines of God and extended its morality to animals.

Of the few accounts available in Schopenhauer's time, the most reliable was the French Eugène Burnouf's history of Indian Buddhism. First published in 1845, it secures Burnouf's place as the founder of modern Buddhist scholarship in the West. The linguist Burnouf had already written a Pāli grammar in 1826. In 1852 he produced a translation of the *Lotus Sūtra,* the first European translation of a Buddhist scripture. Soon thereafter, Thomas William Rhys Davids of Britain and Hermann Oldenberg of Germany consolidated this new tradition of scholarship with publications that are useful to the present day. In 1877, Rhys Davids, who had lived for eight years in Sri Lanka as a British administrator, published *Buddhism,* a reliable manual that is still useful. In 1879, F. Max Müller, a British-based

German, began to publish as general editor the fifty-one volume translation series Sacred Books of the East, which included several Buddhist texts. In 1881 Rhys Davids founded the Pāli Text Society, still the publisher of the most authoritative texts and translations of the Theravāda scriptures. In the same year Oldenberg published his classic study *Buddha,* and was in the midst of publishing a critical edition of the Pāli *Vinaya Piṭaka,* the volumes of which appeared between 1879 and 1883. In the United States, Henry Clark Warren founded the Harvard Oriental Series in 1891, and in 1896 published as volume three of the series his excellent and still popular *Buddhism in Translations,* an anthology from the Pāli canon.

On a yet more popular level, Edwin Arnold published in 1879 his eulogy of the Buddha: *The Light of Asia,* arguably the most popular of the Victorian epic poems. In 1875, Henry Steel Olcott and Madame Blavatsky founded in New York the Theosophical Society, an organization dedicated to popularizing Eastern spirituality in the West. Olcott published his *Buddhist Catechism* in 1881, and the German Friedrich Zimmerman published a similar catechism in 1888. Soon thereafter, the World's Parliament of Religions, held in conjunction with the 1893 Chicago World's Fair, became the watershed marking the beginning of widespread Western interest in Eastern religions.

Starting with the Swede Sven Hedin in 1895, a series of explorer treasure seekers began to fill the museums of Europe and north America with priceless Buddhist manuscripts and artifacts collected in crate loads from the then uncharted wilds of Central Asia. These novelesque adventurers included Marc Aurel Stein of Britain, Paul Pelliot of France, Albert von Le Coq of Germany and Langdon Warner of the United States. Their exploits remain sources of inspiration or outrage, depending upon whether one takes the view of the countries with the museums or of those with the plundered archaeological sites.

The first half of the twentieth century witnessed the consolidation of Buddhist studies in Western universities. Until the second World War and the greater global awareness which came in its wake, however, academic programs in Buddhist studies remained small and confined largely to a handful of prestigious European universities. Within these programs labored most of the pioneers of modern scholarship on Buddhism. Scholars and academic programs have been of vital importance in the development of Buddhism in the West. With the possible exception of Japan, the West now leads the world in Buddhist scholarship, to the great enrichment of Buddhism as well as Western intellectual life.

Nonetheless, the present survey must confine itself primarily to the development of Buddhism as an ideology among rank and file Westerners.

For this purpose, Buddhism as believed and practiced in the West may be divided conveniently into the four categories treated below. In roughly the chronological order of their introduction, these are: Chinese, Japanese, Theravāda, and Tibetan Buddhism.

Chinese Buddhism in the West

Like the gradual accumulation in the West of reliable information about Buddhism, the beginnings of Buddhist practice in the West also passed unnoticed by most Westerners. Though unrelated to the aforementioned scholarly and quasi-scholarly efforts, the advent of Buddhist practice on a significant scale began at more or less the same time, in the 1840s and 1850s, when thousands of Chinese immigrated to the United States as participants in the California Gold Rush. Most of these immigrants were uneducated, working class Cantonese whose arrival made very little impression upon Western civilization as a whole. Few if any made their fortunes in the gold fields, but these immigrants proved to be industrious and temperamentally suited to life in the capitalist West. Soon a Chinatown developed in San Francisco, the first of the many Chinatowns that have become features of many Western cities. The first Chinese temples appeared without fanfare in San Francisco's Chinatown in the early 1850s. These temples, like the many that followed in other American cities, reflected the religious needs of the Chinese immigrant population. Therefore, they were not specifically Buddhist temples, but rather reflected the popular synthesis of Buddhism, Daoism and folk religion prevalent among the working-class Chinese of the time. Virtually all of these temples, however, incorporated an altar dedicated to Guan Yin (Kuan Yin), the Chinese equivalent of Avalokiteśvara, bodhisattva of compassion.

In China at the time, this syncretistic form of religion was being suppressed by the Manchurian Qing (Ch'ing) dynasty (1644-1911), which favored Tibetan-style Buddhism. As a result, the Buddhist-Daoist-folk religion in China operated mostly through secret societies. In Qing China, these secret societies were suppressed as potential sources of rebellion. In the United States, they could operate openly. For the most part they did so, although elements of these societies gained notoriety as the feared "tongs" of Chinese organized crime in the United States. Most temples were openly sponsored by one society or another, and as a result were not only places of worship, but also centers for social life and the education of children. Thus the first Chinese immigrants to North America, like the European immigrants before them, took advantage of a freedom of religion not available in their native country.

Nonetheless, until very recent times, anti-Chinese discrimination among Americans of European descent has been rife, confining most Chinese immigrants to ghettos in major American cities. These China-towns proliferated after the Civil War, when Chinese were dispersed across America in the course of helping to build the first trans-continental railroad. After the second World War — particularly after the advent of the civil rights movement and a more egalitarian society in the United States — Chinese Americans began to enter the mainstream of society, and classical forms of Chinese Buddhism began to attract Western converts. The most influential Chinese Buddhist group among non-Chinese in the West is the eclectic Sino-American Buddhist Association, founded in San Francisco in 1968 by the monk Xuan Hua (Hsüan Hua) from Hong Kong. The most widely practiced classical form of Chinese Buddhism in the West is Tian Tai, though Chan, the Chinese version of Zen, also has a significant following. On the whole, however, Chinese Buddhism in the West is practiced primarily by ethnic Chinese living in North America and reflects the popular Chinese synthesis of Buddhism, Daoism, and Confucianism. The presence of Chinese-style Buddhism in the West was strengthened considerably after the Vietnam war ended in 1975. Since then, well over half-a-million Vietnamese refugees have settled in the West, primarily in North America, but also notably in France and Australia. Many of these are Catholics, but most practice Chinese-style Buddhism.

Japanese Buddhism in the West

Japanese Buddhism, Zen in particular, has been far more successful than Chinese Buddhism in appealing to the spiritual aspirations of Westerners. Like Chinese Buddhist practice, Japanese Buddhist practice entered the Western world in the form of immigration to the United States. This immigration began in the latter half of the nineteenth century, first to Hawaii, at that time a territory of the United States. In 1869 the first Japanese immigrants to North America settled near Sacramento as part of a failed scheme to cultivate silkworms. By 1900 there were over 24,000 Japanese immigrants in the United States, mostly in California. Unlike the first Chinese immigrants, these Japanese were mostly skilled workers and students.

During these early years, the Methodist church in particular attempted to gain converts by ministering to the needs of this growing population of newcomers. Most notably, the Methodists provided English classes, which were attended by practically all Japanese immigrants of the time.

Methodism's success among the early Japanese immigrants alarmed committed Japanese Buddhists in California. These Buddhists petitioned Jōdo Shinshū (True Pure Land) authorities in Japan to send a counter-vailing mission to the Buddhists of San Francisco.

This petition led to the formation in 1898 of a YMBA or Young Men's Buddhist Association in San Francisco. In subsequent years, YMBAs were formed in Seattle, San Jose and Oakland. In 1904, these associations were re-named "Buddhist Churches." This designation became official in the midst of World War II, when Japanese citizens of America were stripped of their rights and imprisoned in concentration camps across the country. In 1944, Buddhist Church authorities confined at the Topaz Relocation Center in Utah petitioned the state of California for incorporation of "The Buddhist Churches of America." In 1945, after the conclusion of the war and the release of the thousands of interned Japanese Americans, "Buddhist Churches of America" became the official designation of an organization that is to the present day the primary sponsor of Japanese-style Buddhism in the Western world. The membership of the Buddhist Churches of America remains almost exclusively ethnic Japanese, though most of these are thoroughly integrated, third and fourth generation Americans. With about 200,000 members, the Buddhist Churches of America is probably the second largest denomination of Buddhism in the West, next to Nichiren Shōshū, which will be discussed shortly.

Though now autonomous, the Buddhist Churches of America remains affiliated with the Jōdo Shinshū sect in Japan and espouses True Pure Land belief and practice, a form of Buddhism that has not proved appealing to non-Japanese Westerners. The forms of Japanese Buddhism that have appealed to Westerners of European descent are Zen and Nichiren. This appeal reveals little about the spiritual preferences of ethnic Europeans, for these two forms of Buddhism are diametrically opposed. Zen represents the ultimate in self-reliance and individualism, while Nichiren represents an extreme of regimentation and reliance upon supernatural means to salvation. Zen has by far the longer history and the more profound influence in Western civilization. For this reason it is best to deal with Nichiren first and briefly.

Nichiren Buddhism entered the Western world in 1960, once again through California, as an outreach program of the Sōka Gakkai directed primarily toward Japanese Americans. Sōka Gakkai is a twentieth-century Japanese political movement affiliated with the Nichiren Shōshū, the most hierarchical and authoritarian subsect of Nichiren Buddhism. The Nichiren Shōshū mission was remarkably successful among Japanese Americans, and by 1965 it was attracting a thousand new members per month. In 1967, the Nichiren Shōshū Academy was formed in order to attempt to attract non-Japanese Americans to the sect. This membership drive was extremely successful, and the Nichiren Shōshū now has chapters throughout North America, as well as in Central and South America. (Brazil in particular has a large Japanese population of about 500,000, most of whom are Buddhists and many of whom follow Nichiren.) Nichiren Shōshū became the first form of Buddhism in the West to attract significant numbers of Blacks and Hispanics in addition to Caucasians. In all, the current membership of Nichiren Shōshū in the Americas is probably in the neighborhood of a quarter-million. The large majority of this membership is non-Japanese. Starting in the 1970s, the sect's leaders ordered a slackening of missionary efforts, so that one is less likely now to encounter Nichiren evangelists at airports or shopping centers. Nonetheless, Nichiren Shōshū is probably the largest single denomination of Buddhism in the Western world, a situation that is all the more remarkable given its recent transplantation.

In terms of pervasive influence on Western culture, however, no form of Buddhism surpasses Zen. Like many forms of Eastern spirituality, Zen's influence in the West began at the 1893 World's Parliament of Religions in Chicago. Representing Zen at this meeting was a Japanese Roshi (meditation master) of the Rinzai school named Sōen Shaku (1858-1919). At the time, the Hindu Swami Vivekananda was the sensation of the Parliament, but in the end the Zen master's influence upon the West was more profound. At the Parliament, Sōen Shaku impressed a San Francisco couple, Mr. and Mrs. Alexander Russell, who in 1905 traveled to Japan to seek instruction in Zen from the Roshi. Sōen Shaku returned to the United States with the Russells and stayed for nine months as their guest. During this time he traveled widely, gaining firsthand experience of the North American scene.

Convinced that America was ready for Zen, Sōen Shaku dispatched two of his students, Nyogen Senzaki and Sokatsu Shaku, who arrived in California in 1905 and 1906 respectively. Sokatsu Shaku stayed only briefly in the United States, between 1906 and 1910, and taught primarily Japanese students. Consequently his influence in the West was less pronounced than that of Nyogen Senzaki. Nonetheless, he is credited with founding in San Francisco the first Zen meditation center in the West. Through the work of his disciple Shigetsu Sasaki (better known as Sokei-an) this center survives with a modest following, transplanted to New York, as the First Zen Institute.

Nyogen Senzaki established a meditation center in San Francisco in 1927, and another in Los Angeles in 1931. The Los Angeles center, known as Mentorgarten Meditation Hall, became his headquarters and remained so until his death in 1958 at the age of eighty-two. Of Nyogen Senzaki's many disciples, the best known is Robert Aitken Roshi, founder of the Diamond Saṅgha in Honolulu and still active as a Zen teacher in North America, Europe, and occasionally Australia.

Of the disciples of Sōen Shaku, the most influential in the West was without doubt Daisetz Teitaro Suzuki (1870-1966). D.T. Suzuki was sent by Sōen Shaku to LaSalle, Illinois, in 1897 to serve as an editor for the Open Court Publishing Company. Paul Carus, the owner of Open Court and himself a well-known writer on Buddhism — e.g. *The Gospel of Buddhism,* 1894 — was another American impressed by Sōen Shaku at the 1893 World's Parliament of Religions. When an opportunity arose to appoint a new editor at Open Court, Carus employed Suzuki upon the recommendation of Sōen Shaku. For eleven years, until 1909 when Suzuki returned to Japan, he not only worked for Open Court, but also resided in the Carus home. Most of Suzuki's prolific output in English on Zen occurred while he and his American wife Beatrice Lane Suzuki were co-editors of the *Eastern Buddhist,* an English language publication based at Ōtani University in Kyōto, where D.T. Suzuki was Professor of English. D.T. Suzuki again resided in the United States from 1936 until the second World War, and again from 1950 to 1958. During this last period of residence, he gave a series of influential lectures at several American universities, including Columbia and Harvard. Most Westerners know what they know of Zen either directly or indirectly as a result of D.T. Suzuki's writings.

Of the Western writers on Zen who were directly influenced by D.T. Suzuki, the best known are the British Christmas Humphreys and the British-American Alan Watts. Though both authors are generally reliable, their exuberant individual personalities occasionally adorn their writings with interpretations of Zen that are dubious from a traditional point of view. In North America, Alan Watts became a leading figure in the "beat generation" of the 1950s and then in the "counter-culture" of the 1960s and 1970s. Humphreys, by contrast, was a controversial but conservative British barrister and court judge often featured in the press for the eccentricity of his legal opinions. Quasi-scholarly popularizations such as those of Humphreys and Watts led in turn to the incorporation of Zen into extremely popular, modern literature, most notably Jack Kerouac's *The Dharma Bums,* 1958.

As Zen in the West attained a faddish, often distorting notoriety on the one hand, on the other hand it continued to develop its deeper roots. This development was given impetus by the return of American troops, often with Japanese brides, following the American occupation of Japan after World War II. Paradoxically, the United States' involvement in the Korean War of the 1950s and the Vietnam War of the 1960s and 1970s also increased awareness of and interest in Buddhism, particularly Zen.

Zen Buddhism is prominent in Japan, Korea and Vietnam, but more to the point, it is traditionally the Buddhism of the warrior. Many Western soldiers returned from duty in these countries with a deep respect for the courage and skill of their erstwhile adversaries, and often with training in oriental martial arts. Such training almost inevitably involves some exposure to Zen, and many Westerners now gain their first experience of meditation and Eastern culture in martial arts classes.

For those who wish to pursue Zen practice as such, most major Western cities, and many smaller communities, now offer some form of Zen group. Many of these are affiliated with institutions founded by Westerners who have been trained and acknowledged as Roshis by Japanese masters. These include among others Phillip Kapleau of the Rochester Zen Center, Richard Baker of the San Francisco Zen Center and Jiyu Kennett, British-born abbess of the Mount Shasta Abbey in northern California. Even small public libraries now usually have some reliable material on Zen Buddhism, and many colleges and universities offer academic instruction and extra-curricular practice in Zen and other forms of Buddhism. For some, an introduction to Buddhism, usually Zen, comes through the Christian church in the form of study groups or meditation classes. Catholicism in particular seems drawn to Buddhism, presumably because of a shared emphasis upon monasticism, meditation and *mantras* (repeated sacred utterances such as "Hail Mary"). Fr. Thomas Merton, a personal friend of D.T. Suzuki and a champion of Buddhism, was particularly influential in forging spiritual ties between Zen and Catholicism. Catholic-sponsored Zen retreats are now common. Others encounter Zen, sometimes without realizing it, in the course of psychological counseling and hospice care. Even more pervasive than these overt examples of Zen influence in the West is a general infiltration of the Western aesthetic by Japanese art, architecture, interior decorating and landscaping, all of which are recognized in Japan as aspects of Zen training.

Theravāda Buddhism in the West

Whereas Zen is by far the most influential form of Buddhism among North Americans of European descent, in Europe itself, particularly Britain, Theravāda Buddhism also has a strong following. This situation is partly due to the early arrival of European powers as colonists in Sri Lanka. First the Portuguese and then the Dutch dominated Sri Lanka in the sixteenth through the eighteenth centuries. As a result of these occupations, however, only very limited knowledge of Theravāda Buddhism filtered through to Europe, mostly in the form of distorted polemic. The situation improved slightly under British colonial administration during the early years of the nineteenth century, which saw the first reliable translations of Pāli texts.

The real beginnings of Theravāda Buddhism's influence in the West may be traced to 1873 and the Great Debate of Pānadura, a town south of Sri Lanka's capital, Colombo. British missionaries had been successfully challenging Sri Lankan monks to public debates since the 1840s as part of their program of converting the populace to Christianity. At Pānadura, however, the monk Migeṭṭuvate Guṇānanda turned the tables on his Christian adversaries both in Sri Lanka and in the West. First, newspaper reports of the event reached the West, and in 1873 itself, the entire text of the debate was published in Battle Creek, Michigan. This caught the attention of H.S. Olcott, who initiated a regular correspondence with Guṇānanda, providing the monk with advice and intellectual ammunition against his missionary adversaries. Olcott and Madame Blavatsky founded the Theosophical Society in 1875. The Theosophical Society is dedicated to the propagation of Eastern wisdom combined with Madame Blavatsky's own peculiar mysticism, but in the early years of the organization its founders were particularly enamored of Buddhism and Sri Lanka. While the efforts of Olcott and Blavatsky contributed greatly to a Buddhist revival in Sri Lanka, the Theosophical Society was not to be Theravāda Buddhism's primary conduit to the West.

In 1881, Olcott did publish in Sri Lanka his *Buddhist Catechism,* re-issued in Boston in 1885. This attempt to popularize Theravāda Buddhism in the West, however, was preceded by far superior scholarly treatments by T.W. Rhys Davids in Britain *(Buddhism,* 1877) and Hermann Oldenberg in Germany *(Buddha,* 1881). Oldenberg's book remains a classic study, based on traditional sources, of the life of the Buddha and the early history of Buddhism. Also in 1881, Rhys Davids founded the Pāli Text Society, the primary publisher of Theravāda scriptures and translations in the West. He was succeeded as President of the PTS by his energetic wife C.A.F. Rhys Davids and then by I.B. Horner, the Western world's first great female scholar of Buddhism. T.W. Rhys Davids was also founding president in 1907 of the Buddhist Society of Great Britain and Ireland, which functioned until 1926. These pioneering scholarly efforts in Europe outshone and outlasted the somewhat eccentric efforts of the Theosophists.

Nonetheless, indigenous Theravādin attempts to proselytize in the West began with a visit to Sri Lanka by Colonel Olcott and Madame Blavatsky in 1880. Heroes of Sri Lanka's Buddhist revival, they arrived to a rapturous welcome from the island's Buddhists. Among the welcoming crowds was one David Hewavitarne. Better known by his adopted

Buddhist name, Anagārika Dharmapāla (1864-1933), he founded the Mahābodhi Society in Sri Lanka in 1891. In 1892 he established an Indian branch of the society in Calcutta. Originally dedicated to the restoration of the site of the Buddha's enlightenment at Bodh Gaya, the Mahābodhi Society became one of the most important early publishers of popular Theravāda religious materials in English. In 1893, Dharmapāla represented Sri Lanka at the World's Parliament of Religions in Chicago. His speeches to the Parliament attracted considerable attention, including that of Paul Carus. In 1896, at the invitation of Carus, Dharmapāla returned to the United States, and in 1897 he opened an American branch of the Mahābodhi Society. He toured the United States a third time in 1902-1904, and in 1926 he established in London a British branch of the Mahābodhi Society.

These early ties between Sri Lankan Buddhism and the United States notwithstanding, the first Westerners to become Theravāda monks were Europeans ordained in Burma. The British Allan Bennett McGregor was ordained in 1902 as Ānanda Metteyya, and the German violinist Anton Gueth was ordained in 1904 as Nyanatiloka. Ānanda Metteyya founded the Buddhasāsana Samāgama, an international Buddhist society headquartered in Rangoon. Nyanatiloka founded a monastery in Sri Lanka on Polgasduwa Island where many Europeans were ordained. Nyanatiloka and his foremost disciple Nyanaponika, also of German descent, are best known for their English language scholarship and translation of Theravāda texts.

Also in Burma, in the 1890s, the Burmese monk U Nārada initiated a Burmese revival of meditation on the basis of ancient texts, thus becoming the founder of the "Burmese school" of meditation. This Burmese style of meditation emphasizes concentration upon the rise and fall of the diaphragm rather than on the spot where the breath touches the nose, which is the preëminent meditation object in the Pāli scriptures and in the Sri Lankan school of meditation. U Nārada's most famous disciple, Mahasi Sayadaw, became extremely prominent in the 1950s and founded in Rangoon a large meditation center. In the 1950s and 1960s, before the Burmese government's imposition of severe visa restrictions, several Westerners — as well as Burmese and non-Burmese Asians — trained at this center and were recognized as qualified teachers. Through their efforts, as well as through translations of Mahasi Sayadaw's works, Burmese-style meditation is now accessible if not prominent in the West.

A second school of Burmese meditation has become probably, though not demonstrably, the most widely practiced Theravāda meditation system in the West. This form of practice, which deviates considerably from ancient scriptural norms, appears to have originated with the Burmese master Saya Thet Gyi in the early 1900s. The practice, which involves attempting to perceive the body as an effervescent froth of sensations, was popularized in Burma by Sayagyi U Ba Khin and spread beyond Burma in both the East and the West by S.N. Goenka. Neither U Ba Khin nor Goenka ever took monastic vows. U Ba Khin, in fact, was Accountant General of Burma, and at one time headed four government departments while still teaching at his International Meditation Center in Rangoon. S.N. Goenka was a successful businessman and a Hindu before becoming a follower of U Ba Khin. In 1969, Goenka began teaching meditation courses in India, thus circumventing the Burmese government's visa restrictions on foreigners. Since then he has attracted thousands of followers, several of whom now teach his non-traditional though highly respected system of meditation in North America, Europe, Japan and Australia.

Just as the revival of Theravāda meditation practice went hand-in-hand with its introduction and spread in the West, so did a modern revival of the rational, analytical philosophy that is the basis of the Buddhist Eightfold Path. After the pioneering efforts of Anagārika Dharmapāla, the Sri Lankan academic K.N. Jayatilleke (1920-70) is the preëminent figure in this philosophical revival. Some would prefer to call this "revival" a "reformation," in that its proponents not only eschew non-scriptural, superstitious accretions, they also de-emphasize radically the miraculous and non-rational elements of the Pāli canon itself, portraying Theravāda Buddhism as a pre-European form of scientific rationalism. Be that as it may, Theravāda modernists such as Jayatilleke have been very adept at substantiating in the ancient scriptures a philosophical and moral doctrine that is remarkably comfortable in the contemporary Western forum of philosophical discourse.

Tibetan Buddhism in the West

Western fascination with Tibet dates back at least to the time of Marco Polo, who reported upon the isolated mountain kingdom in his famous thirteenth-century travelogue. An entire popular mythology developed around the Utopian land of Shangrila, presumed to be located in Tibet. A few bona fide European travelers, mostly missionaries, visited Tibet in the eighteenth century, and by the nineteenth century, reliable scholarly accounts had begun to emerge, most notably those of the Jesuit missionary Ippolito Desideri (1684-1733) and the Hungarian scholar-adventurer Csoma de Koros (1784-1842). By 1904 the British had sent a military expedition under Francis Younghusband and concluded the Treaty of

Lhasa. Throughout the first half of the twentieth century, reliable scholarly accounts of Tibetan history and literature continued to emerge, most notably those of W.Y. Evans-Wentz and Giuseppe Tucci.

The first Tibetan Buddhist temples in the West were established by a community of displaced Mongols who were settled in Freehold Acres, New Jersey, following World War II. For most Westerners, however, Tibet remained a mysterious land of fantasy until the communist Chinese invasion in 1950 attracted limited press coverage. One of the first to recognize the threat communism posed to Buddhism in Tibet was the Gelugpa lama Geshe Wangyal — actually a Mongolian lama living in Tibet — who left in 1951. In 1955, he joined the Mongolian community in Freehold Acres, where he established the first Tibetan Buddhist monastery and teaching center in the West. Among his first Western students were Robert Thurman and Jeffrey Hopkins, who have since established influential programs in Tibetan studies at Columbia University and the University of Virginia.

Following the outright Chinese takeover of Tibet in 1959, about a hundred thousand Tibetans, following the lead of the fourteenth Dalai Lama, fled the country and established refugee communities, first in neighboring India and then throughout the Western world. Now Tibetan lamas teach in several Western Universities; Tibetan Buddhist centers are found in many Western cities, and Tibet has become a standard item in the news and on the political agenda of the Western world. In a single generation, Tibet has emerged from the daydreams of Westerners into the stark light of their day-to-day realities. Tibetan Buddhism has been transformed from a remote fantasy into a readily accessible alternative. Numerous figures are responsible for this remarkable flowering of Tibetan Buddhism in the West. For the sake of brevity and in order to present a representative coverage of the most prevalent schools of Tibetan Buddhism in the West, the following account focuses upon three figures. These are: Chogyam Trungpa of the Kagyudpa, Tarthang Tulku [sPrul-sKu] of the Nyingmapa, and the fourteenth Dalai Lama himself, head of the Gelugpa.

Chogyam Trungpa, the eleventh Trungpa incarnation (*sPrul-sKu*), is well known in the West through his several publications, the most popular being his autobiography *Born in Tibet* and the instruction manual *Meditation in Action*. Like most Tibetans in the West, Chogyam Trungpa fled Tibet for India in 1959 — at the age of twenty — in the wake of the Chinese takeover. In 1963, he became one of the first Tibetans to migrate to the West, to England, where he attended Oxford University. In 1967 he established in Scotland the Samye Ling meditation center, the first full-scale Tibetan center in the West.

Chogyam Trungpa migrated to the United States in 1970, and in the same year founded his Tail of the Tiger Meditation Center in Vermont. In 1971, he founded his third and best known community, the Karma Dzong Meditation Center in Boulder Colorado, home of the University of Colorado. Also in Boulder, in 1974, he founded the Naropa Institute, which in 1986 became the first Buddhist college in the West to grant state-accredited degrees. In addition to his fame as a teacher, Chogyam Trungpa has also become somewhat infamous for his fondness for beer and his occasionally earthy language and behavior. It must be remembered, however, that unconventional behavior is revered in the great masters of the Kagyudpa school: Tilopa, Nāropa, Marpa and Milarepa.

A more conventional representative in the West of the Kagyudpa school has been its head, the sixteenth Karmapa, who passed away in 1981. In 1950 he fled Tibet with some 150 followers and took up residence in the ruined Rumtek Monastery near Gantok, Sikkim. From this headquarters, Karmapa pursued an extensive program of teaching, publication of Tibetan scriptures, and foundation of branch monasteries, all of which involved travel throughout the world. Before his death, he made two tours of the West, visiting and teaching in North America and Europe. His efforts, in conjunction with those of Chogyam Trungpa, have attracted to the Kagyudpa a significant following in the West. This success in the West represents something of a revival of the Kagyudpa vis-à-vis the Gelugpa, which in pre-1959 Tibet had eclipsed without dominating the other schools of Tibetan Buddhism.

Also relatively more prominent in the West than in Tibet is the Nyingmapa school. The best known proponent of Nyingmapa Buddhism in the West — and in the world for that matter — is Tarthang Tulku. In 1959 he fled to Sikkim, but in 1962 the Dalai Lama sent him to Varanasi, India, where he taught Buddhist philosophy at Sanskrit University. There he embarked upon a program of publishing numerous lesser-known Tibetan scriptures in their original language. After moving to the United States in 1968, he began to supplement this publication program with several of his own works in English. In 1969, he founded in Berkeley, California, the Tibetan Nyingma Meditation Center, now housed in a converted fraternity house. As opposed to Chogyam Trungpa, Tarthang Tulku maintains a strictly traditional, guru-disciple mode of spiritual instruction, requiring of students the arduous initiation procedures once required in Tibet. In 1973, he supplemented his Meditation Center with the Nyingma Institute, also in Berkeley. This institute concentrates on intellectual as opposed to meditational aspects of Tantric Buddhism, grants degrees, and does not require formal initiation of students. Both the Meditation Center and the Institute have since been expanded with branches elsewhere in

California and interstate. By 1981, Tarthang Tulku and his followers had produced and published in the United States the most complete edition to date of the Tibetan Buddhist canon, the Kanjur and Tanjur.

In modern times, particularly since the advent of a common oppressor in the form of communist China, the various schools of Tibetan Buddhism are no longer in competition. Nevertheless, the Gelugpa is by far the dominant school in the West, as it was in Tibet before 1959. Of the many eminent Gelugpa teachers in the West, indeed of all Tibetan teachers in the West, none is so prominent as the fourteenth Dalai Lama, spiritual head of the Tibetan people and recipient in 1989 of the Nobel Peace Prize. From the headquarters of his government in exile in Dharamsala, a village in the Himalayan foothills of northern India, His Holiness has waged a persistent though·unobtrusive campaign to create international awareness of the plight of the Tibetan people.

In the course of this campaign and the frequent world travel it entails, the Dalai Lama has consistently found time to nurture the development of Buddhism in the West without ever a hint of proselytization. In addition to his numerous meetings with heads of state, government officials and religious leaders throughout the world, he has also given countless public lectures and written several important books on Buddhist doctrine. When his itineraries permit, he routinely visits Buddhist centers the world over — and not only Tibetan centers — conveying upon even humble communities a level of recognition that emperors in the past have coveted in vain. He has broken with tradition by performing some of the rarest and most important Tantric initiations for followers in the West. Any one of these ceremonies in Tibet would have constituted the major event of any given decade, and would have attracted thousands of participants, many of whom would have parted gladly with their life's savings and traveled hundreds of miles on foot in order to attend.

In less than a generation, Buddhism's most exalted personage has been transformed from a seldom-glimpsed God-king into a familiar — though always inspirational — news item. This personal transformation symbolizes an equally profound transformation in Buddhism as a whole. The opening of the twentieth century found Buddhism scattered among traditional communities practicing uncritically an age-old and in many cases enervated faith with little remaining consciousness of its global mission. At the dawn of the twenty-first century, Buddhism stands confidently in its place as one of the universally acknowledged moral, intellectual and spiritual systems guiding all humanity into the third millennium of the common era.

Abbreviations

A	Aṅguttara Nikāya, PTS edition, followed by volume and page numbers
BCE	Before Common Era, i.e. B.C.
c.	"circa," approximately
CE	Common Era, i.e. A.D.
Chi.	Chinese
D	Dīgha Nikāya, PTS edition, followed by volume and page numbers
d.	"died," followed by the date of a person's death
Jap.	Japanese
Kor.	Korean
M	Majjhima Nikāya, PTS edition, followed by volume and page numbers
P.	Pāli
PTS	Pāli Text Society, original Pāli texts series
r.	"reigned," followed by the years a monarch held office
S	Saṁyutta Nikāya, PTS edition, followed by volume and page numbers
Skt.	Sanskrit
Tib.	Tibetan
tsl.	translation
V	Vinaya Piṭaka, PTS edition, followed by volume and page numbers

Pronunciation Guide

Every effort has been made in this book to facilitate the reading and pronunciation of words and names in the several languages involved. In each case, the starting point has been: Randall K. Barry, *ALA-LC Romanization Tables: Transliteration Schemes for Non-Roman Scripts,* Library of Congress, Washington, D.C., 1991. This publication, containing transliteration systems approved by the Library of Congress and the American Library Association, is available from the Cataloguing Distribution Service, Library of Congress, Washington, D.C. 20541.

The ALA-LC transliteration systems were adequate for Sanskrit, Pāli, Japanese and Korean, except that for Sanskrit "sh" had been used instead of "ṣ", and "ri" has been used instead of "ṛ". This is common practice, makes pronunciation clearer, and avoids daunting transliterations such as Kṛṣṇa (Krishna). For Mongolian, Burmese, Khmer, Lao and Thai it was possible to avoid special transliteration schemes by sticking to Pāli, Sanskrit and Tibetan forms of names and terms, or by using standard English renditions, such as "Genghis Khan". The ALA-LC guide gives no advice for Vietnamese, and so no diacritical marks have been used. The standard Romanization system for Vietnamese is extremely cumbersome, involving up to three diacritical marks for some letters. In this book's short section on Vietnam, avoidance of diacritical marks creates no ambiguity and gives an adequate approximation of pronunciation.

The present book departs from the ALA-LC recommendation in the cases of Chinese and Tibetan. For Chinese, the ALA-LC system specifies the antiquated Wade-Giles transliteration system. Until recently, most Western publications on China used this system. The Peoples' Republic of China, however, has devised its own standard Romanization system, known as Pinyin, which is bound to become the absolute standard in the near future. This system is more rational than the Wade-Giles system, and has been adopted almost universally by Western media. Soon, no doubt, scholarly publications will also adopt the Pinyin system. In the meantime, the present book attempts to cater to both worlds by providing in brackets the Wade-Giles rendition after the first occurrence of each Chinese word or name in Pinyin. When this is not done, it means that the Wade-Giles and the Pinyin are the same. The Wade-Giles transliteration is also given for items included in the Glossary, and the Index contains a complete set of Pinyin–Wade-Giles equivalents. To facilitate reference, the Wade-Giles transliterations of all Chinese words in the text are also entered alphabetically in the Index and followed by their Pinyin equivalents in parentheses. The Index thus provides a complete key for transposing from Wade-Giles to Pinyin and from Pinyin to Wade-Giles for the Chinese words and names in this book. To clarify which is which, only the Pinyin forms of Chinese names and terms in the Index are followed by page numbers.

Any Romanization of Chinese provides at best a rough approximation of the true pronunciation. Having noted this, in the Pinyin system, words are pronounced *approximately* as they are spelled, except that *c* is pronounced "ts"; *q* is pronounced "ch"; *x* is pronounced "sh"; and *z* is pronounced "ds"; *zh*, however, is pronounced "j". Because each Chinese character represents a separate syllable, this book renders them separately, without hyphenation, thus the Pinyin: Mao Ze Dong, rather than Mao Zedong, for the Wade-Giles Mao Tse-tung, Mao Tse-Tung, or Mao Tse Tung. For place-names that remain current in the present day, however, the standard practice of writing syllables together has been adopted (following *The New International Atlas*, Rand McNally, 1980), for example Beijing rather than Bei Jing. No attempt has been made to indicate the four "tones" of Chinese pronunciation.

Tibetan transliteration and pronunciation present something of a problem for the uninitiated. This book follows the ALA-LC guidelines except that herein "capitalization of base consonants" is followed in order to facilitate pronunciation. There are no capital or lower case letters in Tibetan, so that a direct rendition, for example *bka' rgyud pa,* gives little indication of pronunciation ("ka-gyud-pa"). With the base consonants capitalized, as in *bKa' rGyud pa,* pronunciation often becomes much clearer, since the base consonant is usually the first pronounced consonant in a given syllable. Many simple syllables, like *pa,* are unambiguous and require no such capitalization. In this case, *bKa' rGyud pa* is the name of a prominent sect of Tibetan Buddhism. As a result, the more or less standard English transliteration Kagyudpa has evolved. Where widely accepted transliterations have evolved, this book uses them and gives the correct Tibetan spelling in brackets following the first occurrence of the name or term, for example, Kagyudpa [bKa' rGuyd pa]. The correct Tibetan spelling is given again for items included in the Glossary, and the Index contains a complete key to correct Tibetan spelling for names and terms used in this book. To facilitate reference, the Index also contains a complete listing of these Tibetan names and terms entered according to their correct Tibetan spellings.

When there is no standard English rendition of a Tibetan name or term, and the capitalization of base consonants does not help with pronunciation, a rough indication of pronunciation is given in brackets after the first occurrence of the word and again in the Glossary and Index, for example 'Pyong rGyas [Chong Gye]. This means that sometimes brackets enclose the correct Tibetan spelling, and sometimes brackets enclose a rough guide to pronunciation. These cases should be easy to distinguish, as the correct Tibetan spelling usually has extra letters and usually looks impossible to pronounce. When this is not obvious, the pronunciation is enclosed in quotation marks, for example, Sras ["Sray"]. Hyphens have no counterpart in Tibetan script, and are used herein impressionistically, primarily to tie minor syllables — like *pa, po, ma,* and *mo,* which mean something like the English suffixes -ist or -er — into their larger contexts.

Sanskrit and Pāli transliterations may at first look daunting, but actually they are relatively easy to pronounce. The vowels are pronounced like Spanish or Italian vowels, the diphthongs *ai* (as in "tie") and *au* (as in "now") representing combinations of these pure vowel sounds. The vowel *e* is always pronounced as in "play", never as in "free". If vowels are marked long, as *ā, ī,* and *ū,* the vowel sounds are lengthened, and accents fall on those syllables. Otherwise, accent all syllables equally. The consonants are usually pronounced as an English speaker would expect, except that *c* is always soft, as in "cheer", never hard as in "cat". For all but the perfectionist, dots under t, d, and n — *ṭ, ḍ,* and *ṇ* — can be ignored. A dot over *n* or under *m* — *ṅ* or *ṃ* — indicates an *ng* sound as in "thing". The letter *h* seldom occurs alone in Sanskrit or Pāli, except at the beginning of a word. When *h* appears in transliteration, it is almost always in one of the following combinations: *kh, gh, ch, jh, ṭh, ḍh, th, dh, ph,* or *bh.* Each of these is pronounced by saying the initial consonant and puffing out an *h* sound. For example, the *dh* in "Buddha" is pronounced like the *dh* in "adhere". Similarly, *ph* is pronounced as in "top-hat", never as in "photo", and *th* is always pronounced as in "cathouse", never as in "the". This should not be difficult, but if it is, one is better off ignoring the *h.* Thus, for *Theravāda* the slight mispronunciation "tare-a-vāda" is infinitely better than the grotesque rendition "there-a-vāda". An "h" with a dot under it *(ḥ)* usually occurs only at the end of a word, and is in this and other instances best left unpronounced by the uninitiated. At the beginning of a word, *h* is pronounced as in "hat". There are three sibilant sounds in Sanskrit, *s, ś* and *sh* (which is sometimes transliterated as *ṣ*). The plain *s* is pronounced as in "see", and the other two are well enough rendered by the beginner like the *sh* in "she".

Suggestions for Further Reading

The following bibliography is organized according to the chapter divisions of this book. This entails repetition of entries which are relevant to more than one chapter, but will facilitate further study in particular areas of the history of Buddhism. The selection is intended to be a practical, introductory guide for further reading or research on the history of Buddhism. It is by no means an exhaustive bibliography. It contains only books and monographs — no journal articles — and confines itself where possible to accessible works with significant historical and/or sociological content. Most of the works listed are in English and in print, or at least widely available in libraries. In some areas, so little material is available that the above guidelines have had to be abandoned in order to offer any material at all.

General

Bechert, Heinz and Richard F. Gombrich, eds., *The World of Buddhism*, Thames and Hudson, London, 1984.

Ch'en, Kenneth K.S., *Buddhism: The Light of Asia*, Baron's, Woodbury, NY, 1968.

Conze, Edward, *A Short History of Buddhism*, Unwin, London, 1980.

de Bary, William Theodore, ed., *The Buddhist Tradition in India, China and Japan*, Modern Library, New York, 1969.

Eliot, Charles, *Hinduism and Buddhism: An Historical Sketch*, 3 vols., Routledge, London, 1921; Barnes and Noble, New York, 1921.

Harvey, Peter, An Introduction to Buddhism: Tea*chings, History and Practices,* Cambridge University, Cambridge, U.K., 1990.

Kitagawa, Joseph Mitsuo, and Mark D. Cummings, *Buddhism and Asian History,* Macmillan, New York, 1989.

Morgan, Kenneth William, *The Path of the Buddha: Buddhism Interpreted by Buddhists,* Ronald Press, New York, 1956.

Prebish, Charles S., *Buddhism: A Modern Perspective,* Pennsylvania State University, University Park, PA, 1975.

Reynolds, Frank E., et al., *Guide to Buddhist Religion,* G. K. Hall, Boston, 1981 (a useful, annotated bibliography organized by place and subject).

Robinson, Richard H. and Willard L. Johnson, *The Buddhist Religion: A Historical Introduction*, Dickenson (now Wadsworth), Belmont, CA, 1977.

Zürcher, Erik, *Buddhism, Its Origin and Spread in Words, Maps, and Pictures*, Brill, Leiden, 1959; St. Martin's, New York, 1962.

See listings below under "Chapter V: Buddhism in India" for somewhat less general works which apply to Chapters I-IV.

I. The Buddha in Legend and History

Foucher, Alfred Charles Auguste, *The Life of the Buddha According to the Ancient Texts and Monuments of India*, Greenwood, Westport, CT, 1972 (1st French ed., 1949; 1st English ed., 1963).

Ñāṇamoli, *The Life of the Buddha According to the Pali Canon*, Buddhist Publication Society, Kandy, Sri Lanka, 1972.

Nārada, *The Buddha and His Teachings*, Vajirārāma, Colombo, Sri Lanka, 1973 (Part I, pp. 1-269).

Oldenberg, Hermann, *Buddha: His Life, His Doctrine, His Order*, Indological Book House, Varanasi, 1971 (1st German ed., Stuttgart, 1881; 1st English ed., London, 1882).

Pye, Michael, *The Buddha*, Duckworth, London, 1979.

Rockhill, William Woodville, *The Life of the Buddha and the Early History of His Order Derived from Tibetan Works*, Orientalia Indica, Varanasi, 1972 (1st ed., Boston, 1884).

Saddhatissa, Hammalawa, *The Life of the Buddha*, Harper and Row, New York, 1976.

Schuman, Hans Wolfgang, T*he Historical Buddha*, Penguin, London, 1989 (1st German ed., Köln, 1982).

Thomas, Edward Josep, The *Life of the Buddha in Legend and History*, Routledge, London and New York, 1949 (1st ed., 1927).

II. Early Developments in the Saṅgha

Bareau, Andre, *Les premiers concils bouddhiques*, Presses Universitaires, Paris, 1955.

Bareau, Andre, *Les sectes bouddhiques du petit véhicule*, École Française d'Extrême-Orient, Saigon, 1955.

Dutt, Nalinaksha, *Buddhist Sects in India,* Motilal, Delhi, 1978 (1st ed., Calcutta, 1970).

Dutt, Nalinaksha, *Early History of the Spread of Buddhism and the Buddhist Schools,* Rajesh, Delhi, 1980 (1st ed., London, 1925).

Dutt, Nalinaksha, *Early Monastic Buddhism,* Mukhopadhyay, Calcutta, 1971; Oriental Book Agency, Calcutta, 1960 (1st ed., London, 1924).

Dutt, Sukumar, *Buddhist Monks and Monasteries of India,* Unwin, London, 1962 (Part I, pp. 19-97).

Dutt, Sukumar, *Early Buddhist Monachism,* Munshiram Manoharlal, Delhi, 1984 (1st ed., London, 1924).

Dutt, Sukumar, *The Buddha and Five After Centuries,* S. Samsad, Calcutta, 1978; Luzac, London, 1957.

Frauwallner, Erich, *The Earliest Vinaya and the Beginnings of Buddhist Literature,* Istituto Italiano per il Medio ed Estremo Oriente, Rome, 1956.

Oldenberg, Hermann, *Buddha: His Life, His Doctrine, His Order,* Indological Book House, Varanasi, 1971 (1st German ed., Stuttgart, 1881; 1st English ed., London, 1882).

Wijayaratna, Mohan, *Buddhist Monastic Life,* Cambridge University, Cambridge, 1990.

III. The Teachings of the Historical Buddha

Conze, Edward, *Buddhism: Its Essence and Development,* Cassirer, Oxford, 1951; Harper and Row reprint, New York, 1975 (Parts I-IV).

Conze, Edward, *Buddhist Thought in India,* Unwin, London, 1962; University of Michigan, Ann Arbor, 1967 (Parts I-II).

Glasenapp, Helmuth von, *Buddhism: A Non-theistic Religion,* Braziller, New York, 1966 (1st German ed., Munchen, 1954).

Gombrich, Richard F., *Theravāda Buddhism: A Social History from Ancient Benares to Modern Colombo,* Routledge, London, 1988.

Jayatilleke, K.N., *Early Buddhist Theory of Knowledge,* Unwin, London, 1963.

Jayatilleke, K.N. (posthumous ed., Ninian Smart), *The Message of the Buddha,* Unwin, London, 1974; Macmillan, New York, 1975.

Kalupahana, David J., *Buddhist Philosophy: A Historical Analysis,* University of Hawaii, Honolulu, 1976 (Chapters 1-7).

Lamotte, Étienne, *The Spirit of Ancient Buddhism,* Istituto per la collaborazione culturale, Venice, 1961.

Nārada, *The Buddha and His Teachings,* Vajirārāma, Colombo, Sri Lanka, 1973 (Part II, pp. 270-695).

Oldenberg, Hermann, *Buddha: His Life, His Doctrine, His Order,* Indological Book House, Varanasi, 1971 (1st German ed., Stuttgart, 1881; 1st English ed., London, 1882).

Pande, Govind Chandra, *Studies in the Origins of Buddhism,* Motilal, Delhi, 1974 (1st ed., Allahabad, 1957).

Piyadassi, *The Buddha's Ancient Path,* Rider, London, 1964.

Rahula, Walpola, *What the Buddha Taught,* Grove Press, New York, 1974 (1st ed., Bedford, U.K., 1959).

Saddhatissa, H., *The Buddha's Way,* Unwin, London, 1971.

Schumann, Hans Wolfgang, *Buddhism: An Outline of its Teachings and Schools,* Theosophical Publishing House, Wheaton, Ill., 1973 (Chapters I-II).

Thomas, Edward Josep, *The History of Buddhist Thought,* Routledge, London, 1933 (Chapters 1-12).

Wijayaratna, Mohan, *Buddhist Monastic Life,* Cambridge University, Cambridge, 1990.

IV. The Development of Mahāyāna Buddhism

Conze, Edward, *Buddhism: Its Essence and Development,* Cassirer, Oxford, 1951; Harper and Row reprint, New York, 1975.

Conze, Edward, *Buddhist Thought in India,* Unwin, London, 1962; University of Michigan Press, Ann Arbor, 1967.

Dayal, Har, *The Bodhisattva Doctrine in Buddhist Sanskrit Literature,* Routledge, London, 1932; Motilal, Delhi, 1970.

Kalupahana, David J., *Buddhist Philosophy: A Historical Analysis,* University of Hawaii, Honolulu, 1976.

Schumann, Hans Wolfgang, *Buddhism: An Outline of its Teachings and Schools,* Theosophical Pub. Hse., Wheaton, Ill., 1973 (Chapters III and IV).

Suzuki, Daisetz Teitaro, *Outlines of Mahāyāna Buddhism,* Schoken Books, New York, 1963 (1st ed., London, 1907).

Thomas, Edward Josep, *The History of Buddhist Thought,* Routledge, London, 1933.

Williams, Paul, *Mahāyāna Buddhism,* Routledge, London, 1989.

V. Buddhism in India

N.B. Most of the items in this section relate as well to Chapters I-IV above.

Conze, Edward, *Buddhism: Its Essence and Development,* Cassirer, Oxford, 1951; Harper and Row reprint, New York, 1975.

Conze, Edward, *Buddhist Thought in India,* Unwin, London, 1962; University of Michigan Press, Ann Arbor, 1967.

Dutt, Sukumar, *Buddhist Monks and Monasteries of India,* Unwin, London, 1962.

Lamotte, Étienne, *History of Indian Buddhism,* Institut Orientaliste, Louvain, 1988 (1st French ed., Louvain, 1958).

Ling, Treavor Oswald, *Buddhist Revival in India: Aspects of the Sociology of Buddhism,* St. Martin's, New York, 1980.

Ling, Treavor Oswald, *The Buddha: Buddhist Civilization in India and Ceylon,* Temple Smith, London, 1973.

Nakamura, Hajime, *Indian Buddhism: A Survey with Bibliographical Notes,* Hirakata, Japan, 1980; Motilal, Delhi, 1987.

Warder, Anthony Kennedy, *Indian Buddhism,* Motilal, Delhi, 1980 (1st ed., 1970).

Kashmir

Bamzai, Prithivi Nath Kaul, *A History of Kashmir — Political, Social, Cultural — From the Earliest Times to the Present Day,* Metropolitan, Delhi, 1962.

Dutt, Nalinaksha, *Buddhism in Kashmir,* Eastern Book Linkers, Delhi, 1985.

Ganhar, J.N., *Buddhism in Kashmir and Ladakh,* Munshiram Manoharlal, New Delhi, 1956.

Khosla, Sarla, *History of Buddhism in Kashmir,* Sagar, New Delhi, 1972.

Ray, Sunil Chandra, *Early History and Culture of Kashmir,* Munshiram Manoharlal, New Delhi, 1969, 2nd revised ed., 1970.

Central Asia

Eliot, Charles, *Hinduism and Buddhism,* Routledge, London; Barnes and Noble, New York, 1921 (vol. III, pp. 188-222).

Litvinsky, Boris Anatolevitch, "Outline History of Buddhism in Central Asia", *Kushan Studies in the U.S.S.R.* (pp. 53-132), Indian Studies Past and Present, Calcutta, 1970.

Puri, Baij Nath, *Buddhism in Central Asia,* Motilal, Delhi, 1987.
Saha, Kshanika, *Buddhism and Buddhist Literature in Central Asia,* Mukhopadhyay, Calcutta, 1970.
Snellgrove, David L., *Indo-Tibetan Buddhism: Indian Buddhists and their Tibetan Successors,* Serindia, London, 1987; Shambhala, Boston, 1987 (pp. 324-62).

VI. Buddhism in Sri Lanka

Adikaram, E.W., *Early History of Buddhism in Ceylon,* Gunasena, Colombo, 1953.
Bechert, Heinz, ed., *Buddhism in Ceylon and Studies on Religious Syncretism in Buddhist Countries,* Vandenhoeck and Ruprecht, Göttingen, 1978.
Carrithers, Michael B., *The Forest Monks of Sri Lanka: An Anthropological and Historical Study,* Oxford University, Delhi, 1983.
de Silva, K.M., *A History of Sri Lanka,* Hurst, London, 1981; University of California, Berkeley, 1981.
Evers, Hans Dieter, *Monks, Priests and Peasants: A Study of Buddhism and Social Structure in Central Ceylon,* Brill, Leiden, 1972.
Geiger, Wilhelm, *Culture of Ceylon in Mediaeval Times,* Harrassowitz, Wiesbaden, 1960.
Gombrich, Richard F., and Gananath Obeyesekere, *Buddhism Transformed: Religious Change in Sri Lanka,* Princeton University, Princeton, NJ, 1988.
Gombrich, Richard F., *Precept and Practice: Traditional Buddhism in the Rural Highlands of Ceylon,* Clarendon, Oxford, 1971.
Gombrich, Richard F., *Theravāda Buddhism: A Social History from Ancient Benares to Modern Colombo,* Routledge, London, 1988.
Gunawardana, R.A.L.H., *Robe and Plough: Monasticism and Economic Interest in Early Mediaeval Sri Lanka,* University of Arizona, Tuscon, 1979.
Ludowyk, Evelyn Fredrick Charles, *The Footprint of the Buddha,* Unwin, London, 1958.
Malalgoda, Kitsiri, *Buddhism in Sinhalese Society, 1750-1900,* University of California, Berkeley, 1976.
Rahula, Walpola, *History of Buddhism in Ceylon: The Anurādhapura Period,* Gunasena, Colombo, 1966 (1st ed., 1956).
Smith, Bardwel L., ed., *Religion and the Legitimation of Power in Sri Lanka,* Anima, Chambersburg, PA, 1978.

Smith, Bardwell L., *The Two Wheels of Dhamma: Essays on the Theravāda Tradition in India and Ceylon,* American Academy of Religion, Chambersburg, 1972.

VII. Buddhism in Southeast Asia

General

Coedès, George, *The Making of Southeast Asia,* Routledge, London, 1966 (1st French ed. 1962).
Coedès, George, *The Indianized States of Southeast Asia,* Australian National University, Canberra, 1975 (1st French ed., Paris, 1948).
Hall, Daniel George Edward, *A History of Southeast Asia,* Macmillan, London, 1981 (1st ed., 1955).
Smith, Bardwell L., ed., *Tradition and Change in Theravāda Buddhism: Essays on Ceylon and Thailand in the 19th and 20th Centuries,* Brill, Leiden, 1973.

Ancient Kingdoms

Coedès, George, *The Indianized States of Southeast Asia,* Australian National University, Canberra, 1975 (1st French ed., 1948).
Eliot, Charles, *Hinduism and Buddhsim,* Routledge, London, 1921; Barnes and Noble, New York, 1921 (vol. III, pp. 137-87).
Gómez, Luis O., and Hiram W. Woodward, *Barabuḍur: History and Significance of a Buddhist Monument,* University of California, Berkeley, 1981.
Hall, Daniel George Edward, *A History of Southeast Asia,* Macmillan, London, 1981 (1st ed., 1955).
Miksic, John, *Borobudur, Golden Tales of the Buddhas,* Bamboo, London, 1990.
Soekmono, J.G. de Dasparis and Jacques Dumarçay, *Borobudur: Prayer in Stone,* Thames and Hudson, London, 1990.

Cambodia

Audric, John, *Angkor and the Khmer Empire,* Hale, London, 1972.
Bizot, François, *Recherches sur le bouddhisme khmer,* vols. I-V, École Française d'Extrême-Orient, Paris, 1976-89.

Briggs, Lawrence Palmer, *The Ancient Khmer Empire,* American Philosophical Society, Philadelphia, 1951.

Chandler, David P., *A History of Cambodia,* Westview, Boulder, 1992 (1st ed., 1983).

Chatterji, Bijan Raj, *Indian Cultural Influence in Cambodia,* University of Calcutta, Calcutta, 1964.

Coedès, George, *Angkor: An Introduction,* Oxford University, Hong Kong, 1963 (1st French ed., 1929-32 serial).

Dutt, Sukumar, *Buddhism in East Asia,* Bhatkal, Bombay, 1966 (pp. 87-102).

Eliot, Charles, *Hinduism and Buddhism,* Routledge, London, 1921; Barnes and Noble, New York, 1921 (vol. III, pp. 100-36).

Leclère, Adhemard, *Le bouddhisme au Cambodge,* AMS, New York, 1975 (1st ed., Paris, 1899).

MacDonald, Malcolm, *Angkor and the Khmers,* Oxford University, Singapore, 1987 (1st ed., U.K., 1937).

Yang Sam, *Khmer Buddhism and Politics from 1954 to 1984,* Khmer Studies Institute, Newington, CT, 1987.

Laos

Archimbault, C., *Structures religieuses lao: Rites et mythes,* Vithanga, Vientiane, 1973.

Jumsai, M.L. Manich, *History of Laos,* Chalermnit, Bangkok, 1971 (1st ed. 1967).

Smith, Bardwell L., ed., *Religion and the Legitimation of Power in Thailand, Laos and Burma,* Anima, Chambersburg, PA, 1978.

Stuart-Fox, Martin, *Laos: Politics, Economics and Society,* Pinter, London, 1986; Rienner, Boulder, 1986.

Viravong, Maha Sila, *History of Laos,* Paragon, New York, 1964 (1st ed., 1959).

Zago, Marcello, *Rites et cérémonies in milieu bouddhiste lao,* University Gregoriana, Rome, 1972.

Burma

Eliot, Charles, *Hinduism and Buddhism,* Routledge, London, 1921; Barnes and Noble, New York, 1921 (vol. III, pp. 46-77).

Hall, Daniel George Edward, *Burma,* Hutchinson's, London, 1960 (1st ed., 1950).

Htin Aung, *Folk Elements in Burmese Buddhism,* Oxford University, London, 1962.

King, Winston Lee, *A Thousand Lives Away: Buddhism in Contemporary Burma,* Cassirer, Oxford, 1964; Harvard University, Cambridge, MA, 1964.

Mendelson, E. Michael, *Saṅgha and State in Burma,* Cornell University, Ithaca, NY, 1975.

Ray, Niharranjan, *An Introduction to the Study of Theravāda Buddhism in Burma,* University of Calcutta, Calcutta, 1946; 1977.

Ray, Niharranjan, *Sanskrit Buddhism in Burma,* H.J. Paris, Amsterdam, 1936.

Sarkisyanz, E., *Buddhist Backgrounds of the Burmese Revolution,* Nijhoff, The Hague, 1965.

Smith, Bardwell L., ed., *Religion and the Legitimation of Power in Thailand, Laos and Burma,* Anima, Chambersburg, PA, 1978.

Smith, Donald Eugene, *Religion and Politics in Burma,* Princeton University, Princeton, NJ, 1965.

Spiro, Melford E., *Buddhism and Society: A Great Tradition and its Burmese Vicissitudes,* Unwin, London, 1971.

Than Tun, *Essays on the History and Buddhism of Burma,* Kiscadale, Isle of Arran, Scotland, 1988.

Thailand

Bunnag, J., *Buddhist Monk, Buddhist Layman: A Study of Urban Monastic Organization in Central Thailand,* Cambridge University, Cambridge, 1973.

Eliot, Charles, *Hinduism and Buddhism,* Routledge, London, 1921; Barnes and Noble, New York, 1921 (vol. III, pp. 78-99).

Gard, Richard, *The Role of Thailand in World Buddhism,* World Fellowship of Buddhists, Bangkok, 1971.

Ishii, Yoneo, *Saṅgha, State and Society: Thai Buddhism in History,* University of Hawaii, Honolulu, 1986.

Jackson, Peter, *Buddhism, Legitimation and Conflict: The Political Functions of Urban Thai Buddhism,* Institute of Southeast Asian Studies, Singapore, 1989.

Rajadhon, Phya Anuman, *Life and Ritual in Old Siam,* HRAF Press, New Haven, CT, 1961.

Smith, Bardwell L., ed., *Religion and the Legitimation of Power in Thailand, Laos and Burma,* Anima, Chambersburg, PA, 1978.

Suksamran, Samboon, *Buddhism and Politics in Thailand,* Institute of Southeast Asian Studies, Singapore, 1982.

Suksamran, Samboon, *Political Buddhism in Southeast Asia,* St. Martin's, New York, 1976.

Tambiah, Stanley J., *Buddhism and the Spirit Cults in Northeast Thailand,* Cambridge University, Cambridge, 1970.

Tambiah, Stanley J., *The Buddhist Saints of the Forest and the Cult of Amulets: A Study in Charisma, Hagiography, Sectarianism and Millennial Buddhism,* Cambridge University, Cambridge, 1984.

Tambiah, Stanley J., *World Conqueror World Renouncer: A Study of Buddhism and Polity in Thailand against a Historical Background,* Cambridge University, Cambridge, 1976.

Wells, Kenneth E., *Thai Buddhism: Its Rites and Activities,* AMS, New York, 1982 (1st ed., Bangkok, 1939).

Vietnam

Dutt, Sukumar, *Buddhism in East Asia: An Outline of Buddhism in the History and Culture of the Peoples of East Asia,* Bhatkal, Bombay, 1966 (pp. 103-111).

Eliot, Charles, *Hinduism and Buddhism,* Routledge, London, 1921; Barnes and Noble, New York, 1921 (vol. III, pp. 137-50; 340-44).

Gheddo, Piero, *The Cross and the Bo-Tree: Catholics and Buddhists in Vietnam,* Sheed and Ward, New York, 1970.

Truyen, Mai Tho, *Le Bouddhisme au Vietnam: Buddhism in Vietnam: Phat-Giao Viet-Nam,* Pagoda Xa Loi, Saigon, 1962.

Thai, Van Kiem, *Vietnam, Past and Present,* UNESCO, Saigon, 1957.

Thien-an, Thich (= Rev.), *Buddhism and Zen in Vietnam in Relation to the Development of Buddhism in Asia,* Tuttle, Tokyo and Rutland, VT, 1975.

VIII. Buddhism in China

Ch'en, Kenneth K.S., *Buddhism in China: A Historical Survey,* Princeton University, Princeton, NJ, 1964.

Ch'en, Kenneth K.S., *The Chinese Transformation of Buddhism,* Princeton University, Princeton, NJ, 1973.

Chan, Wing-tsit, *Religious Trends in Modern China,* Columbia University, New York, 1953; Octagon, New York, 1969.

Dumoulin, Heinrich, *Zen Buddhism: A History — Volume 1: India and China,* Macmillan, New York, 1988 (1st German ed., Bern 1985).

Eliot, Charles, *Hinduism and Buddhism,* Routledge, London, 1921; Barnes and Noble, New York, 1921 (vol. III, pp. 223-335).

MacInnis, Donald E., *Religion in China Today: Policy and Practice,* Orbis, Maryknoll, N.Y., 1989.

Overmeyer, Daniel L., *Religions of China: The World as a Living System,* Harper and Row, San Francisco, 1986.

Reischauer, Edwin O., *Ennin's Travels in T'ang China,* Ronald Press, New York, 1955.

Weinstein, Stanley, *Buddhism under the T'ang,* Cambridge University, Cambridge, MA, 1987.

Welch, Holmes, *Buddhism under Mao,* Harvard University, Cambridge, MA, 1972.

Welch, Holmes, *The Buddhist Revival in China,* Harvard University, Cambridge, MA, 1968.

Welch, Holmes, *The Practice of Chinese Buddhism: 1900-1950,* Harvard University Press, Cambridge, MA, 1967.

Wright, Arthur F., *Buddhism in Chinese History,* Stanford University, Stanford, CA, 1971 (1st ed., 1959).

Zürcher, Erik, *The Buddhist Conquest of China: The Spread and Adaptation of Buddhism in Early Medieval China,* 2 vols., Brill, Leiden, 1972 (1st ed., 1959).

IX. Buddhism in Korea

Buswell, Robert E., *The Korean Approach to Zen: The Collected Works of Chinul,* University of Hawaii, Honolulu, 1983 (translation of Chinul with extensive historical introduction, pp. 1-95).

Chang, Byung-kil (= Pyong-gil), *Religions in Korea,* Korean Overseas Information Service, Seoul, 1984.

Chun, Shin-yong, ed., *Buddhist Culture in Korea,* Si-sa-yong-sa Publishers, Seoul, 1982.

Clark, Charles Allen, *Religions of Old Korea,* Garland, New York, 1981 (1st ed., New York, 1932).

Grayson, James Huntley, *Early Buddhism and Christianity in Korea,* Brill, Leiden, 1985.

Grayson, James Huntley, *Korea: A Religious History,* Clarendon, Oxford, 1989.

Han, Woo-keun, *The History of Korea,* University of Hawaii, Honolulu, 1971.

Kim, Duk-Whang, *A History of Religions in Korea,* Daeji Moonwha-sa, Seoul, 1988.

Lancaster, Lewis R., and Chai-shin Yu, *Introduction of Buddhism to Korea*, Asian Humanities Press, Berkeley, CA, 1989.

Lancaster, Lewis R., and Chai-shin Yu, *Assimilation of Buddhism to Korea*, Asian Humanities Press, Berkeley, CA, 1989.

Lee, Ki-baik, *A New History of Korea*, Harvard Yenching Institute, Cambridge, MA, 1984.

Yu, Chai-shin, and R. Guisso, eds., *Shamanism: The Spirit World of Korea*, Asian Humanities Press, Berkeley, CA, 1988.

Yu, Chai-shin, *Korean and Asian Religious Tradition*, University of Toronto, Toronto, 1977.

X. Buddhism in Japan

Anesaki, Masaharu, *History of Japanese Religion,with Special Reference to the Social and Moral Life of the Nation*, Tuttle, Tokyo and Rutland, VT, 1983 (1st ed., London, 1930).

Anesaki, Masaharu, *Nichiren, the Buddhist Prophet*, P. Smith, Gloucester, MA, 1966.

Bellah, Robert N., *Tokugawa Religion: The Cultural Roots of Modern Japan*, Free Press, New York, 1985; Macmillan, London, 1985 (1st ed., Glencoe, IL, 1957).

Dobbins, James C., *Jōdo Shinshū: Shin Buddhism in Medieval Japan*, Indiana University, Bloomington, 1989.

Dumoulin, Heinrich, *Zen Buddhism: A History — Volume 2: Japan*, Macmillan, New York, 1990 (1st German ed., Bern, 1986).

Eliot, Charles, *Japanese Buddhism*, Routledge, London, 1935; Barnes and Noble, New York, 1959.

Erhart, H. Byron, *Japanese Religion: Unity and Diversity*, Wadsworth, Belmont, CA, 1974 (1st ed., Belmont, 1969).

Hanayama, Shinsho, *A History of Japanese Buddhism*, Bukko Dendo Kyokai, Tokyo, 1960.

Ichiro, Hori, et al., eds., *Japanese Religion: A Survey by the Agency for Cultural Affairs*, Kodansha, Tokyo, 1972.

Kitagawa, Joseph M., *Religion in Japanese History*, Columbia University, New York, 1966.

Matsunaga, Daigan and Alicia, *Foundation of Japanese Buddhism*, 2 vols., Buddhist Books International, Los Angeles and Tokyo, 1974.

Morrell, Robert, *Early Kamakura Buddhism: A Minority Report*, Asian Humanities Press, Berkeley, CA, 1987.

Nakamura, Hajime, *A History of the Development of Japanese Thought from A.D. 592 to 1868,* 2 vols., Kokusai Bunka Shinkokai, Tokyo, 1969.

Thomsen, Harry, *The New Religions of Japan,* Tuttle, Tokyo and Rutland, VT, 1963.

Watanabe, Shoko, *Japanese Buddhism,* Kokusai Bunku Shinkokai, Tokyo, 1970 (1st ed., 1964).

XI. Buddhism in Tibet

Chattopadhyaya, Alaka, *Atīśa and Tibet,* Indian Studies Past and Present, Calcutta, 1967.

Dargyay, Eva, *The Rise of Esoteric Buddhism in Tibet,* Motilal, Delhi, 1977.

Ekvall, Robert Brianard, *Religious Observances in Tibet: Patterns and Functions,* University of Chicago, Chicago, 1964.

Eliot, Charles, *Hinduism and Buddhism,* Routledge, London, 1921; Barnes and Noble, New York, 1921 (vol. III, pp. 345-401).

Hoffmann, Helmut, *The Religions of Tibet,* Macmillan, New York and London, 1961 (1st German ed., 1956).

Karmay, Samten G., *The Treasury of Good Sayings: A Tibetan History of Bon,* Oxford University, London, 1972.

Norbu, Thubten and Colin M. Turnbull, *Tibet,* Simon and Schuster, New York, 1968; Penguin (Pelican), U.K., 1972.

Richardson, Hugh E., *Tibet and its History,* Oxford University, London, 1962 (also published as *A Short History of Tibet,* Dutton, New York, 1962).

Snellgrove, David L., and Hugh E. Richardson, *A Cultural History of Tibet,* Weidenfeld and Nicholson, London 1968; Praeger, New York, 1968; Prajñā, Boulder, 1980.

Snellgrove, David L., *Indo-Tibetan Buddhism: Indian Buddhists and their Tibetan Successors,* Serindia, London, 1987; Shambhala, Boston, 1987.

Stein, R.A., *Tibetan Civilization,* Faber, London 1972; Stanford University, Stanford, 1972 (1st French ed., Paris, 1962).

Tucci, Giuseppi, *The Religions of Tibet,* Routledge, London, 1980; University of California, Berkeley, 1980 (1st German ed., Stuttgart, 1970).

XII. Tibetan Buddhism Beyond Tibet

General

Snellgrove, David L., *Buddhist Himalaya*, Cassirer, Oxford, 1957.
Tucci, Giuseppi, *The Ancient Civilization of Trans-Himalaya*, Barrie and Jenkins, London, 1973.

Nepal

Furer-Haimendorf, Christoph von, *The Sherpas of Nepal: Buddhist Highlanders*, University of California, Berkeley, 1964.
Ortner, Sherry B., *High Religion: A Cultural and Political History of Sherpa Buddhism*, Princeton University, Princeton, NJ, 1989.
Petech, Luciano, *Medieval History of Nepal, c. 750-1480*, Istituto Italiano per il Medio ed Estremo Oriente, Rome, 1958.
Ram, Rajendra, *A History of Buddhism in Nepal*, Motilal, Delhi, 1978.
Shakya, Min Bahadur, *A Short History of Buddhism in Nepal*, YMBA, Kathmandu, 1984.
Snellgrove, David L., *Indo-Tibetan Buddhism: Indian Buddhists and their Tibetan Successors*, Serindia, London, 1987; Shambhala, Boston, 1987 (pp. 362-80).

Ladakh

Francke, August Hermann, *A History of Ladakh: With Critical Introduction and Annotations by S.S. Gergan and F.M. Hassnian*, Sterling, New Delhi, 1977 (Originally *History of Western Tibet*, London, 1907).
Petech, Luciano, *The Kingdom of Ladakh, c. 950-1842 A.D.*, Istituto Italiano per il Medio ed Estremo Oriente, Rome, 1977.
Shakspo, Nawang Tsering, *A History of Buddhism in Ladakh*, Ladakh Buddhist Vihara, Delhi, 1988.
Snellgrove, David L. and Tadeusz Skorupski, *The Cultural Heritage of Ladakh*, 2 vols., Aris and Phillips, Warminster, U.K., 1979-80.

Lahaul Spiti

Bajpai, Shiva Chandra, *Lahul-Spiti: A Forbidden Land in the Himalayas*, Indus, New Delhi, 1987.

Tobdan, *History and Religions of Lahul: From Earliest times to Circa A.D. 1950*, Books Today, New Delhi, 1984.

Kinnaur

Bajpai, Shiva Chandra, *Kinnaur a Restricted Land in the Himalaya*, Indus, New Delhi, 1991.

Bajpai, Shiva Chandra, *Kinnaur in the Himalayas*, Concept, New Delhi, 1981.

Chib, Sukhdev Singh, *Kinauras of the Himalaya*, Ess Ess Publications, New Delhi, 1984.

Raha, Manis Kumar, and Satya Narayan Mahato, *The Kinnaurese of the Himalayas*, Anthropological Survey of India, Calcutta, 1985.

Singh, Jogishwar, *Banks, Gods and Government: Institutional and Informal Credit Structure in a Remote and Tribal Indian District*, Steiner Verlag, Stuttgart, 1989.

Bhutan

Aris, Michael V., *Bhutan: The Early History of a Himalayan Kingdom*, Aris and Phillips, Warminster, U.K., 1979.

Chakravarti, Balaram, *A Cultural History of Bhutan*, 2 vols., Hilltop Publishers, Chittaranjan, West Bengal, 1979-1980.

Olschak, Blanche C., *Ancient Bhutan*, Swiss Foundation for Alpine Research, Zürich, 1979.

Sikkim

Bhattacharyya, Prandab Kumar, *Aspect of Cultural History of Sikkim: Studies in Coinage*, (sic) K.P. Bagchi, Calcutta, 1984.

Chopra, P.N., *Sikkim*, S. Chand, New Delhi, 1979.

Coelho, V.H., *Sikkim and Bhutan*, Vikas, Delhi and North Harrow, Middlesex, U.K, 1971 (not recommended for Bhutan).

Kotturan, George, *The Himalayan Gateway: History and Culture of Sikkim*, Sterling, New Delhi, 1983.

The Mongols

Grousset, René, *The Empire of the Steppes: A History of Central Asia*, Rutgers University, New Brunswick, NJ,1970.

Heissig, Walther, *The Religions of Mongolia*, University of California, Berkeley, 1979 (1st German ed., 1970).

Hyer, Paul, and Sechin Jagchid, *A Mongolian Living Buddha*, State University of New York, Albany, NY, 1983.

Jagchid, Sechin, and Paul Hyer, *Mongolia's Culture and Society*, Westview, Boulder, 1979.

Miller, Robert James, *Monasteries and Culture Change in Inner Mongolia*, Harrassowitz, Wiesbaden, 1959.

Moses, Larry William, *The Political Role of Mongolian Buddhism*, Indiana University, Bloomington, 1977.

XIII. Buddhism in the West

de Jong, J.W., *A Brief History of Buddhist Studies in Europe and North America*, Bharat-Bharati, Varanasi, India, 1976 (reprinted from *The Eastern Buddhist*, vol. 7, 1974); updated ed. (covering also 1973-83), Sri Satguru, Delhi, 1986.

Fields, R., *How the Swans Came to the Lake: A Narrative History of Buddhism in America*, Shambhala, Boston and London, 1992 (1st ed., Boulder, CO, 1981.

Hecker, Hellmuth, *Buddhismus in Deutschland*, Deutsche Buddhistische Union, Hamburg, 1978.

Humphreys, Christmas, *Sixty Years of Buddhism in England (1907-1967)*, Buddhist Society, London, 1968.

Kashima, Tetsuden, *Buddhism in America: The Social Organization of an Ethnic Institution*, Greenwood, London and Westport, CT, 1977.

Layman, Emma McCloy, *Buddhism in America*, Nelson-Hall, Chicago, 1976.

Oliver, Ian P., *Buddhism in Britain*, Rider, London, 1979.

Peiris, William, *The Western Contribution to Buddhism*, Motilal, Delhi, 1973.

Prebish, Charles, *American Buddhism*, Wadsworth, Belmont, CA, 1979.

Notes

[Items cited in Suggestions for Further Reading
are minimally referenced in these notes.]

1. See Abbreviations. The colon separates volume and page numbers, which refer to the Pāli Text Society editions of the Pāli originals. These page numbers are included in the PTS English translations and often in alternative translations as well. As a result, their use is the standard way of locating material in the Pāli canon.
2. E. Conze, *Buddhist Thought in India,* Unwin, London, 1962, pp. 31-2; *Thirty Years of Buddhist Studies,* Cassirer, Oxford, 1967, pp. 1-13.
3. See A. Bareau, *Les sectes bouddhiques du petit véhicule,* Saigon, 1955 for the classical study of these schools. See also A.K. Warder, *Indian Buddhism,* 2nd edition, Delhi, 1980, pp. 288-351; and E. Lamotte, *Histoire du Bouddhisme Indien,* Louvain, 1958, pp. 571-606; English translation, Louvain, 1988, pp. 517-48. For more recent articles, see Charles Prebish, "A Review of Scholarship on the Buddhist Councils," *Journal of Asian Studies,* vol. 33, no. 2, Feb. 1974, pp. 239-54. See also Jan Nattier and Charles Prebish, "Mahāsaṅghika Origins," *History of Religions,* vol. 16, no. 3, Feb. 1977, pp. 237-72.
4. See: Anesaki, "Some Problems of the Textual History of the Buddhist Scriptures" and "The Four Buddhist Āgamas in Chinese," *Transactions of the Asiatic Society of Japan,* vol. 35, nos. 2 and 3, 1908. See also: Thich Minh Chau, *The Chinese Madhyama Āgama and the Pāli Majjhima Nikāya,* The Saigon Institute of Higher Buddhist Studies, n.d. but probably 1964.
5. L. de la Vallée Poussin, Théorie des douze causes, Luzac, London, 1913. N.A. Sastri, *Ārya Śālistamba Sūtra,* Adyar Library, Madras, 1950. N. R. Reat, *The Śālistamba Sūtra,* Motilal Banarsidass, Delhi, 1993.
6. Early formulations of this theory include: Edward Conze, *Buddhist Thought in India,* London, 1962, p. 31; "Recent Progress in Buddhist Studies," *The Middle Way,* vol. 34, 1959, Reprinted in: E. Conze, *Thirty Years of Buddhist Studies,* Oxford, 1967. See also Constantin Regamey, "Der Buddhismus Indiens," in *Christus und die Religionen der Erde,* vol. 3, Vienna, 1951, pp. 231-317 (reprinted in *Der Christ in der Welt,* series 17, vol. 6, Zürich, 1964, pp. 1-103). See also Regamey, "Le problème du Bouddhisme primitif et les derniers travaux de Stanislaw Schayer," *Rocznik Orientalistyczny,* vol. 21,

1957, pp. 37-58. See S. Schayer, "Precanonical Buddhism," *Archiv Orientální,* vol. 7, fasc. 2, 1935, pp. 121-132; and "New contributions to the Problem of Pre-hīnayānistic Buddhism," *Polski Biuletyn Orientalistyczny,* vol. 1, 1937, pp. 8-17. See the response to Schayer's work by A.B. Keith, "Pre-Canonical Buddhism," *Indian Historical Quarterly,* vol. 12, no. 1, 1936, pp. 1-20. See also M. Falk, *Nāma-rūpa and Dharma-rūpa,* Calcutta, 1943.

7. Śāntideva's *Śikshāsamuccaya;* Yaśomitra's *Abhidharmakośa-sphutārtha;* Prajñākaramati's, *Bodhicaryāvatāra-pañjikā;* Candra-kīrti's *Madhyamaka-kārikā-prasannapadā.*

8. See, for example: *Kena Upanishad* I.3.7; *Brihadāraṇyaka Upanishad* II.3.6; IV.4.1-25 and IV.5.13-15; *Chāndogya Upanishad* VII.24.1; VIII.11 and 12. *Taittirīya Upanishad* II.9.

9. N.R. Reat, *The Śālistamba Sūtra,* Delhi, 1993, para. 34.

10. Reat, *The Śālistamba Sūtra,* para. 3; M1:262, etc.

11. D2:354; S1:227; S3:54.

12. The Jains and Ājīvakas appear to have been something of an exception.

13. E.g., *Katha Upanishad* I.3.

14. *Taittirīya Upanishad* II.2-5; III.2-6. See *Paiṅgala Upanishad* II.7.

15. E.g., M1:111; D1:222-23; D2:62. See: N.R. Reat, "Some Fundamental Concepts of Buddhist Psychology," *Journal of the International Association of Buddhist Studies,* 1987, no. 17, pp.15-28.

16. D1:184; A4:451-54.

17. A.K. Warder, *Indian Buddhism,* 1980, p. 486.

18. B.A. Litvinsky, "Outline History of Buddhism in Central Asia," *Kushan Studies in the U.S.S.R.,* 1970, pp. 58-9.

19. Tsl. by James Legge, *A Record of Buddhistic Kingdoms,* Oxford, 1886, Oriental Publishers reprint, Delhi, 1971, pp. 101-7.

20. Tsl. by Samuel Beal, *Buddhist Records of the Western World,* London, 1884, Motilal Banarsidass reprint, Delhi, 1981, vol. II, p. 247.

21. *Cūlavaṃsa,* chapter 60, lines 4-8.

22. *The Temporal and Spiritual Conquest of Ceylon,* tsl. S.G. Perera, Colombo, 1930.

23. G. Coedès, *The Indianized States of Southeast Asia,* 1975, p. 178.

24. David Hawk, *WCRP Report on Kampuchea,* New York, 1981, p. 4.

25. *Mahāvaṃsa* chapter XII, lines 44-55.

26. Charles Backus, *The Nan-chao Kingdom and T'ang China's Southwestern Frontier,* Cambridge University, Cambridge, U.K., 1981, pp. 46-52.

27. *A Record of Buddhistic Kingdoms,* tsl. by James Legge, Oxford, 1886, Oriental Publishers reprint, Delhi, 1971, p. 12.

28. The *Wei Lüe* itself does not survive, but it is extensively quoted in a commentary on the well-known *San Guo Zhi* or *History of the Three Kingdoms.* See Kenneth Ch'en, *Buddhism in China,* 1964, pp. 29-34.

29. Stanley Weinstein, *Buddhism under the T'ang,* 1987, pp. 147-49.

30. Holmes Welch, *The Buddhist Revival in China,* 1968, p. 10.

31. James H. Grayson, *Early Buddhism and Christianity in Korea,* 1985, p. 19.

32. *The Hye Ch'o Diary,* Asian Humanities Press, Berkeley, 1989.

33. Nichiren, *Kaimoku-shū,* conclusion. See Anesaki, *History of Japanese Religion,* 1963, p. 198.

34. J.M. Kitagawa, *Religion in Japanese History,* 1966, p. 291.

35. H.E. Richardson, *Tibet and Its History,* 1962, p. 6.

36. Snellgrove and Richardson, *A Cultural History of Tibet,* 1980, pp. 76-78.

37. W.Y. Evans-Wentz, tsl., *Tibet's Great Yogī: Milarepa,* Oxford University, London, 1928. Lobsang P. Lhalungpa, tsl., *The Life of Milarepa,* Dutton, New York, 1977. Herbert V. Guenther, tsl., *The Life and Teaching of Nāropa,* Oxford University, Oxford, 1963. Chogyam Trungpa, tsl., *The Life of Marpa the Translator,* Prajñā, Boulder, CO, 1982. Khenpo K. Gyaltsen, tsl., *The Great Kagyu Masters,* Snow Lion, Ithaca, NY, 1990.

38. W.Y. Evans-Wentz, *Tibet's Great Yogī: Milarepa,* Oxford University, Oxford, 1928, p. 2.

39. Translated by Garma C.C. Chang, *The Hundred Thousand Songs of Milarepa,* Harper, New York, 1962.

40. Translated by Herbert V. Guenther, Rider, London, 1959.

41. See W.Y. Evans-Wentz, *Tibetan Yoga and Secret Doctrines,* Oxford University, Oxford, 1935, pp. 155-252 for a fuller explanation of the Six Teachings of Nāropa.

42. Translated by W.Y. Evans-Wentz, Oxford University, Oxford 1927, and by Francesca Freemantle and Chogyam Trungpa, Shambhala, Boulder, CO, 1975.

43. Ippolito Desideri, *An Account of Tibet,* Routledge, London, 1931; revised ed. Broadway Travellers, London, 1937. *Documenti dei missionari nel Tibet e nel Nepal,* serialized in *Nuovo Ramuso,* Rome, 1952-56. See also Snellgrove and Richardson, *A Cultural History of Tibet,* 1980, pp. 220-24.

44. Notably recorded in the works of Charles Bell and L.A. Waddell, though the latter is somewhat biased against Tibet and Buddhism.

45. Translated in: A.H. Franke, *Antiquities of Indian Tibet, vol. II,* Calcutta, 1926.

46. D. Snellgrove and T. Skorupski, *The Cultural Heritage of Ladakh,* 1977, pp. 6-8.
47. D. Snellgrove, *Indo-Tibetan Buddhism,* 1987, p. 472.
48. L. Petech, *The Kingdom of Ladakh,* 1977, pp. 19-20.
49. A.H. Franke, *A History of Ladakh,* 1977, pp. 93-4.
50. A.H. Franke, *A History of Ladakh,* 1977, pp. 100-101.
51. See above, Chapter V, final section "The Modern Buddhist Revival in India".
52. Michael Aris, *Bhutan,* 1979, p. 23, but see also pp. 6-8.
53. Michael Aris, *Bhutan,* 1979, pp. 51-2.
54. *Kindly Bent to Ease Us,* 3 vols., tsl. Herbert V. Guenther, Dharma, Emeryville, CA, 1976.
55. Michael Aris, *Bhutan,* 1979, p. 153
56. C. Bawden, *The Modern History of the Mongols,* Praeger, New York, 1968.
57. Walther Heissig, *The Religions of Mongolia,* 1980, p. 1 (1st ed., 1970).
58. These conservative estimates are based on Peter Harvey, *An Intro-duction to Buddhism,* 1990, chapter 13, which in turn is based primarily upon estimates by the American Buddhist Congress and the Buddhist Union of Europe.
59. E.B. Cowell, preface to *The Jātaka,* Vol. I, Cambridge University, Cambridge, U.K., 1895, p. vii.
60. T.W. Rhys Davids, *The Questions of King Milinda,* Vol. I, Clarendon, Oxford, 1890, pp. xix-xx.
61. J.W. de Jong, *A Brief History of Buddhist Studies in Europe and America,* 1976, pp. 5-6.

Glossary

[Items herein are alphabetized in the "letter-by-letter" mode; e.g., "Annam" comes before "An Shi Gao."]

abbacy — the office of abbot

abbot — the head of a monastery or monastic order

Abhayagiri — a monastery and the second lineage of Sri Lankan Theravāda (after the Mahāvihāra), established in 29 BCE, associated with scriptural and doctrinal innovations originating in India, thus forming a more liberal, quasi-Mahāyāna branch of the Sri Lankan Saṅgha, abolished by Parakrama Bāhu I (r. 1153-86) — see Jetavana

Abhidhamma — (P.) see Abhidharma

Abhidharma — (Skt.) the third section of the canon in the various forms of Nikāya Buddhism, containing complex philosophical and psychological material doubtfully attributed to the historical Buddha (P. Abhidhamma)

Abhidharma Kośa — a treatise by Vasubandhu purporting to systematize and explain the meaning of the Abhidharma teachings of Nikāya Buddhism

absolutism — belief in an impersonal, ultimate, metaphysical reality that underlies the universe and accounts for its existence

Ado — according to tradition, the second Buddhist monk in Korea, said to have arrived in Koguryŏ from northern China in 383 CE

Advaita — the "non-dual" school of Hindu Vedānta founded by Śaṅkara

Āgama — a section of the Sanskrit canon of non-Mahāyāna Buddhism, analagous to the Nikāyas of the Pāli canon

Āgama Buddhism — the several schools of non-Mahāyāna Buddhism, now represented only by the Theravāda (see Nikāya Buddhism)

aggregates, five — (P. *khandha*, Skt. *skandha*) according to Theravāda Buddhism, the constituents of the individual human being: 1) body (P. and Skt. *rūpa*), 2) feelings (P. and Skt. *vedanā*), 3) perceptions (P. *saññā*, Skt. *saṃjñā*), 4) mental formations (P. *saṅkhārā*, Skt. *saṃskārā*) and 5) consciousness (P. *viññāna*, Skt. *vijñāna*)

Ājīvakas — pre-Vedic, pre-Buddhist, yogic religion of ancient India

Alexander the Great — (356-323 BCE) Macedonian monarch who conquered Greece, northern Africa, and a swath of Asia through to India

Altaic — (from Altai Mountains of Mongolia) a language family of which Korean, Mongolian, Manchurian, Turkish, Korean and Japanese are members

Altan Khan — (r. 1543-83) Mongol chieftain who bestowed the title of Dalai Lama upon the reincarnating head of the Gelugpa sect of Tibetan Buddhism

Alu Vihāra — Sri Lankan monastery at which the Pāli canon was first written down in the first century BCE

Amarapura Nikāya — the branch of the Sri Lankan Saṅgha that serves the middle castes, founded in 1803-7 by delegations sent to Burma (see Siam and Ramana Nikāyas)

Amaterasu — goddess of the sun, the supreme deity of Shintō

Amida — Japanese for Sanskrit Amitābha

Amitābha — the mythological "Buddha of infinite radiance," whose "Western Paradise" is the goal of Pure Land devotion

Amitāyus — the Buddha of infinite life

Anagārika Dharmapāla — (1864-1933) originally David Hewavitarne, founder of the Mahābodhi Society in Sri Lanka in 1891

anātman — (Skt.) without soul (P. *anatta*)

anatta — (P.) without soul (Skt. *anātman*)

Angkor — ancient Khmer kingdom founded in the ninth century, precursor of modern-day Cambodia

Angkor Wat — Vaiśnavite temple-mountain in Cambodia, built under Sūryavarman II (r. 1113-50)

Aṅguttara Nikāya — the "numerical" section of the Pāli canon, containing material grouped according to the number of items discussed

anicca — (P.) impermanent (Skt. *anitya*)

anitya — (Skt.) impermanent (P. *anicca*)

Annam — central Vietnam (see Tonkin and Cochin China)

An Shi Gao (An Shih-kao) — (second century) a Central Asian, the first major translator of Buddhist scriptures into Chinese

Anurādhapura — the first capital of Sri Lanka, circa 250 BCE to 1000 CE

Anuruddha — (r. 1044-77) the Burman king who overthrew the Mon, unified Burma, established Pagan as his capital, aided Sri Lanka against the Tamils in 1067, and in 1073 provided a delegation of monks to Sri Lanka in order to re-establish the Saṅgha there

arahat — one who has realized nirvāṇa by following the Buddha's teachings (also spelled arahant, arhat, and arhant)

arūpa jhāna — (P.) one of four "formless" meditational states of absorption in Theravāda Buddhism

Āryadeva — (second century) pupil of Nāgārjuna

Asaṅga — (fourth century CE) along with his brother Vasubandhu, generally regarded as co-founder of the Vijñānavāda or "Consciousness school" of Mahāyāna Buddhism

Ashikaga period — (1336-1600) tumultuous period of Japanese history in

which the Ashikaga clan dominated the nation while the emperor
ruled in name only (also known as the Muromachi period)

Aśoka — (r. circa 270-230 BCE) India's foremost royal patron of Buddhism and the first monarch to rule over a united India

Aśvaghosha — (first or second century CE) one of the first Mahāyāna
scholars, author of the *Buddha-carita* or "Life of the Buddha," and
dubiously credited with *The Awakening of Faith in the Mahāyāna*

Atīśa (982-1054) — Indian scholar-monk, founder of the Kadampa sect of
Tibetan Buddhism after his arrival in Western Tibet in 1042

ātman — (Skt.) soul (P. *atta*)

atta — (P.) soul (Skt. *ātman*)

Avadāna — in several schools of Nikāya Buddhism, a section of scripture
roughly corresponding to the Theravādin *Khuddaka Nikāya* (miscellaneous collection)

Avalokiteśvara — the bodhisattva of compassion

Avataṃsaka Sūtra — a mammoth Mahāyāna sūtra containing several
independent texts, supposedly delivered by the celestial Buddha
Vairocana

Ayutthaya — ancient Thai capital from circa 1350 to 1781

Bali — an Indonesian island that still bears significant traces of its ancient
Buddhist and Hindu heritage (see Sumatra and Java)

Bangkok — the capital of Thailand since 1781

Bar Do — according to Tibetan Buddhism, the "intermediate state" between death and rebirth

Bashō — (1664-94) Zen poet, credited with inventing the *haiku*

Bayon — twelfth-century Mahāyāna Buddhist temple-mountain near
Angkor Wat in Cambodia

Beijing — (Peking) during and after the Yuan (Mongol) dynasty (1280-
1368), the primary capital of China

Bhagavad Gītā — the first Hindu scripture to espouse *bhakti,* or devotionalism, probably composed between 200 BCE and 200 CE

bhakti — devotionalism, loving worship of a savior deity

Bhāvaviveka — (sixth century) Indian Buddhist logician, generally regarded as the founder of the Svātantrika branch of Madhyamaka
Buddhism (see Buddhapālita)

Bhutan — Buddhist kingdom in the southeastern Himalayas

bKa' gDams-pa — see Kadampa

bKa' 'Gyur — see Kanjur

bKa' rGyud-pa — see Kagyudpa

bKra Shis Lhun-po — see Tashilhunpo

bLama — see lama

Blavatsky, Madame — (1831-91) co-founder, with H.S. Olcott, of the

Theosophical Society

bodhi — (P. and Skt.) enlightenment, literally "awakening"

Bodhidharma — the first patriarch of Chinese Chan (Jap. Zen) Buddhism, supposedly an Indian meditation master (though probably from Central Asia) who arrived in China around 500 CE

bodhisatta — (P.) in the Theravāda tradition, the Buddha before he realized enlightenment (Skt. bodhisattva)

bodhisattva — (Skt.) in the Mahāyāna tradition, one who renounces nirvāṇa in order to lead other beings to salvation; also a supernatural savior figure (P. *bodhisatta*)

bodhisattva, celestial — a savior deity of Mahāyāna Buddhism

Bon — the indigenous, pre-Buddhist religion of Tibet

Bon-po — a follower of the Bon religion

Borobudur — eighth-century Buddhist temple-mountain on Java, one of the largest religious monuments ever built

brahman — according to Hinduism, the ultimate metaphysical principle, the source and resolution of the universe

Brāhmaṇas — Hindu texts relating to the performance of Vedic ritual, most composed between 1000 and 500 BCE

Brahmanism — conventional designation for the ancient Vedic religion before it developed into Hinduism

Brahma-vihāra meditations — contemplative practices, prominent in Theravāda Buddhism, whereby one is to cultivate and extend to all beings a mental attitude of benevolence *(metta)*, compassion *(karuṇā)*, sympathetic joy *(muditā)* and equanimity *(upekkhā)*

Brahmin — (Skt. Brāhmaṇa) a member of the priestly caste of Hinduism

'Brog-mi [Dog-mi] — (992-1072) founder of the Sakyapa sect of Tibetan Buddhism

'Brom sTon [Dom-ton] — (1008-64) immediate disciple of Atīśa, consolidator of the Kadampa sect of Tibetan Buddhism

bSam-yas — see Sam-ye

bSod-Nams rGya-mTsho [Sonam Gyatso] — (1543-88) the third Dalai Lama, who received the title from the mongol chieftain Altan Khan (r. 1543-83)

bsTan 'Gyur — see Tanjur

Buddha-carita — epic poem by Aśvaghosha recounting the legendary life of the Buddha

Buddhaghosa — (fifth-century) editor of the Pāli commentaries of Theravāda Buddhism and author of the *Visuddhimagga*

Buddha-nature — very generally, in Mahāyāna Buddhism, the quality of truth believed to be inherent in all things

Buddhapālita — (sixth century) Indian Buddhist philosopher, generally regarded as the founder of the Prāsaṅgika branch of Madhyamaka Buddhism, though Nāgārjuna himself was like-minded (see Bhāvaviveka and Candrakīrti)

Burma — a Theravāda Buddhist country of Southeast Asia

Burman — Tibeto-Burmans in particular, as opposed to "Burmese," which refers to the mixed population of Burma as a whole

Bu sTon — (1290-1364) Tibetan Buddhist monk, author of the first comprehensive history of Buddhism in Tibet, renowned as the scholar primarily responsible for organizing and editing the standard Tibetan canon (the Kanjur and Tanjur)

Byang-Chub rGyal-mTshan [Jang-chub Gyal-tsan] — (fourteenth century) liberated Tibet from Mongol overlordship and revived the ancient Tibetan tradition of monarchy by founding the Phag-mo Gru [Phag-mo-du] dynasty (c. 1350-1480)

cakravartin — mythological "wheel turning monarch" destined to rule the entire earth

Cambodia — a Theravāda Buddhist country of Southeast Asia (previously Kampuchea)

Candrakīrti — (seventh century) Indian Madhyamaka philosopher who established the ascendancy of the Prāsaṅgika school with his famous treatise, the *Prasannapadā*

canon — a set of scriptures recognized as authoritative

Cao Dong (Ts'ao Tung) — one of the two surviving lineages of Chan Buddhism in China, transmitted to Japan as Sōtō Zen

caste system — the hereditary social system of Hindu India

catush-koṭi — "four corners," according to Buddhism the four logical possibilities: a thing or proposition may be 1) x, 2) not x, 3) both x and not x, 4) neither x nor not x

Central Asia — an ill-defined area stretching between the Aral Sea in the west to the Gobi Desert in the east and including in the south modern-day Afghanistan, northern Pakistan, Kashmir, and western Tibet

Chajang — (608-686) eminent Korean monk of Silla, associated with the Vinaya school, a contemporary of Wŏnhyo (617-687) and Ŭisang (625-702)

Chakri dynasty — founded in 1781, the present royal family of Thailand

Champa — an ancient Southeast Asian kingdom located along the southeastern coast of present-day Vietnam, not survived by any modern state

Chan (Ch'an) — (Chi. for "meditation," Skt. *dhyāna*) the Meditational school of Chinese Buddhism, better known by its Japanese name Zen

Chang An (Ch'ang An) — alternative name for Xi'an, an ancient Chinese capital (see Luoyang)

Chao Phraya — a river in Thailand

Chenla — the ancient Khmer kingdom that succeeded Funan in the seventh century, precursor of Angkor

Chiang Mai — ancient Thai capital in the north of the country

Chimyŏng — Korean monk who returned from China in 602 and is credited with founding the Vinaya school in Silla

Chinhŭng — (r. 540-76) Pŏphŭng's successor as king of Silla

Chinŏn — one of the two Korean branches of the Chinese Zhen Yan (Chen Yen) or Tantric school

Chinp'yŏng — (r. 579-632) king of Silla and personal friend of the monk Wŏn'gwang

Chinul — (1158-1210), widely regarded as the most influential Buddhist in the history of Korea, attempted to synthesize the Sŏn (Zen) and Hwaŏm (Hua Yan) schools of Buddhism

Chogyal [Chos rGyal] — "Dharma King," traditional title of the king of Sikkim

Chola — a Hindu kingdom of southern India (see Paṇḍu)

Ch'ŏnt'ae school — Korean counterpart of the Chinese Tian Tai school of Buddhism

Chosŏn dynasty — (1392-1910) Korean dynasty which suppressed Buddhism, Confucianism and Christianity

Chulalongkorn — see Rāma V

citta — mind, thought

Clement of Alexandria — second-century Greek Christian theologian

Cochin China — southern Vietnam (see Annam and Tonkin)

Colombo — modern capital of Sri Lanka

commentarial tradition — orthodox Theravāda Buddhism, based upon commentaries (edited by Buddhaghosa) explaining the meaning of the Pāli canon

commentary — a treatise purporting to explain the meaning of a scripture

common era — abbreviated "CE," the period of time more commonly designated A.D.

conditioned arising — (P. *paticcasamuppāda,* Skt. *pratītyasamutpāda*) the Buddhist doctrine of causation, normally given in a twelvefold formula: 1) ignorance conditions 2) mental formations . . . 3) consciousness . . . 4) name-and-form . . . 5) the six senses (including mind) . . . 6) sensual contact . . . 7) feeling . . . 8) desire . . . 9) grasping . . . 10) existence . . . 11) birth (i.e. rebirth) . . . 12) ageing and death

Confucius — (551-479 BCE) founder of the Chinese religious and political system known as Confucianism

Consciousness school — see Vijñānavāda

Council (P. *saṅgīti*) — one of several authoritative gatherings of Buddhist monks held to standardize accepted versions of the teachings of the Buddha

coup — coup d'état, a sudden, usually forceful usurpation of a government

Cūlavaṃsa — Sri Lankan historical chronicle, supplement to the *Mahāvamsa*

Cullavagga — section of the Pāli Vinaya Piṭaka containing accounts of the First and Second Councils (see Council)

Dalai Lama — title of the head of the Gelugpa sect of Tibetan Buddhism, but widely recognized as the head of all Tibetan Buddhism as well as the Tibetan state

dao — (*tao*) the "Way" of nature, doctrinal basis of Daoism

Dao De Jing (Tao Te Ching) — (sixth century BCE) foundational text of Daoism, doubtfully attributed to Lao Zi

Daoism — (Taoism) Chinese religion founded by Lao Zi and based on the *dao* or "Way" of nature

Dark Ages — stagnant period of European history between approximately 500 and 1000 CE

Daśabhūmika Sūtra — Mahāyāna *Sūtra of Ten Stages* (on the path to enlightenment)

Dengyō Daishi — (766-822) see Saichō

Devānampiya Tissa — (r. circa 250-207 BCE) the first historical king of Sri Lanka, enthroned as a direct result of the introduction of Buddhism under Emperor Aśoka of India

devotionalism — (Skt. *bhakti*) loving worship of a savior deity

dGe 'Dun Grub [Ge-dun Dup] — (1391-1475) nephew of Tsong Kha-pa, eventually recognized as the first Dalai Lama of Tibet, though the title did not exist in his lifetime (see Dalai Lama)

dGe 'Dun rGya mTsho — (1475-1553) the second Dalai Lama, though the title did not exist in his lifetime (see Dalai Lama)

dGe Lugs-pa — see Gelugpa

dGe sLong — (Tib. for Skt. *bhikshu*) a Buddhist monk (see lama)

dhamma — (P.) truth, the teachings of the Buddha (Skt. dharma)

Dhammapada — an important verse scripture of Theravāda Buddhism

Dhammayut Nikāya — founded by King Rāma IV, the second major branch of Thai Buddhism in addition to the ancient Mahānikāya

dharma — (Skt.) truth, the teachings of the Buddha (P. *dhamma*)

Dharma-kāya — in Mahāyāna Buddhism, the "truth-body" of the Buddha, conceived as a universal metaphysical principle

Dharmakīrti — (seventh century) Indian logician, author of the *Nyāya-bindu,* a follower of and commentator upon Dignāga *dhyāna* — meditation (P. *jhāna*, Chi. *chan*, Jap. *zen*)

Dhyāna — a school of Mahāyāna Buddhism emphasizing meditation, transmitted from India to China (as Chan) and then to Japan (as Zen)

dialectic — branch of logic concerned with critically evaluating the truth-value of theories, opinions or statements

Dīgha Nikāya — section of the Pāli canon containing the long discourses of the Buddha

Dignāga — (c. 400 CE) generally regarded as the founder of Buddhist logic, pupil of Vasubandhu

Di Lun (Ti Lun) — (Chi.) *Daśabhūmika Sūtra*

Dinh dynasty — (969-81) the first indigenous rulers of Vietnam

Dīpavaṃsa — quasi-historical Buddhist chronicle compiled in Sri Lanka in the fourth century CE

Dōgen — (1200-1253) author of the *Shōbōgenzō*, and the Japanese Zen master usually credited with introducing the Cao Dong branch of Chinese Chan into Japan, where it came to be known as Sōtō Zen

Dolma [sGrol-ma] — (Tib.) the "Savioress," consort of Avalokiteśvara (Skt. Tārā)

Dolma, Green — the Nepalese wife of King Srong bTsan sGam-po of Tibet (see Dolma)

Dolma, White — the Chinese wife of King Srong bTsan sGam-po of Tibet (see Dolma)

Dōsen — (702-60) Japanese name for a Chinese Buddhist missionary who brought extensive commentaries on the *Avataṃsaka Sūtra* to Japan in 736 and is generally recognized as the founder of Kegon Buddhism in Japan

Dōshō — (628-700) founder in Japan of the Hossō or Vijñānavāda school, arguably the most influential monk in seventh-century Japan

Dravidian — the non-Indo-European race and languages of India, primarily Tamil, possibly descended from the Indus Valley Civilization

Drepung ['Bras sPungs] — second largest monastery of the Gelugpa sect of Tibetan Buddhism, founded in the early fifteenth century near Lhasa

Drugpa ['Brug-pa] — a subsect of the Kagyudpa sect of Tibetan Buddhism, now found almost exclusively in the northwestern Himalayas and Bhutan

duḥkha — (Skt.) see P. *dukkha*

dukkha — (P.) suffering, the first Noble Truth of Buddhism: "To exist is to suffer." (Skt. *duḥkha*)

Dunhuang (Tun-huang) — gateway to imperial China, the meeting point of the northern and southern branches of the Silk Road, which skirt the Takla Makan desert

326 Buddhism: A History

Dvaravati — early Mon kingdom in the Chao Phraya river valley of
Thailand
edict — decree issued by a monarch or other authority
Eightfold Path — according to Nikāya Buddhism, the path to enlightenment, comprised of right view, right thought, right speech, right
action, right livelihood, right effort, right mindfulness, and right
concentration
eight teachings — Tian Tai doctrine that the Buddha taught different
doctrines according to the ability of his audience, intended to harmonize the conflicting doctrines of the various schools
Eisai — (1141-1215) usually considered to be the first successful proponent of Zen in Japan, founder of the Rinzai school
Elder — (P. *Thera*, Skt. *Sthavira*) an eminent Theravādin monk, one of
the conservative monks who refused to go along with the Mahāsaṅghika schism at the Second Council (about 350 BCE)
elements, four great — earth, water, fire and air, the atomic constituents
of the universe according to early Buddhism
emptiness — (Skt. *śūnyatā*) according to Mahāyāna Buddhism, the ultimate nature of all phenomena
Fa Shun — (557-640) generally regarded as the founder of Hua Yan Buddhism in China
Fa Xian (Fa Hsien) — Chinese pilgrim who visited India and Sri Lanka
during the Gupta period in 399-414 CE
Fa Xiang (Fa Hsiang) school — see Wei Shi school
Fa Zang (Fa Tsang) — (643-712) third patriarch of the Hua Yan school in
China, systematizer of its doctrines
five periods — Tian Tai doctrine that the Buddha taught different doc-
trines during differerent periods in his career, intended to harmonize
the conflicting doctrines of the various schools
Four Noble Truths — see Noble Truths
Funan — an ancient Southeast Asian kingdom, comprising territory sur-
rounding the Mekong River delta, appears to have emerged as a po-
litical entity in the first century of the common era, at about the time
Indian civilization began to exert a sustained influence in the region
Ganden [dGa' lDan] — the first monastery of the Gelugpa sect of Tibetan
Buddhism, founded by Tsong Kha-pa on an isolated mountain top
about twenty-five miles from Lhasa
Gandhāra — ancient Kingdom to the northwest of India in which Bud-
dhism was prominent from Aśokan times (see Kashmir)
Ganjin — (688-763) — Japanese name of the Chinese monk who
founded in Japan the Ritsu school, counterpart to the Chinese Lü or
Vinaya school, in 753

Gelugpa [dGe Lugs-pa] — the "Model of Virtue Sect," the largest and youngest sect of Tibetan Buddhism, founded by Tsong Kha-pa (1357-1419) and headed by the reincarnating lineage of Dalai Lamas

Genghis Khan — (1162-1227) the first Mongol emperor

geomancer — in China and Japan, diviners thought to be able to read portents in the landscape

gLang Dar-ma (r. 836-42) — the last of the old lineage of kings of Tibet, remembered for his persecution of Buddhism

Godan Khan — (d. 1251) son of Ogodai Khan, he appointed Sakya Paṇḍita viceroy of Tibet

gong an — (*kung an*) — (Chi.) a meditational riddle employed in Lin Ji Chan (Jap. Rinzai Zen) Buddhism (Jap. *kōan*)

Gotama — family name of the Buddha (also spelled Gautama)

gShen — (Tib.) a shaman

gShen Rab — "Great Shaman," the legendary founder of the Bon religion of Tibet

gTer-ma — "treasure texts," in Tibetan Buddhism and Bon, religious texts supposedly hidden in the distant past and discovered at a much later date (see *gTer-sTon*)

gTer sTon — "treasure finder," one who discovers *gTer-ma* or "treasure texts" (see *gTer-ma*)

Guge — a principality of Western Tibet, associated with modern-day Kinnaur

Guo Min Dang (Kuo Min Tang) — the "Nationalist party" of China, led by Chiang Kai-shek, which was defeated by communists in 1949 and now rules on the island of Taiwan

Gupta dynasty — (320 to circa 500 CE) the first truly Hindu dynasty of India

Gurkhas — the dominant (mostly Hindu) ethnic group in modern-day Nepal

Gushi Khan — (d. 1656) Mongol chieftain named King of Tibet in 1642 (a title retained by his successors until 1720), the fifth Dalai Lama's Mongol patron (also spelled Gusri and Gushri)

Gyer sPungs — a great Tibetan shaman supposed to have saved Bon from the persecution of the Buddhist King Khri Srong lDe bTzan

Gyōgi — (670-749) — followed Dōshō as patriarch of the Hossō school in Japan and initiated the Ryōbu or "Double Aspect" Shintō movement which sought to identify Buddhist and Shintō deities and thus to combine the two religions

Haedong Kosŭng Chŏn — ("Biographies of Eminent Korean Monks") a traditional Korean history

Haedong school — Korean school of Buddhism related to the Hua Yan school of China, also known as the Pŏpsŏng school

haiku — a poem containing three lines of five, seven and five syllables, associated with Zen Buddhism and especially the poet Bashō

Han dynasty — (206 BCE-220 CE) Chinese dynasty that saw the introduction of Buddhism to China

Hanoi — ancient and present-day capital of Vietnam, situated in the north of the country

Harappa — one of the two major cities of the Indus Valley Civilization (see Mohenjo Daro)

Harsha — (r. 606-647) last great Buddhist emperor of India

Heian period — (794-1185) the period of Japanese history when Kyōto (Heian Kyō) was the actual center of Japanese government, though it was nominally the capital until 1868

Heian schools of Buddhism — the schools of Buddhism founded in the Heian period of Japanese history: Tendai and Shingon schools

Hideyoshi — Toyotomi Hideyoshi (1536-99), the second of a series of allied generals who overthrew the Ashikaga shogunate (see Nobunaga and Ieyasu)

Hieronymus — (c. 340-420) St. Jerome, monk and scholar of the Latin Church

Himachal Pradesh — a northwestern state of modern India

Himalayas — mountain range to the north of India

Hīnayāna — derogatory term for non-Mahāyāna Buddhism (see Nikāya Buddhism)

Hōnen — (1133-1212) founder of the Jōdo or Pure Land sect in Japan, author of the *Senchaku-shū*

Hong Ren (Hung Jen) — (602-75) the fifth patriarch of Chinese Chan Buddhism

Hossō school — Japanese counterpart of the Chinese Wei Shi or Consciousness school, established in Japan in approximately 653 by the Japanese monk Dōshō

Hua Yan (Hua Yen) — the "Avatamsaka" school of Chinese Buddhism, which takes its name from the *Avataṃsaka (Hua Yan) Sūtra* (Jap. Kegon)

Hué — an ancient capital of Vietnam, now a city in the center of the country

Hui Neng — (638-713) according to the southern lineage of Chinese Chan, the sixth patriarch of the school, now universally regarded as such (see Shen Xiu)

Hui Yuan — (334-417) founder of the Pure Land Society in 402, regarded as the first Chinese patriarch of the Pure Land school

Hwaŏm school — Korean counterpart of the Chinese Hua Yan school

Ieyasu — Tokugawa Ieyasu (1542-1616), the third of a series of allied generals who overthrew the Ashikaga shogunate, founder of the Tokugawa regime (see Hideyoshi and Nobunaga)

immaterialism — the philosophical position that the universe is a projection of the mind rather than a material reality

Indo-Europeans — ancestors of most of the racial and linguistic groups from Europe through to northern India

Indonesia — the cluster of islands between Southeast Asia and Australia

Indravarman III — the first Theravādin king of Angkor

Indus Valley — valley of the Indus River, in present-day Pakistan, in which an ancient Indian civilization lived in the third millennium BCE

Inner Mongolia — southern, Chinese Mongolia

Irrawaddy — a river in Burma

Jain — a follower of Jainism

Jainism — a pre-Vedic, pre-Buddhist, yogic religious tradition of India

Jammu and Kashmir — northernmost state of India, partially disputed by Pakistan; in ancient times, Gandhāra and Kashmir

Jātaka Tales — fanciful scriptures of Theravāda Buddhism recounting the supposed lives of the Buddha (usually as an animal) prior to his birth as Siddhattha Gotama

Java — an Indonesian island, once Buddhist and Hindu, now primarily Muslim

Jayavarman I — (d. 514) the greatest of the kings of Funan and its last powerful ruler

Jayavarman II — founder of the Khmer kingdom of Angkor in approximately 800 CE

Jayavarman VII — (r. 1181-1218) first Buddhist king of Angkor, builder of the Mahāyāna temple-mountain known as Bayon and the grand Khmer capital Angkor Thom

Jayavarman VIII — (r. until 1295) the last of the old dynasty of Angkor, probably a Hindu, usurped by Indravarman III, the first Theravādin king of Angkor

Jebtsundamba Khutuktu — one of a series of eight powerful, reincarnating lamas in Mongolia from 1649 to 1924 (Tib. rJe bTsun Dam-pa)

Jesuits — a Roman Catholic religious order founded by Ignatius Loyola in 1534, renowned for their educational achievement and missionary zeal

Jetavana — Sri Lankan monastery and lineage that occupied a middle doctrinal position between the liberal Abhayagiri and the conservative Mahāvihāra, founded by King Mahāsena (r. 334-61), abolished by Parakrama Bāhu I (r. 1153-86)

jhāna — a meditational absorption or "trance" (Skt. *dhyāna*)

Jin (Chin) dynasty (1115-1234) — a minor Manchurian dynasty in China that overlapped with the dominant Song (Sung) dynasty (960-1279)

Jing Tu (Ching T'u) school — Pure Land school of Chinese Buddhism (see Jap. Jōdo and Jōdo Shinshū)

Jōdo — Japanese counterpart of the Jing Tu or Pure Land sect of Chinese Buddhism, generally reckoned to have been established in Japan with the publication in 1175 of the treatise *Senchaku-shū* by Hōnen (1133-1212)

Jōdo Shinshū — the "True Pure Land" sect of Japanese Buddhism (no Chinese counterpart), founded by Shinran (1173-1262), a disciple of Hōnen

Jōjitsu school — a Japanese branch of the Chinese Ju She or Abhidharma school of Nikāya Buddhism, founded in Japan in 625 by the Korean monk Ekan (see Kusha school)

Jo Khang Temple — Buddhist temple in central Lhasa supposedly founded by King Srong bTsan sGam-po

Ju She (Chü She) school — Chinese school of Buddhism based on the *Abhidharma Kośa* of Vasubandhu (Chi. *ju she* = Skt. *kośa*, "treasure house")

Kadampa [bKa' gDams-pa] — reformed sect of Tibetan Buddhism founded by the Indian monk Atīśa (982-1054)

Kagyudpa [bKa' rGyud-pa] — sect of Tibetan Buddhism systematized by sGam-po-pa (1079-1153) fifth in the line of founding masters (after Tilopa, Nāropa, Marpa, and Milarepa)

Kamakura Buddhism — the four sects of Japanese Buddhism that developed during the Kamakura period — Jōdo, Jōdo Shinshū, Nichiren, and Zen

Kamakura period — (1185-1333) the period of Japanese history during which warlords of the Minamoto clan exercised actual authority over Japan, even though the emperor continued nominally to rule in Kyōto

Kamalaśila — (c. 700-750) pupil of Śāntarakshita, a monk from India who successfully argued the Indian side in a great debate between Chinese and Indian Buddhism held in about 792 at the Sam-ye Monastery in Tibet

kami — in Shintō a deity or spirit, but also an impersonal, supernatural force thought to inhabit certain objects, natural phenomena, and people

Kammu — (r. 781-806) Japanese emperor responsible for moving the capital to Kyōto, a patron of Saichō and Tendai Buddhism

Kampuchea — see Cambodia

Kandy — the former highland capital of Sri Lanka

Kanishka — (r. 78-123 CE) patron of Buddhism and the first great emperor of the Kushan dynasty in India and Central Asia

Kanjur [bKa' 'Gyur] — section Tibetan Buddhist which contains sacred teachings attributed to the Buddha, his immediate disciples and to mythological sources (see Tanjur)

Kapilavastu — the site of the Buddha's early life, the actual location of the ancient city is in dispute between India and Nepal

Kargil — primarily Muslim district of Ladakh

karma — "volitional action," supposed to have good or bad consequences in this or a future life

Karmapa sect — a subsect of the Kagyudpa sect of Tibetan Buddhism

Karmapa, first — (1110-93), one of the chief disciples of sGam-po-pa, first in a reincarnating lineage of Karmapas that continues to the present day

Karmapa, sixteenth — (1923-1981) one of the foremost propagators of Tibetan Buddhism in the West

Kashgar — a city-state on the Silk Road

Kashmir — an ancient state northwest of India (covering roughly what is now officially known as Jammu and Kashmir) in which Buddhism was prominent from Aśokan times (see Gandhāra)

Kathmandu Valley — central valley of modern-day Nepal, the territory of ancient Nepal

kāya — (P. and Skt.) body

Kegon school — Japanese counterpart of the Chinese Hua Yan or Avataṃsaka school, founded in Japan by a Chinese missionary known to the Japanese as Dōsen (702-60)

Khmer — the primary ethnic group of Cambodia

Khmer Rouge — "Red Khmers," radical communists under General Pol Pot who ruled Cambodia from 1975 to 1979 and virtually eradicated Buddhism there

Khotan — a city-state on the Silk Road

Khri Srong lDe bTsan [Ti Song De Tsan] — (742-98) the fifth successor to King Srong bTsan sGam-po, remembered as the great restorer of Buddhism in Tibet (after its persecution by King gLang Dar-ma); he was probably the first truly Buddhist king of Tibet

Khuddaka Nikāya — miscellaneous section of the Pāli canon

khutuktu — Mongolian term for a reincarnating lama

Kinnaur — largely Buddhist district in the modern Indian state of Himachal Pradesh

kLong Chen-pa — (1308-63) long resident in Bhutan, the foremost systematizer of the Nyingmapa sect of Tibetan Buddhism

kōan — (Jap.) a meditational riddle employed in Rinzai Zen (Chi. Lin Ji

Chan) Buddhism (Chi. *gong an* or *kung an*)

Kōbō Daishi — (773-835) see Kūkai

Koguryŏ — (c. 12-668 CE) the first Korean state, situated in the north of the peninsula

Korea — the peninsula between China and Japan

Koryŏ — (918-1392) Korean kingdom descended from Koguryŏ, in name and territory the direct ancestor of modern Korea

Krishṇa — Hindu deity, supposedly an incarnation of Vishṇu, who appears in the *Bhagavad Gītā*

Kublai Khan (d. 1294) founder of the Mongol or Yuan dynasty of China (1280-1368)

Kucha — a city-state on the Silk Road

Kuddhaka Nikāya — the "Miscellaneous" section of the Pāli canon (see *Avadāna*)

Kūkai — (773-835) better known as Kōbō Daishi, founder of the Shingon (Tantric) school of Buddhism in Japan

Kulu — a district in the modern Indian state of Himachal Pradesh

Kumārajīva — (344-413) Central Asian monk from Kucha, active in China, the most illustrious translator of Buddhist scriptures into Chinese

Kun dGa' sNying-po — (1092-1158) systematizer of the teachings brought back from India by 'Brog-mi, thereby a founder of the Sakyapa sect of Tibetan Buddhism

Kusha school — the Japanese counterpart of the Chinese Ju She or Abhidharma school of Nikāya Buddhism; like its Chinese counterpart, named after and based upon the *Abhidharma Kośa* of Vasubandhu; *kośa* (Skt. "treasure house") = *ju she* = *kusha*

Kushan dynasty — (78-225 CE) Buddhist rulers of northern India and a large part of Central Asia

Kyanzittha — usurper of the Burmese throne in 1086, probably the first Theravādin king to rule all Burma

Kyo school — artificially unified "Doctrinal" school of Korean Buddhism

Kyōto — capital of Japan from 794 to 1868, though the actual seat of imperial power only from 794 to 1185

Ladakh — a largely Buddhist district of the Indian state of Jammu and Kashmir

Lahaul Spiti — a largely Buddhist district in the modern Indian state of Himachal Pradesh

Lalita-vistara — an early Mahāyāna scripture dealing with the life of the Buddha

lama — (Tib. *bLama;* Skt. *guru*) conventionally, a Tibetan Buddhist monk, strictly speaking an eminent monk (see dGe sLong)

Lam Te — Vietnamese for Lin Ji or Rinzai Zen Buddhism

Laos — Theravāda Buddhist country of Southeast Asia

Lao Zi (Lao Tsu) — (sixth century BCE) quasi-historical founder of the Chinese religion Daoism

Latter Koguryŏ — (901-18) Korean kingdom (see Koguryŏ and Koryŏ)

Latter Le dynasty — the fifth Vietnamese dynasty, which ruled from 1428 until the end of the eighteenth century, though only nominally after the mid-sixteenth century (see Nguyen and Trinh)

Latter Paekche — (832-936) Korean kingdom (see Paekche)

Le dynasty — (981-1009) the second Vietnamese dynasty, during which the first complete Chinese Tripiṭaka was imported, establishing the scriptural basis of Vietnamese Buddhism

Leh — primarily Buddhist district of Ladakh

Lepchas — the indigenous inhabitants of Sikkim

Lha — (Tib.) a god

Lha-pa — an extinct subsect of the Kagyudpa, once powerful in Bhutan

Lhasa — the capital of Tibet

Liao dynasty — (907-1124) a minor Mongol dynasty in China that overlapped with the dominant Song (Sung) dynasty

Licchavi dynasty of Nepal — though sympathetic to Buddhism, a primarily Hindu dynasty of the Kathmandu Valley that ruled from 704 until the eleventh century

Ligdan Khan — (1603-34) Mongol chieftain under whom the Kanjur was translated into Mongolian in 113 volumes

Lin Ji (Lin Chi) — one of the two surviving lineages of Chinese Chan Buddhism, transmitted to Japan as Rinzai Zen

Lokakshema — (second century) a Kushan, traditionally regarded as the founder of Mahāyāna Buddhism in China

Lotus Sūtra — an early Mahāyāna scripture encouraging devotionalism

Lü school — the Vinaya school of Chinese Buddhism

Luang Phrabang — capital of Laos from the fourteenth to the sixteenth century (see Vien Chan)

Lumbinī — birthplace of the Buddha, in what is today southern Nepal

Luoyang — (also Loyang) an ancient Chinese capital (see Xi'an)

Ly dynasty — (1010-1225) the third Vietnamese dynasty, which spanned the golden age of Vietnamese independence and prosperity

Madhyamaka — the "dialectical" school of Mahāyāna Buddhist philosophy founded by Nāgārjuna

Mahābodhi Society — founded by Anagārika Dharmapāla in Sri Lanka in 1891, an organization dedicated to preserving Buddhist holy sites and spreading Buddhism in the West

Mahāmudra — "Great Gesture" tantric tradition practiced by the

Kagyudpa sect of Tibetan Buddhism

Mahānikāya — the largest order of the Thai Saṅgha, tracing back to the Mahāvihāra lineage of Sri Lanka

Mahāsaṅghika — the group of liberal monks who split from the conservative Elders in about 350 BCE and became the forebears of Mahāyāna Buddhism

Mahāvaṃsa — quasi-historical Buddhist chronicle compiled in Sri Lanka in the fifth century (see Cūlavaṃsa)

Mahāvastu — Mahāyāna scripture relating the legendary life of the Buddha

Mahāvihāra — "Great Monastery," the first Buddhist monastery and ordination lineage established in Sri Lanka and the ultimate source of all existing Theravāda ordination lineages

Mahāyāna — the "Great Vehicle" form of Buddhism now practiced in Tibet, China (tenuously), Korea, Mongolia, Japan, Vietnam and some Himalayan regions to the north of India (see Theravāda and Nikāya Buddhism)

Mahinda — Aśoka's son, Buddhist monk and head of the first Buddhist mission to Sri Lanka in c. 250 BCE

Maitreya — the future Buddha

Maitreya Society — a Chinese lay Buddhist group that looked to the coming of Maitreya (the future Buddha) as a messianic incentive to rebellion (see White Cloud and White Lotus Societies)

Majjhima Nikāya — the collection of middle-length teachings of the Buddha in the Pāli canon

Malaysia — once Buddhist, now a primarily Muslim country forming the southernmost extreme of the Southeast Asian peninsula

Malla dynasty of Nepal — Hindu rulers of Kathmandu Valley from about 1200 to 1768

Manchu — see Manchurian

Manchurian — Mongol racial group originating from Manchuria, territory northeast of China

maṇḍala — a mystical diagram or painting

Mandalay — a city in northern Burma

Mañjuśrī — bodhisattva of wisdom

mantra — a short, repetitive incantation or prayer

Mao Zedong (Mao Tse-tung) — (1893-1976) leader of the Chinese communists who seized power in 1949

Marco Polo — (c. 1254-1324) Venetian traveler who wrote a popular account of his extensive travels in Asia

Marpa — (1012-96) first Tibetan master of the Kagyudpa lineage of Tibetan Buddhism, disciple of the Indian tantric master Nāropa

Maurya dynasty — (270-185 BCE) the Indian dynasty to which Aśoka belonged

Meiji restoration — (1868-1945) the period of Japanese history (between the fall of the Tokugawa regime and the end of World War II) when the emperor wielded real power for the first time since 1185

Mekong — a river forming most of the border between Laos and Thailand, flowing through Cambodia, with its delta in Vietnam

Menandros — (r. circa 155-130 BCE), Greek king of northwesten India, reputedly a Buddhist (P. Milinda)

mendicant — a wandering holy person who lives by begging

metaphysics — philosophical speculation concerning the ultimate reality or realities upon which the physical universe is based

miko — in Japanese Shintō, a shaman, almost always female, thought to be able to communicate with and influence the supernatural spirit world

Milarepa [Mi-la Ras-pa] — (1040-1123) disciple of Marpa, thereby the second Tibetan master in the tantric lineage that gave rise to the Kagyudpa sect of Tibetan Buddhism

Milinda — (r. circa 155-130 B.C.) see Menandros

Milinda Pañha — *Questions of King Milinda* a Theravāda scripture purportedly recording a famous debate between the Greek king Milinda and the Buddhist monk Nāgasena

Minamoto — Japanese clan that dominated the nation during the Kamakura period (1185-1333)

Mindon — (r. 1853-78) reformist king of Burma who convened a fifth Buddhist Council (in the tradition of Aśoka and Kanishka) to create a modern, revised edition of the Pāli Tipiṭaka

Ming, Emperor — (r. 58-75 CE) Han dynasty emperor traditionally said to be responsible for the introduction of Buddhism to China

Ming dynasty — (1368-1644) the so-called "enlightened," ethnic Chinese dynasty that replaced the Mongol dynasty

Mohenjo Daro — one of the two major cities of the Indus Valley civilization (see Harappa)

moksha — final, spiritual release from suffering and rebirth within saṃsāra

Mon — the earliest known inhabitants of present-day Burma and Thailand, largely responsible for the transmission into Southeast Asia of Indian influences in general and of Theravāda Buddhism in particular

mondō — in Zen Buddhism, question-answer exchanges between master and pupil, intended to test progress and precipitate enlightenment

Mongkut — see Rāma IV

Mongolia — homeland of the Mongols, an ill-defined area north of China (see Inner and Outer Mongolia)

Mou Zi (Mou Tzu) — early (Han dynasty) Buddhist treatise, named after its author Mou Zi, appearing to be a defence of Buddhism against Confucian critics

Mt. Fuji — a volcanic cone in Japan regarded as sacred by Shintō and some forms of Japanese Buddhsim

Mt. Hiei — a mountain near Kyōto on which the Tendai school established an enormous complex of temples as its headquarters

Mt. Kōya — a mountain about fifty miles from Kyōto on which the Shingon school established a headquarters and temple complex that came to rival the Tendai complex on Mt. Hiei

mudra — mystical hand gestures believed to have supernatural power

Mukhoja — traditionally the first Buddhist monk in Silla, he arrived during the reign of King Nulchi (r. 417-458)

mundane — associated with the material world

Muromachi period — see Ashikaga period

Nāgārjuna — (second century CE) founder of the Madhyamaka school of Mahāyāna Buddhism

Nālandā — ancient Buddhist University in present-day state of Bihar, India

Namgyal dynasty — rulers of Sikkim from 1642 to 1975

Nam-myōhō-renge-kyō — Japanese for "Homage to the *Lotus Sūtra*," the repeated prayer of Nichiren Buddhists

Namu Amida Butsu — Japanese for "Homage to Amitābha Buddha," the repeated prayer of the Jōdo and Jōdo Shinshū sects

Nan Zhao — (Nan Chao) an ancient Thai kingdom that occupied territory in the present Chinese province of Yunnan

Nara — capital of Japan from 710 to 794

Nara period — (593-784) the period of Japanese history during which the city of Nara was the focus of Japanese civilization, especially the absorption of Buddhism and Chinese culture

Nara schools of Buddhism — six schools of Japanese Buddhism founded during the Nara period: the Sanron, Jōjitsu, Kusha, Hossō, Kegon, and Ritsu schools

Nāropa — (1016-1100) abbot of Nālandā (some sources say Vikramaśilā) University in India until 1057, thereafter a member of the founding lineage of the Kagyudpa sect of Tibetan Buddhism, a disciple of Tilopa

nembutsu — the phrase *"Namu Amida Butsu,"*

neo-Confucianism — Confucianism with a Buddhist admixture

neo-Daoism — Daoism with a Buddhist admixture

Nepal — Hindu and Buddhist country in the southeastern Himalayas

Newars — earliest known inhabitants of Nepal, centered upon the Kathmandu Valley, today numbering only about half a million

New Tantras — Tantric texts that are recognized by all sects of Tibetan Buddhism and contained in the Kanjur, as opposed to the "Old Tantras" of the Nyingmapa

Nguyen family of Vietnam — de facto rulers of southern Vietnam from the mid-sixteenth to the eighteenth century

nibbāna — (P.) cessation of suffering and rebirth, the ultimate goal of Buddhism (Skt. nirvāṇa)

Nichiren — (1222-82) founder of the Nichiren sect of Japanese Buddhism

Nichiren Buddhism — a Japanese form of Buddhism founded by Nichiren (1222-82) which split into several sub-sects all characterized by repetition of the phrase *Nam-myōhō-renge-kyō* — "Homage to the *Lotus Sūtra*"

Nichiren Shōshū — a subsect of the Nichiren sect founded in the thirteenth century, shortly after Nichiren's death, by his disciple Nikkō, now the largest single Buddhist denomination in Japan

Nikāya — one of the five sections of the Sutta Piṭaka (collection of discourses) of Theravāda Buddhism

Nikāya Buddhism — the several schools of non-Mahāyāna Buddhism, now represented only by the Theravāda (see Āgama Buddhism)

Nine Mountain schools — a collective designation for the nine schools of Korean Sŏn (Zen) Buddhism, because of the location of their principal monasteries on nine sacred mountains in Korea

Nirmāṇa-kāya — the physical, manifest body of the Buddha (see Dharma-kāya)

nirvāṇa — (Skt.) cessation of suffering and rebirth, the ultimate goal of Buddhism (P. *nibbāna*)

Noble Eightfold Path — see Eightfold Path

Noble Truths — the four fundamental doctrinal propositions of Buddhism: 1) Mundane existence is suffering (P. *dukkha*, Skt. *duḥkha*). 2) Desire is the cause of suffering. 3) Nirvāṇa is the cessation of suffering. 4) Buddhism provides a practical method for realizing this awakening (see Eightfold Path).

Nobunaga — Oda Nobunaga (1534-1582), the first of a series of allied generals who overthrew the Ashikaga shogunate (see Hideyoshi and Ieyasu)

Nulchi — (r. 417-458) according to Korean tradition, king of Silla when Buddhism was introduced

Nyi-ma mGon — see sKyid lDe Nyi-ma mGon

Nyingmapa [rNying-ma-pa] — the "Ancient Ones," the first sect of Tibetan Buddhism, reputedly founded by Padma-sambhava

Olcott, Henry Steel — (1832-1907) co-founder, with Madame Blavatsky, of the Theosophical Society

Old Tantras — tantric texts preserved by the Nyingmapa sect of Tibetan Buddhism, as opposed to the "New Tantras" preserved in the standard Kanjur

Outer Mongolia — northern, Russian Mongolia

Padma-sambhava — Tantric master credited with having decisively won Tibet over to Buddhism during the reign of King Khri Srong lDe bTsan (742-98)

Paekche — (c. 200-660) the second Korean state to emerge, situated in the southwest of the peninsula

Pagan — the ancient capital of Burma established by King Anuruddha (r. 1044-77) and still famed for its magnificent Buddhist ruins

pagoda — a monument (usually Buddhist), associated primarily with China and Japan, in the form of a tower with protruding eaves on each story

Pahlavas — (Parthians) Iranian peoples who, along with the related Śakas, dominated northwest India from c. 100 BCE-75 CE

Pāla dynasty — ruled present-day Bihar and Bengal from about 650 to 950, the last royal patrons of Buddhism in India after the death of Emperor Harsha in 647

P'algwanhoe — a great Buddhist ceremony of Silla to bless the departed spirits of soldiers

Pāli — the dialect of Sanskrit in which the scriptures of Theravāda Buddhism are preserved

Pāli canon — the scriptures of Theravāda Buddhism

Pāli Text Society — founded in London in 1881 by T.W. Rhys Davids, the primary publisher of the Pāli canon in Roman text and English translation

palladium — a sacred image or object believed to protect a nation supernaturally

Panchen Lamas — established by the fifth Dalai Lama, a second reincarnating lineage of Gelugpa lamas, headquartered at the Tashilhunpo Monastery in Shigatse, Tibet

Paṇḍu — a Hindu kingdom of south India (see Chola)

Parakrama Bāhu I — (r. 1153-86) Sri Lankan king who reunited the island and abolished the Abhayagiri and Jetavana monasteries, giving the Mahāvihāra lineage a monopoly on the island's Buddhism

Parakrama Bāhu II — (r. 1236-70) the last great Buddhist monarch of Sri Lanka, recaptured Polonnaruwa from the Tamils in 1244

Paramārtha — (c. 498-569) the great Indian translator who was primarily responsible for the introduction of Vijñānavāda (Consciousness school) ideas into China

Parhae — a minor Korean state which endured from 698 until 926 as a buffer state, subservient to the Tang dynasty, between China and independent Silla

Parthians — see Pahlavas

Patan — ancient Buddhist city of Nepal, near Kathmandu

paṭiccasamuppāda — (P.) see "conditioned arising" (Skt. *pratītya-samutpāda*)

patriarch — in Buddhism, one of the early leaders of a sect or lineage, particularly Chan or Zen

Peking — see Beijing

People's Republic of China — communist China, founded in 1949

Phag-mo Gru ["Phag-mo-du"] — Tibetan dynasty (c. 1350-1480), named after the Phag-mo Gru branch of the Kagyudpa sect of Tibetan Buddhism

'Phags-pa — (1235-1280) Tibetan Buddhist scholar of the Sakyapa sect, nephew of Sakya Paṇḍita, inventor of the Mongolian script, and vice-roy of Tibet under Kublai Khan

Pha-jo — (c. 1208-76) quasi-historical figure of Bhutan, supposed to have established there the Drugpa subsect of Tibetan Buddhism

Phayao — an ancient Thai capital

Phnom Penh — capital of Cambodia since the fifteenth century

Phra Bang — the palladium of Laos, a Buddha image brought to the country from Angkor by the teacher of King Fa Ngum

Phra Keo — Thailand's most sacred Buddha image, captured from Laos in 1778 and now housed in the Wat Phra Keo in Bangkok

Phun Tshog — (r. 1642-70) the first Chogyal of Sikkim, founder of the Namgyal dynasty

Plutarch — first-century Greek biographer

Podŏk — Korean monk who founded the Yŏlban (Nirvāṇa) school in Silla

Polonnaruwa — primary capital of Sri Lanka from the eleventh to the thirteenth century

Pŏmnang — (seventh century) founder in Korea of Sŏn (Zen) Buddhism, studied in China under the third successor to Bodhidharma himself

Pŏphŭng — (r. 514-540) according to Korean tradition, the first Buddhist king of Silla

Pŏpsŏng school — see Haedong school

Prajñā Pāramitā — the "Perfection of Wisdom" literature which forms the basis of the Madhyamaka school of Mahāyāna Buddhism

Prakrit — any one of the several dialects of Sanskrit

Prāsaṅgika — one of the two branches of the Madhyamaka school of

Mahāyāna Buddhism, associated with Nāgārjuna, Āryadeva and Candrakīrti (see Svātantrika)

pratītyasamutpāda — (Skt.) see "conditioned arising" (P. paṭicca-samuppāda)

pre-canonical Buddhism — a very early form of Buddhism which supposedly existed before the Mahāsaṅghika schism of approximately 350 BCE

precepts, five — (pañca-sīla or sikkhā-pada) ethical rules enjoined upon Theravāda Buddhist laypeople: avoidance of 1) violence toward anything that breathes, 2) taking that which is not freely given, 3) false, harsh or harmful speech, 4) sexual misconduct, and 5) abuse of drugs or alcohol.

principality — a state ruled by a prince

Pudgalavādins — "those who affirm the person," a school of Nikāya Buddhism that came so close to affirming a soul that they were regarded as heretics by all other schools of Buddhism

Pure Land — a Buddhist paradise; a school of Buddhism devoted to gaining rebirth in this paradise (Skt. Sukhāvatī, Chi. Jing Tu)

Pyu — a Tibetan people prominent in Burma from about 650 to 850 CE

Qing (Ch'ing) dynasty — (1644-1912) the most powerful Manchurian dynasty of China

Rāma I — (r. 1782-1809) the first king of the Chakri dynasty of Thailand, initiated modern reform of Thai Buddhism

Rāma II — (r. 1809-24) second Chakri king of Thailand

Rāma III — (r. 1824-51) third Chakri king, sent delegations to Sri Lanka in 1840 and 1843 to secure authoritative versions of the Pāli canon in order to rectify the Thai canon

Rāma IV — (r. 1851-68) also known as Mongkut, the fourth and arguably the greatest Chakri king, a contemporary of King Mindon of Burma (r. 1853-78)

Rāma V — (r. 1868-1910) also known as Chulalongkorn, the last of the great Chakri reformers of Thai Buddhism

Rāmādipati — founder of the Thai kingdom of Ayutthaya in 1350

Rāma Khamhaeng — (died c. 1299) recognized as king in 1287 by an alliance of the three principal kingdoms of the Thai (Chiang Mai, Sukhothai and Phayao) he extended his power over most of the area of present-day Thailand, in effect founding the nation

Ramana Nikāya — the branch of the Sri Lankan Saṅgha that serves the lower castes, founded in 1863 by a delegation sent to Burma (see Siam and Amarapura Nikāyas)

regent — one who rules as a monarch without having the title

Republic of China — now confined to Taiwan, formerly (1912-49) mainland China (see People's Republic of China)

Republican period — (1912-49) the period of Chinese history between the last traditional dynasty and the advent of communism

Rig Veda — the primary scripture of the Indo-Europeans who migrated into India in the second millennium BCE

Rin Chen bZang-po — (958-1055) a Buddhist monk of Western Tibet renowned for his prolific translation activities, a contemporary of Atīśa

Rinzai — Japanese counterpart of the Chinese Lin Ji (Lin Chi) tradition of Zen (Chi. Chan) Buddhism (see Sōtō)

Ritsu school — Japanese counterpart of the Chinese Lü or Vinaya school, established in Japan in 753 by the Chinese monk known in Japan as Ganjin (688-763)

rNying-ma-pa — see Nyingmapa

Ryōbu Shintō — "Double Aspect" Shintō, a syncretistic movement initiated by Gyōgi (670-749) which sought to identify Buddhist and Shintō deities and thus to harmonize the two religions

Saichō — (766-822) better known as Dengyō Daishi, the founder of Tendai Buddhsim in Japan

Saigon — (also Ho Chin Minh City) the major city of southern Vietnam

Śailendra dynasty — eighth-century Buddhist dynasty on Java, builders of Borobudur

Śaivite — worshipper of the Hindu god Śiva

Śakas — (Scythians) Iranian peoples who, along with the related Pahlavas, dominated northwest India from about 100 BCE to about 75 CE

Sakyapa [Sa-sKya-pa] — sect of Tibetan Buddhism, founded by 'Brog-mi [Dog-mi — 992-1072] and emphasizing tantric practices

Sakya Paṇḍita — (d. 1251) the Sakyapa scholar appointed viceroy of Tibet by Godan Khan

Śālistamba Sūtra — the *Stalk of Rice Sūtra*, a very early Mahāyāna text on *pratītyasamutpāda*

Salween — a river in Burma

samādhi — meditational concentration

samatha — calmness meditation

saṃsāra — the realm of repeated death and rebirth, the mundane world

Sam-ye [bSam-yas] — the first Buddhist monastery in Tibet, founded by King Khri Srong lDe bTsan (742-98)

Saṃyutta Nikāya — the section of the Pāli canon arranged according to subject matter

Saṅgha — Buddhist community of monks and nuns

Saṅghamittā — Aśoka's daughter, supposed to have brought to Sri Lanka the nun's Saṅgha and a cutting from the original Bodhi tree

342   Buddhism: A History

San Jie Jiao (San Chieh Chiao) — Three Ages school, founded in the sixth
    century by Xin Xing (Hsin Hsing), the only important school of Bud-
    dhism developed in China that failed to take root in Japan
Śaṅkara — (eighth century) first major systematizer of classical Hinduism
    and founder of the Advaita (non-dual) Vedānta school
San Lun school — school of "Three Treatises" (Chi. *san lun*), the Chinese
    Madhyamaka school (Jap. Sanron), based on three works translated
    by Kumārajīva: Nāgārjuna's *Madhyamaka Kārikā* and two works by
    his disciple Āryadeva
Sanron school — Japanese counterpart of the Chinese San Lun or
    Madhyamaka school of Buddhism
Sanskrit — classical language of ancient India
Śāntarakshita — (c. 680-740) an eminent Indian monk (author of the
    Tattva-saṃgraha) who is credited with having masterminded the
    ascendancy of Indian-style Budhism in Tibet under King King Khri
    Srong lDe bTsan (742-98)
Śāntideva — (eighth century) Indian Buddhist monk and author of the
    Bodhicaryāvatāra and *Śikshā Samuccaya*
Sarvāstivāda — a school of Nikāya Buddhism, split from the Sthaviravāda
    in approximately 350 BCE
sati — (P.) mindfulness meditation
Sautrāntikas — "those concerned only with the sūtras," a school of
    Nikāya Buddhism that broke away from the Sarvāstivāda specifically,
    but rejected the Abhidharma and commentarial literature of all
    schools
schism — the splitting of a religious tradition into two or more factions
Schwegon Nikāya — a strict Burmese order of Theravāda monks formed
    under King Mindon (r. 1853-78) as an alternative to the long-
    established and much larger Sudhamma Nikāya of Burma
Scythians — see Śakas
Senchaku-shū — the foundational treatise of the Jōdo or Pure Land sect
    in Japan, written by Hōnen (1133-1212)
Sera — largest monastery of the Gelugpa sect of Tibetan Buddhism,
    founded in the early fifteenth century near Lhasa
sGam-po-pa — (1079-1153) fifth in the line of founding masters of the
    Kagyudpa sect of Tibetan Buddhism (after Tilopa, Nāropa, Marpa,
    and Milarepa), systematizer of the sect's teachings in his *Jewel Orna-
    ment of Liberation*
sGrol-ma — see Dolma
Shaku, Sōen — see Sōen Shaku
shaman — general term for a person thought to have developed the
    ability to communicate with and influence the spirit world (see *miko*)

shamanism — religion based upon the function of shamans

Shen Hui — (670-762) disciple of Hui Neng, orchestrated the ascendancy of the southern school of Chinese Chan Buddhism

Shen Xiu (Shen Hsiu) — (600-706) according to the northern lineage of Chinese Chan, the sixth patriarch of Chan or Zen (see Hui Neng)

Shigatse — the second largest city in Tibet, some 150 miles west of Lhasa

Shingon school — Japanese counterpart to the Chinese Zhen Yan or Tantric school, founded in Japan by Kūkai or Kōbō Daishi (773-835)

Shinin — one of the two Korean branches of the Chinese Zhen Yan (Chen Yen) or Tantric school, better known by the Japanese name Shingon, (see Chinŏn)

Shinran — (1173-1262) disciple of Hōnen and founder of the Jōdo Shinshū or True Pure Land sect of Japanese Buddhism

Shintō — "Way of the Gods," the indigenous, pre-Buddhist religion of Japan

shōgun — a Japanese warlord, associated with the Kamakura and Ashikaga periods, who exercised real political power by virtue of military might, while in theory the emperor ruled the nation

shogunate — the office of shōgun

Shōtoku — (573-621) Japanese prince who came to power in 593 and established Buddhism in Japan

Siam Nikāya — the branch of the Sri Lankan Saṅgha that serves the higher castes, founded in 1753 by a delegation sent to Thailand (Siam) in order to re-establish proper ordination on the island (see Amarapura and Ramana Nikāyas)

Siddhārtha — (Skt.) the given name of the Buddha (P. Siddhattha)

Siddhatta — (P.) the given name of the Buddha (Skt. Siddhārtha)

Sikh — Indian religion combining elements of Hinduism and Islam

Sikkim — a Himalayan Buddhist kingdom between Nepal and Bhutan, became the twenty-second state of India by referendum in 1975

Silk Road — the ancient trade route between China and the Mediterranean world

Silla — (c. 350-935) the third Korean state to emerge, situated in the southeast of the peninsula

Silla period — (668-935) the period of Korean history when the kingdom of Silla was dominant

Śiva — Hindu deity associated with yoga and asceticism

skillful means — (P. and Skt. *upāya*) specifically, the technique of tailoring the difficulty of teachings to the intellectual level of the audience; generally, any effective method of imparting spiritual knowledge

sKyid lDe Nyi-ma mGon — great-grandson of the Tibetan king gLang

Dar-ma, consolidated the Himalayan region of Western Tibet sometime around 950

Sōen Shaku — (1858-1919) Japanese master representing Zen Buddhism
at the 1893 World's Parliament of Religions in Chicago, teacher of the
teachers primarily responsible for Zen Buddhism's introduction to
the Western world, primarily D.T. Suzuki

Sōka Gakkai — a powerful political and economic movement in Japan
that characterizes itself as the lay organization of the Nichiren Shōshū
sect

Sŏn — (Kor.) Korean counterpart of Japanese Zen and Chinese Chan
Buddhism

Song (Sung) dynasty — (960-1279) the primary Chinese dynasty of its
time, but it overlapped with the Liao and Jin dynasties

Sosurim — (r. 371-84) according to tradition, king of Koguryŏ when Buddhism was introduced to the Korean peninsula in 372

Sōtō — branch of Japanese Zen derived from the Chinese Cao Dong
(Ts'ao Tung) branch of Chan Buddhism (see Rinzai)

sPrul-sKu — see Tulku

Śrikshetra — (c. 650-850 CE) the ancient Pyu state in Burma

Sri Lanka — island-nation off the southern tip of India, the primary homeland of Theravāda Buddhism

Śri Vijaya — a blanket term for several primarily Buddhist (though Hindu-
influenced) states that developed on the Malay Peninsula and the
islands of Sumatra and Java from about 600 to 800 CE

Srong bTsan sGam-po [Song Tsan Gampo] — (r. circa 627-50) traditionally, the Tibetan king under whom Buddhism was introduced to
Tibet

Sthavira — (Skt.) see Elder (P. Thera)

Sthaviravāda — (Skt.) "School of the Elders," the oldest school of Nikāya
Buddhism (P. Theravāda)

stūpa — a dome-shaped Buddhist monument

Sudhamma Nikāya — the largest order of the Burmese Saṅgha (see
Schwegon Nikāya)

Sui dynasty — (581-618) the northern "barbarian" dynasty responsible for
the reunification of China in 589

Sukhothai — ancient Thai capital, prominent from 1250 to 1350

Sumatra — an Indonesian island, once Buddhist and Hindu, now primarily Muslim

Sumisan — "Sumi Mountain," the ninth and last school of Korean Sŏn
(Zen), founded in 911 by Iŏm

Sundo — according to tradition, the first Buddhist monk in Korea, said to
have arrived in Koguryŏ from northern China in 372 CE

Śuṅga dynasty — (185-85 BCE) an early Indian dynasty favoring Brahmanism
śūnyatā — see emptiness
supra-mundane — transcending the material world
Sūryavaṃsa — (r. 1637-1694) the last king of a unified Lao state
Sūryavarman II — (r. 1113-50) Khmer king who built Angkor Wat
sūtra — (Skt.) a discourse of the Buddha or one of his foremost disciples
(P. sutta)
Sūtra in Forty-two Sections — traditionally the first Buddhist sūtra available in China
sutta — (P.) a discourse of the Buddha or one of his foremost disciples
(Skt. sūtra)
Sutta Nipāta — a very ancient Theravāda text in the *Kuddhaka Nikāya*
Sutta Piṭaka — the section of the Pāli canon containing the discourses of
the Buddha and some of his foremost disciples
Suzuki, Daisetz Teitaro — (1870-1966) a pupil of Sōen Shaku, arguably
the most influential figure in establishing Zen in North America
svabhava — (Skt.) self-existence, inherent nature
Svātantrika — one of the two branches of the Madhyamaka school of
Mahāyāna Buddhism, associated with Bhāvaviveka (see Prāsaṅgika)
syncretism — the combination in one religion of elements derived from
two or more religions
T'aejo — (r. 1392-1398) founder of the Chosŏn dynasty of Korea (see Yi
Sŏng-gye)
Taiwan — an island off the coast of China to which the Guo Min Dang
fled after their defeat in 1949, and which remains to the present day
an independent nation claiming to represent the legitimate government of China (see Republic of China)
Tai Wu Di (T'ai Wu Ti) — (r. 424-51) Chinese emperor of the Northern
Wei dynasty who ordered the first Chinese persecution of Buddhism
in 446
Tai Zong (T'ai Tsung) — (r. 618-26)) first emperor of the Tang dynasty,
also known as Gao Zi (Kao Tsu); another Tai Zong (r. 626-49) was
the second Tang emperor
Takauji — (r. 1336-1358) the first Ashikaga shōgun
Takla Makan desert — impassable area of far western China skirted by
the northern and southern branches of the Silk Road
Tamil — a Dravidian racial and linguistic group dominant in southern
India
Tang (T'ang) dynasty — (618-907) after the Han, generally regarded the
most glorious of Chinese dynasties
Tanjur [bsTan 'Gyur] — section Tibetan Buddhist canon which contains

venerated (but not sacred) writings attributed to the great teachers of the religion (see Kanjur)

Tantra — esoteric forms of Buddhism or Hinduism

Tao Te Ching — see *Dao De Jing*

Tashilhunpo [bKra Shis Lhun-po] — Gelugpa monastery, seat of the Panchen Lama, founded by dGe 'Dun Grub, the first Dalai Lama (1391-1475), in Shigatse

Tathāgata — a title of the Buddha

Taxila — Buddhist archaeological site in northern Pakistan, once a major monastic center

temple-mountain — Buddhist or Hindu temple comprised of a series of stone terraces, e.g. Borobudur and Angkor Wat

Tendai school — Japanese counterpart of the Chinese Tian Tai school, founded in Japan by Saichō (766-822)

Thai — the primary ethnic group of Thailand

Thailand — a Theravāda Buddhist country in Southeast Asia

theism — belief in a supreme God who created and governs the universe

Theosophical Society — founded New York in 1875 by Henry Steel Olcott and Madame Blavatsky, an organization dedicated to popularizing Eastern spirituality in the West

Thera — (P.) see Elder

Theravāda — (P.) the "Way of the Elders," the form of Buddhism now practiced in Sri Lanka, Burma, Thailand, Cambodia, and Laos (Skt. Sthaviravāda)

Thon-mi Sam-Bho-ta — Tibetan scholar credited with the single-handed creation of the written Tibetan language, under King Srong bTsan sGam-po (r. circa 627-50)

Three Ages school — a Chinese school of Buddhism based on the doctrine of progressive decay of the dharma during successive ages

Three Kingdoms period of Chinese history — (c. 220-280 CE) the period following the fall of the Han dynasty; not to be confused with the overlapping but much longer Three Kingdoms period of Korean history (c. 200-668 CE).

Three Kingdoms period of Korean history — (c. 200-668 CE) a period of conflict among the three contenders to Korean domination (Koguryŏ, Paekche and Silla); not to be confused with the Three Kingdoms period of Chinese history (c. 220-80 CE)

tian (t'ien) — (Chi.) the sky or heaven; according to Confucianism, an impersonal force that stands over the affairs of humankind as the celestial vault stands over the earth

Tiananmen (T'ien-an-men) Square — the enormous central plaza of Beijing where, in 1989, hundreds of protestors were massacred by government troops

Tian Tai (T'ien T'ai) — school of Chinese Buddhism named after the mountain on which its founder Zhi Yi (538-97) habitually resided (Jap. Tendai)

Tibeto-Burmans — after the Pyu, a second wave of Tibetan peoples to migrate into Burma; the primary ancestors of the present-day Burmese

Tilopa — (988-1069) the first historical figure in the Indian tantric lineage that eventually resulted in the Kagyudpa sect of Tibetan Buddhism; the teacher of Nāropa

Tipiṭaka — (P.) the Buddhist canon, especially Theravāda (Skt. Tripiṭaka)

Tokugawa period — (1601-1867) the period of Japanese history in which the Tokugawa clan dominated Japan even though the emperor continued to rule nominally

T'ong pulgyo — "Unified Buddhism," the eclectic brand of Korean Buddhism initiated by Wŏnhyo

Tonkin — (also Tonking) northern Vietnam (see Annam and Cochin China)

tooth relic — supposedly a tooth of the Buddha brought to Sri Lanka during the reign of King Meghavaṇṇa (r. 352-379) and now housed in Kandy

Tran dynasty — (1225-1400) the fourth Vietnamese dynasty

Trinh family of Vietnam — de facto rulers of northern Vietnam from the mid-sixteenth to the eighteenth centuries

Tripiṭaka — (Skt.) the Buddhist canon (P. Tipiṭaka)

Triple Gem of Buddhism — the Buddha, the Dharma and the Saṅgha

Truc Lam — a Vietnamese synthesis of Chan–Pure Land Buddhism with Confucianism and Daoism, initiated by King Tran Nhan Ton (r. 1258-1308)

True Pure Land — founded in Japan by Honen (1133-1212), a more radical form of Pure Land Buddhism

Tsong Kha-pa (1357-1419) — founder of the Gelugpa sect of Tibetan Buddhism, author of the *Lam Rim Chen-mo* or "Great Treatise on the Stages of the Path"

Tulku [sPrul-sKu] — (Tib.) literally, the "manifest body" of the Buddha; but in the Tibetan tradition, a major reincarnating lama (Skt. *nirmāṇa-kāya*)

Turfan — a city-state on the Silk Road

Tōkyō — the capital of Japan since 1868

Tārā — "Savioress," the consort of Avalokiteśvara Bodhisattva (see Dolma)

Ŭisang — (625-702) eminent Korean monk of Silla, a Master of Hua Yan

(Kor. Hwaŏm) Buddhism and a great promoter of monastery and temple building, a contemporary of Wŏnhyo (617-687) and Chajang (608-686)

Ulan Bator — capital of Outer Mongolia

untouchables — members of the lowest castes of Hinduism, whom higher caste Indians are forbidden even to touch

Upanishads — scriptures composed in India between approximately 800 and 300 BCE, the earliest texts containing clear elements of classical Hinduism

upāya — see skillful means

uposatha — days of the new and full moon, upon which gatherings of Buddhist monks and nuns are held to confess and punish lapses of discipline

Vairocana — the celestial Buddha whose name means "Radiant One," associated with the sun in Buddhist mythology, and thereby with Amaterasu in the Japanese Shintō religion

Vaishṇavite — follower of the Hindu god Vishṇu

Vasubandhu — (fourth century CE) along with his brother Asaṅga, generally regarded as co-founder of the Vijñānavāda or "Consciousness school" of Mahāyāna Buddhism

Vedānta — "culmination of the Vedas," those schools of classical Hinduism based on the *Upanishads, Brahma Sūtras,* and the *Bhagavad Gītā*

Vedas — scriptures of the Indo-Europeans who migrated into India

viceroy — one who rules in the name of, or in place of, a king

Vien Chan (Vientiane) — capital of Laos since the sixteenth century

Vietnam — Mahāyāna Buddhist country of easternmost Southeast Asia

vijñāna — (Skt.) consciousness (P. *viññana*)

Vijñānavāda — the "Consciousness school" of Mahāyāna Buddhism, which maintained that the universe is a projection of the mind

Vikramaśilā — (sometimes Vikramaśila) Buddhist university in ancient India

Vinaya Piṭaka — the section of the Buddhist scriptures containing rules for monks and nuns

Vinītaruci — The history of Vietnamese Buddhism as such begins in 580, with the arrival of Vinītaruci, an Indian monk who had studied in China with the third patriarch of Chan (Zen) Buddhism, before it split into northern and southern schools.

vipassanā — insight meditation

Vishṇu — the primary deity of Hindu devotionalism (*bhakti*)

Visuddhimagga — the *Path of Purity* an important manual of Theravāda doctrine by Buddhaghosha

Wang Kŏn — founder of the Korean kingdom of Koryŏ

warlord — one who exercises the prerogatives of political power by virtue of military might rather than as a result of a lawful political process

Warring States period — (c. 453-221 BCE) a period of disunity and strife in Chinese history

Wei Shi (Wei Shih) — Chinese Vijñānavāda school of Buddhism, also known as the Fa Xiang (Fa Hsiang) school (Jap. Hossō)

Western Tibet — the conventional name of a kingdom established by an exiled remnant of the Tibetan royal family in the ninth century, centered upon present-day Ladakh, in far-north India

White Cloud Society — a Chinese lay Buddhist group that looked to the coming of Maitreya (the future Buddha) as a messianic incentive to rebellion

White Lotus Society — a Chinese lay Buddhist group that looked to the coming of Maitreya (the future Buddha) as a messianic incentive to rebellion

Wŏn'gwang — (d. 631) the most influential of the early Korean pilgrims to study Buddhism in China, a personal friend of King Chinp'yŏng of Silla

Wŏnhyo — (617-687) eminent Korean monk of Silla, said to have achieved enlightenment at age 32, a contemporary of Chajang (608-686) and Ŭisang (625-702)

World's Parliament of Religions — held in conjunction with the 1893 Chicago World's Fair, the watershed marking the beginning of widespread Western interest in Eastern religions

wu — (Chi.) non-being

Wu of Northern Zhou — (r. 561-77) emperor responsible for the second Chinese suppression of Buddhism in 574

wu wei — (Chi.) "non-action," not in the sense of inactivity, but in the sense of effortless action in harmony with the Way (*dao*), especially in Daoism

Wu Yan Tong (Wu Yen T'ung) — (d. 826) initiated the second Zen lineage in Vietnam, studied in China with Hui Neng, the sixth patriarch and founder of the southern school of Chan

Wu Ze Tian (Wu Tse T'ien) — (r. 683-705) the first and only empress of China, who supported Buddhism lavishly, but declared the San Jie Jiao sect heretical

Wu Zong (Wu Tsung) — (r. 840-46) emperor of the Tang dynasty responsible for the third Chinese suppression of Buddhism

xenophobic — fearing or hating foreigners

Xi'an (Hsi-an) — an ancient capital of China, pronounced "Shi-an" and known in ancient times as Chang An (see Luoyang)

Xin Xing (Hsin Hsing) — (late sixth century) founder of the San Jie Jiao school

Xiong Nu (Hsiung Nu) — marauding hordes that threatened ancient China, possibly related to the Huns

Xuan Zang (Hsüan Tsang) — (602-664) Chinese monk who traveled in India from about 630-45 and returned to China with crateloads of Buddhist scriptures

Yi Jing (I Ching, sometimes I Tsing) — (635-713) Chinese Buddhist pilgrim who left an important record of his journey to India and Buddhist kingdoms in Indonesia

yoga — religious discipline, usually associated with meditation, intended to release the soul from rebirth

Yogācāra — "Yoga-practice" school of Mahāyāna Buddhism also known as Vijñānavāda

Yuan dynasty — (1280-1368) the most powerful Mongol dynasty of China, founded by Kublai Khan

Yue Zhi (Yüeh Chih) — Chinese name for the Kushans

Zanskar — ancient principality of Western Tibet, today a primarily Buddhist district of Ladakh

Zen — the Japanese counterpart of Chinese Chan or "Meditation" Buddhism, usually regarded as having been introduced to Japan by Eisai (1141-1215). The term *"zen"* is a Japanese pronunciation of the Chinese word *chan,* which in turn is a rendition of the Sanskrit term *dhyāna,* meaning "meditation."

Zhabs Drung ["Zhab Drung"] — ("Most Reverend") titular head of the Drugpa subsect of Bhutan

Zhen Yan (Chen Yen) — Tantric school of Chinese Buddhism (Jap. Shingon)

Zhi Yi (Chih I) — (538-97) founder of Tian Tai Buddhism

Zhou (Chou) dynasty — (1025-453 BCE) ancient Chinese dynasty; to be distinguished from the Northern Zhou (557-581 CE)

Zoroastrianism — ancient religion of Iran or Persia

Index

[Items herein are alphabetized in the "letter-by-letter" mode; e.g., "Southeast Asia" comes before "South Korea." Chinese names and terms are listed under both Pinyin and Wade-Giles forms, with page numbers listed only after the Pinyin entries. Ambiguous surnames, like Tarthang Tulku, are listed under both possibilities.]

Mohenjo Daro 2
moksha (release) 4, 6, 33
mondō 208-9
Mongka Khan 241-42
Mongkut (see Rāma IV) 125-26
Mongolian Buddhism
— introduction of 273-74
— canon of 275
— Chinese influence upon 273
— Manchurian influence upon 275
— Russian influence upon 276-77
— Tibetan influence upon 241-43, 246-52
— communism and 276-77
— shamanism and 273-74, 276
Mongolian Kanjur and Tanjur 275
Mongols xi, 92, 102, 116-17, 122, 129-30, 150, 158, 160-61, 165, 181-82, 206, 210, 221, **241-43**, 246-49, 251, 253, 257-58, 270-72, **273-77**, 280, 291
Mons 100, **113-16**, 121-23
monsoon 7, 14
Mormonism 184
Morye 168
Mount (see Mt.)
Mou Tzu (see Mou Zi)
Mou Zi (Mou Tzu) the author 139
Mou Zi (Mou Tzu), the text 139
Mt. Fuji 206
Mt. Hiei 194-95, 197-98, 201-202, 204, 207-208, 211, 213-14

Mt. Kōya 197-98
Mt. Shasta Abbey 287
mudra 231
Muhammad 1
Muhammad Ghūrī 76
Mukhoja 168
Müller, F. Max 280
Munjong, king of Koryŏ 179
Musō Soseki 210-11
Mussolini 217
Myŏngjong, king of Koryŏ 182
Naemul, king of Silla 168
Nāgārjuna 46, 54, 58, 62, **67-69, 74-75**, 88, 150, 189-90, 236, 244, 259
Nāgasena 78
Nālandā 68, 72, 76, 83, 102, 146, 150, 236
Nagpur 82
Namgyal dynasty of Sikkim 272
Nan Chao (see Nan Zhao)
Nan Zhao (Nan Chao) kingdom 114
Nara period of Japan **189-94**, 196, 199, 201 207, 210, 219
Nārada, U 289
Naresuan, king of Thailand 124
Nāropa 73, **236-40**, 292
Naropa Institute 292
Nationalist China 162-63
National League for Democracy 120
Nazis 217, 223
Nehru, Jawaharlal 82
nembutsu 201-203, 205
neo-Confucianism 147, 159-61, 182, 280
neo-Daoism 140, 142, 147, 156-57, 159